Educational Psychology

Educational Psychology offers a comprehensive overview of how key advances in social, developmental and cognitive psychology impact upon the role of educational psychologists working today. Written by leading researchers, the book also explores controversies and dilemmas in both research and practice, providing students with a balanced and cutting-edge introduction to both the field and the profession.

Fully revised throughout, the new edition is written to encourage students to integrate their understanding of core psychological disciplines, as well as to consider what 'evidence-based practice' really means. Organised into two broad sections related to learning and behaviour, the book features a selection of vignettes from educational psychologists working in a range of contexts, as well as tasks and scenarios to support a problem-orientated approach to study.

By integrating both research and everyday practice, the book is unique in engaging a critical appreciation of both the possibilities and limitations of educational psychology. It is the ideal book for any student wishing to engage with this important and evolving field of study.

Tony Cline is Co-Director of the CPD Doctorate in Educational Psychology at University College London, UK.

Anthea Gulliford is D App Ed Psy Joint Programme Director in the School of Psychology at the University of Nottingham, UK, and Senior Educational Psychologist at Nottingham City Council, UK.

Susan Birch is Co-Director of the CPD Doctorate in Educational Psychology, University College London and Senior Educational Psychologist at Buckinghamshire County Council, UK.

Topics in Applied Psychology

Series Editor: Graham Davey, Professor of Psychology at the University of Sussex, UK, and former president of the British Psychological Society.

Topics in Applied Psychology is a series of accessible, integrated textbooks ideal for courses in applied psychology. Written by leading figures in their field, the books provide a comprehensive academic and professional overview of the subject area, bringing the topics to life through a range of features, including personal stories, case studies, ethical debates, and learner activities. Each book addresses a broad range of cutting-edge topics, providing students with both theoretical foundations and real-life applications.

Clinical Psychology
Second Edition
Graham Davey

Educational Psychology
Second Edition
Tony Cline, Anthea Gulliford and Susan Birch

Work and Organizational Psychology
Second Edition
Ian Rothmann and Cary Cooper

Sport and Exercise Psychology
Second Edition
Andy Lane

Health Psychology
Second Edition
Charles Abraham

Criminal Psychology
Second Edition
David Canter

Educational Psychology

Topics in Applied Psychology

Second edition

Edited by
**Tony Cline,
Anthea Gulliford and
Susan Birch**

Routledge
Taylor & Francis Group

LONDON AND NEW YORK

Second edition published 2015
by Routledge
27 Church Road, Hove, East Sussex BN3 2FA

and by Routledge
711 Third Avenue, New York, NY 10017

Routledge is an imprint of the Taylor & Francis Group, an informa business

First edition published by Hodder Education 2008

British Library Cataloguing in Publication Data
A catalogue record for this book is available from the British Library

Library of Congress Cataloging in Publication Data
Educational psychology / edited by Tony Cline, Anthea Gulliford and
    Susan Birch. – Second edition.
    pages cm. – (Topics in applied psychology)
    Revised edition of: Educational psychology / Norah Frederickson, Andy
    Miller, Tony Cline. London : Hodder Education, 2008.
    I. Cline, Tony, editor of compilation, author. II. Gulliford, Anthea,
    editor of compilation, author. III. Birch, Susan, editor of compilation,
    author.
    LB1051.F733 2015
    370.15 – dc23
    2014036844

ISBN: 978-1-84872-330-6 (hbk)
ISBN: 978-1-84872-331-3 (pbk)
ISBN: 978-1-31571-996-2 (ebk)

Typeset in Bembo and Univers
by Florence Production Ltd, Stoodleigh, Devon, UK

Contents

Contributors to the second edition

Susan Birch, University College London and Buckinghamshire Educational Psychology Service, UK

Tony Cline, University College London, UK

Norah Frederickson, University College London and Buckinghamshire Educational Psychology Service, UK

Anthea Gulliford, University of Nottingham and Nottingham City Community Educational Psychology Service, UK

Ben Hayes, University College London and Kent Educational Psychology Service, UK

Nathan Lambert, University of Nottingham and Birmingham Educational Psychology Service, UK

Andy Miller, University of Nottingham, UK

Series preface

Psychology is still one of the most popular subjects for study at undergraduate degree level. As well as providing the student with a range of academic and applied skills that are valued by a broad range of employers, a psychology degree also serves as the basis for subsequent training and a career in professional psychology. A substantial proportion of students entering a degree programme in psychology do so with a subsequent career in applied psychology firmly in mind, and, as a result, the number of applied psychology courses available at undergraduate level has significantly increased over recent years. In some cases, these courses supplement core academic areas and, in others, they provide the student with a flavour of what they might experience as a professional psychologist.

The original series of *Texts in Applied Psychology* consisted of six textbooks designed to provide a comprehensive academic and professional insight into specific areas of professional psychology. The texts covered the areas of *Clinical Psychology*, *Criminal and Investigative Psychology*, *Educational Psychology*, *Health Psychology*, *Sports and Exercise Psychology*, and *Work and Organizational Psychology*, and each text was written and edited by the foremost professional and academic figures in each of these areas.

These texts were so successful that we are now able to provide you with a second edition of this series. All texts have been updated with details of recent professional developments, as well as relevant research, and we have responded to the requests of teachers and reviewers to include new material and new approaches to this material. Perhaps most significantly, all texts in the series will now have back-up web resources.

Just as in the first series, each textbook is based on a similar academic formula that combines a comprehensive review of cutting-edge research and professional knowledge with accessible teaching and learning features. The books are also structured so that they can each be used as an integrated teaching support for a one-term or one-semester course in their relevant area of applied psychology. Given the increasing importance of applying psychological knowledge across a growing range of areas of practice, we feel this series is timely and comprehensive. We hope you find each book in the series readable, enlightening, accessible and instructive.

Graham Davey
University of Sussex, Brighton, UK
August 2014

Preface to the second edition

This book builds on the content and methods of the First Edition, and we wish to pay tribute to those editors of the first edition who have handed on the baton at this stage – Norah Frederickson and Andy Miller. We have written two new chapters and substantially revised and updated all the rest. This new edition reflects important changes that have occurred in research and practice in educational psychology over the last decade. Many scenarios and vignettes in this edition have been supplied by educational psychologists, based on their work in the field. We hope that these will enhance readers' sense of engagement with the practice of this profession and the evidence about childhood and schooling provided. We are grateful to Esther Adelman, Rachel Grace, Rachael Green, Emma-Kate Kennedy, Louise Lomas and Bridget Simms for the contributions they made on the basis of their professional experience. We are also grateful to Karen Wicks for constructive comments on an early draft of Chapter 8.

HOW CAN THIS BOOK BE USED?

In this preface we outline, for students and tutors, the range of ways in which this book can be used to support teaching and learning about educational psychology. We first consider *purpose* – *why* you may have decided to open the book. We then discuss *approach* – *how* the chapters are structured and may be used to achieve each of a number of goals. In the third part, we focus on *content* – what areas of knowledge and understanding are addressed and what sequencing options are available. We finish this introduction with some thoughts about what is involved in applying psychology to education.

PURPOSE

We first consider a number of different purposes for which this textbook might be used, focusing in particular on the needs and priorities of different target readerships.

Advanced level undergraduate psychology degree option

The primary audience we have had in mind in writing this book comprised advanced level undergraduate psychology students and tutors. Tutors will find material suitable for a one-term or one-semester Level 2 or Level 3 undergraduate course. Subject benchmarking statements for psychology suggest that a virtuous circle often exists 'between theory and empirical data, the results of which may find their expression in applications to educational, health, industrial/commercial and other situations' and specify that degree programmes should develop 'the ability to extrapolate and comprehend the applications of knowledge within the areas of psychology' (QAA, 2002, p. 4). The book will support the achievement of this goal in the area of educational psychology.

For students, educational psychology has a number of advantages in supporting this purpose. The main context of application in educational psychology is the school context. Although there are other, important areas of educational psychology practice, in families and in the community, we will only touch on them occasionally in this book, which will focus mainly on the school. All students have had experience of school, which in most cases is recent. We hope this broad familiarity will enable a ready grasp of the applications of psychology that are described. In addition, students are encouraged, specifically in Chapter 1, to think about other possible applications to schools from the courses studied in the first and second years of the degree programme.

Application to educational psychology training

For anyone who might be interested in applying for professional training as an educational psychologist, Chapter 1, 'What do educational psychologists do?', is an obvious starting point for finding out about the professional role and training. For the serious applicant, each chapter offers insights about aspects of professional practice and ways in which psychology can be applied in educational contexts. The criteria used by selection panels for educational psychology training programmes commonly include: *knowledge of ways in which psychology can be applied in educational, childcare and community contexts* and/or *experience of applying psychology theory and research in work with children.* This book will contribute to the knowledge required by the first of these criteria and will assist both in planning and reflecting on relevant experience for addressing the second criterion.

Professional training in educational psychology

In the initial stages of doctoral professional training programmes in educational psychology, there is often a need for trainees to update their knowledge of psychological theory and research relevant to professional practice. Although many trainees will have completed their undergraduate psychology degree within the previous couple of years, some will have completed it a number of years prior to that, and for some there may have been less emphasis on the actual application of psychology in educational contexts. We hope that this book will serve these purposes well and be of value on the initial set reading list for these programmes.

APPROACH

This book is designed to be used to support a range of different course formats:

- a one–term/–semester lecture course;
- a seminar group meeting weekly, alongside a lecture course;
- a problem–based learning (PBL) course, structured as a series of tutor-facilitated or self-directed learning group meetings (for example, see Dunsmuir and Frederickson, 2014).

Across each of these formats, the text is designed to encourage and support a problem–orientated approach to learning. This orientation has been selected to engage interest and develop critical analysis. It also aids the presentation of issues in practice contexts in ways that facilitate the representation of different perspectives and the development of a realistic appreciation of both the contributions and current limitations in the application of psychology.

The problem–orientated approach is reflected in a number of different ways. The titles of the chapters pose questions highlighting controversies and dilemmas in research and practice. For example: 'Why does mathematics make so many people fearful?' and 'Educating children with autism: What use are psychological theory and research?'. Most chapters contain at least one focus box that features a suitable stimulus or 'trigger' for use by a PBL or seminar group as a starting point for the topic in question. This will often be a vignette or case study from the professional practice of educational psychologists, but newspaper reports and other relevant material are also included. Information on current theories and research is presented in relation to issues arising from the case study material. Using a variety of activities in the text, students are encouraged to critically evaluate potential implications of the different areas of research reviewed for practice and policy in education and to identify limitations of current methods and knowledge in the pursuit of 'evidence-based' practice.

New topics are frequently introduced in a way that encourages students to access (and, where working in groups, to share) existing knowledge of relevance to the scenarios presented. This is intended to assist them in building upon, extending to a more advanced level, and, crucially, seeking to integrate, information from topics covered in the core domains during the first two years of their degree: biological, cognitive, developmental, personality and individual differences, and social psychology.

Each of the chapters follows a similar overall structure:

- An introductory paragraph (chapter summary) orientates the reader to the topic.
- A set of intended learning outcomes is then presented.
- The text is organised in a number of sections, addressing different facets of the topic and focused around boxes containing stimulus material, activities, examples of applications and more detailed discussion of methodological or ethical issues.
- A summary of the main issues addressed in the chapter is presented.
- Key concepts and terms are listed.
- Recommendations for further reading are provided.
- Sample essay titles are suggested.

The problem-orientated approach is represented throughout. For example, the sample essay titles suggested include two representatives of this approach, such as:

- Design an evidence-based intervention programme for Alex (Activity Box 1.1), justifying the approaches you decide to include, with reference to relevant literature.
- You have been asked to give a talk to sixth-form volunteers on 'Supporting children with ASD in school: Key insights from psychology'. Explain what you will include in your talk and why.

Alongside these are two more conventional essay titles, such as:

- To what extent can a 'theory of mind' deficit account for the triad of impairments in autism?
- Evaluate the strengths and weaknesses of research evidence on the use of social stories with children who have ASD.

It is our objective throughout to maximise the flexibility with which the book can be used to meet the purposes of different tutors and groups of learners.

CONTENT

In Part I, an introductory chapter (Chapter 1) focuses on the role and training of educational psychologists. This chapter both provides a basis for those that follow and seeks to draw together some overarching themes and encourage learners to make connections with information from topics from the core domains – biological, cognitive, developmental, personality and individual differences and social psychology – covered during the first two years of the undergraduate psychology degree. Chapter 1 closes with some consideration of the processes used by educational psychologists in establishing links between theory and practice. A further introductory chapter, Chapter 2, extends this and addresses questions raised by the notion of 'evidence-based practice', considering the range of methods that contribute to our understanding of what constitutes evidence. This chapter addresses those who are interested to understand how research methods in psychology can support our understanding of complex real-life problems, and helps in the evaluation of evidence presented later in the volume.

The remaining chapters are organised into two further parts. Part II, 'Cognition, learning and instruction', contains chapters that reflect educational psychologists' work in relation to the core purposes of schools of promoting learning and raising achievement. They draw primarily on cognitive development, cognitive psychology and individual differences. Part III, 'Social, emotional and behavioural issues in school', contains chapters that reflect educational psychologists' work in relation to the social context and ethos of the school and schools' responsibilities in providing for the behaviour and well-being of the pupils. They draw primarily on social development and social psychology.

It is recommended that Chapter 1 be used as both the starting and finishing points of the course. Initially, it will provide an orientation to the work of educational psychologists. At the end of the course, an educational psychologist from a neighbouring educational psychology service might be invited to give a talk on their work. This may be particularly useful where there is no chartered educational psychologist on the staff. The suggested essay questions for Chapter 1 will also be most appropriately addressed at the end of the course, as they seek to integrate topic areas, allow more scope for individual interests to be followed, and challenge the highest-achieving students.

Otherwise, with the aim of allowing maximum flexibility, the chapters have been written so that they can be studied in any order. Sufficient background is provided in each chapter for it to stand alone, so that chapters can readily be used to support contributions to other Level 3 courses, for example contributing four lectures on educational psychology to a course on applied psychology. The associated disadvantage is that, although there are a small number of themes that recur across chapters, this recurrence is not flagged up in the text.

APPLYING PSYCHOLOGY TO EDUCATION

In Chapter 1, the work of educational psychologists will be introduced, and the way in which they operate as scientist–practitioners is highlighted. Chapter 2 makes a case for the importance of psychologists understanding the methods used to generate the evidence they may choose to draw upon in practice. However, it has long been recognised that the application of psychology to education is not a matter of direct translation:

> You make a great, a very great mistake if you think that psychology, being the science of minds' laws, is something from which you can deduce definite programmes and schemes and methods of instruction for immediate classroom use. Psychology is a science and teaching is an art: and sciences never generate arts directly out of themselves. An intermediary, inventive mind must make the application, by using its originality.
>
> (James, 1899/1958, pp. 23–4)

In this book, we hope to illustrate both elements in William James's formula for the successful application of psychology to education: first, the basis in psychological science, which allows clear principles and guidelines to be developed in particular areas of practice; second, the creativity, inventiveness and 'professional artistry' that are also involved in undertaking the process of translation into practice, with different people, in different contexts. It is this combination, we believe, that makes educational psychology such a fascinating field of study and practice.

Tony Cline
Anthea Gulliford
Susan Birch
May 2014

REFERENCES

Dunsmuir, S. and Frederickson, N. (2014). Problem-based learning in professional training: Experiences of school psychology trainers in the UK. *Training and Education in Professional Psychology*. First publication online, 17 March 2014. Available at: http://dx.doi.org/10.1037/tep0000040 (accessed 27 November 2014).

James, W. (1899). *Talks to Teachers*. New York: Norton (republished 1958).

QAA (2002). *Psychology Subject Benchmark Statements*. Gloucester, UK: Quality Assurance Agency for Higher Education.

Overview

Overview | 1

1 What do educational psychologists do?

Susan Birch, Norah Frederickson and Andy Miller

CHAPTER SUMMARY

Educational psychology *seems to be rather a mysterious profession. An education officer who claimed to have read over 1,000 reports written by educational psychologists (EPs) wrote an article entitled, 'Okay then: What do EPs do?' (Wood, 1998). UK governments have appeared similarly baffled, in that four reviews of the role and function of EPs have been carried out since the turn of the century, one in Scotland (Scottish Executive, 2002) one in England and Wales (DfEE, 2000), and a further two in England (Farrell et al., 2006; DfE, 2011). Our main objective is that, by the end of this chapter, you will be able to answer the question in the title, and will have gained an appreciation of some of the issues in the professional practice of educational psychology that lead to the question being asked.*

We begin this chapter by identifying the different levels at which EPs work (from individual child to local authority (LA)) and the core activities that they undertake. We consider similarities and differences between the work of EPs in different places and at different times in the history of the profession. A case study of an EP's work in response to a teacher's concern about a child is presented to illustrate the way in which different activities are typically integrated and informed, both by psychological theory and research and professional ethics and practice guidelines. The resulting central conceptualisation of the role of the EP as 'scientist–practitioner' is then examined, with a number of current issues and possible future developments being highlighted. The chapter concludes with information on training as an EP.

LEARNING OUTCOMES

When you have studied this chapter, you should be able to:

1 describe what EPs do and identify some of the key issues in their practice;
2 evaluate the extent to which EPs can be described as scientist–practitioners;
3 outline the requirements for training as an EP and locate more detailed information if required.

HOW MUCH DO DIFFERENT ACCOUNTS OF EDUCATIONAL PSYCHOLOGY PRACTICE AGREE?

In this section, we examine different descriptions of EPs' work – from individual EPs, from government reports and from information provided to the public from LA educational psychology services. In Activity Box 1.1, we start by looking at what EPs say they do.

ACTIVITY 1.1

What do educational psychologists say they do?

Read the following four descriptions by EPs of their work. Apart from their obvious enthusiasm, what do they have in common? How many different aspects of EPs' work are mentioned?

Use just the information in these four extracts to write a one-paragraph description of what EPs do. If possible, compare your paragraph with that produced by someone else. As you read the rest of the chapter, annotate your paragraph to reflect the further information you obtain.

> EPs need to be able to multitask while simultaneously being able to prioritise their work. They need to be able to think on their feet while helping others to think through labyrinthine problems; listen carefully to what adults are saying about a child while keeping the child's perspective in mind. There doesn't seem to be a typical day; there are some cases that are more straightforward than others, but at the heart of them all is an attempt to gain some insight in to the child's worldview. I find my job varied, interesting and rewarding. No two days are the same and I am frequently challenged by new experiences that need researching and learning more about.
>
> (Louise Lomas, Buckinghamshire Educational Psychology Service)

My experience reflects the role of the EP in a service that has recently begun trading their services with schools in addition to providing the local authority core offer. I feel that schools still really value the involvement of the EP in casework, particularly when they feel the need to develop a better understanding of a young person. Once involvement has been agreed, and with consultation, schools are quite open to the direction and assessment route that the EP wants to take. While some schools still hang on to the traditional role of the EP in cognitive assessment I feel schools are increasingly open to alternative approaches such as consultation, a problem-solving approach. Within schools, EPs are joint problem solvers working with staff and parents to develop a better understanding of a presenting problem in order to inform hypotheses to identify interventions or ways forward. The EP draws upon problem-solving skills from psychological theory to steer the problem solving towards an agreeable way forward. This process can occur at multiple levels: individual, group or whole school and places EPs in a unique position of working at strategic and systemic levels within schools and Local Authorities.

(Bridget Simms, South Gloucestershire Educational Psychology Service)

EPs work at multiple levels – with individual children and families, groups of students or parents/carers and at the level of the organisation. The latter may involve working at an EP service level, within a wider Local Authority (LA) structure or in a school or early years setting. While it has been recognised that the impact of applied psychology at the level of the organisation can be of significant benefit, it can sometimes prove challenging to negotiate the time and relevant brief to operate helpfully in such a context. One piece of work I am currently engaged in with senior leadership colleagues relates to raising the standard of teaching across the whole school. It is hugely exciting, and provides the opportunity to apply multiple psychological skills, including psychological theory and research on effective teamwork. I am involved in diverse work such as participating in the training of teachers in coaching models that enhance their listening, empathising and questioning skills; designing processes such as coaching contracts and supervision structures and much more. Because of the change to role and boundaries across staff in the school, it has also included reflecting together on issues such as workload management, staff health and well-being and effective work-based strategies to support motivation and engagement in high quality learning. There is no job like that of the EP, where you are privileged to enter the worlds of children, families and those who work with them. The insight afforded through the application of high quality psychology is valued across a range of stakeholders and makes a significant, measurable difference to the lives of our children and young people!

(Emma-Kate Kennedy, Child and Family Support Team Manager and Consultant Educational Psychologist, Redriff School, London)

What does an EP do? Such a simple question but often so difficult to answer succinctly. Over the years I have come to the following response: 'applies skills and knowledge of psychology to bring about change, maybe with a child or adults or systems around a child'. What varies from EP to EP and situation to situation is the 'type of change', 'the person or people we are helping to bring about change for', the 'how we do it' and increasingly the 'where'/ working context. For me the keys to good practice are being interested in, and good at solving, problems by thinking creatively; being able to look at yourself and reflect on your role and impact in any situation; being able to really understand, or help understand, what a person wants, how they think and feel and work with that; having a strong and wide ranging base of knowledge about different psychological and learning theories and approaches and an ability to assess the evidence base of each and being open minded and open to new ideas. The work of an EP is rarely easy or straightforward. You are often entering situations where people are stuck, frustrated, angry or upset. However, it is enormously rewarding to see such situations move forward, people to become unstuck, and resourceful enough to know what to do next and feel positive. To me the ultimate measure of success is the (unscientific and difficult to measure) 'Ah-ha' moment. The moment when someone says, 'Ah-ha, I know what I could do, I could try . . .' or 'Ah-ha I can do this now!' – positive change in action!

(Rachael Green, Educational Psychologist, working
independently in a range of contexts)

On the website of the Department for Education, the role of an EP in England is described as follows:

EPs work in a variety of ways to address the problems experienced by children and young people in education. They have a central role in the statutory assessment and statementing procedures for children with special educational needs. They work directly with a wide range of other professionals to deliver their work.

(August 2013)

In the last 10 years, reviews of educational psychology services in England and Wales (DfEE, 2000) and in Scotland (Scottish Executive, 2002) have identified very similar levels of work and core activities. The examples of work across levels and core activities shown in Table 1.1 are taken from the Scottish report. Notice the same levels that you will have already identified in the accounts given by practising EPs in Activity Box 1.1.

One issue that emerges from the international literature is a potentially confusing difference in terminology. In North America, psychologists undertaking the range of core activities carried out by EPs in Great Britain are called 'school psychologists'. As can be seen from Table 1.2, the American Psychological Association has a separate

TABLE 1.1 Examples of the levels of work and core activities of educational psychologists

Core functions

Level	Consultation	Assessment	Intervention	Training	Research
Child and family	Individual discussions Contribution to IEPs Home visits Parents' meetings Review meetings, as appropriate	Overall assessment in context Standardised assessment instruments Identifying special needs	Behaviour management programmes Individual and family therapy Working with small groups (e.g. self-harm, social skills, anger management)	Talk to groups of children (e.g. anti-bullying groups) Parenting skills	Single case studies Interactive video research with families (SPIN)
School or establishment	Joint working with staff Advice on programmes for children and young people Contribution to strategic planning Policy advice for schools, children's homes Review meetings, as appropriate	Contribution to school assessment policy and procedure	Contribution to whole-establishment interventions (e.g. anti-bullying programmes, playground behaviour, discipline, raising achievement) Contribution to special exam arrangements Contribution to curricular innovation/initiatives Joint working with class/subject teacher/LST Supporting inclusion Supporting special college placements	Staff training Disseminating evidence-based practice	Design, implementation and evaluation of action research in single establishments and groups of schools
EA/Council	Contribution to strategic planning	Contribution to authority assessment policy and procedure Contribution to best-value reviews	Contribution to establishing authority-wide interventions (e.g. anti-bullying initiatives, alternatives to exclusion, promoting social inclusion, resource allocation)	Authority-wide training in all areas relevant to psychology Input to multidisciplinary conferences	Design, implementation and evaluation of authority-wide action research (e.g. early intervention, raising achievement) Informing evidence-based policy and practice

Source: Scottish Executive, 2002

TABLE 1.2 American Psychological Association divisions of educational and school psychology

Division 15: Educational psychology	Concerned with theory, methodology and applications to a broad spectrum of teaching, training and learning issues
Division 16: School psychology	Composed of scientific-practitioner psychologists . . . engaged in the delivery of comprehensive psychological services to children, adolescents, and families in schools and other applied settings

division for EPs who are academic psychologists, such as cognitive or social psychologists, whose field of study is the processes of teaching and learning. In the UK, the term *educational psychologist* used to refer to both academic and practitioner psychologists working in education. However, in 2009, the profession of educational psychology became a regulated profession, through the operation of the *Health and Care Professions Council* (HCPC; www.hcpc-uk.org.uk). All practising EPs have to register with the HCPC, and only psychologists registered with the HCPC may use the title 'educational psychologist'. In this book, 'educational psychologist/psychology' will therefore be used to refer to these applied practitioners and their work.

More recent reports that include a focus on the role of the EP suggest that the range of work completed continues to be recognised and valued. In 2011, the DfE undertook a review of 'EP training' that not only drew attention to the role of EPs in working with children with special educational needs (SEN), but also in 'improving the opportunities of all children and young people, both in terms of LA statutory responsibilities and more universal early intervention and preventative support' (DfE, 2011, p. 5). Similarly, the role of the EP described in the final report of the National Child and Adolescent Mental Health Services Review (DOH, 2008) included reference to the SEN aspects of the role, as well as to a range of other functions:

> Their role is much wider . . . and can include therapeutic work, consultation and advice, parent training, staff training, support to schools on organisational issues such as behaviour management and specialist work with those in care and in contact with the youth justice system.
>
> (p. 46)

Therefore, EPs work across a number of different levels, in a range of contexts, with a range of different people, influencing children's development in the broadest sense.

Despite the similarities in educational psychology practice apparent internationally, there is an increasingly varied picture in terms of the models of service delivery being developed in different LAs in Great Britain. In the past, the majority of EPs were employed by LAs in one centralised specialist team, and schools were able to access a free service. However, the number of authorities where this remains the case has decreased. A report published by the Association of Educational Psychologists in 2011 suggested two key factors impacting on the variation that now exists: first, the degree of integration of EP services within multi-agency teams, and, second, sources of funding for services. The 2012 and 2013 Educational Psychology Workforce Surveys (NCTL, 2013; Truong and Ellam, 2014) reported a large number of EP services nationally utilising a 'mixed model' of funding, with many services trading directly with schools and, on occasions, other organisations, who were then invoiced for the cost of that work. Educational psychology services are increasingly developing skills in marketing and trading. How this will develop over future years, with the potential even for services to become social enterprise businesses, rather than being based almost entirely within LAs, will be interesting to see.

Allen and Hardy (2013), in a paper written for the *British Psychological Society* (BPS) book celebrating 100 years of educational psychology practice, note other key developments that are likely to influence the shape of service delivery, notably: the impact of legislative changes and the political context, the impact of technology, the increasing priority given to children's mental health, the raising of the school leaving age and the role of EPs in promoting the evidence base that informs our work. Dunsmuir and Kratochwill (2013) reflect further on this last development and on the key role of EPs as 'agents of change' through the translation and dissemination of research to practitioners.

ACTIVITY 1.2

What do educational psychology services say they do?

Despite recent developments in the design and funding of EP services, most EPs continue to be employed by LAs. Visit the websites of at least six LAs, including the one in which you are living. How do the accounts of what the educational psychology services say they do fit into the grid shown in Table 1.1? Update the paragraph you produced in Activity 1.1 describing what EPs do (keeping your description as succinct as possible). Note also whether the website talks about trading – activities that schools (and/or others) can buy. Which of the activities are available free, and to whom? Which are traded? How does this vary across services?

Can you find accounts of services offered by EPs who are not employed by LAs? Again, how do the services offered by these EPs map on to Table 1.1?

EDUCATIONAL PSYCHOLOGY: A HISTORICAL PERSPECTIVE

The first LA EP in the UK was appointed by London County Council in 1913 and held the half-time post for almost 20 years. The individual appointed to the post was Cyril Burt, who was later to become head of the psychology department at University College London and, later still, the subject of one of the most widely publicised controversies in modern psychology, concerning research ethics and data falsification (Macintosh, 1995). Burt was given the following brief:

- to report on problematic cases referred by teachers, doctors or magistrates for individual investigation;

- to construct and standardise tests;
- to organise and carry out surveys of large and representative samples of the entire school population;
- to be ready to report on any specific problem raised by the education officer or committee.

There are clear parallels with the range of practice apparent today. In addition, Burt's description of his work with individual children indicates an interactionist perspective that appears strikingly contemporary almost 90 years later.

> Whatever the problem might be, instead of calling each child up to the office . . . I always found it far more effective to study him, as it were, *in situ*, and that of course meant visiting him in the school, calling at his home, and watching him with his play fellows larking in the streets.
>
> (Burt, 1964 address to the Association of Educational Psychologists' Conference, transcribed and reported in Rushton, 2002, p. 565)

Of particular interest also, given our discussion later in this chapter of the conceptualisation of the role of the EP as that of scientist–practitioner, is the place Burt saw for research in all aspects of professional practice, including individual case work: 'All my work in the Council's schools was of the nature of research. Even the individual cases . . . had each to form the subject of a small intensive investigation' (Burt, 1964, in Rushton, 2002, p. 565).

Although Burt's model of practice was highly regarded by his employers in London (Maliphant, 1998), it did not immediately become established nationwide. Initially, the number of EPs increased slowly, and many were based in child guidance clinics run by health authorities, rather than in the education departments of LAs. The child guidance clinic teams comprised child psychiatrists, psychiatric social workers and EPs, offering the potential advantage of a multidisciplinary approach. However, there were many tensions. The psychiatrists were usually designated as team leaders and often adopted a narrow medical model that the psychologists did not consider appropriate to educational and social problems. The psychologists generally had a much more limited role than the one Burt had created, which, in some cases, became confined primarily to *psychometric testing*.

The report of the first committee of inquiry into the work of EPs, the Summerfield Report (DES, 1968), recommended that EPs should be administratively responsible to LA education departments, but did not challenge the narrow focus on individual case work. Indeed, in 1975, a DES circular identified the desirability of obtaining an assessment report from an EP in the special education ascertainment procedures run by the school doctors. This created something of a dilemma for EPs:

> On the one hand they would like to spend more time on advisory and treatment activities, but on the other hand their 'coming of age' relies on their having achieved official recognition for their contribution to assessment procedures as required in Circular 2/750.
>
> (Quicke, 1982, p. 39)

Many argued for change, for a reconstruction of the EP's role. In an influential edited volume (Gillham, 1978), three main directions for change were advocated:

- decreasing emphasis on individual work with children individually referred;
- increasing emphasis on indirect methods aimed at the organisation, policy and structure of schools and the attitudes and behaviour of adults towards children;
- increasing emphasis on preventative work, especially through courses for parents and teachers.

This period has been described 'as a time when the profession was beginning to gird its loins and drag itself out of . . . the sterile treadmill of individual casework, psycho-metrics, and the professional suffocation of child guidance' (Dessent, 1992, p. 34). However, the 1981 Education Act enshrined in legislation and extended the role for EPs in advising on the special educational needs of individual children that had been introduced in the 1975 guidance circular. The new legal requirement to produce psychological advice to inform the *Statement of Special Educational Needs* issued by the LA led to pessimism about reconstructing a broader professional role. 'Under the 1981 Education Act procedures, educational psychologists are firmly nailed and fastened as assessors of needs and definers of resources. They are likely to find themselves seeing and assessing an ever increasing number of individual pupils' (Dessent, 1988, p. 74).

Balancing the demands for statutory and other assessments with prevention and intervention continued (and continues) to be an issue. It was the stimulus for the governmental review of the work of EPs following the 1997 Green Paper, which set out the government's vision for raising the achievement of children with SEN:

> The Green Paper recognised the wide ranging responsibilities of educational psychologists. In doing so it observed that the growing pressure for statements has led to educational psychologists spending more of their time carrying out statutory assessments, at the expense of providing early intervention and support when the child's needs are first identified. The Green Paper made a commitment to explore ways of changing the balance of educational psychologists' work to ensure their expertise is used more effectively.
>
> (DfEE, 2000, p. 1)

Rather than coming up with radical solutions, however, this report focused on publicising descriptions of strategies some services had found to be successful in balancing conflicting demands and shifting practice.

Given the 32-year gap between the publication of the previous two governmental reports on the work of EPs, it is perhaps surprising that the next one was to appear only 6 years later. This report (Farrell *et al.*, 2006) was commissioned to review the functions and contribution of EPs in England and Wales in light of the government's priorities for services for children at the time. Although the government framework has changed, many of the themes discussed by Farrell *et al.* (2006) are still reflected in EP practice today, for example:

- a focus on improving outcomes for children;
- shifting the focus of service delivery from school to community;

- an emphasis on multi-agency involvement and specialist educational psychology input;
- defining the distinctive contribution of EPs, with an emphasis on psychology.

One final word about the fourth of the above points. It was argued that identification of the distinctive contribution that EPs can make, as opposed to other professionals, should drive decisions about the balance of activities they undertake. 'The general view that the EPs' distinctive contribution lies in their psychological skills and knowledge would suggest that agreed clarity of the EP role should be focused around the particularly psychological function within it' (Farrell *et al.*, 2006).

It is interesting that almost exactly the same conclusion was reached almost 40 years earlier, in the Summerfield Report: 'The particular contribution of psychologists in education services derives from their specialized study of psychological science and its application to education and to other aspects of human development. It should be the main criterion in determining their work' (DES, 1968, p. xi).

The most recent reform of legislation and regulations around SEN (DfE, 2014) suggests that EPs are to have a continuing role within statutory assessment, although whether the EP completing the psychological advice will be employed by a LA, as in the previous legislation, or whether parents will be able to employ their own psychologist for the purposes of the assessment, is still unclear.

The most significant of the anticipated implications for EPs in the new legislation is likely to be the need to develop work with young people up to the age of 25. The new legislation supports the provision of education for young people with the most complex needs up to this age, where special educational provision continues to be required to enable them to work towards unmet educational and training outcomes, as specified in their *Education, Health and Care Plan* (the replacement for the statement of SEN), outcomes aimed at enabling the young person to prepare for adulthood (DfE, 2014). Hence, there is likely to be a role for EPs in supporting planning for the transition between child and adult services, in supporting provision for young adults with complex needs, and in further developing person-centred approaches for working with young people and their families in preparation for adulthood.

So, although there would appear to be a continuing role for EPs in statutory assessments for the foreseeable future, there is also a recognition of their work in other areas. It may be that local priorities and budgets will, to some extent, dictate the shape of educational psychology services of the future. Many services are already operating mixed models, with core statutory services being funded by the LA and with more creative and preventive work being commissioned by schools and other services.

EDUCATIONAL PSYCHOLOGY PRACTICE TODAY: A CASE STUDY

In this section of the chapter, we present a case study that illustrates the integrated way in which different core activities and levels of work may be incorporated into the EP's everyday practice. The starting point for this case study is a typical one for an EP engaged in consultative work with a school – a request from a school for advice about an individual pupil who is causing concern, made to the EP during one of their regular visits to the school.

Although the specifics of policy and practice vary between LAs, educational psychology practice in responding to requests of this kind is guided by the framework for psychological assessment (see Figure 1.1) contained in the BPS Division of Educational and Child Psychology (DECP) *Professional practice guidelines* (BPS, 2002). The process cycle contained in this model is essentially a *problem-solving* process, and it has been argued that the applied psychology professions are, at their core, problem-solving professions (Pearson and Howarth, 1982). The method cycle to which it links describes stages in a *consultation* between an EP and adults concerned about a child's progress. A widely accepted definition of consultation makes this link clear: 'an indirect problem-solving process between a [consultant] and one or more [consultees] to address concerns presented by a client' (Sheridan *et al.*, 1996, pp. 341–2). Models of consultation commonly used by EPs in the US (Gutkin and Curtis, 1999) and the UK

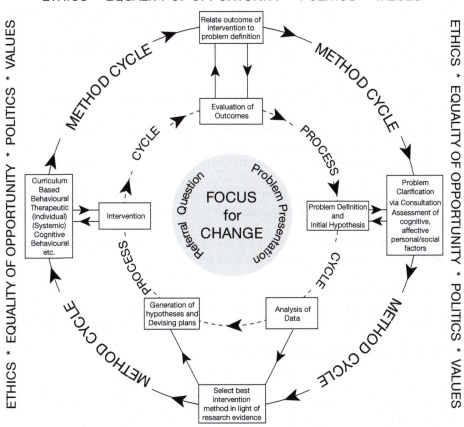

FIGURE 1.1 DECP framework for psychological assessment and intervention

Source: © British Psychological Society, *Professional Practice Guidelines*, 2002, Division of Educational and Child Psychology. Reproduced with permission of the British Psychological Society

(Woolfson *et al.*, 2003) utilise a closely similar set of stages. The psychologist in this case study used a six-stage problem analysis framework (Monsen and Frederickson, 2008; Annan *et al.*, 2013).

Lukasz case study

Phase 1: collect background information, clarify role and expectations

On one of the EP's regular visits to a primary school in south-east England, a special educational needs co-ordinator (SENCo) requested EP involvement for Lukasz, a 6-year-old pupil in her Year 1 class. She was concerned about both his learning and behaviour. She had been concerned about Lukasz for some time and had obtained written consent from his parents to consult the EP about him, in line with the BPS *Code of Ethics and Conduct* (BPS, 2006) and the HCPC *Standards of Conduct, Performance and Ethics* (HCPC, 2012). After an initial exploration of the level of concern and of strategies tried previously, it was agreed that this was an appropriate case for EP involvement.

During the initial consultation meeting, the main areas of concern highlighted were that Lukasz appeared to have difficulty in:

- initiating and sustaining verbal interaction with adults and peers in a range of social situations;
- engaging in turn-taking and sharing of learning materials with peers;
- communicating needs and views to adults and peers;
- behaving in a positive, non-disruptive manner within the classroom.

In addition, some background information was collected; for example, Lukasz lived with both his parents and two younger siblings, and the first language of the home was Polish.

At the end of this initial consultation meeting, it was agreed that an intervention would be considered successful if Lukasz could:

- sit on the carpet without distracting others;
- speak up more frequently within class and social settings;
- engage in appropriate turn-taking behaviour and share things with his peers.

Phase 2: initial guiding hypotheses

On the basis of the information collected from the consultation with the teacher, the EP begins to generate tentative initial guiding hypotheses, drawing both on the unique details of the presenting problem situation and the knowledge base within the discipline of psychology, as can be seen below:

1   Could a range of environmental contingencies be maintaining and reinforcing inappropriate social behaviour (Spence, 2003)?
2   Could there be insufficient motivational factors in class to encourage verbal interaction (Gresham *et al.*, 2001)?

3   Could Lukasz's expressive and receptive language skills in Polish and/or English be delayed (Conti-Ramsden and Botting, 2004)?
4   Could Lukasz's temperament predispose him to behave in a shy and introverted manner (Crozier and Alden, 2005)?
5   Could Lukasz's social problem-solving skills be delayed (Webster-Stratton and Reid, 2003)?
6   Could there be insufficient social opportunities for modelling/teaching of appropriate social behaviours (Spence, 2003)?
7   Could English as an additional language be a factor (Snow, 2002)?

Initial guiding hypotheses focus and direct subsequent assessment activities, the purpose of which is the collection of data to test the applicability and relevance of these hypotheses to the problem situation surrounding Lukasz. In this case, the EP and class teacher agreed that the EP would carry out structured classroom observations, arrange an interview with Lukasz's parents and conduct some assessments of language competencies and social cognition with Lukasz. The teacher agreed to keep a record of specific behaviours, together with information about events occurring before and after the behaviour, to help build up a picture of exactly when the difficult behaviours occurred.

Phase 3: identified problem dimensions

From the assessment information collected, the following were identified as the main features of relevance in understanding the situation for Lukasz:

1   There were insufficient motivational factors within the classroom context to encourage verbal interaction. The teacher tended to ask a series of questions, to which Lukasz could respond by nodding or shaking his head. Also, other pupils often responded on his behalf.
2   There was a range of environmental contingencies that appeared to be maintaining inappropriate social behaviour. From the behavioural record being kept by his teacher, it was apparent that her attention was often secured by disruptive behaviour, and that Lukasz was sometimes able to retain and use resources that he had snatched from others or refused to share with them.
3   Lukasz presented in many social situations as shy and reserved.
4   Lukasz's expressive language skills in Polish, as well as English, were below average for his age.
5   Lukasz's social skills and social problem-solving skills appeared delayed.

These aspects, along with strengths and assets, would be used to inform intervention planning. A particular relevant strength was Lukasz's good oral comprehension skills, despite some vocabulary difficulties and despite the fact that English was his second language.

Phase 4: problem analysis

This is the case conceptualisation or formulation that attempts to integrate the problem dimensions and represent relationships between them. In this case, it was argued that the following three within-pupil factors could all be acting to form barriers to Lukasz's social participation: shy personality, limited knowledge of what is appropriate within social situations, and delayed expressive language skills. It was expected that the limited level of social contact would further perpetuate Lukasz's difficulties by limiting opportunities for him to model and practise appropriate social skills (Spence, 2003).

In addition to these within-child factors, the lack of sufficient environmental factors to motivate Lukasz's oral communication (Gresham *et al.*, 2001) and the presence of environmental contingencies that reinforced competing inappropriate social behaviours (Spence, 2003) were contributing to the low occurrence of verbal social communication and the higher-than-average levels of inappropriate social behaviour. This can be represented visually on an *interactive factors framework* (IFF) (see Figure 1.2, in Method Box 1.1), which also assists in the formulation of intervention plans.

Phase 5: agreed action plan

Table 1.3 summarises the actions that were discussed and agreed in an intervention planning meeting between the EP, the class teacher, Lukasz's parents and the school SENCo, who is responsible for managing arrangements within the school to meet pupils' SEN. In addition, Lukasz's class teacher suggested that she might begin to explore available resources for supporting children's expressive language development, for example as provided by the local speech and language therapy service's website.

Phase 6: monitoring and evaluation of outcomes

Table 1.4 shows how outcomes were evaluated in relation to two intervention goals for Lukasz. It can be seen that the EP again interviewed the class teacher and again

TABLE 1.3 Agreed action plan for Lukasz

Priority problem dimensions	Objectives and actions
1 Social interaction and problem-solving skills	To teach explicitly appropriate responses in various social situations:
	Agreed action: Lukasz's class teacher and learning support assistant to develop an initial social story (Smith, 2003) for Lukasz, focused around 'sitting appropriately' for carpet time.
	To promote a positive and cooperative class environment to encourage socially appropriate behaviour:
	Agreed action: The EP and Lukasz's class teacher to have a follow-up consultation to share strategies and plan actions to promote cooperation in the classroom, including reviewing the whole class and Lukasz's individual behaviour management plan (See Webster-Stratton's framework for the Incredible Years' Teacher Classroom Management Programme; Webster-Stratton, 2011).
2 Expressive language in social situations	To increase the need for verbal communication by altering environmental contingencies:
	Agreed action: Lukasz's class teacher to work with the EP to agree strategies for communicating with Lukasz, e.g. how to give him attention for positive behaviour and for asking for things appropriately, and considering the use of questions with him (see Chapter 6).

METHOD 1.1

Interactive factors framework

The IFF (see Frederickson and Cline, 2009) was developed from the causal modelling framework (Morton and Frith, 1995; Morton, 2004). The IFF displays all of the problem dimensions identified, together with other relevant aspects of the problem situation for which there is evidence. The integrating hypothesis or hypotheses are shown via arrows indicating the connections between the behavioural, cognitive, affective, environmental and biological variables, as argued in the integrating statement. As can be seen from the dotted lines in Figure 1.2, the IFF diagram also represents the expected effects of suggested interventions on the priority problem dimensions.

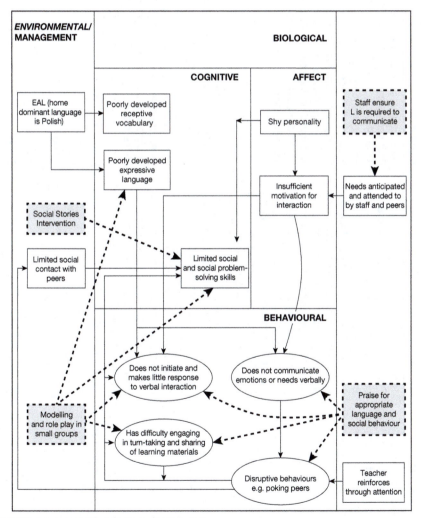

FIGURE 1.2 Interactive factors framework

TABLE 1.4 Evaluation of outcomes

Aims of intervention	Pre-intervention measures	Post-intervention measures	Interpretation
Sitting on carpet square with hands and feet to self (does not poke peers; socially appropriate response):	TME completed in teacher interview Pre-intervention (baseline): rated as a concern: 8 out of 10 Baseline descriptor: needs reminding constantly by TA and ends up being moved to sit by teacher in 4 morning carpet sessions out of 5; disrupts teaching and distracts other children. L pokes his peers: 'can't seem to keep himself to himself' Target set (expected): teacher rating of 4 (i.e. he may still need reminders and may be moved once a week)	TME completed in teacher interview Post-intervention: rated as a concern: 2 out of 10 Post-intervention descriptor: occasionally L needs a reminder, but generally he keeps his hands and feet to himself. He likes to sit on his square and has also found having something to hold a useful distractor – 'He does not poke his peers anymore'	L's targeted inappropriate behaviour was no longer a cause for concern L exceeded the initial target set for him
Increases frequency of verbal interaction in class with peers and teacher:	Teacher interviews Pre-intervention: 'L tends to be quiet in class. Compared with the rest of the class, he talks less to his peers and to me' Observation using interval sampling (with attempts at establishing social validity by observing L along with two randomly selected classmates, one girl (G) and one boy (B))	Teacher interview Post-intervention: 'L has begun to respond more to me, will initiate questions and answers and will talk about his work' Observation using interval sampling (with attempts at establishing social validity by observing L along with same two other pupils in class)	L has shown improvement in his targeted behaviour
Initiates conversation with teacher:	Pre-intervention: –L (0x) –G (2x) –B (1x)	Post-intervention: L (2x) G (7x) B (1x)	
Responds to teacher:	L (7x) G (17x) B (19x)	L (4x) G (1x) B (4x)	
Initiates conversation with peers:	L (1x) G (2x) B (1x)	L (13x) G (13x) B (11x)	

carried out observation in the classroom, using interval sampling (where the presence or absence of a particular target behaviour within each of a number of short time intervals is noted). In addition, the *target monitoring and evaluation* (TME) method was used. This approach was developed by Dunsmuir *et al.* (2009) as a method that could be used efficiently and effectively by EPs working through consultation in applied practice. TME allows practitioners to consider whether progress is as expected, better than expected or worse than expected, through the setting of 'specific measurable outcome descriptors that reflect the progress of an individual, group, agency or system receiving the intervention' (Dunsmuir *et al.*, 2009, p. 57). TME is well suited to negotiating 'hoped-for' outcomes for a particular child from a particular intervention, and also for reviewing perceived progress made. It can be used alongside other measures of progress, for example standardised scores on a checklist of a child's social skills. TME can be used in casework and also in the evaluation of a wider range of work, for example in the use of video interaction guidance with teaching assistants in secondary schools (Hayes *et al.*, 2011) and in the evaluation of CBT-based interventions for behaviour in schools (Brown *et al.*, 2012).

Although this is a thorough evaluation, concerns are often expressed that this is an aspect of educational psychology practice that is given insufficient attention (Leadbetter, 2000). Kratochwill and Stoiber (2000), writing in an American context, suggest that, owing to pressure of work, 'school psychologists may fall into "crisis routines", rather than follow systematic procedures for intervention planning, monitoring and evaluation' (p. 247). EPs have an ethical duty to evaluate the outcomes of advice given in supporting children and young people, so that effectiveness can be maximised and any unanticipated negative outcomes identified and rectified. In addition, successful work at the individual level can lead to invitations from schools to undertake organisational-level work that can efficiently impact on the learning and development of a larger number of pupils. For example, following the work with Lukasz, the EP was asked by the SENCo to deliver training on the social stories intervention approach to the whole staff. (More information on this can be found in Chapter 9.) The headteacher was very interested in the awareness the class teacher had developed about ways in which she and Lukasz's classmates had unwittingly been reinforcing undesirable behaviour. As a consequence, the EP was invited to a school senior management team meeting to discuss the possibility of carrying out a systems project in the school on 'behavioural awareness', involving staff and pupils. (More information on systems work by EPs at a whole-school level can be found in Chapters 8 and 13.)

EDUCATIONAL PSYCHOLOGISTS AS SCIENTIST–PRACTITIONERS

The central role of *hypothesis testing* in practice frameworks such as the problem analysis framework described above demonstrates how EPs function as scientist–practitioners. In keeping with other applied psychologists, this is a mantle that EPs have frequently aspired to adopt, often finding themselves acting as 'midwife' to the contribution of science to complex social problems (Lane and Corrie, 2006). Or, as Elliot (2000) puts it, 'the educational psychologist represents an important link between the worlds of academic psychology and education'.

At its simplest level, and a simplistic one at that, as it turns out, the term 'scientist–practitioner' might conjure up notions of an expert researcher, or an expert conversant with pertinent research, who is able to draw on this knowledge to advise others or engage directly in various activities designed to help others, especially those in some form of need. This was indeed a conceptualisation to which early practitioners attempted to adhere.

The origins of the scientist–practitioner

The idea of the applied psychologist as a scientist–practitioner originated from the Boulder Conference, held in Colorado in 1949, in an attempt to forge the identity of the new profession of clinical psychology, which was felt to be engaged in an 'erratic process of expansion'. Basically, this professional group was faced with a choice between allying itself somehow to psychiatry and other therapeutic approaches, or establishing itself as a separate profession, built upon academic and research-based psychology. As a result of that conference, it chose the latter.

No sooner had this decision been taken than a fundamental tension began to reveal itself, a pull between two positions that is still felt to this day and is exemplified by the two quotations in Focus Box 1.1 that illustrate extreme ends of a spectrum.

FOCUS 1.1

An example of a competing pull on the priorities of the applied psychologist as scientist–practitioner

We must be careful not to let social need interfere with scientific requirements.

(Eysenck, 1949)

Even after 15 years, few of my research findings affect much of my practice. Psychological science *per se* doesn't guide me one little bit . . . My clinical practice is the only thing that has helped me in my practice to date.

(Matarazzo, cited in Bergin and Strupp, 1972)

Further dilemmas and challenges for EPs as scientist–practitioners

Other tensions and competing pulls became apparent as EPs, who also adopted an identity as scientist–practitioners, attempted to develop this role and to deal with the increasing demands and expectations placed upon them by wider society (see Miller and Frederickson, 2006). Some of these issues, which recur in different forms throughout this book, are now briefly introduced.

Unidirectional or bidirectional influences?

In many successful fields of human endeavour, such as medicine and engineering, there is a well-established tradition that 'basic research' (in laboratories) informs 'applied research' (in 'simplified' field settings) that, in turn, after a period of development, informs professional practice (Tizard, 1990). Can we automatically assume that this unidirectional influence will also hold for psychology? Or might we equally, or more plausibly even, look to the everyday problems brought to the attention of applied psychologists as the starting points for the investigations of academic research psychologists? After all, the study of cases of acquired neurological problems has been valuable in learning about normal neurological processing (e.g. Shallice and Warrington, 1975), and the study of cases of atypical development in seeking to learn about normal development (e.g. Snowling and Hulme, 1989).

Generalisable results and idiographic problems

A major goal of psychological research is to arrive at a generalised account of some underlying psychological process or processes (Clarke, 2004). In order to do this, research is usually carried out with groups of participants where only a few 'variables' are subjected to study. For educational, and other applied, psychologists, the situations where their help is being sought – either with individuals, groups or organisations – are usually idiographic and complex in nature. Significant findings from group studies offer an indication of likely efficacy, not a prescription. For children and adolescents with all kinds of psychological problems, the 'best available' treatment does not work in up to one-third of cases, and some children deteriorate in response to intervention (Carr, 2000). Therefore, 'evidence-based practice' (see Chapter 2) is necessary, but not sufficient. EPs following the framework for evidence-based practice put forward by the APA (APA Presidential Task Force on Evidence-Based Practice, 2006) will not only take into account the available research around the efficacy of the intervention and the knowledge base in terms of psychological theory, but will also consider the context of the client and their own professional skills in recommending and devising interventions. These interventions will then be carefully monitored and evaluated so that the EP can be sure that they are not doing harm, as well as contributing to the collection of 'practice-based evidence' – what works, for whom, and in which context, in educational psychology practice (Fox, 2011; Maliphant et al., 2013).

The systemic context of individual problems

Individual problems of learning or development are typically embedded within a complex pattern of cause and effect, inside a system where changing one aspect can potentially affect others. This dynamic context means that interventions aimed at an individual may stand no chance of success if other interfering organisational features cannot also be controlled or modified. Traditionally, most academic research has been conducted outside such contexts, leading to possibly successful outcomes in the research context, but poor transfer into a child's everyday environment. Within developmental psychology, Bronfenbrenner (1974) argued that development should be studied in its ecological context and criticised 'the study of the strange behaviour of children in strange situations for the briefest possible period of time'. Instead, the developmental systems approach apparent in the bio-ecological model of human development incorporates investigation of *process* (activity engagement that promotes development), *personal* attributes of the people involved, the *context* in which development is taking place and *time* (see Bronfenbrenner and Morris, 2006). It promotes the use of structural equation modelling and other statistical techniques that have been developed to handle this kind of complexity.

Statistical sophistication is not the same as rigorous scientific method

Historically, EPs have been closely associated with the use of norm-referenced, psychometric tests – especially 'intelligence tests'. Although such tools appear to lend a high degree of sophistication to assessments, permitting fine discriminations to be made and the performance of individuals to be closely compared with that of much larger groups, they are not usually well suited to informing interventions or evaluating their impact. There have been repeated calls for more rigorous evaluation of interventions at both group and individual levels. At a group level, there is a demand for the systematic evaluation of local innovatory programmes and local implementations of national initiatives generated by an increasing focus on accountability requirements and evidence-based practice in education (Sebba, 2004, and see Chapter 2). The field of implementation science, which 'focuses on understanding the processes and factors related to successful integration of evidence based interventions in a specific type of setting, such as a school' (Forman *et al.*, 2013, p. 80), may have much to offer EPs involved in this type of work.

At an individual level, Kratochwill and Stoiber (2000) argue that, 'concerted effort should be given to developing viable resource tools that permit flexible and adaptable use of empirically supported interventions and that incorporate progress monitoring strategies as part of the evaluation process' (p. 247).

'Giving psychology away' – what if some people don't seem to want it?

Many EPs responded enthusiastically to George Miller's classic injunction to 'give psychology away' (Miller, 1969). The needs of young people were too many and too widespread, and the potential benefits to them, their teachers and parents too substantial not to adopt this approach. As an academic subject with practical applications, psychology was being incorporated into the training of teachers, social workers and childcare professionals. Likewise, many EPs appreciated the potential advantages of putting useful elements of their own knowledge and practice into the hands of, and then supporting, frontline professionals and parents who were in regular contact with young people. It came as a shock, therefore, to find that advice was sometimes not followed, and recommended interventions were not implemented. However, instead of construing these responses as 'non-compliance' or 'resistance', EPs were moved to an exploration of the barriers to the implementation of psychological advice and interventions, a field of study now often incorporated within the rubric of 'consultation' (Noell *et al.*, 2005; DuPaul *et al.*, 2006), but that could also be understood within the framework of implementation science (Forman *et al.*, 2013).

The 'political' context of EPs' work

A final challenge for EPs attempting to work as scientist–practitioners lies in the political context in which they operate, political in the sense that their time is a scarce resource that is inevitably distributed in favour of a few, however those particular recipients come to be selected. How EPs spend their time remains a preoccupation. In advising LAs on how to distribute their resources, both in terms of money and professional time, there is a danger that EPs can become seen or used by their employers and others as 'street level bureaucrats' (Lipsky, 1971). In the light of expectations such as these, it can take a determined effort from within the educational psychology profession itself in order to maintain and promote the benefits of practice as scientist–practitioners. Both the recognition of the centrality of psychological science in determining the EP role (Farrell *et al.*, 2006) and recent developments in the way that LAs are viewing the importance of evidence and research in determining resourcing and provision should be helpful in this regard: 'with politicians and senior managers insisting that they focus their funding on what works' (Allen and Hardy, 2013, p. 144), EPs are well placed to advise.

TRAINING AS AN EDUCATIONAL PSYCHOLOGIST

The requirements for HCPC registration to practise as an EP are: an undergraduate degree in psychology that confers the *graduate basis for chartered membership* (GBC) registration with the BPS, followed by a 3-year postgraduate programme of supervised training and practice accredited by the BPS. The arrangements for training in Scotland are different from those in the rest of the UK. In Scotland, two universities, Dundee and Strathclyde, offer a 2-year accredited Master's programme, following which trainee EPs obtain a post in an educational psychology service, accredited by the BPS to provide a final year of supervised practice leading to the BPS Qualification in Educational Psychology (Scotland) (stage 2). In England, Wales and Northern Ireland, 3-year doctoral training programmes are offered by the following higher-education institutions: Birmingham University, Bristol University, Cardiff University, Exeter University, the Institute of Education in London, Manchester University, Newcastle University, Nottingham University, Queens University Belfast, Sheffield University, Southampton University, the Tavistock Clinic in London, University College London and the University of East London.

Teaching experience is no longer a requirement for training as an EP in any part of the UK. However, the application process is highly competitive (a programme might typically receive 200 applications for ten funded places), and applicants are unlikely to be successful in obtaining an interview unless they can demonstrate relevant experience of working with children within educational, childcare or community settings. Examples of settings in which relevant experience is likely to be gained include work as: a graduate assistant in an educational psychology service, a school teacher, a learning support assistant, an educational welfare officer, a learning mentor, a speech and language therapist, a care worker or a worker in early years settings. Voluntary experience of various kinds over a number of years may assist applicants in demonstrating a breadth of relevant experience. Whatever kind of work has been done, universities will be primarily interested in what applicants have learned from their experiences that is relevant to work as an educational psychologist, and how they have been able to apply the knowledge of psychology gained through their first degree.

Funding is available through 3-year bursaries for educational psychology training in England, Wales and Northern Ireland. Readers who are interested in training as an educational psychologist are advised to visit the BPS website (www.BPS.org.uk), the DfE website (www.gov.uk/educational-psychology-funded-training-scheme) and the websites of the training providers listed above, for up-to-date information.

Educational psychology also has its own trade union, the Association of Educational Psychologists (AEP), and you will be able to find information on the AEP website (www.aep.org.uk) about a wide range of issues, including pay and conditions for EPs. The AEP, in collaboration with the publishers Taylor & Francis, also produces the most widely read UK professional journal for EPs, *Educational Psychology in Practice*, which you would be well advised to read if you are thinking of applying for educational psychology training.

The content of professional training as an EP

The course centres listed above all offer BPS-accredited training as a professional EP and, therefore, all offer, with distinctive individual variations, a 3-year programme that follows the BPS core curriculum for such training. Looking through the range of topics covered in this book, intended primarily for final-year undergraduates, the casual observer might wonder why a further 3 years of postgraduate study is necessary before a person can qualify to practise as an EP. To answer such a query, it must first be acknowledged that, owing to space constraints, these chapters are selective in their breadth of coverage and restricted in their depth of coverage. Second, there are many more school-focused topics requiring study than are covered in this volume. Examples include: working with pupils deemed to have attention deficit hyperactivity disorder, the special strengths and needs of deaf children, and working with the staff and students of schools that have experienced violent or tragic events. Finally, there are important areas of educational psychology practice that are not addressed in the rest of this book: for example, work specifically focused on the child below school age, on children in their families, on work with parents and carers in home and community settings, on work with multidisciplinary teams such as Child and Adolescent Mental Health Services, and on young people post-school or in the juvenile justice system.

However, training as an effective and highly skilled professional requires considerably more than an intensive period of advanced knowledge acquisition. This is only one of three strands of the BPS accreditation requirements; a minimum of 300 days supervised professional practice and a high level of research training are the other two. So, aspiring EPs spend 2 years placed within an educational psychology service, developing their problem-solving, consultation, assessment and intervention skills, as well as having to study advanced research methods and carry out a major piece of empirical research, in order to acquire and demonstrate the knowledge and skills expected from a postgraduate researcher.

Finally, all elements of the training will need to integrate, with the whole representing more than the sum of the parts. It is in the 2-year professional placements in particular that trainees are expected to demonstrate a high level of what might be termed 'professional artistry' (Schon, 1987) – interpersonal skills, agile problem-solving abilities and a self-questioning, reflective stance. No amount of knowledge can improve outcomes for a vulnerable child if this knowledge cannot be utilised appropriately, communicated effectively, tailored to the contexts and understandings of those in the best position to help and conceptualised within a set of values that are truly humanistic and person centred. This is what constitutes the training challenge – a challenge that, if met, places applied psychology in a position where it can make major contributions to the education, welfare and safety of all children and young people.

SUMMARY OF MAIN ISSUES ADDRESSED IN THIS CHAPTER

- Educational psychologists carry out a range of activities aimed at promoting the learning and development of children and young people through the application of psychology. They spend most time working with schools and other education providers, but also work in preschool settings, and with children and their families and with other agencies.
- The first EP in the UK was appointed in London in 1913 and fulfilled a broad role, including work with individual children experiencing problems and research and development work across the LA. However, there has long been a tension between providing detailed assessments of special educational needs for a small number of pupils and engaging in prevention, intervention and training that can benefit a whole school and wider community.
- The distinctive contribution of EPs derives from their specialist knowledge of psychology. However, their role, both historically and currently, has also been determined by political imperatives and the availability of other staff to carry out key functions.
- Educational psychologists' consultation, assessment and intervention work is carried out with regard to the BPS DECP professional practice guidelines. Underpinning these is a problem-solving process model that involves hypothesis generation and testing as a central activity.
- Like other applied psychologists, EPs are conceptualised as scientist–practitioners. A number of the tensions and issues surrounding this conceptualisation are identified and discussed.
- Professional training in educational psychology in the UK requires a 3-year undergraduate degree in psychology that confers graduate basis for chartered membership with the BPS, followed by a 3-year postgraduate programme of supervised training and practice approved by the HCPC.
- The title 'educational psychologist' is now a legally protected title, and all EPs must register with the HCPC, meeting standards of proficiency, conduct, performance and ethics, and for continuing professional development.

KEY CONCEPTS AND TERMS

- Educational psychology
- School psychology
- Hypothesis testing
- Problem solving
- British Psychological Society (BPS)
- Consultation
- Psychometric testing

- Statement of Special Educational Needs
- Education, Health and Care Plan
- Interactive factors framework (IFF)
- Target monitoring and evaluation (TME)

- Chartered status
- Graduate basis for chartered membership (GBC)
- Health and Care Professions Council (HCPC)

RECOMMENDATIONS FOR FURTHER READING

Journal articles

Annan, M., Chua, J., Cole, R., Kennedy, E., James, R., Markusdottir, I., Monsen, J., Robertson, L. and Shah, S. (2013). Further iterations on using the problem-analysis framework. *Educational Psychology in Practice*, *29*(1), 79–95.

Cameron, R.J. (2006). Educational psychology: The distinctive contribution. *Educational Psychology in Practice*, *22*(4), 289–304.

Books

BPS (2013). *British Educational Psychology: The first hundred years* (HoPC Monograph No. 1). C. Arnold and J. Hardy (eds). Leicester, UK: BPS Publications.

Farrell, P., Woods, K., Lewis, S., Rooney, S., Squires, G. and O'Connor, M. (2006). *A Review of the Functions and Contribution of Educational Psychologists in England and Wales in Light of 'Every Child Matters: Change for children'*. Nottingham, UK: DfES Publications.

Miller, A. and Frederickson, N. (2006). Generalisable findings and idiographic problems: Struggles and successes for educational psychologists as scientist-practitioners. In D. Lane and S. Corrie (eds), *The Modern Scientist–Practitioner: Practical approaches to guide how professional psychologists think*. London: Routledge.

Squires, G. and Farrell, P.T. (2007). Educational psychology in England and Wales. In S.R. Jimerson, T.D. Oakland and P.T. Farrell (eds), *The Handbook of International School Psychology*. London: SAGE, pp. 81–90.

Topping, K.J., Smith, E., Barrow, W., Hannah, E. and Kerr, C. (2007). Professional educational psychology in Scotland. In S.R. Jimerson, T.D. Oakland and P.T. Farrell (eds), *The Handbook of International School Psychology*. London: SAGE, pp. 339–50.

SAMPLE ESSAY TITLES

1   To what extent can EPs be described as scientist–practitioners?
2   Select any psychology course from the first two years of your degree and critically evaluate its applicability to educational psychology practice.
3   Identify any area of psychological theory and research that you think is relevant to the practice of educational psychology and that is not featured in a chapter of this book. Produce an up-to-date review of the literature in this area and outline its implications for educational psychology practice.

REFERENCES

Allen, A. and Hardy, J. (2013). The future of educational psychology. In C. Arnold and J. Hardy (eds), *Educational Psychology the first One Hundred Years*. HoPC Monograph No. 1. Leicester, UK: British Psychological Society.

Annan, M., Chua, J., Cole, R., Kennedy, E., James, R., Markúsdóttir, I., Monsen, J., Robertson, L. and Shah, S. (2013). Further iterations on using the problem-analysis framework. *Educational Psychology in Practice*, *29*(1), 79–95.

APA Presidential Task Force on Evidence-Based Practice (2006). Evidence-based practice in psychology. *The American Psychologist*, *61*(4), 271–85.

Association of Educational Psychologists (AEP) (2011). *The Delivery of Educational Psychology Services*. Durham, UK: AEP.

Bergin, A. and Strupp, H. (1972). *Changing Frontiers in the Science of Psychotherapy*. Chicago, IL: Aldine.

British Psychological Society (BPS) (2002). *Professional Practice Guidelines. Division of Educational and Child Psychology*. Leicester, UK: British Psychological Society.

British Psychological Society (BPS) (2006). *Code of Ethics and Conduct*. Leicester, UK: British Psychological Society.

Bronfenbrenner, U. (1974). Developmental research, public policy and the ecology of childhood. *Child Development*, *45*, 1–5.

Bronfenbrenner, U. and Morris, P.A. (2006). The bio-ecological model of human development. In R.M. Learner and W. Damon (eds), *Handbook of Child Psychology (6th edn): Vol 1, Theoretical Models of Human Development*. Hoboken, NJ: John Wiley, pp. 793–828.

Brown, E.L., Powell, E. and Clark, A. (2012). Working on what works: Working with teachers to improve classroom behaviour and relationships. *Educational Psychology in Practice*, *28*(1), 19–30.

Carr, A. (ed.) (2000). *What Works with Children and Adolescents? A critical review of psychological interventions with children, adolescents and their families*. London: Routledge.

Clarke, D.D. (2004). 'Structured judgement methods' – the best of both worlds? In Z. Todd, B. Nerlich, S. McKeown and D.D. Clarke (eds), *Mixing Methods in Psychology. The integration of qualitative and quantitative methods in theory and practice*. London: Routledge.

Conti-Ramsden, G. and Botting, N. (2004). Social difficulties and victimization in children with SLI at 11 years of age. *Journal of Speech, Language, and Hearing Research*, *47*(1), 145–61.

Crozier, R.W. and Alden, L.E. (2005). Introduction: the development of social anxiety. In R.W. Crozier and L.E. Alden (eds). *The Essential Handbook of Social Anxiety for Clinicians*. New York: Wiley, pp. 27–32.

DES (1968). *Psychologists in Education Services* (Summerfield Report). London: HMSO.

Department for Education (DfE) (2011). *Developing Sustainable Arrangements for the Initial Training of Educational Psychologists*. London: HMSO.

Department for Education (DfE) (2014). *Draft Special Educational Needs and Disability Code of Practice: 0 to 25 years. Statutory guidance for organisations who work with and support children and young people with special educational needs and disabilities*. London: HMSO.

Department for Education and Employment (DfEE) (2000). *Educational Psychology Services (England): Current role, good practice and future directions* (Report of the Working Group). London: HMSO.

Department of Health (2008). *Children and Young People in Mind: The final report of the National CAMHS Review*. Available online at http://webarchive.nationalarchives.gov.uk/2013 0107105354/http://www.dh.gov.uk/en/Publicationsandstatistics/Publications/Publications PolicyAndGuidance/DH_090399 (accessed 18 November 2014).

Dessent, T. (1988). Educational psychologists and the resource issue. In N. Jones and J. Sayer (eds), *Management and the Psychology of Schooling*. Lewes, UK: Falmer Press, pp. 73–88.

Dessent, T. (1992). Educational psychologists and the 'case for individual case work'. In S. Wolfendale, T. Bryans, M. Fox, A. Labram and A. Sigston, *The Profession and Practice of Educational Psychology: Future directions*. London: Cassell, pp. 34–48.

Dunsmuir, S., Brown, E., Iyadurai, S. and Monsen, J. (2009). Evidence-based practice and evaluation: From insight to impact. *Educational Psychology in Practice, 25*(1), 53–70.

Dunsmuir, S. and Kratochwill, T.R. (2013). From research to policy and practice: Perspectives from the UK and the US on psychologists as agents of change. *Educational and Child Psychology, 30*(3), 60–71.

DuPaul, G.J., Jitendra, A.K., Volpe, R.J., Tresco, K.E., Lutz, J.G., Junod, R.E.V., Cleary, K.S., Flammer, L.M. and Mannella, M.C. (2006). Consultation-based academic interventions for children with ADHD: Effects on reading and mathematics achievement. *Journal of Abnormal Child Psychology, 34*(5), 635–48.

Elliott, J. (2000). Editorial. Psychological influences upon educational interventions. *Educational and Child Psychology, 17*(3), 4–5.

Eysenck, H.J. (1949). Training in clinical psychology: An English point of view. *American Psychologist, 4,* 173–6.

Farrell, P., Woods, K., Lewis, S., Rooney, S., Squires, G. and O'Connor, M. (2006). *A Review of the Functions and Contribution of Educational Psychologists in England and Wales in Light of 'Every Child Matters: Change for children'*. Nottingham, UK: DfES Publications.

Forman, S.G., Shapiro, E.S., Codding, R.S., Gonzales, J.E., Reddy, L.A., Rosenfield, S.A. and Stoiber, K.C. (2013). Implementation science and school psychology. *School Psychology Quarterly, 28*(2), 77–100.

Fox, M. (2011). Practice-based evidence – overcoming insecure attachments. *Educational Psychology in Practice, (27)*4, 325–35.

Frederickson, N. and Cline, T. (2009). *Special Educational Needs, Inclusion and Diversity. A textbook* (2nd edn). Buckingham, UK: Open University Press.

Gillham, B. (1978). *Reconstructing Educational Psychology*. London: Croom Helm.

Gresham, F.M., Watson, T.S. and Skinner, C.H. (2001). Functional behavioural assessment: Principles, procedures, and future directions. *School Psychology Review, 30*(2), 156–72.

Gutkin, T.B. and Curtis, M.J. (1999). School-based consultation: Theory and practice. In C.R. Reynolds and T.B. Gutkin (eds), *The Handbook of School Psychology* (3rd edn). New York: Wiley.

Hayes, B., Richardson, S., Hindle, S. and Grayson, K. (2011). Developing teaching assistants' skills in positive behaviour management: An application of Video Interaction Guidance in a secondary school. *Educational Psychology in Practice, 27*(3), 255–69.

Health and Care Professions Council (HCPC) (2012). *Standards of Conduct, Performance and Ethics*. London: HCPC.

Kratochwill, T.R. and Stoiber, K.C. (2000). Empirically supported interventions and school psychology: Conceptual and practice issues – Part II. *School Psychology Quarterly, 15,* 233–53.

Lane, D. and Corrie, S. (eds) (2006). *The Modern Scientist–Practitioner: Practical approaches to guide how professional psychologists think*. London: Routledge.

Leadbetter, J. (2000). Patterns of service delivery in educational psychology services: Some implications for practice. *Educational Psychology in Practice, 16*(4), 449–60.

Lipsky, M. (1971). Street-level bureaucracy and the analysis of urban reform. *Urban Affairs Review, 6*, 391–409.

Macintosh, N.J. (ed.) (1995). *Cyril Burt: Fraud or framed?* Oxford, UK: Oxford University Press.

Maliphant, R. (1998). Educational psychology training: History and lessons from history. *Educational and Child Psychology, 50 years of professional training in educational psychology* (special edn), 17–26.

Maliphant, R., Cline, T. and Frederickson, N. (2013). Educational psychology practice and training: The legacy of Burt's appointment with the London County Council? *Educational and Child Psychology, 30*(3), 46–59.

Miller, A. and Frederickson, N. (2006). Generalisable findings and idiographic problems: Struggles and successes for educational psychologists as scientist–practitioners. In D. Lane and S. Corrie (eds), *The Modern Scientist–Practitioner: Practical approaches to guide how professional psychologists think*. London: Routledge.

Miller, G. (1969). On turning psychology over to the unwashed. *Psychology Today, 3*(7), 53–4, 66–8, 70, 72, 74.

Monsen, J.J. and Frederickson, N. (2008). The problem analysis framework: A guide to decision making, problem solving and action within applied psychological practice. In B. Kelly, L. Wolfson and J. Boyle (eds), *Frameworks for Practice in Educational Psychology: A textbook for trainees and practitioners*. London: Jessica Kingsley.

Morton, J. (2004). *Understanding Developmental Disorders: A causal modelling approach*. Oxford, UK: Blackwell.

Morton, J. and Frith, U. (1995). Causal modelling: A structural approach to developmental psychopathology. In D. Cilchette and D.J. Cohen (eds), *Manual of Developmental Psychopathology* (vol. 1). New York: Wiley, pp. 357–90.

National College for Teaching and Leadership (NCTL) (2013). *Educational Psychology Workforce Survey 2012*. London: HMSO.

Noell, G.H., Witt, J.C., Slider, N.J., Connell, J.E., Gatti, S.L., Williams, K.L., Koenig, J.L., Resetar, J.L. and Duhon, G.J. (2005). Treatment implementation following behavioural consultation in schools: A comparison of three follow-up strategies. *School Psychology Review, 34*(1), 87–106.

Pearson, L. and Howarth, I.C. (1982). Training professional psychologists. *Bulletin of the British Psychological Society, 35*, 375–6.

Quicke, J. (1982). *The Cautious Expert*. Milton Keynes, UK: Open University Press.

Rushton, J.P. (2002). New evidence on Sir Cyril Burt: His 1964 speech to the Association of Educational Psychologists. *Intelligence, 30*, 555–67.

Scottish Executive (2002*). Review of Provision of Educational Psychology Services in Scotland*. Edinburgh, UK: Scottish Executive Education Department.

Schon, D. (1987). *Educating the Reflective Practitioner*. San Francisco, CA: Jossey Bass.

Sebba, J. (2004). Developing evidence-informed policy and practice in education. In G. Thomas and R. Pring (eds), *Evidence-Based Practice in Education*. Maidenhead, UK: Open University Press/McGraw-Hill Education, pp. 34–43.

Shallice, T. and Warrington, E.K. (1975). Word recognition in a phonemic dyslexic patient. *Quarterly Journal of Experimental Psychology, 27*(2), 187–99.

Sheridan, S.M., Welch, M. and Orme, S.F. (1996). Is consultation effective: A review of outcome research. *Remedial and Special Education, 17,* 341–54.

Smith, C. (2003). *Writing and Developing Social Stories.* Bicester, UK: Speechmark.

Snow, C.E. (2002). Second language learners and understanding the brain. In A.M. Galaburda, S.M. Kosslyn and C. Yves (eds), *The Languages of the Brain.* Cambridge, MA: Harvard University Press, pp. 151–65.

Snowling, M. and Hulme, C. (1989). A longitudinal case study of developmental phonological dyslexia. *Cognitive Neuropsychology, 6*(4), 379–401.

Spence, S.H. (2003). Social skills training with children and young people: Theory, evidence and practice. *Child and Adolescent Mental Health, 8*(2), 84–96.

Tizard, B. (1990). Research and policy: Is there a link? *The Psychologist, 3,* 435–40.

Truong, Y. and Ellam, H. (2014). *Educational Psychology Workforce Survey. Research Report 2013.* National College for Teaching and Leadership. London: HMSO.

Webster-Stratton, C. (2011). *The Incredible Years. Parents, Teachers and Children's Training Series. Program content, methods, research and dissemination, 1980–2011.* Seattle, WA: Incredible Years.

Webster-Stratton, C. and Reid, J.M. (2003). Treating conduct problems and strengthening social and emotional competence in young children: The dinosaur treatment programme. *Journal of Emotional and Behavioural Disorders, 11*(3), 130–43.

Wood, A. (1998). Okay then: What do EPs do? *Special Children, May,* 11–13.

Woolfson, L., Whaling, R., Stewart, A. and Monsen, J.J. (2003). An integrated framework to guide educational psychologist practice. *Educational Psychology in Practice, 19*(4), 283–302.

2 Evidence-based practice in educational psychology

The nature of the evidence

Anthea Gulliford

CHAPTER SUMMARY

The chapter begins by exploring the term evidence-based practice, *raised in Chapter 1, and reviews a number of challenges to the notion, particularly as they relate to applied psychology. The journey from* evidence *to* practice *will lead us to consider the nature of the methods used in the generation of evidence bases for applied educational psychology and to touch upon different* paradigms *of knowledge. A distinction is drawn between the evidence available through controlled methods and through exploratory qualitative methods, and the extent to which researchers wish to understand the effects of an intervention versus the mechanisms of change it involves. A review of methodological considerations will lead to a particular focus upon single-case experimental designs (SCEDs), before consideration of the way in which qualitative approaches may illuminate questions faced by educational psychologists. The chapter offers this overview of methodological approaches in research evidence in order to assist with critical evaluation of some of the evidence presented later in this volume.*

LEARNING OUTCOMES

When you have studied this chapter, you should be able to:

1 explain the origins and key features of 'evidence-based practice';
2 identify some of the key critical challenges to the evidence-based practice approach;
3 understand the relationship of scientific methods to evidence-based practice knowledge bases;
4 explain the role of qualitative approaches to research in contributing to the knowledge base for educational psychology;
5 explain the key features of SCED methods;
6 critically evaluate the evidence underpinning practice in later chapters in this volume.

INTRODUCTION

Educational psychology, as we saw in Chapter 1, has long debated its precise identity. It has, arguably, been clearer about its *function*, namely the support for any area of a child's development, in any context, but this can sometimes translate into questions about role and activities. A further area of interrogation for professional educational psychology is that of the paradigms to which the profession wishes to affiliate itself. As Chapter 1 explored, the *scientist–practitioner* model comes with some challenges for this branch of applied psychology. Enquiry here revolves around the following questions:

• How can the notion of evidence-based practice inform the work of an educational psychologist?
• Upon what epistemological and methodological foundations are the knowledge bases for educational psychology practice built?

These questions will be explored below, drawing upon themes from Chapter 1 and pointing to evidence presented in later chapters in this volume. The questions will take us from a traditional, *post-positivist* view of scientific methods to one that can be described as *post-modern*. Although many allied topics of relevance lie on the periphery of this journey, such as questions of *epistemology* and ontology, these cannot be explored in depth here, but readers may feel encouraged to undertake further exploration through studying the recommendations for further reading at the close of the chapter, through Robson (2011), for example.

EVIDENCE-BASED PRACTICE

Evidence–based practice is a phrase with resonance in the provision of social policy and its underpinning practices. Originating in the field of health, the term has grown in significance for applied psychologists, with an ever greater focus upon accountability within public services bringing questions about *what* interventions are likely to work best, and *for whom*, and therefore *why* (Frederickson, 2002; Spring, 2007; Lilienfeld *et al.*, 2013). Its aim, at the outset, was to generate systematic and reliable insights regarding what constituted the likely *efficacy* of an intervention in a given field, for example, medications of choice for particular populations identified with common ailments (Cochrane and Fellowship, 1972; Pring and Thomas, 2004). Evidence-based practice aspired to overcome the local and national variations whereby practitioners' professional decision-making might be driven by personal preference, anecdotal report or local cultures of practice, where the artefact of historical accident might determine whether patients received particular treatments. Instead, through the systematic analysis of evidence drawn from accumulations of randomised controlled trials (RCTs), the likely *efficacy* of particular interventions for particular populations can be delineated, and, in turn, a practitioner is enabled to make decisions based upon judgements regarding the best available evidence. The *evidence* in question was, at the outset, presumed to be the kind of evidence that described the outcomes of interventions. This focus, it was argued, was pivotal in evidence-based practice precisely because *the effects* of an intervention, for example a medication or a psychological therapy, needed to be made clear. Increasingly, practitioners and researchers drew attention to the question of the various *processes* involved in delivering those effects. Were they not as important to capture, when attempting to explain the journey from problem to solution? This question is one that we shall explore further below.

Unless a strong protocol is applied when journeying from evidence to practice, there are hazards whereby well-intentioned practitioners may inadvertently adapt their practice according to the findings of a recent study, slipping towards incidental or accidental choices. The possible threats to *internal validity* contained in a study can be overlooked at the expense of the well-known human preference (on the part of researcher and practitioner) for significant findings (Kirkham *et al.*, 2010; Button *et al.*, 2013). Countering this, and at its heart, the evidence-based-practice pathway seeks to employ meta-analytic approaches, *systematic reviews* of evidence that are aggregated either numerically or qualitatively (Petticrew and Roberts, 2008; Petticrew *et al.*, 2013). The systematic review of studies allows key features of context to be identified, together with an overview of the methods used, and aggregation of data, ideally with an understanding and awareness of the implications of statistical analysis, including effect size, for aggregating evidence (Moher *et al.*, 2009). One approach to systematic evidence review that has proved useful in professional educational psychology is Gough's (2007) weight of evidence model. Gough advises working through a number of criteria by which to evaluate each study included in a review: (a) the methodological *quality* of the study *on its own terms*; (b) the methodological *relevance* of a study for the question being addressed by the reviewer – for example, whether the study contains the methods that are likely to illuminate the question; (c) the *relevance* of the *topic* and research question for the systematic reviewer's question; leading to (d) an *overall* weighting of a study's evidence quality for the review.

Despite the approach's aim of enhancing effective professional practices, evidence-based practice has faced many theoretical critiques (Hammersley, 2005; Nevo and Slonim-Nevo, 2011). To begin with, the processes developed by Cochrane and colleagues rely heavily upon traditional perspectives of 'scientific' endeavour, where

Evidence-based practice in educational psychology

As an example of research aiming to secure a clear picture of the effects of a commonly used intervention, and to link those effects with a hypothesised theoretical mechanism, Frederickson *et al.* (2005) undertook a study evaluating the effects of a 'Circle of Friends'(CoF) intervention with pupils in mainstream school. CoF is a peer intervention, designed to draw together a problem-solving, peer-support group around a focus pupil, who may have additional needs, in order to promote their educational and social inclusion. The approach is popular in many quarters and can be found in the practice of educational psychologists, particularly those aiming to support the inclusion of pupils in mainstream school who may experience difficulties in social or behavioural functioning, for example with autism (see Chapter 9).

Evidence from a controlled study by Frederickson *et al.* (2005), however, suggested that, although the CoF intervention enhanced social 'acceptance' and decreased 'rejection' on sociometric measures immediately following an initial whole-class meeting of the CoF group, there seemed to be a later fall-off in social acceptance levels and a return towards normal levels of social 'rejection'. This finding, of the diminution of effects over time, was replicated in a further investigation using single-case methods (see below) by James (2011). This work again highlighted that more needed be done to maintain the CoF intervention over time, if any gains made in the initial phase were to be developed.

In terms of evidence-based practice, the study by Frederickson *et al.* (2005) modelled neatly how the interventions that hold intuitive appeal and that often prove popular with school staff struggling with vulnerable pupils require the close scrutiny and measurement by enquiring investigators to explore the favoured practice, to understand both its effects and how to optimise delivery.

FOCUS 2.1

a notion of objective, deductive methods predominates. The 'hierarchy of methods', often cited, underpins evidence-based practice, giving precedence to positivist, fixed experimental designs, and less weight to those designs founded upon 'softer' approaches, as it was argued (Ramey and Grubb, 2009):

- systematic reviews of several RCTs or group studies;
- single RCTs;
- quasi–experiments;
- case studies;
- expert opinion.

The activities implied by evidence-based practice, of evaluating research evidence quality, have therefore been dominated by a positivist–empiricist view of scientific endeavour, allied to epistemologies and methods that aim to discern *causal* associations and explanations (Shadish *et al.*, 2001). This position depends upon a *positivist epistemology* and on research activities involving *objectivity*, allowing for consensus upon measurement and for *nomothetic, realist* explanations, described as *modernist* (Ramey and Grubb, 2009). As we saw in Chapter 1, evidence-based practice was the inevitable consequence of applied psychology's affiliation with the scientist–practitioner model (Dilillo and Mcchargue, 2007). Yet the precepts in the *hierarchy of evidence* reverberate across the profession of educational psychology, creating both consensus and fragmentation (Frederickson, 2002; Fox, 2003; Miller *et al.*, 2008; Burnham, 2013).

In its demand for causal associations and explanations, evidence-based practice risks the charge of reductionism, through mutating complex research narratives into quantification for the purposes of comparisons of 'effect'. Extensive debate can be found upon this issue (Oakley, 2002; Hammersley, 2005), with many authors arguing for '*softer*' types of evidence to be included in reviews of evidence. The concern relates to the extent to which studies are able to identify the relevant contextual variables that contribute to the successes or failures of an intervention: in their core processes, the evidence-based-practice models obscure, the arguments goes, the key features of contexts and interventions that contribute to the causal inferences being drawn (Hammersley, 2005; Schraw and Patall, 2013). If a 'what works' paradigm is adopted (Carr, 2013), there may be a focus on *outcomes* at the expense of insights into the *mechanisms* involved in the *processes of change*.

In respect of this concern, as noted above, much consideration has been given to the question of what information *does* constitute evidence. There have been questions as to whether evidence-based-practice approaches can sustain the necessary theorising for developments in a field. Research has an important role to play in 'learning about' the intervention, as much as about the *effects* of the intervention itself, it is argued (Petticrew *et al.*, 2013). Paving the way for this notion, in traditional scientific methods, is the problem of 'treatment integrity' and its often-noted absence from empirical research accounts (Hagermoser Sanetti and Fallon, 2011). Description of an intervention's core features is essential to allow for comparison and replication, as well as for the generation of theoretically explanatory accounts regarding the mechanisms of an intervention. This is critical in complex applied contexts such as education, where the goal is, ultimately, to enhance positive outcomes for children and young people. Controlled studies that do give robust accounts of intervention features, and their relationship to the psychosocial context in which they were delivered, are rare.

An alternative view, however, more likely to be presented by researchers from *qualitative* traditions, explicitly positions such features as central to the research account – the details of interventions, as *perceived* by those delivering them, and their *contingencies* with the environment in which they are implemented – capturing, rather than controlling or reducing, their complexity (Stufflebeam, 2003; Ling, 2012). Proponents of 'soft' evaluation, of 'implementation science' and of some mixed-methods studies have argued that quantitative insights must, at very least, be supplemented by qualitative ones, precisely in order to supply the critical details of the relationship of the intervention to its ecology (Palinkas and Aarons, 2011; Cook and Odom, 2013). A broad history of evaluation research stands behind such ideas, with very different goals from those of RCTs. Whereas an empiricist view of evaluation methods has seen their core function as identifying cause and effect (Ling, 2012), for others, *evaluation* methods have held at their heart the need to gain insight into the participant perceptions and give accounts of environmental detail coloured by *postmodern* epistemology (Koenig, 2009). More recently, *realistic evaluation* (Pawson and Tilley, 1997; Pawson and Greenhalgh, 2005) has gained momentum in theoretical popularity, as an approach aiming to identify and pattern the relationships between the mechanism of an intervention, its context and its outcome, and, in doing so, appearing to offer the best of both worlds, through striving for causal explanations that are specific to the context of study, but avoiding fully *nomothetic* explanations. In order to do this, the positivist *realist ontology* of science is softened to *critical realism*, which allows both for measurement and subjective inferences (Clegg, 2005).

Chapter 1 explored a number of pathways to evidence-based practice, through the use of problem-solving frameworks that aim to systematise the selection of evidence. To enhance the legitimacy and validity of the evidence-based-practice process, a research-to-practice sequence is suggested by Schraw and Patall (2013), a *policy*-driven approach that involves scrutiny of evidence by expert (and varied) groups, and the application of criteria for valid causal inference. The proposed sequence involves 'generating data, aggregating data, summarizing aggregated data into prioritized EBP strategies, and implementing and evaluating those strategies in the field in conjunction with stakeholders' (Schraw and Patall, 2013, p. 346). Such an approach, showing collegiality in its steps to analysis and implementation, is demonstrated in the work of many national policy units, and these scrutiny processes do something to bring the traditional evidence-based-practice movement closer to the world of the practitioner and, indeed, to the consumers and the policymakers of services (Cartwright *et al.*, 2009), while also enhancing the robustness of quality controls in the evidence-based-practice process.

The translation of evidence into practice requires the unique skills *of practitioners* in delivering interventions, and, when the translation of ideas from *theoretical evidence* to *applied practice* is considered, evidence-based practice has been criticised for potentially undermining the intuitive skills of the practitioner (Nevo and Slonim-Nevo, 2011). Models that quantify data, it has been argued, overlook the contribution of the practitioner in interpreting and delivering interventions. Included in this is the practitioner's therapeutic rapport skill in their work, known to be a significant contributor to the client's or recipient's perception of, and response to, an intervention (APA Presidential Task Force on Evidence-Based Practice, 2006). It has been noted that practice might be evidence-*led*, but that other factors will influence policy and practice developments, including *values* that influence delivery of interventions, and policy-planning developments (Wilcox, 2003). A further dilemma for practice that aims to be evidence based is that where the evidence is communicated in such a way as to obscure the practical implications of a theoretical finding, the translational pathway from 'laboratory' to 'clinic' is obscured (Dozois, 2013).

Other concerns focus upon 'client' or recipient characteristics, which are likely to vary from those reported in studies, despite attempts by original authors to describe external validity (Callahan *et al.*, 2013). The RCT, or group design, carries the difficulty that individual response to interventions is masked by the dependence of such designs upon measures of central tendency – average effects obscure those details that are needed in order to gain insight into the likely effects of an intervention for individuals or for the population from which they are drawn (Smith, 2013).

Meta-analyses, in this view, only compound the problem, through aggregation. In short, statistical inference is a solution to many questions, but generates many others for the practitioner. Larger samples, which contribute to greater internal and external validity and statistical power in a study, obscure relevant detail regarding *individual* characteristics (Callahan *et al.*, 2013), and it has been noted, for example, that minority populations may be less well-represented in studies (Sue and Zane, 2006; Ramey and Grubb, 2009). Although studies may seek to describe sample characteristics closely, those features of an individual that are relevant to functioning or to responding to an intervention may go obscured, or unrecorded, and this can be a fundamental issue for intervention programmes.

EVIDENCE IN PRACTICE

In reality, within applied journals, caution regarding the external validity of findings is not rigidly articulated, with journals requiring 'recommendations for practice' from authors, for example (Vaughn and Fuchs, 2013). It is all too easy for authors to omit the qualifiers that curtail the implications of their studies, or for practitioners to assume that the most recent piece of evidence is the most reliable or most pertinent. Rather than using the careful evidence selection processes described in Chapter 1, professionals may appear to adopt theoretical preferences (Fox, 2011). In order to overcome dispositional biases, training programmes in applied psychology must ensure skills in data scrutiny (Bauer, 2007; Schraw and Patall, 2013), and, for UK educational psychologists now trained under doctoral arrangements, the review of large datasets through systematic review or meta-analysis is a core skill (Dunsmuir and Kratochwill, 2013). The extent to which practitioners employ those skills in guiding their own judgements of the evidence in relation to casework activity is a question that requires further investigation (Annan and Priestley, 2011).

An overarching concern regarding the notion of evidence-based practice is the extent to which its precepts can encompass the long chains of correlation or causality found in circumstances other than direct medical intervention, from whence the paradigm originated (Kelly *et al.*, 2010). This question is explored by Kelly and colleagues in relation to public health policy, which draws upon evidence linking across domains: for example, from social interaction (GP–patient), to patient behaviour (patient uptake of advice), to health outcomes (measurable patient well-being). Each domain, we might argue, depends upon different modes of measurement and must be only cautiously and carefully linked. Transposed to the field of education, the linking of input variables to outcome variables becomes even more complex (Cartwright *et al.*, 2009), where very often the interventions being studied may have longer chains of causation or correlation than can easily be captured within a controlled study. An example of this complexity in studying complex social processes when intervening to support pupils in educational contexts is given in Focus Box 2.2.

Despite the increased presence of systematic reviews in the professional literature, the relationship of evidence to practice may continue to be variable, with indications throughout professional educational psychology that practice moves on apace, followed by the search for evidence. An example of this is seen in the domain of solution-focused (SF) practice. SF approaches aim to support client change, through working through

FOCUS 2.2

Generating evidence: the case of Circles of Adults

Despite the articulated role for educational psychologists in supporting evidence-based practices in the world of education (Frederickson, 2002), there are other examples of interventions that are popular among educational psychologists, but that may not have underpinnings in research evidence (Styles, 2011). In viewing some of these, the task of rigorous investigation appears highly complex.

Circles of Adults (CoAs) (Newton and Wilson, 2006) is an approach used to guide adults through a group problem-solving process. It can help staff involved in supporting a student who is experiencing difficulties within the school setting, or beyond, by guiding them through a problem-solving sequence aiming to enhance their insights into the pupil's needs and possible adaptations to provision. It is an approach with some popularity, but with only anecdotal evidence published as yet in terms of its *outcomes* (Bennett and Monsen, 2011). Recent unpublished research has begun to explore and address this concern. CoA is hypothesised to be based on a number of core mechanisms, akin to those of *other* problem-solving and staff-sharing processes, identified from exploratory case studies, such as Bozic and Carter's (2002). Explorations of participant perceptions of other similar group processes have indicated that participating staff find it helpful to be part of a *support group* and *receive emotional containment through the process*; to expand their *understanding of the young person's background and needs*; to enhance the *hypotheses they bring as explanations regarding a young person's needs*; and to *amplify the potential solutions and ways forward in working with the young person*.

As the process aims to help with the inclusion of children in school, it is important that its *efficacy* is investigated, in line with that of other approaches to supporting collaborative problem-solving (Jones *et al.*, 2013). Should the *mechanisms* within the *process* be the focus of attention? Or, in line with the 'what works' movement, is the greatest imperative to understand whether or not the process results in changes in *pupil outcomes*? If the latter, how can causal inferences be confidently drawn between a problem-solving group process among adults and effects upon pupil functioning, where many intervening variables (threats to internal validity) will occur? Some of these issues have been noted as methodological concerns in respect of person-centred planning approaches of this kind, elsewhere in the literature (e.g. Holburn, 2002).

Using exploratory interpretative methods (Interpretative Phenomenological Analysis), which allowed a fine-grained investigation of the experiences of young people and adults, Dawson (2013) noted the capacity of the CoA process to heighten adult perceptions of pupil need in schools, apparently influencing interactional dynamics between adults and student. Syme (2011) investigated the causal pathways between the CoA process and pupil outcomes through case studies incorporating controlled single-case experiments (see below). One key finding was that the influence of extraneous factors in the pupil's life, beyond the control of the CoA process, was so great as to create a threat to any potential explanatory causal pathways between the CoA and pupil outcomes. This, nevertheless, highlighted the importance of a strong consideration of 'risk factors' for a pupil, within the process.

Both Syme (2011) and Dempsey (2012) (through a quasi-experimental design) reviewed the effects of the CoA upon teacher *causal attributions* (see Chapter 10), with the former noting some effects, but the latter none. Both authors noted the difficulties in reliable measurement of key variables and in securing sufficient *power* to support the investigation. They also found no significant effects of the process upon *teacher self-efficacy*.

Such studies illustrate the importance of close investigation of the *mechanism* and processes likely to optimise behaviour change, while also illustrating and illuminating the difficulties for a researcher involved in the analysis of causal pathways around complex social processes. It is helpful to be reminded of the ethos statement of the Evidence-Based Practice Unit: 'All research is provisional. All research raises as many questions as it answers' (Anna Freud Centre, 2014).

FOCUS 2.2 *continued*

careful reviews of the narrative constructed by an individual around their current experience (*problem-free talk*), their possible goals (*miracle question*) and elicitation of perceptions upon the narrative elements and upon possible and preferable futures (*scaling*). Evidence of the popularity of SF approaches in practice is to be found in many quarters (Redpath and Harker, 1999; Burns and Hulusi, 2005; Stobie, 2005). A systematic review of the effects of the SF approach, however (Bond *et al.*, 2013), identified relatively low levels of evidence of positive outcomes for children and young people. Tentative conclusions are offered by these authors regarding the possible positive effects of the approach upon internalising and externalising behaviours in children and young people. In this example, practice is ahead of the evidence in terms of popularity, usage and, possibly, confidence. Anecdotal practitioner evidence suggests that, when combined with the wider professional skill set of an applied psychologist in working with those around a vulnerable young person, SF approaches can have successes. However, the evidence, analysed through a meta-analytic framework, is only partial at this stage. Bond and colleagues identify the need for more evidence: for the practitioner, the challenge is to generate greater *practice-based evidence*, potentially using single-case examples, and the challenge for the researcher is to develop approaches that allow such a complex and individualised approach to be evaluated through group designs.

In contrast to the example above, a further example, in Focus Box 2.3, illustrates a phenomenon whereby practice in educational psychology and recent evidence now appear to be 'on the same page' regarding interventions for children and young people described as having Attention Deficit and Hyperactivity Disorder (ADHD).

Practice and ADHD: the need for evidence

For many years, assessment, diagnosis and intervention in respect of children and young people with high levels of activity, impulsivity or challenging behaviour have been an area of significant contention (Divoky and Schrag, 1975; Visser and Jehan, 2009). Whereas, from the perspective of psychiatry, a child showing high levels of difficult behaviour may merit consideration of a diagnosis of ADHD, practitioners in educational psychology have tended to be aware of the potency of *psychosocial* environments for child development and behaviour and, therefore, of the impact of the educational and familial environments upon behaviour at any given time. This has led to less confidence in assessments of behaviours as being pervasive across all domains of a child's life, and in the more categorical and diagnostic approaches taken by clinical staff.

This critical perspective regarding diagnosis leads in turn to questions regarding the prevalent use of medication to 'treat' children and young people with ADHD, particularly as stimulant medication is known to carry the risk of long-term side-effects. Consonant with the profession's remit of supporting functioning in context, educational psychologists have in any case focused on approaches to behaviour management, underpinned by various paradigms (see Chapter 10), but above all with a strong ecological focus.

The available evidence indicates that psychosocial interventions for ADHD do indeed have the likelihood of good efficacy (Evans *et al.*, 2013). A systematic review of treatments for adolescents with a diagnosis of ADHD (Sibley *et al.*, 2014) highlights that, although medication and behavioural therapy (interventions) combined are likely to bring gains for a young person, behavioural therapy alone offers *greater* efficacy. The US authors note that this contradicts the guidance of the American Academy of Pediatrics and the American Academy of Child and Adolescent Psychiatry, where stimulant medication is the recommended treatment.

FOCUS 2.3

For some, the answer to these dilemmas, and others, is to describe the process as 'evidence-informed practice' (Nevo and Slonim-Nevo, 2011), signalling by this the softer approach to adoption of evidence in practice, an approach that embraces the skills, the varied knowledge bases and, above all, the creativity of the practitioner.

DEVELOPING THE EVIDENCE: EXPERIMENTAL METHODS

Applied research must, by its very nature, sacrifice the control achieved in the laboratory. In the 1960s, traditional scientific method was supported in its complex transition to the applied world, where multiple variables defy easy rational control, by *post-positivist* methods (Shadish *et al.*, 2001), which allow for robust accounts of the *threats to internal validity* (Cook and Odom, 2013) to be thoroughly described in reports of research seeking causal explanations. In addition, to enable the high reliability of studies in the natural world, there is a need for thorough and close descriptions of populations under study, sampling procedures, random allocation to groups (Torgerson and Torgerson, 2001) and treatment integrity, as a minimum (Flay *et al.*, 2005).

Accounts of experimental methods in research *by* educational psychologists were rarer until recent times (Miller and Frederickson, 2006). This picture has evolved since the inception of doctoral training in educational psychology, however, with increasing instances of practitioner studies employing group-controlled designs available (Rodgers and Dunsmuir, 2013; Squires and Caddick, 2012; Lamb and Gulliford, 2011; Cole *et al.*, 2012). The context for such studies, together with the resource restrictions faced by practitioner–researchers, often means that a significant challenge is that of recruiting sufficient participants, leading to low power overall in the final statistical inferences (Button *et al.*, 2013). However, the *ecological validity* (Burns, 2011) of such studies, that is, their relationship to, and significance for, the real world is arguably enhanced through their applied nature, deriving from local contexts, from which the researcher can extract insights, often through mixed-methods studies (Frost *et al.*, 2010; Symonds and Gorard, 2010). To overcome the challenges of group designs, research and practice-based evidence relevant to educational psychology can be drawn from single-case designs, an approach possibly underused in the UK.

DEVELOPING THE EVIDENCE: THE SPECIAL CASE OF SINGLE-CASE EXPERIMENTAL DESIGNS

Despite an important focus upon *universal* and, therefore, *preventive* work (Burns, 2011), educational psychology is very often concerned with the development of atypical populations: for example, children and young people with autistic-spectrum needs, or those who show challenging behaviour, are among the key client groups for many educational psychologists (Odom *et al.*, 2005; Kratochwill *et al.*, 2012). Inter-individual variance within such populations renders the generation of practice-based evidence through group designs a significant difficulty. The quest for evidence here leads us towards the study of single (or a few) cases. An opportunity to join this quest with the principles of post-positivist, modernist scientific thought presents itself in SCED methods.[1]

---

1 Synonyms include *single-subject* and *single-participant* experiments. In the US, *brief-experimental-analysis* approaches have also been adopted, which are less formal than the methods described here, but have a similar aim.

Despite the tendency to assume the primacy of group methods in psychological research, the origins of psychological research and theory are founded upon single-subject interrogations of a question, which played a role in the investigations of operant conditioning in the 1950s and 1960s (Kazdin, 2011). Retrospective *case study* methods have a limited capacity to generate scientifically plausible evidence regarding the association of any change detected in an individual with any features of an intervention they might be receiving. Kazdin (2011) highlights the question of psychotherapy as an example, where controlled measurement was warranted in order to boost the causal explanations people wished to attach to various forms of intervention, historically.

The insight giving rise to single-case methods was the notion that, rather than grappling with the challenge of matching subjects across conditions in order to create experimental control (Jarrold and Brock, 2004; Thomas *et al.*, 2009), the subject could act as *his or her own control* (Barlow *et al.*, 2009). In order for this to be achieved, certain features must be present: baseline and intervention *phases*; multiple data points, rather than measurements of key variables at (typically two) single time points; and, crucially, the use of repeated measures with clear definition and objectivity, which could allow for *high reliability* in measurement (Barlow *et al.*, 2009; Hitchcock and Horner, 2014). If the subject is to act as his or her own control, there is a risk of autocorrelation, that is, each data point having some interdependence (Todman *et al.*, 2012). SCED methodology attempts to overcome this problem, through robust measurement procedures and through steps in analysis, although there is significant variation in how these are employed (Parker and Vannest, 2012).

Experimental validity in SCEDs

The simplest form of SCED offers a comparison between two phases, A (baseline) and B (intervention) (AB design), where sufficient confidence in the validity of the baseline data must be established, for example through a minimum of five data points showing relative stability (Kratochwill *et al.*, 2012). Confidence in internal validity is enhanced through elaboration upon this core design. A return to the baseline phase measures a participant's responses when the intervention is withheld, but this (technically known as a *withdrawal* design) is difficult ethically where a treatment is proving to be beneficial. An ABAB design may offer some help, in that respect, with the restoration of the intervention, for further comparison.

A further design utilised to support internal validity explanations is that of the *multiple-baseline* design, which involves a number of delayed parallel investigations, with a time variation prospectively specified between each investigation, to allow for confidence in inferences drawn regarding effects found. For this design, variance can come from multiple participants (across-subjects design), or from multiple targets (within-subject design). There are considerable practical difficulties with this design in reality (see Activity Box 2.1, below), but the use of additional subjects can be helpful in explaining

FOCUS 2.4

FOCUS 2.4 *continued*

features of change in individuals. SCEDs risk the same *threats to internal validity* (Shadish *et al.*, 2001) as do group experimental designs, with a particular risk being any practice effects from measures taken that involve any form of self-report.

For the empirical scientist, the absence in SCEDs of a large sample through which to test hypotheses is problematic. In effect, the null hypothesis is not being tested; rather, the subject's progress against baseline attainments is noted. It is difficult, though not impossible, to develop the use of inferential statistics in this case. For some, therefore, the use of SCEDs is exploratory, *inductive* and *post*modern in its scientific epistemology (Plavnick and Ferreri, 2013). For others, SCEDs are a valid use of the *deductive* scientific process at the level of the individual, allowing us to generate explanations of causal inference. As these are explanations at the level of the individual, the key element that will enhance the external validity of such practice-based evidence is a *clear description of the population being investigated*, whereby consumers of such research are able to identify for themselves the relevance of this evidence for their setting (Hitchcock and Horner, 2014).

In theory, SCEDs have the potential to liberate the resource-challenged practitioner, who nevertheless wishes to generate high-quality, practice-based evidence. In *practice*, achieving highly reliable data can be a challenge. The greatest test in SCEDs for the practitioner is the challenge of drawing a tight frame, such that repeated instances of measurement have an optimal chance of reliability. This, more than any potential question of statistical inference, is at the heart of SCED designs. (Wolery, 2012) and their capacity to describe cause and effect.

SCED offers a route to achieve both practice-based evidence, at a case level, and externally facing data that may support theory building within the profession (Kazdin, 2011).

Single-subject designs have been noted to offer ecological and social validity (Barlow and Nock, 2009; Hitchcock and Horner, 2014), and it can be argued that their use of repeated measurement, while aiming for scientific control, potentially allows for explorations of *ideographic data* – *patterns* in the environment and features that can be indicated as relevant to the changes observed, or to the progress of the intervention. This can bring insight into the *mechanisms* of an intervention, not merely its effects, thereby addressing many of the concerns noted in the early part of this chapter regarding the evidence needed for evidence-based practice. Slack (2013) for example, analysed responses of young people with a diagnosis of autistic spectrum needs to an adapted cognitive behavioural therapy (CBT)-based intervention, FRIENDS, adapted to accommodate the learning needs of participants. Working with this specific

ACTIVITY 2.1

Developing a multiple-baseline SCED

An educational psychologist wishes to measure the effects of the 5-week intervention '*In Our Street*' programme being introduced to support the phonic skills of 8-year-olds in one school. It is hypothesised that there will be effects upon reading accuracy. There are five pupils, and measures of reading accuracy will be taken with them using daily 1-minute probes (specially formulated check sheets) for each pupil. For each pupil, the baseline phase lasts one full week before the intervention is then introduced. A multiple-baseline design would allow each pupil to set off using the same intervention, at weekly intervals, with any incremental gains seen across all pupils giving greater confidence in the explanation that can be offered as to the efficacy of the programme. The study progresses as follows:

- *Week 1*: Pupil A begins her programme. The 5-day baseline period reveals high variability, meaning that the baseline phase does not show stability, that is, does not reveal a *typical* level of reading functioning. Despite this, Pupil A must begin her intervention at the start of Week 2, for fear of disappointing her parents, who have been promised by the class teacher that the intervention will begin.
- *Week 2*: Pupil B's baseline phase is developed, and he makes good progress. The positive trend evident in his data during the baseline phase suggests that he is *already* beginning to make increasing progress. Nevertheless, he commences the intervention, where his accuracy scores continue this positive trajectory.
- *Week 3*: Pupil C begins the baseline phase, but for 3 out of the 5 days is absent. With a baseline phase of two data points, the school nevertheless wishes to move forward with the intervention as soon as possible. (This takes place in Week 5; see next.)
- *Week 4*: The school's Special Educational Needs Co-ordinator (SENCo) reports that the teaching assistant delivering the intervention has been called to jury service. No one is available to replace this person until Week 5.
- *Week 5*: Pupil D commences their baseline phase. Although the educational psychologist is pleased with the baseline data from Pupil D, the opportunity to deliver the intervention will now have to wait until after the Easter holidays.

Threats to internal validity describe threats that jeopardise the causal explanations that can be drawn from the data obtained.

1 Identify threats to internal validity in the example given above.
2 Next, identify which of these threats could be overcome in this very real example of applied investigation, and how.

population allowed the closely repeated measurement of responses and, therefore, the possibility of elucidating causal pathways in any outcomes from the intervention and tracing patterns of change in how individual young people were responding, thereby illuminating their behavioural response to different features of the CBT programme.

As SCEDs are concerned with measuring progress and change in an individual, in response to an intervention, it is common for that change to be noted through data collected upon behavioural change, that is, external manifestations of change. Some studies explore self-report too (White and Kratochwill, 2005). The link here to applied behaviour analysis is clear, which, from its inception, has depended upon the measurement of behavioural change, and this will be seen in Chapter 9.

Journal searches suggest a low use of the approach by educational psychologists in the UK, but the potential for rigorous exploration of case-based evidence through SCEDs has been illustrated through a robust literature from the US, generating data to investigate practical and theoretical hypotheses. In the UK, there is less evidence (although an emerging unpublished literature in doctoral theses: see Beeson, 2013; Vivian, 2013), but studies have illustrated the potential for the approach to support the educational psychologists' work with atypical populations, as well as to investigate the power of instructional features of a programme for more typically developing young people with mild delays in skills acquisition (Reason and Morfidi, 2001).

DEVELOPING THE EVIDENCE: EXTENDING THE PARADIGMS

Unlike in the US, where it has been possible to state, 'Research and the scientific method is the foundation for school psychology practice' (Burns, 2011, p. 32), within the UK, the relationship of educational psychology with the natural sciences is complex. The discussion above has already noted the pull of interpretive methods for educational researchers, and educational psychology, more than other applied psychologies, experiences the call of both of its home disciplines. In the UK, the manifest tension between the influence of the natural sciences and that of the humanities can be found in the variety of research submitted to professional journals, in contrast to those of academic educational psychology (Miller *et al.*, 2008). For some, the profession commenced with the work of measuring intelligence and has continued with other nomothetic presuppositions (Miller and Frederickson, 2006). For others, such supposedly scientific activity not only is unreliable in casework activity, but remains incompatible with the espoused values of the professional practice of educational psychology when research is undertaken (Miller *et al.*, 2008). It might be argued that educational psychology, as practised in the UK, has long shown wariness towards approaches perceived to be driven by causal models. For example, conjoint behavioural consultation, which is favoured in the US (Sheridan and Bovaird, 2012), features less often in reports of UK professional practice, where there appears to be a preference for conceptually eclectic and, therefore, highly adaptable models of consultation (Wagner, 2000). Whereas a call for the abandonment of a medical model in favour of ecological approaches (Sheridan and Gutkin, 2000) could be described, at the turn of the century in the US, as 'revolutionary' (Burns, 2011), such perspectives had long been integral to the *relativist* and *postmodern* thinking of much of the profession in the UK. Evidence-based-practice approaches have, therefore, appeared to challenge the epistemological foundations of a profession that has sought to retain its position as a profession that accepts both empiricist and constructive precepts (Miller *et al.*, 2008). Burnham (2013) suggests that the supposed epistemological divide within the profession may be given unwarranted prominence and calls our attention to the need for educational psychology to adopt questions and solutions according to relevance and expediency, ensuring a strong methodological foundation for any approaches adopted.

QUALITATIVE METHODS: EXPLORATION AND INSIGHT

The scientific, *positivist* position was fractured open during the latter half of the twentieth century, through arguments suggesting that, not only in the case of applied psychology, there was a need for a widening of horizons to include methods that could discern evidence regarding the features of interventions and their contexts, which could provide greater understanding than purely causal associations (Pressley *et al.*, 2006; Trainor and Graue, 2014). The challenges above, for some, rendered the search for causal inference in complex settings such as schools insufficiently helpful in explaining either the phenomenon under investigation or its effects. For those who wished to attend to the very complexity of detail that defies causal explanation, the solution was not to attempt such arguably invalid inferences and struggle to make the case for implausible external validity, but to focus upon restricted (low external validity) explanations of local questions, underpinned by problem exploration and insight. Qualitative approaches were needed, from this viewpoint, in order to reveal just that: the essential *quality* of a phenomenon, or an intervention, illustrated by rich detail to capture the diverse perceptions of those involved on the ground. Many diverse methodologies rest under these superordinate purposes. Relying upon various processes of collation and analysis of participant perceptions, through semi-structured interviews or focus groups, for example, such studies typically aim to capture both *synthesis* and depth of *detail*, with the mode of analysis often becoming the method (in the case of *discourse analysis* or *grounded theory*, for example; refer to Willig, 2013, for further detail).

Qualitative research has consistently been shown to be valuable in the field of education in exploring features of phenomena or the perspectives of the various stakeholders involved. Studies of teacher education and professional development have identified that capturing the experiences of those involved in the delivery of curriculum changes was of strong value in supporting professional practice changes, for example (Goodnough, 2011), or that pupil perspectives of school experience could be captured to enhance their stake and positioning in a school's ethos (Flutter, 2006) or the nature of provision (Michael and Frederickson, 2013). Although the methods, retrospective and often case-study based, may be anathema to a natural scientist, the percolation of such qualitative paradigms in educational studies quickly led to their predominance in that field (Torgerson and Torgerson, 2001).

The *epistemological* foundation for such methods is broadly postmodern, *interpretive* and *inductive* – the notion that individual or group *experience* and *perceptions* are important features in their own right to be captured, in order to inform those around them, or a wider community. *Constructivist* and *interpretive* methodologies typically acknowledge and even invite the express positioning of the researcher in the construction or interpretation of data obtained with participants, in the concept known as 'reflexivity' (Ramey and Grubb, 2009; Willig, 2013; Trainor and Graue, 2014). This is in contrast to traditional methods, where *objective* measurement is paramount. Qualitative approaches are less interested in 'measurement' of phenomena, than in description and illumination and, indeed, typically assume that little can be done to 'measure' the complex social phenomenon under investigation through measurement of single variables. Underlying this view is the notion that there is no single measurable external reality, only multiple perceptions to be captured. Nevertheless, qualitative studies often undertake activities of classification and categorisation, which can be described as precursors to the notion of measurement, often giving implicit scales of value to data rather than explicit ones, for example in reporting the emphasis or value found by the researcher in the data's attributes; as Clarke says, 'There is no hard and fast boundary between quality and quantity' (2004, p. 81). Despite abandoning a search for 'external validity', research reports may often *seem* to seek generalisable truths.

Investigating the social phenomenon of bullying

The domain of anti-bullying research is an interesting one for methodological reflection. Studies investigating how schools can best reduce instances of bullying, or enhance the positive social skills of all pupils (see Chapter 11), must deal with the variable influence of contexts and of within-pupil differences, making cross-study comparisons exceptionally challenging. Although experimental control is difficult to achieve in the complex psychosocial environments in which bullying typically occurs, such investigations have also demonstrated *precisely* that some kind of control of variables is needed: we do need to understand *what works* and *why*. Systematic reviews have identified, however, limited confidence in the capacity of particular interventions to effect changes for children in school, for the reasons already explored in this chapter (Farrington and Ttofi, 2009; Ttofi and Farrington, 2011).

Miller *et al.* (2008), on the other hand, note that bullying is a domain in which there is a significant amount of qualitative data available. This illustrates the dilemmas for the would-be evidence-based practitioner: to explore the multiple threats to validity in controlled studies and employ effect size as a guide to *efficacy* of an intervention, or be guided by the perceptions of the students and staff involved in problem situations and their interventions? Insights from both types of study can and must make a valuable contribution to understanding the *nature* of a concern and how it is experienced by those involved, as well as to how to intervene, optimally.

The notion of *typologies of evidence* rather than *hierarchies of evidence* is helpful in this respect. It has been suggested that focusing upon what *type of question* can be addressed by what *type of evidence* is of greater importance, allowing for a spectrum of methods to address different facets of a problem scenario (Petticrew and Roberts, 2003).

FOCUS 2.5

In terms of evidence-based practice, then, there is for some an important opportunity to draw upon close, detailed knowledge of local contexts, valuable precisely because the data illuminate the setting from which they are drawn and do not attempt to create nomothetic explanations; instead, the focus is upon questions for that localised context, or, at most, insights that may, for example, contribute to generalisable explanations of mechanisms in an intervention, for example.

The evidence-based-practice movement has evolved some way towards consideration of non-RCT data in systematic reviews, for example, through the inclusion of qualitative data in meta-analyses (Clegg, 2005; Anderson *et al.*, 2013). Qualitative data can be seen to play a role by allowing for the illumination of relevant questions, by key stakeholders, and perceptions of key participants, described in any case by various authors as a *sine qua non* of evidence-based practice and attuned to the zeitgeist of addressing the needs and views of policy consumers (Kelly *et al.*, 2010).

Such concern to capture the participants' perceptions of a scenario resonates with *action research* (AR) models. AR assumes the capacity of practitioners (from any domain) to generate answers to their own complex problems through systematic and rigorous review (see Chapter 13, for an example of a school-based AR intervention), but is not prescriptive regarding its precise methods, giving primacy to its *strategic conceptualisation* of activities. In this way, AR has been seen as having low external validity and as being able to offer only localised explanations. Perhaps, the unification of evidence-based practice with more stakeholder scrutiny is the best way forward, conjoining some of the practitioner features and epistemological positioning of the AR paradigm with the claimed rigour of the evidence-based-practice paradigm.

CONCLUSIONS

Evidence-based practice as an approach has exerted a powerful influence across disciplines and has made a significant contribution to the general understanding of the need to examine and understand interventions used to support well-being in diverse areas of practice. It is a complex process, open to critique: those who challenge evidence-based practice tend to soften its terms of reference from those of 'traditional science' to include a broader range of 'evidence'. Professional educational psychology, historically, has grappled with dilemmas regarding its affiliations in terms of preferred types of 'evidence', but ultimately has capacity to embrace evidence from many diverse methodologies, in order to address many different types of question. The move among applied psychology professions, and other disciplines in social policy, to evidence-based practices has highlighted some pertinent questions regarding the epistemological foundations of the profession. Rather than this becoming a battleground between nomothetic and idiographic approaches, effort must focus on the struggle to enhance the quality of evidence on its own terms. How a practitioner receives and deploys such evidence will depend on their clarity of purpose, rendering much of the debate regarding methodological preferences secondary to the primary concern of rigour and quality in research.

SUMMARY OF MAIN ISSUES ADDRESSED IN THIS CHAPTER

- Evidence-based practice is an approach that aims to enhance the rigour and understanding of interventions to support, in this case, children and young people. It has a background in the field of health, but has made a transition to other fields.
- Evidence-based practice draws upon research that investigates causal inferences regarding interventions.
- Difficulties, in the view of some, with evidence-based practice include its focus upon causal explanations, through reductionist approaches, its possible neglect of population characteristics, and the skills of practitioners in implementation.
- Moving from evidence to practice requires tight procedures, and these can valuably be informed by *stakeholders* in the research, such as client groups and practitioners.
- Post-positivism has supported the translation of traditional, deductive positivist methods to applied contexts, through allowing researchers to describe threats to internal validity.
- An alternative, possibly underused, approach to applied studies is that of *SCEDs*, allowing for controlled experimental study of the *individual*.
- Qualitative methods make a contribution to the study of applied contexts, and many educational psychologists espouse relativist, interpretivist or constructivist approaches in practice, and this informs approaches to research and research evidence, too.
- Some approaches to evaluation, such as realist evaluation, aim to use qualitative approaches to draw some causal inferences.

KEY CONCEPTS AND TERMS

- Evidence based-practice
- Scientist–practitioner
- Educational psychology
- Epistemology

- Positivism
- Hierarchy of evidence
- Systematic reviews
- Practice-based evidence
- Paradigms

- Single-case experimental designs
- Qualitative methods
- Evaluation

RECOMMENDATIONS FOR FURTHER READING

Journal articles

APA Presidential Task Force on Evidence-Based Practice (2006). Evidence-based practice in psychology. *The American Psychologist*, *61*(4), 271–85.

Burnham, S. (2013). Realists or pragmatists? 'Reliable evidence' and the role of the educational psychologist. *Educational Psychology in Practice*, *29*(1), 19–35.

Frederickson, N. (2002). Evidence-based practice and educational psychology, *Educational and Child Psychology*, *19*, 96–111.

Gough, D. (2007). Weight of evidence: A framework for the appraisal of the quality and relevance of evidence. *Research Papers in Education*, *22*(2), 213–28.

Kratochwill, T.R., Hitchcock, J.H., Horner, R.H., Levin, J.R., Odom, S.L., Rindskopf, D.M. and Shadish, W.R. (2012). Single-case intervention research design standards. *Remedial and Special Education*, *34*(1), 26–38.

Books

Barlow, D., Nock, M. and Hersen, M. (2009). *Single Case Experimental Designs: Strategies for studying behavior change*. Boston, MA: Allyn & Bacon.

Cohen, L., Manion, L. and Morrison, K. (2011). *Research Methods in Education*. London. Routledge.

Petticrew, M. and Roberts, H. (2008). *Systematic Reviews in the Social Sciences: A practical guide*. Oxford, UK: Blackwell.

Robson, C. (2011). *Real World Research: A resource for users of social research methods in applied settings*. Chichester, UK: Wiley.

Chapters

Miller, A., Billington, T., Lewis, V. and DeSouza, L. (2006). Educational psychology. In C. Willig and W. Stainton-Rogers (eds), *The SAGE Handbook of Qualitative Research in Psychology*. London: Sage.

SAMPLE ESSAY TITLES

1 What support does the evidence-based-practice movement offer to educational psychology?
2 Describe some of the difficulties with the concept of evidence-based practice when applied to the practice of professional educational psychology.
3 What methods can a practitioner–researcher draw upon to generate practice-based evidence?
4 Discuss the potential contribution of qualitative methods to educational psychology practice.

REFERENCES

Anderson, L., Oliver, S. and Michie, S. (2013). Investigating complexity in systematic reviews of interventions by using a spectrum of methods. *Journal of Clinical Epidemiology*, *66*, 1223–9.

Anna Freud Centre (2014). Available online at www.annafreud.org/pages/about-ebpu.html (accessed 28 November 2013).

Annan, J. and Priestley, A. (2011). A contemporary story of school psychology. *School Psychology International*, *33*(3), 325–44.

APA Presidential Task Force on Evidence-Based Practice (2006). Evidence-based practice in psychology. *The American Psychologist*, *61*(4), 271–85.

Barlow, D.H. and Nock, M.K. (2009). Why can't we be more idiographic in our research? *Perspectives on Psychological Science*, *4*(1), 19–21.

Barlow, D., Nock, M.K. and Hersen, M. (2009). *Single Case Experimental Designs: Strategies for studying behavior change*. Boston, MA: Allyn & Bacon.

Bauer, R.M. (2007). Evidence-based practice in psychology: Implications for research and research training. *Journal of Clinical Psychology*, *63*(7), 685–94.

Beeson, P. (2013). Investigating the incorporation of precision teaching assessment methods within a structured approach for children with autism. Unpublished DAppEdPsy thesis, University of Nottingham.

Bennett, S. and Monsen, J. (2011). A critical appraisal of four approaches which support teachers' problem-solving within educational settings. *Educational Psychology in Practice*, *27*(1), 19–35.

Bond, C., Woods, K., Humphrey, N., Symes, W. and Green, L. (2013). Practitioner review: The effectiveness of solution focused brief therapy with children and families: A systematic and critical evaluation of the literature from 1990 to 2010. *Journal of Child Psychology and Psychiatry, and Allied Disciplines*, *54*(7), 707–23.

Bozic, N. and Carter, A. (2002). Consultation groups: Participants' views. *Educational Psychology in Practice*, *18*(3), 189–201.

Burnham, S. (2013). Realists or pragmatists? 'Reliable evidence' and the role of the educational psychologist. *Educational Psychology in Practice*, *29*(1), 19–35.

Burns, K. and Hulusi, H. (2005). Bridging the gap between a learning support centre and school: A solution-focused group approach. *Educational Psychology in Practice*, *21*(2), 123–30.

Burns, M.K. (2011). School psychology research: Combining ecological theory and prevention science. *School Psychology Review*, *40*(1), 132–9.

Button, K.S., Ioannidis, J.P., Mokrysz, C., Nosek, B.A., Flint, J., Robinson, E.S. and Munafò, M.R. (2013). Power failure: Why small sample size undermines the reliability of neuroscience. *Nature reviews. Neuroscience*, *14*(5), 365–76.

Callahan, J.L., Heath, C.J., Aubuchon-Endsley, N.L., Collins, F.L. and Herbert, G.L. (2013). Enhancing information pertaining to client characteristics to facilitate evidence-based practice. *Journal of Clinical Psychology*, *69*(12), 1239–49.

Carr, A. (2013). *What Works with Children and Adolescents? A critical review of psychological interventions with children, adolescents and their families*. London: Routledge.

Cartwright, N., Goldfinch, A. and Howick, J. (2009). Evidence-based policy: Where is our theory of evidence? *Journal of Children's Services*, *4*(4), 6–14.

Clarke, D.D. (2004). 'Structured judgement methods' – the best of both worlds? in Z. Todd, B. Nerlich, S. McKeown and D.D. Clarke (eds) (2004). *Mixing Methods in Psychology: The integration of qualitative and quantitative methods in theory and practice*. Hove, UK: Psychology Press.

Clegg, S. (2005). Evidence-based practice in educational research: A critical realist critique of systematic review. *British Journal of Sociology of Education*, *26*(3), 415–28.

Cochrane, A. and Fellowship, R. (1972). *Effectiveness and Efficiency: Random reflections on health services*. London: Royal Society of Medicine Press & Nuffield Trust.

Cole, R.L.,Treadwell, S., Dosani, S. and Frederickson, N. (2012). Evaluation of a short-term, cognitive-behavioral intervention for primary age children with anger-related difficulties. *School Psychology International, 34*(1), 82–100.

Cook, B. and Odom, S. (2013). Evidence-based practices and implementation science in special education. *Exceptional Children, 79*(2), 135–44.

Dawson, K. (2013). An interpretative analysis of key adults' and children's experiences of school and their relationship before and after a Circle of Adults intervention. Unpublished DEdCPsy thesis, University of Sheffield.

Dempsey, K. (2012). A mixed-method study investigating a Circle of Adults approach to group work in schools. Unpublished thesis, University of Nottingham.

Dilillo, D. and Mcchargue, D. (2007). Implementing elements of evidence-based practice into scientist–practitioner training at the University of Nebraska–Lincoln. *Journal of Clinical Psychology, 63*(7), 671–84.

Divoky, D. and Schrag, P. (1975). *The Myth of the Hyperactive Child and Other Means of Child Control*. Harmondsworth, UK: Penguin.

Dozois, D. (2013). Psychological treatments: Putting evidence into practice and practice into evidence. *Canadian Psychology/Psychologie canadienne, 54*(1), 1–11.

Dunsmuir, S. and Kratochwill, T. (2013). From research to policy and practice: Perspectives from the UK and the USA on psychologists as agents of change. *Educational and Child Psychology, 30*(3), 60–71.

Evans, S.W., Owens, J.S. and Bunford, N. (2013). Evidence-based psychosocial treatments for children and adolescents with attention-deficit/hyperactivity disorder. *Journal of Clinical Child and Adolescent Psychology, 43*(4), pp. 1–25.

Farrington, D. and Ttofi, M. (2009). *School-Based Programs to Reduce Bullying and Victimization*. London: The Campbell Collaboration.

Flay, B., Biglan, A. and Boruch, R. (2005). Standards of evidence: Criteria for efficacy, effectiveness and dissemination. *Prevention Science, 6*(3), 151–75.

Flutter, J. (2006). 'This place could help you learn': Student participation in creating better school environments. *Educational Review, 58*(2), 183–93.

Fox, M. (2003). Opening Pandora's Box: Evidence-based practice for educational psychologists. *Educational Psychology in Practice, 19*(2), 91–102.

Fox, M. (2011). Practice-based evidence – overcoming insecure attachments. *Educational Psychology in Practice, 27*(4), 325–35.

Frederickson, N. (2002). Evidence-based practice and educational psychology. *Educational and Child Psychology, 19*, 96–111.

Frederickson, N., Warren, L. and Turner, J. (2005). 'Circle of Friends' – An exploration of impact over time. *Educational Psychology in Practice, 21*(3), 197–217.

Frost, N., Nolas, S. and Brooks-Gordon, B. (2010). Pluralism in qualitative research: The impact of different researchers and qualitative approaches on the analysis of qualitative data. *Qualitative Research, 10*(4), 1–19.

Goodnough, K. (2011). Examining the long-term impact of collaborative action research on teacher identity and practice: The perceptions of K–12 teachers. *Educational Action Research, 19*(1), 73–86.

Gough, D. (2007). Weight of evidence: A framework for the appraisal of the quality and relevance of evidence. *Research Papers in Education, 22*(2), 213–28.

Hagermoser Sanetti, L.M. and Fallon, L.M. (2011). Treatment integrity assessment: How estimates of adherence, quality, and exposure influence interpretation of implementation. *Journal of Educational and Psychological Consultation, 21*(3), 209–32.

Hammersley, M. (2005). Is the evidence-based practice movement doing more good than harm? Reflections on Iain Chalmers' case for research-based policy making and practice. *Evidence & Policy: A Journal of Research, Debate and Practice, 1*(1), 85–100.

Hitchcock, J. and Horner, R. (2014). The what works clearinghouse single-case design pilot standards: Who will guard the guards? *Remedial and Special Education, 35*(3), 145–52.

Holburn, S. (2002). How science can evaluate and enhance person-centered planning. *Research and Practice for Persons with Severe Severe Disabilities, 27*(4), 250–60.

James, R. (2011). An evaluation of the 'circle of friends' intervention used to support pupils with autism in their mainstream classrooms. Unpublished DAppEdPsy thesis, University of Nottingham.

Jarrold, C. and Brock, J. (2004). To match or not to match? Methodological issues in autism-related research. *Journal of Autism and developmental Disorders, 34*(1), 81–6.

Jones, D., Monsen, J. and Franey, J. (2013). Using the staff sharing scheme to support school staff in managing challenging behaviour more effectively. *Educational Psychology in Practice, 29*(3), 258–77.

Kazdin, A. (2011). *Single-case Research Designs: Methods for clinical and applied settings.* New York: Oxford University Press.

Kelly, M., Morgan, A., Ellis, S., Younger, T. and Swann, C. (2010). Evidence based public health: A review of the experience of the National Institute of Health and Clinical Excellence (NICE) of developing public health guidance in England. *Social Science & Medicine, 71*(6), 1056–62.

Kirkham, J., Dwan, K. and Altman, D. (2010). The impact of outcome reporting bias in randomised controlled trials on a cohort of systematic reviews. *British Medical Journal, 340*(7747), 637–40.

Koenig, G. (2009). Realistic evaluation and case studies stretching the potential. *Evaluation, 15*(1), 9–30.

Kratochwill, T.R., Hitchcock, J.H., Horner, R.H., Levin, J.R., Odom, S.L., Rindskopf, D.M. and Shadish, W.R. (2012). Single-case intervention research design standards. *Remedial and Special Education, 34*(1), 26–38.

Lamb, D. and Gulliford, A. (2011). Physical exercise and children's self-concept of emtional and behavioural well-being: A randomised controlled trial. *Educational and Child Psychology, 28*(4), 66–74.

Lilienfeld, S.O., Ritschel, L.A., Lynn, S.J., Cautin, R.L. and Latzman, R.D. (2013). Why many clinical psychologists are resistant to evidence-based practice: Root causes and constructive remedies. *Clinical Psychology Review, 33*(7), 883–900.

Ling, T. (2012). Evaluating complex and unfolding interventions in real time. *Evaluation, 18*(1), 79–91.

Michael, S. and Frederickson, N. (2013). Improving pupil referral unit outcomes: Pupil perspectives. *Emotional and Behavioural Difficulties, 18*(4), 407–22.

Miller, A., Billington, T., Lewis, V. and DeSouza, L. (2008). Educational psychology. In W. Stainton-Rogers and C. Willig (eds), *The SAGE Handbook of Qualitative Research in Psychology*. Milton Keynes, UK: The Open University.

Miller, A. and Frederickson, N. (2006). Generalisable findings and idiographic problems: Struggles and successes for educational psychologists as scientist–practitioners. In D. Lane and S. Corrie (eds), *The Modern Scientist–Practitioner: Practical approaches to guide how professional psychologists think*. London: Routledge.

Moher, D., Liberati, A., Tetzlaff, J. and Altman, D.G. (2009). Preferred reporting items for systematic reviews and meta-analyses: The PRISMA statement. *PLoS Medicine, 6*(7), 1–6.

Nevo, I. and Slonim-Nevo, V. (2011). The myth of evidence-based practice: Towards evidence-informed practice. *British Journal of Social Work, 41*(6), 1176–97.

Newton, C. and Wilson, D. (2006). Circles of Adults. Inclusive solutions. Available online at www.inclusive-solutions.com (accessed 30 November 2014).

Oakley, A. (2002). Social science and evidence-based everything: The case of education. *Educational Review, 54*(3), 277–86.

Odom, S., Brantlinger, E. and Gersten, R. (2005). Research in special education: Scientific methods and evidence-based practices. *Exceptional Children, 71*(2), 137–48.

Palinkas, L. and Aarons, G. (2011). Mixed method designs in implementation research. *Administration and Policy in Mental Health, 38*, 44–53.

Parker, R. and Vannest, K. (2012). Bottom-up analysis of single-case research designs. *Journal of Behavioral Education, 21*(3), 254–65.

Pawson, R. and Greenhalgh, T. (2005). Realist review – A new method of systematic review designed for complex policy interventions. *Journal of Health Services Research and Policy, 10*(1), 21–34.

Pawson, R. and Tilley, N. (1997). *An Introduction to Scientific Realist Evaluation*. Thousand Oaks, CA: SAGE.

Petticrew, M., Rehfuess, E. and Noyes, J. (2013). Synthesizing evidence on complex interventions: How meta-analytical, qualitative, and mixed-method approaches can contribute. *Journal of Clinical Epidemiology, 66*, 1230–43.

Petticrew, M. and Roberts, H. (2003). Evidence, hierarchies, and typologies: Horses for courses. *Journal of Epidemiology & Community Health, 57*(7), 527–9.

Petticrew, M. and Roberts, H. (2008). *Systematic Reviews in the Social Sciences: A practical guide*. Oxford, UK: Blackwell.

Plavnick, J.B. and Ferreri, S.J. (2013). Single-case experimental designs in educational research: A Methodology for causal analyses in teaching and learning. *Educational Psychology Review, 25*(4), 549–69.

Pressley, M., Graham, S. and Harris, K. (2006). The state of educational intervention research as viewed through the lens of literacy intervention. *The British Journal of Educational Psychology, 76*(1), 1–19.

Pring, R. and Thomas, G. (2004). *Evidence-Based Practice in Education*. Maidenhead, UK: McGraw-Hill.

Ramey, H.L. and Grubb, S. (2009). Modernism, postmodernism and (evidence-based) practice. *Contemporary Family Therapy, 31*(2), 75–86.

Reason, R. and Morfidi, E. (2001). Literacy difficulties and single-case experimental design. *Educational Psychology in Practice*, *17*(3), 227–44.

Redpath, R. and Harker, M. (1999). Becoming solution-focused in practice. *Educational Psychology in Practice*, *15*(2), 116–21.

Rodgers, A. and Dunsmuir, S. (2013). A controlled evaluation of the 'FRIENDS for Life' emotional resilience programme on overall anxiety levels, anxiety subtype levels and school adjustment. *Child and Adolescent Mental Health*, DOI: 10.1111/camh.12030

Schraw, G. and Patall, E.A. (2013). Using principles of evidence-based practice to improve prescriptive recommendations. *Educational Psychology Review*, *25*(3), 345–51.

Shadish, W.R., Cook, T.D. and Campbell, D.T. (2001). *Experimental and Quasi-Experimental Designs for Generalized Causal Inference* (2nd edn). Boston, MA: Cengage Learning.

Sheridan, S. and Bovaird, J. (2012). A randomized trial examining the effects of conjoint behavioral consultation and the mediating role of the parent–teacher relationship. *School Psychology Review*, *41*(1), 23–46.

Sheridan, S. and Gutkin, T. (2000). The ecology of school psychology: Examining and changing our paradigm for the 21st Century. *School Psychology Review*, *29*(4), 485–501.

Sibley, M.H., Kuriyan, A.B., Evans, S.W., Waxmonsky, J.G. and Smith, B.H. (2014). Pharmacological and psychosocial treatments for adolescents with ADHD: An updated systematic review of the literature. *Clinical Psychology Review*, *34*(3), 218–32.

Slack, G. (2013). An evaluation of the FRIENDS for Life intervention with an autism spectrum population: Evaluating the impact on children's anxiety. Unpublished DAppEdPsy thesis, University of Nottingham.

Smith, T. (2013). What is Evidence-Based Behavior Analysis?, *The Behavior Analyst*, *1*(1), 7–33.

Spring, B. (2007). Evidence-based practice in clinical psychology: What it is, why it matters, what you need to know. *Journal of Clinical Psychology*, *63*(7), 611–31.

Squires, G. and Caddick, K. (2012). Using group cognitive behavioural therapy intervention in school settings with pupils who have externalizing behavioural difficulties: An unexpected result. *Emotional and Behavioural Difficulties*, *17*, 25–45.

Stobie, I. (2005). Solution-focused approaches in the practice of UK educational psychologists: A study of the nature of their application and evidence of their effectiveness. *School Psychology International*, *26*(1), 5–28.

Stufflebeam, D.L. (2003). The CIPP model for evaluation. In *International Handbook of Educational Evaluation*, Dordrecht, Netherlands: Kluwer, pp. 31–62.

Styles, A. (2011). Social stories™: Does the research evidence support the popularity? *Educational Psychology in Practice*, *27*(4), 415–36.

Sue, S. and Zane, N. (2006). How well both evidence-based practices and treatment as usual satisfactorily address the various dimensions of diversity. In *Evidence-Based Practices in Mental Health: Debate and dialogue on the fundamental questions*. Washington, DC: American Psychological Association, pp. 329–74.

Syme, W. (2011). An evaluation of the impact of 'Circles of Adults'. Unpublished thesis, University of Nottingham.

Symonds, J. and Gorard, S. (2010). Death of mixed methods? Or the rebirth of research as a craft. *Evaluation & Research in Education*, *23*(23), 121–36.

Thomas, M.S.C., Annaz, D., Ansari, D., Scerif, G., Jarrold, C. and Karmiloff-Smith, A. (2009). Using developmental trajectories to understand developmental disorders. *Journal of Speech, Language, and Hearing Research*, *52*(April), 336–58.

Todman, J., File, P. and Dugard, P. (2012). *Single-Case and Small-N Experimental Designs: A practical guide to randomization tests*. Hove, UK: Taylor & Francis.

Torgerson, C. and Torgerson, D. (2001). The need for randomised controlled trials in educational research. *British Journal of Educational Studies*, *49*(3), 316–28.

Trainor, A.A. and Graue, E. (2014). Evaluating rigor in qualitative methodology and research dissemination. *Remedial and Special Education*, (March), 1–8.

Ttofi, M. and Farrington, D. (2011). Effectiveness of school-based programs to reduce bullying: A systematic and meta-analytic review. *Journal of Experimental Criminology*, 7, 27–56.

Vaughn, S. and Fuchs, L. (2013). Staying within one's data to make recommendations for practice in primary educational research journals. *Educational Psychology Review*, *25*(3), 339–43.

Visser, J. and Jehan, Z. (2009). ADHD: A scientific fact or a factual opinion? A critique of the veracity of attention deficit hyperactivity disorder. *Emotional and Behavioural Difficulties*, *14*(2), 127–40.

Vivian, R. (2013). The impact of a paired reading literacy intervention on literacy skills, academic self-concept and reading confidence for looked after children. Unpublished DAppEdPsy thesis, University of Nottingham.

Wagner, P. (2000). Consultation: Developing a comprehensive approach to service delivery. *Educational Psychology in Practice*, *16*(1), 9–18.

White, J.L. and Kratochwill, T.R. (2005). Practice guidelines in school psychology: Issues and directions for evidence-based interventions in practice and training. *Journal of School Psychology*, *43*(2), 99–115.

Wilcox, A. (2003). Evidence-based youth justice? Some valuable lessons from an evaluation for the Youth Justice Board. *Youth Justice*, *3*(1), 21–35.

Willig, C. (2013). *Introducing Qualitative Research in Psychology. Adventures in theory and method.* Maidenhead, UK: Open University Press.

Wolery, M. (2012). A commentary: Single-case design technical document of the what works clearinghouse. *Remedial and Special Education*, *34*(1), 39–43.

Cognition, learning and instruction

3 What use is 'intelligence'?

Tony Cline

CHAPTER SUMMARY

The concept of intelligence *has been influential in psychology, and that influence has often been portrayed as malign. This chapter will analyse how ideas about intelligence have developed in recent years among the general public and within psychology. Applications of these ideas in education will be illustrated by examining two specific areas:*

- *the identification of moderate and severe learning difficulties;*
- *the notion of* multiple intelligences.

The chapter ends with a discussion of the changes that have occurred over time in the role that the assessment of intelligence has played in the practice of educational psychologists.

LEARNING OUTCOMES

When you have studied this chapter, you should be able to:

1 outline how views of the concept of intelligence have changed over time among teachers and the general public and discuss reasons for these changes;
2 explain and evaluate selected theoretical approaches to conceptualising intelligence within psychology;
3 describe some of the ways in which psychologists' ideas about intelligence have been applied in education and discuss the possible value of current applications.

VIEWS OF THE CONCEPT OF INTELLIGENCE AMONG TEACHERS AND THE GENERAL PUBLIC

If someone is described to you as 'intelligent', what might you expect to notice about them when you meet them? When teachers in various countries have been asked questions such as this about the pupils they work with, they have tended to list sets of abilities, such as:

- going beyond the given;
- seeing connections between different ideas;
- seeing patterns in data;
- applying concepts to new contexts;
- thinking logically;
- applying knowledge from one context to another
- demonstrating deep understanding of a concept (Adey *et al.*, 2007).

However, Adey and his colleagues note a paradox: 'These responses explicate professional, intuitive, experienced-based conceptions of general ability. But as soon as you try to suggest that a good word to describe this general ability is "intelligence", you encounter resistance' (p. 76). The term had broader public acceptance in Western countries in the 1940s, but after that time there appears to have been a steady erosion of confidence in the term. Intelligence quotient (IQ) tests were a specific focus of concern. This is reflected in Table 3.1, which records some of the changes found by Shipstone and Burt (1973), who repeated a survey originally conducted by Flugel in 1947. Subsequent surveys have not shown a reversal of the trend, even when they have focused on the views of psychology students (e.g. Swami *et al.*, 2008). Those participating in such surveys within Western cultures would generally agree that some notion of general mental ability is important in the judgements they make about other people. That does not mean that they are all comfortable with the ways in which psychologists have treated this construct. The image of professional practice in educational psychology suffered for many years from an association with the regular

TABLE 3.1 Changes in public opinion recorded by Shipstone and Burt (1973)

	% disagreeing with the proposition in 1947	*% disagreeing with the proposition in 1973*
This sort of measurement of 'general intelligence' would help find the right man for the job	22	41
Intelligence tests are better than ordinary examinations for finding out the brains a person was born with (as distinct from what he has been taught)	16	27
If a child's intelligence is measured when he is between 8 and 10, we can get an idea of how intelligent he will be when he is grown up	41	52

Source: Shipstone and Burt, 1973

administration of intelligence tests. This image became inaccurate over time. Successive surveys by Farrell and Smith (1982), Farrell *et al.* (1989) and Woods and Farrell (2006) recorded slow change within the profession from the routine use of global *intelligence scales* to their highly selective use within a much broader range of assessment strategies. An outline of the rise and fall of educational psychologists' engagement with psychometric practices and with the notion of global intelligence is presented in the final section of this chapter.

Particularly sceptical views on the value of the construct of intelligence have been expressed by commentators on school education. These views have covered a range of issues:

- Theoretical: scepticism that a single construct can explain as much variation in children's learning as had originally been suggested. This view gained empirical support when, for example, the contribution of IQ to predictions of young children's progress in literacy and numeracy was shown to be less than that of more specific cognitive factors, such as working memory (Alloway and Alloway, 2010).
- Practical: doubts among teachers about whether norm-based measures of intelligence can provide useful information for planning how to adapt teaching to the needs of individual children, for example when compared with criterion-referenced forms of assessment (see Chapter 4) or dynamic assessment of learning *potential* (Freeman and Miller, 2001).
- Moral: concern that the measurement of intelligence may be inequitable in its treatment of the performance of children who have had access to limited learning opportunities during early childhood (Scarr, 1984).
- Ideological: worries about racist interpretations of some 'scientific' ideas on group differences in measured intelligence (Mackintosh, 2007).
- Pedagogic: concern that the concept of intelligence suggests that children have a fixed level of ability, and that this will discourage teachers from trying to develop untapped potential (Adey *et al.*, 2007).

In the face of such extensive concerns, why have some psychologists continued to employ the construct of intelligence and to try to develop new theories of intelligence and new ways of measuring it? To understand this, it is necessary to examine first how they and others have conceptualised the construct – their answers to the question, what is intelligence?

THE CONCEPT OF INTELLIGENCE IN PSYCHOLOGY

Cultural influences on how psychologists conceptualise intelligence

Throughout history, the conceptualisation of human abilities in each society has been influenced by the cultural values of that society. This means that there is great variation in the way in which intelligence is described across periods of history and across regions of the world. For example, in classical Chinese traditions, the Confucian image of an intelligent person included a moral perspective, emphasising the use of abilities in the service of 'benevolence' and highlighting the possibility that an individual can enhance their potential through effort. In the Taoist tradition, on the other hand, the concept of intelligence incorporates, not only a capacity for effective action, but also humility and the flexibility to be able to respond to changed circumstances. Yang and Sternberg (1997) studied conceptions of intelligence among heterogeneous samples of adults in two major cities in Taiwan and showed that their ideas about what characterises an intelligent person had different emphases from those typically found in Western populations and reflected values associated with the cultural legacy of Confucianism and Taoism.

Another example of cultural differences in the way people think about intelligence concerns beliefs about the potential to become highly intelligent. Rattan, Savani et al. (2012) found that, in a group of students from California whom they interviewed, participants tended to believe that only some people have the potential to become highly intelligent. In contrast, in a group of students from Bangalore in India, participants tended to believe that most people have the potential to become highly intelligent. This work builds on an extensive body of research on people's beliefs about the nature of intelligence led by Carol Dweck, who became interested in the implications of believing that it is possible (or not possible) for an individual's intelligence to change in the course of their lifetime. She termed the view that a person's intelligence can increase over time an '*incremental* belief', and the view that it is fixed and cannot grow over time an '*entity* belief'. Research on these beliefs had shown that those with an incremental view of intelligence within North American society are more likely to show sustained motivation in the face of difficulty (Blackwell et al., 2007) and to treat those whom they think have low ability in different ways from 'entity theorists' (Rattan, Good et al., 2012). The evidence that there are cultural differences between societies in the frequency with which students espouse a 'universal' view of the potential for high intelligence suggests that there could be similar variation in the frequency of incremental and entity views on intelligence in different societies. Rattan, Savani et al. (2012) showed that such variation may be associated with different views on aspects of public policy. The evolution of Western psychological research on intelligence in the modern era has been deeply influenced by broader ideological assumptions about the nature of individual differences and their social significance.

The first step towards the scientific study of intelligence in psychology

Working within the framework of scientific method, early psychologists tried to base their ideas about intelligence on empirical investigation. The first strategy was to collect systematic data on how a wide range of people performed on a range of short mental tests. Inevitably, the design of their studies was influenced by cultural expectations within their society. Examine the advertisement in Focus Box 3.1, which was circulated on a handbill in London in 1884 by Francis Galton (1822–1911), an energetic polymath from a wealthy Victorian family. On this evidence alone, what aspects of his approach do you think are in line with what would be expected today in terms of ethical requirements and methodology, and what aspects deviate from today's standards?

ANTHROPOMETRIC
LABORATORY
For the measurement in various
ways of **Human Form and Faculty**.

Entered from the Science Collection of the S. Kensington Museum.

This laboratory is established by Mr. Francis Galton for
the following purposes:—

1. For the use of those who desire to be accurately measured in many ways, either to obtain timely
warning of remediable faults in development, or to
learn their powers.

2. For keeping a methodical register of the principal measurements of each person, of which he
may at any future time obtain a copy under reasonable restrictions. His initials and date of birth will
be entered in the register, but not his name. The
names are indexed in a separate book.

3. For supplying information on the methods,
practice, and uses of human measurement.

4. For anthropometric experiment and research,
and for obtaining data for statistical discussion.

Charges for making the principal measurements:
THREEPENCE each, to those who are already on the Register.
FOURPENCE each, to those who are not:— one page of the
Register will thenceforward be assigned to them, and a few extra
measurements will be made, chiefly for future identification.

The Superintendent is charged with the control of the laboratory
and with determining in each case, which, if any, of the extra measurements may be made, and under what conditions.

H & W. Brown, Printers, 20 Fulham Road, S.W.

FIGURE 3.1 Galton's anthropometric laboratory

Source: Flanagan and Harrison, 2005: 4.

That handbill was circulated when Galton established his first laboratory at a Health Exhibition in London. When it closed a year later, he opened another nearby. Eventually, he collected data on approximately 17,000 individuals (Johnson *et al.*, 1985). The large battery of tests that he used included physical measures, such as length and breadth of the head, and functional measures, such as breathing capacity. Among the functional measures was one that later played a significant role in the development of experimental psychology, participants' *reaction times* to visual and auditory stimuli. As we will see, this also later featured in theoretical analyses of the nature of intelligence. However, Galton's own conceptualisation of intelligence was based on a misunderstanding of the operation of perception and cognition that led him to stress the value of measuring sensory acuity as a basis for analysing individual differences in mental ability: 'The only information that reaches us concerning outward events appears to pass through the avenue of our senses; and the more perceptible our senses are of difference, the larger the field upon which our judgment and intellect can act' (Galton, 1883, cited by Wasserman and Tulsky, 2005).

This biological emphasis, along with his interest in the role of heredity in individual differences, illustrates ways in which Galton's historical and cultural position influenced his ideas about intelligence. The study of intelligence since his day has benefited from advances in scientific method, but may be no less subject to the cultural and social factors that influence thinking generally at any time.

Factorial theories of intelligence

The early psychometricians developed a wide variety of mental tests, many of which have stood the test of time and continue in use today. Examples include:

- a *vocabulary* test, in which the participant is presented with a list of words, one at a time, and has to provide a definition of each one to the interviewer;
- a *block design* test, in which the participant is presented with a number of wooden or plastic blocks that have sides that are either all white, or all red, or a mix of red and white. They are required to arrange them according to a two-dimensional pattern that they are shown in a booklet, and they are timed on this task.

Charles Spearman (1863–1945) was a pioneer of factor analysis and emphasised the high correlations that are found between mental tests. He concluded that what matters in human intelligence is some form of mental energy that is captured by a general factor in these correlations, which he called '*g*'. The notion of *g* was thus based on statistical analysis and highlighted the shared variance that had been found when the results of a wide range of mental tests were examined. This core finding has proved remarkably robust. Thus, more than 90 years after Spearman's initial reports on the subject, Jensen (1998) reviewed studies of correlates of *g*, including:

- a record of creative accomplishment in arts and sciences;
- job performance in a wide range of occupations;
- scholastic performance;
- success in training programmes.

Studies of human performance on widely different batteries of tests, with diverse samples of participants, have repeatedly confirmed 'the existence of a unitary higher-level general intelligence construct whose measurement is not dependent on the specific abilities assessed' (Johnson *et al.*, 2008).

However, from a very early stage, there were competing views. For example, Louis L. Thurstone (1887–1955) developed a technique of multiple-factor analysis that made it possible to extract separate 'group factors' when analysing matrices of correlations. On that basis, he argued that too much importance had been given to the notion of a general factor and highlighted the role of what he called *primary mental abilities* (PMAs) in explaining the variance in scores on a battery of mental tests. The 'separate and unique' abilities that he identified were word fluency, number facility, verbal comprehension, perceptual speed, associative memory, spatial visualisation and inductive reasoning. At the time that he developed this model, Thurstone denied the validity of Spearman's general factor, but evidence accumulated during the period 1930–50 that the PMAs were not independent of each other, and that Thurstone's own data had a statistical general factor. By the end of his life, after developing factor analytic techniques further, so as to give more attention to higher-order factors in a

FIGURE 3.2 Block design test

Source: Educational Psychology Group, University College London, UK. Reproduced with permission

matrix, Thurstone was ready to acknowledge the possible existence of *g* at a higher-order level (Wasserman and Tulsky, 2005). Although there were earlier challenges to the notion of a general factor of intelligence (Bartholomew *et al.*, 2009), the most influential revival of interest in the importance of separate and unique abilities has been triggered in recent years by the work of Howard Gardner (1983) whose theory of 'multiple intelligences' will be discussed later in this chapter.

Spearman and Thurstone had each made important contributions to the development of the statistical techniques of factor analysis, but, in their day, this was a laborious process, involving extensive manual calculations. Carroll (1993) undertook a major re-analysis of more than 460 datasets from earlier studies of intelligence, employing contemporary factor analytic techniques and taking advantage of the advances in computer technology that had occurred in the interim. Many of his datasets were from earlier pioneers of intelligence assessment, including Thurstone. The 'three-stratum theory of cognitive abilities' that emerged from his work is a hierarchical model in which there are three types of ability:

- first-order abilities, which are narrow in scope and highly specialised, such as absolute pitch, phonetic coding, spelling ability; these are subsumed by
- second-order abilities, which are broader in scope and subsume a number of first-order abilities; examples include general memory and learning, broad visual perception, broad cognitive speediness; these are subsumed by
- a third-order, general intelligence.

The notion of intelligence as a general core plus special abilities thus has a substantial evidence base, and this model was well received when it was published and continues to be influential (Deary, 2012). Carroll (2005) outlined what he saw as the implications of his model for the practical assessment of individuals by groups such as educational psychologists. Although, ideally, all the abilities in his extensive lists should be tested, that would be impractical. However, it needs to be recognised that, if only *g* is assessed, and this policy is followed strictly, 'many abilities that are important in particular cases would probably be missed' (p. 75).

There is one assumption that has often been associated with the concept of *g*, although it is not a necessary corollary of it. This is that intelligence is a fixed, inherited quality that cannot be enhanced or increased. That assumption has been discredited over the last 40 years, because it has been shown that:

- mean IQ in a society tends to increase over time with increases in affluence or educational opportunities (Flynn, 1999);
- the gap between the IQ scores of black and non-Hispanic white Americans has narrowed as the social and economic circumstances of black Americans have improved (Dickens and Flynn, 2006);
- the measured IQ of deprived children often increases following adoption (O'Connor *et al.*, 2000); and
- mean intelligence measures in a general school population may increase following long-term intervention programmes in school, such as cognitive acceleration (Adey *et al.*, 2007).

Process-based theories of intelligence

Factorial theories of intelligence highlight ways in which human abilities are organised or structured, but do not explain how they work. Another approach to investigating the detailed working of cognitive abilities is to break down intelligence-test tasks to their basic components and analyse the microlevel cognitive processes that underlie cognitive abilities. The findings of cognitive psychology are applied to this analysis, so that the focus shifts over time with changes in the focus of interest in cognitive psychology and in the instrumentation that is available. This can be illustrated by considering the progress over time of research on the relationship between intelligence and what, at one point, was termed *cognitive speed*. In Western cultures, people who are seen as intelligent are often described as 'quick'. Does *speed of information processing* offer an explanation of individual differences in intelligence?

Initially, it was shown that speed of reaction on a simple decision-making task (e.g. pressing a button when a light comes on) did not correlate highly with performance on a range of problem-solving tasks. If the task was made more complex (e.g. if participants had to react as quickly as possible to one or another out of several stimuli), then the correlations with measures of cognitive ability increased significantly. However, the amount of variance in ability test performance that can be explained in this way is limited, as correlations rarely exceed 0.4. In addition, it emerged that the apparently simple reaction-time (RT) task was more complex than had been assumed. To do well on an RT task, participants did not just have to respond quickly to a stimulus; they also had to focus their attention on the target and maintain it there, and they had to move quickly to make a response. Studies of the decline of performance with ageing suggested that it was not speed of processing in itself that explained the correlation between reaction time and ability measures, but a decline in the ability to focus and maintain attention over time (Horn and Blankson, 2005). In Method Box 3.1, you will find an account of an alternative experimental paradigm that was designed to provide a simpler and 'cleaner' test of cognitive speed – *inspection time*.

METHOD 3.1

Inspection time and intelligence

In a typical experiment on inspection time, participants are shown two parallel, vertical lines, one of which is longer than the other. The two lines are joined at the top by a horizontal bar. In one form of the stimulus, the long line is on the right, and, in the other, it is on the left. The difference in length is sufficient so that people with normal vision can discriminate between the longer and shorter lines easily: with sufficient inspection time, they give an error-free performance on every occasion. But what happens if the task is made more difficult? One way of achieving that is to allow participants to view the lines for only a very limited period of time. Another way is to prevent participants from processing information that is available in iconic memory after the stimulus has been removed. This can be done by presenting a visual mask of some kind immediately after the target stimulus.

In order to measure a participant's 'inspection time', the target stimuli are presented randomly, so that the long line is equally likely to appear on the left as on the right side. The duration of the stimulus's appearance on screen will vary, for example between 10 and 300 milliseconds. Each time it appears, participants are required to state whether the long line appeared on the left or on the right. They are told to try to judge it correctly and have no instruction to work quickly. Their accuracy is plotted against the length of exposure of the stimulus. Typically, the longer the figure appears on the screen, the more accurate participants' judgements about it are. Some participants achieve high accuracy scores with much shorter periods of exposure than others: they show themselves able to process simple sensory input relatively quickly. It turns out that these individuals tend also to obtain higher scores on cognitive ability tests. (For a review, see Deary and Stough, 1996.) The aim of the experimental paradigm was to reduce the effect of all other variables, such as movement speed or iconic memory, to a minimum, so that individual differences in performance on the task could be attributed almost entirely to a single variable – inspection time (IT). It was hypothesised that, 'if IT does measure the time required to make a single observation of the sensory input, then such a quantity seems likely to operate as a basic factor limiting perceptual and cognitive performance in general' (Vickers and Smith, 1986, cited by Deary and Stough, 1996, p. 603).

Research on inspection time and intelligence showed that people who obtain high scores on intelligence tests (especially nonverbal intelligence tests) also tend to have the ability to make more accurate judgements when stimuli are visible for very brief periods. Perhaps, then, a fundamental characteristic of intelligence is that it is associated with variation in the speed with which people take in and process very simple stimulus information. There must be some doubt about so sweeping a claim, however, because complex information processing seems to rely on other cognitive components, besides speed of processing, for its successful completion.

In contrast to the Western view that speed of thinking is very important, in some cultures it is assumed that a wise person will take time to think. Research on complex information processing found evidence to support the latter view as well as the former: when the time people take to solve a problem is broken down, it is found that those who obtain higher scores on intelligence tests tend to take longer planning how to tackle the problem and then compensate for that by completing the final stages of problem solution more quickly (Sternberg, 1981). Subsequently, Naglieri and Das (1997) developed an ambitious theory of intelligence that highlighted the role of planning in cognitive activity alongside attention or arousal, simultaneous processing and successive processing – the PASS theory. The components of their model were:

- a planning (P) system, which controls and organises behaviour, develops strategies and monitors performance;
- an attention (A) system, which maintains arousal levels and ensures that the individual focuses on relevant stimuli; and
- a system of information processing that employs simultaneous (S) and successive (S) processing to encode, transform and retain information.

Aspects of the PASS model have been shown to correlate with components of reading performance in both alphabetic languages, such as English (Joseph et al., 2003), and non-alphabetic languages, such as Chinese (Wang et al., 2012).

Biological theories of intelligence

Reducing individual differences in intelligence to basic cognitive processes may not go far enough. An alternative approach is to try to explain them at the biological level. The rapid technical advances made in recent years in genetics and neuroscience have meant that we are closer now to understanding the nature of the challenges in this field than we were just a few years ago. One key lesson has been that having better tools for the job does not, in itself, make the job simple. Thus, advances in molecular genetics led to many studies in which attempts were made to link specific genetic variants to measured differences in intelligence. Several such studies had positive results, but careful attempts at replication were unsuccessful, leading one large research team to give their paper on the subject the provocative title 'Most reported genetic associations with general intelligence are probably false positives' (Chabris and Hebert, 2012).

In contrast to studies in molecular genetics, research in behavioural genetics has investigated twins, adoptive children and broader families, in order to estimate the proportion of the variance in measured intelligence that may be caused by genetic differences and by the aspects of the environment that are shared and not shared by members of the same family. As the methodology of large-scale and longitudinal studies in this field has improved, its main results have been validated, not only through repeated replication, but also through confirmation in studies of the DNA of unrelated individuals (Trzaskowski et al., 2013). The central finding is that there are positive genetic correlations of over 0.5 between a range of different tests of verbal and nonverbal cognitive abilities. This suggests that most of the genes that affect cognitive abilities are highly 'pleiotropic', in the sense that genes that affect one cognitive ability affect all cognitive abilities. This supports the notion of a construct of general intelligence (g). The contribution of genetic factors to variations in performance may change with age and may also be affected by environmental factors (Deary, 2012). The impact of the latter was illustrated in an analysis by Turkheimer et al. (2003) of data they obtained from 319 pairs of twins across the US, when they were 7 years old. They found that the proportion of the variance in IQ test scores attributable to genetic factors was much less for those in impoverished families than for those in affluent families, whereas factors relating to their shared environment had a significantly greater influence.

Neuroscience now has the benefit of improved techniques for imaging and recording the activity of the brain. These laid the basis for challenging the old idea that intelligence is localised in the frontal lobes of the brain. Colom et al. (2006) used structural magnetic resonance imaging to study the brains of adults who had different patterns of scores on various intelligence tests. They found that measures of verbal and nonverbal g (i.e., vocabulary and block design) correlated with the amount of regional grey matter across the frontal, parietal, temporal and occipital lobes, and not just in the frontal lobes. The emerging consensus from a range of studies of this kind is that:

> Intelligence does not reside in a single, narrowly circumscribed brain region such as the frontal lobe. Rather, intelligence seems to be best described as a small-world network. This model implies that high intelligence probably requires undisrupted information transfer among the involved brain regions along white matter fibres.
>
> (Deary et al., 2010, p. 207)

An influential idea from earlier research by Haier was that the critical characteristic of more intelligent people is not that their brains differ structurally from those of others, but that they operate in a more efficient manner. This hypothesis was triggered by the finding that there is a *negative* correlation between glucose uptake across the brain and performance on mental tests such as Raven's progressive matrices (a nonverbal ability test closely related to g). It was argued that, if those who do well on such tests consume less sugar during their performance, they are expending less effort on the task. This was taken further, and it was shown that, if participants in an experiment learn a complex task (such as a task involving visuospatial skills) and then practise it, the brightest of them not only show lower overall glucose metabolism in the brain, but also show higher levels in those specific brain areas that are important to the task that has been learned: they focus their mental efforts more efficiently (Haier, 1993). This interesting notion attracted a good deal of subsequent research, and some of the evidence has been contradictory. At the very least, the impact of 'efficiency' may be moderated by variables such as gender, type or complexity of task, or brain area. It has proved possible to train individuals so that they operate on selected tasks with enhanced neural efficiency. Reviewing 20 years of research, Neubauer and Fink (2009) concluded that the efficiency savings in neural effort would be more likely to occur when individuals were confronted with tasks that they did not find very difficult or had had previous opportunities to practise. If the task was very complex, abler individuals would actually invest more cortical resources in completing it, so that there is a positive correlation between brain usage and cognitive ability.

But is demonstrating such correlations enough? For an educational psychologist, the greatest challenge from psychological theories of the basis of intelligence is to tease out what their implications might be for education. If we have an idea about what intelligence is, does that help us to plan how to improve it? Before you turn to the next section, about the applications of the concept of intelligence in education, reflect on what the possibilities might be by tackling the task in Activity Box 3.1.

APPLICATIONS OF IDEAS ABOUT INTELLIGENCE IN EDUCATION

There have been many applications of ideas about intelligence in education. In the past, intelligence tests have been used to identify children with exceptional gifts and talents and children who might be suitable for an academic style of selective education in grammar schools. During the second half of the twentieth century, confidence in the reliability and validity of these methods was steadily eroded. Curriculum-based testing and close classroom observation were seen as providing a more secure basis for key educational decisions (Sutherland, 1990; Freeman, 1998), and intelligence was seen as only one component of giftedness (Sternberg and Grigorenko, 2002). In addition, the influence of a notion of fixed and unchangeable intelligence came to be seen as fostering a sense of helplessness in teachers and students alike: if intelligence is considered to be something that you are born with, there is nothing you (or your teachers) can do to break out of the limitations it places upon you. In the first part of this section, we will examine the application of a factorial theory of intelligence to the identification of learning difficulties. In the second part, we will consider recent attempts to apply process-based theories of intelligence to support effective education across the ability spectrum.

The identification of moderate and severe learning difficulties

In 1904, the Minister of Public Instruction in France appointed a commission to investigate options for educating the group of children who were then called 'defective', such as special classes. One challenge for those involved was how to decide which children needed to be admitted to the new classes. That was not easy, because there was no agreement about what constituted mental subnormality and no standard method of testing children to identify it. The Commission relied heavily on the work of a psychologist, Alfred Binet, and a psychiatrist, Henri Simon, to overcome this problem. Unlike Galton in England, Binet and Simon played down the importance of psychophysical tests. They thought of intelligence as involving higher-order, more complex skills, including judgement, comprehension and reasoning ability. These early scales were relatively simple and crude, and Binet himself had serious reservations about

ACTIVITY 3.1

How to improve intelligence: a modern fairy tale

In the latter half of the twenty-first century, the citizens of the United Kingdom became disillusioned with the cult of celebrity that had been so influential in their culture for the previous two generations. They ceased to want to read about the wives and girlfriends of leading footballers in their magazines; they ceased to want to watch TV games featuring celebrity contestants; they ceased to want to buy products just because they were endorsed by celebrities. Economists and other members of the intellectual elite in Europe became very worried. The void that had been left by the loss of interest in celebrity must be filled. A special commission was set up and took evidence on what might best replace the cult of celebrity. They rejected many suggestions, such as a cult of physical strength and a cult of temperamental calm, because they did not appear to offer economic advantages over other national groups. The proposal they decided to take forward was that the UK should develop a cult of intelligence. Instead of every child hoping to become famous, the pressures within British culture should inspire every child to try to become more intelligent. But how could this be achieved?

The Commission issued an open invitation to any person in the kingdom to come forward and present their ideas on the steps to be taken to enhance the national level of intelligence. A dietician suggested changing the national diet and was sent away for lack of evidence that this method would work. A geneticist suggested building up a stem-cell bank from the brain material of Fellows of the Royal Society and was sent away because of ethical objections. As the time limit that the Commission had set was approaching, it had no viable ideas to take forward. At last, three wise sages from the discipline of psychology asked to address the Commission. Unfortunately, they had different ideas about what intelligence comprises. The first psychologist had a factorial theory of intelligence and emphasised the importance of identifying which ability factors were weakest in any individual's repertoire and which were strongest. The second psychologist had an information processing theory of intelligence and emphasised the importance of processing speed. The third psychologist had a biological theory of intelligence and emphasised the importance of efficiency.

- If you had the theoretical views of each of those psychologists, what advice would you expect to give the Commission about how to improve the national level of intelligence?
- The ending of our modern fairy tale was lost when the Commission's computer crashed. You may like to speculate about how it ended.

them. Nonetheless, they were seen as achieving their main objective – enabling those responsible for provision for the mentally retarded to identify who needed their services. A historian of psychology has observed:

> If the criteria that authorities were forced to rely upon up to that time are taken into account, the eager welcome given to the Binet–Simon scale does not appear excessive. Some physicians had struggled bravely to devise a way of differentiating between the idiot and the imbecile along the lines suggested by Pinel, who claimed that an idiot's attention was 'fugitive' whereas an imbecile's attention was 'fleeting' . . . Some frankly acknowledged that their judgments were uncertain. Dr. Walter Fernald, head of the Massachusetts School for the Feebleminded, regretted that the best that he had been able to do for the classification of children was to depend on observations of their posture and motor coordination when they stepped from the vehicle that brought them to his institution. Others insisted they could tell more about a child based on feelings about the child or on the twinkle, or lack of a twinkle, in the child's eye than could ever be learned from mental testing. But these voices were drowned in the chorus of approval. In Belgium, Germany, Italy, England, and the United States great interest in Binet's work was aroused. Here at last seemed to be an objective means of classification and a convenient device upon which could be placed the greater part of the responsibility for making decisions.
>
> (Reisman, 1991, p. 60)

During the period since then there have been significant technical advances in the structure of intelligence tests. For example, they no longer rely on a concept of 'mental age', a description of a child's intellectual level as the chronological age for which their overall performance on an intelligence scale is average or typical. This had proved an unreliable and misleading statistic. In addition, they pay more attention to nonverbal skills, in parallel with verbal skills. However, the most remarkable feature of the subsequent history of intelligence testing has been its conservatism. The first American version of Binet's scale was published by Terman in 1916. Almost 100 years later, when an updated and revised fifth edition of the Stanford–Binet Intelligence Scale was published, Binet himself would have recognised many of its features, including the format of some individual items and the procedure for interviewing a testee (Roid, 2003).

That continuity is surprising, because the language used to describe learning difficulties and the ways in which such difficulties are conceptualised have changed radically during that period. The shift in official terminology in the United Kingdom is illustrated in Table 3.2. The changes, of course, signify a rejection of terms and phrases that were seen to have negative connotations. But the shift goes further than that: the earlier terminology implied that the groups who were listed in each column were in completely different mental categories, whereas the more recent terminology places individuals on a dimension that differs only in the severity of the difficulties that they encounter.

The table provides a notional range of IQs for each of the groups. In the past, it would have been expected that children whose IQs were less than 50 would attend one type of special school (for those with severe or profound learning difficulties), and those whose IQs were in the range 51–70 would attend another type (for those with

TABLE 3.2 Official terminology for describing children with learning difficulties

Notional IQ range	0–25	26–50	51–70
1913	Idiot	Imbecile	Feeble-minded or high-grade defective
1944	Educationally subnormal (severe)	Educationally subnormal (severe)	Educationally subnormal (mild)
1981	Severe and profound learning difficulties	Severe and profound learning difficulties	Moderate learning difficulties

Source: Frederickson and Cline, 2009. Reproduced with the kind permission of Open University Press. All rights reserved

moderate learning difficulties). However, studies over an extended time period showed that not all children within those intelligence brackets were required to attend the 'appropriate' type of school. Those who appeared to have moderate learning difficulties, on the basis of IQ, might continue to attend a mainstream school, if their reading attainment level was higher (Rutter et al., 1970), or if they showed relatively fewer behaviour difficulties (Simonoff et al., 2006). Separate placement in a special school has become less and less common as a result of policies of educational inclusion. The category term 'moderate learning difficulties' no longer appears in the text of the Code of Practice on Special Educational Needs drafted to support the implementation of recent SEN reforms (DfE/DoH, 2014). However, that is not the only reason why educational decisions about children with learning difficulties are no longer taken mainly on the basis of assessments of intelligence.

Dissatisfaction with cultural bias in intelligence tests undermined confidence in the validity of the tests for educational purposes (Gipps and Murphy, 1994, Chapter 3). More fundamentally, however, the categorisation of learning difficulties by IQ was undermined by the finding that there is no simple relationship between differences in measured intelligence and patterns of learning behaviour. Knowing the IQ of a child with *moderate and severe learning difficulties* does not give a teacher useful information about whether they are likely to learn in a particular way or to experience particular learning problems. The responses of a group of mainstream secondary-school teachers to a detailed questionnaire on the 'moderate learning difficulties' category indicated high degrees of uncertainty about what it might mean (Ylonen and Norwich, 2012). More attention needs to be paid to motivational and attitudinal factors (Zigler, 1999). Adaptations of pedagogy and curriculum content are more likely to be successful when they are based on a broader analysis of the children's approaches to learning in naturalistic settings, as well as their current knowledge and understanding (Porter, 2005). Concerns of this kind led many educational psychologists to advocate a more balanced approach to assessment, with less reliance on norm-based intelligence scales (Lokke et al., 1997). This shift in opinion and practice among educational psychologists will be discussed in more detail in the final section of this chapter.

Multiple intelligences and special abilities

Thurstone's early work on special abilities has been taken forward in recent years in the form of a theory of 'multiple intelligences' that was developed by Howard Gardner.

Like Thurstone, Gardner argued that human intelligence is not a single, complex entity and does not involve a single, integrated set of processes. His model envisaged several relatively autonomous ability sets, which he called, in the plural, intelligences. Each individual is thought to have a unique profile of these intellectual capacities. They are described as developing out of 'a biopsychological potential to process information that can be activated in a cultural setting to solve problems or create products that are of value in a culture' (Gardner, 1999, p. 33). Thus, he rejected the notion of intelligence as fixed and innate. He drew on empirical data to identify the cognitive abilities that were to be included in the list of multiple intelligences, but the datasets on which he relied were not just from psychological research. He also drew on the results of studies in biology and cultural anthropology. There were explicit criteria for identifying an area of ability as a separate and distinct 'intelligence'. They included, for example, biological criteria: 'An intelligence should be isolable in cases of brain damage, and there should be evidence for its plausibility and autonomy in evolutionary history' (Chen and Gardner, 2005, p. 78). The set of multiple intelligences he listed in his 1983 book included:

- *linguistic intelligence* (used in reading, writing, understanding what people say);
- *logical–mathematical intelligence* (used in solving maths problems, checking a supermarket bill, logical reasoning);
- *spatial intelligence* (used in reading a map, packing suitcases in a car so that they all fit);
- *musical intelligence* (used in playing a musical instrument, appreciating the structure of a piece of music);
- *bodily-kinesthetic intelligence* (used in imitating gestures, dancing, running);
- *interpersonal intelligence* (used in relating to other people, e.g. in understanding another person's behaviour or feelings);
- *intrapersonal intelligence* (used in understanding ourselves and how we can change ourselves).

He emphasised that that was not a definitive list and added to it later. Further, although he thought of these distinct abilities as functioning somewhat independently of each other, he noted that, when we observe intelligent behaviour, it is usually the result of an interaction between intelligences.

This formulation proved popular with educators. It was seen as egalitarian, in that everyone might have an area of intelligence in which they showed strengths, even if they did not do well on tests of *g*. It highlighted the value of teaching outside the core academic skills of literacy and numeracy. It stimulated experiments in pedagogy that were designed to draw on and enrich different 'intelligences' (Klein, 1997). To that end, there were initiatives to develop assessments based on multiple-intelligences theory that would assist teachers to select instructional strategies and materials that would be appropriate for each individual child (Chen and Gardner, 2005). Ironically, that approach runs counter to Gardner's original aspirations, because it risks narrowing individuals' experience of the curriculum and reinforcing a static view of each student. An alternative way of interpreting the multiple-intelligences model is to broaden the experience that all students receive, so as to ensure that every lesson meets the needs of a range of individuals, each with different profiles of multiple intelligences. Where a school system traditionally provides a narrow, teacher-centred experience of, for example, biology, the theory of multiple intelligences can be a stimulus to attractive pedagogic reform (e.g. Özdermir *et al.*, 2006).

However, there have been multiple criticisms of Gardner's multiple intelligences. The justification for the criteria used to define separate intelligences has been criticised as muddled and reliant on individualistic judgements (White, 2004). Critics from within psychology have pointed out that Gardner's intelligences correlate positively with *g* and so, like Thurstone's PMAs, are best thought of as factors of general intelligence (Visser *et al.*, 2006). This position has been supported by empirical studies in which a *g* factor has been shown to be highly significant in the results obtained with multiple-intelligence testing (Almeida *et al.*, 2010). Attempts to measure the various intelligences as distinct constructs have been subjected to detailed critical scrutiny (e.g. MacMahon *et al.*, 2004). Analysts of expert performance have highlighted evidence that outstanding results in a particular field do not simply reflect specific innate abilities, but rely significantly on skills that are acquired through deliberate practice (Ericsson and Charness, 1994). It may be that Gardner's specific model has been less important as a contribution to progress in our understanding of human abilities than the flexible and creative use of the concept of intelligence that he championed. This can be seen in the growth of research on such constructs as *emotional intelligence* (Goleman, 1996) and the development by psychologists (e.g. Sternberg, 2010) and educationalists (e.g. Lucas and Claxton, 2010) of broader conceptualisations of how teachers can best think of their students' mental abilities. Thus, for example, Sternberg's model is called WICS, which is an acronym for wisdom, intelligence and creativity synthesised.

> The basic idea is that citizens of the world need creativity to form a vision of where they want to go and to cope with change in the environment, analytical intelligence to ascertain whether their creative ideas are good ones, practical intelligence to implement their ideas and to persuade others of the value of these ideas, and wisdom in order to ensure that the ideas will help achieve some ethically-based common good, over the long and short terms, rather than just what is good for them and their families or friends.
>
> (Sternberg, 2010, pp. 603–4)

EDUCATIONAL PSYCHOLOGISTS' INVOLVEMENT IN THE ASSESSMENT OF INTELLIGENCE

As concepts of intelligence and the tools for investigating intelligence have developed, what involvement have educational psychologists had in this activity? Early accounts of the work of educational psychologists in child guidance clinics refer to 'a room for the psychologist and his various kinds of test' (Burke and Miller, 1929, quoted by Sampson, 1980, p. 4). At around the same time, an American commentator was protesting, 'It must be borne in mind that the psychologist in the Child Guidance Clinic does a great deal more than the estimating of intelligence quotients by the Binet–Simon and other tests' (Hardcastle, 1933, quoted by Sampson, 1980, p. 10). However, an account of a Scottish clinic in that period located the expertise and responsibilities of the psychologist centrally in this field:

The psychologist is a person trained in the measurement of intellectual capacity and in educational methods . . . He is responsible for the accurate measurement of the child's intelligence and also for an estimation of latent capacity, specific disability and any abnormality of temperament that may appear during the testing of the child.

(Dickson, 1938, p. 24)

As psychological science broadened its scope, psychologists came to see their role in quite different terms. Advances in this aspect of their practice reflected the advances that were made in conceptualising children's cognitive development and mental abilities. When a government committee reported on the work of educational psychologists 30 years after Dickson's publication, they emphasised that:

Efforts have been made by psychologists to supplement general types of assessment with more detailed investigations designed to throw light on ways in which problems are solved and the kinds of difficulty that occur. While it remains invaluable to have accurate and reliable information about a child's intelligence, information is also needed about its underlying constituent processes . . . There are several reasons for this added emphasis. First, many intelligence tests provide little information about the nature of problem solving activities and skills and 'all-or-none' methods of scoring are regarded as too insensitive by many who use these tests. If a child fails a particular item, a psychologist can usually only guess at the reasons for his failure, and cannot necessarily assume that the child is incapable of solving all similar problems. Conversely, success in a particular solution does not mean that it has necessarily been arrived at by the most efficient route. Secondly, more detailed diagnostic study can lead to distinctions between a child's intellectual strengths and weaknesses, and hence to knowledge which could enable a psychologist to help a teacher to devise an appropriate remedial programme for the child. In this way, remedial methods might be planned more scientifically in order to place children who need this kind of help in environments for learning which are adapted to their needs.

(Summerfield Committee, 1968, p. 8)

The Summerfield Committee's survey of how educational psychologists allocated their time indicated that psychological assessment formed an important component. Reports by a DfEE Working Group (DfEE, 2000) and a DfES-appointed research team (Farrell et al., 2006) make clear that the assessment of individual children remains a major element of educational psychologists' work, but, in these reports, there is no mention of intelligence testing as a key part of that task, and assessment is tied to consultation and leads to intervention. The use of intelligence scales features in the professional literature when there is a specific reason for undertaking an assessment of general mental ability, for example, when there has been traumatic brain injury (Bozic and Morris, 2005). However, even in these situations, the assessment of general mental ability is likely to make only a modest contribution to an effective investigation of the presenting problems. In the practice of educational psychology, as in education more generally, the use of intelligence as a concept is now considered of limited value.

There is much greater investment in developing dynamic approaches to assessment (Elliott, 2003; Lauchlan and Carrigan, 2013) and methods of assessing specific functions that relate closely to academic achievement, such as *working memory* (Alloway and Alloway, 2010). It will be seen that the term 'intelligence' appears very infrequently in this volume, outside this chapter.

SUMMARY OF MAIN ISSUES ADDRESSED IN THIS CHAPTER

- Teachers tend to agree on how they identify general ability in their pupils, but they are often resistant to using the word 'intelligence' to describe that.
- Scepticism about the value of a construct of intelligence is based on a range of concerns – theoretical, practical, moral, ideological and pedagogic.
- Psychologists' ideas about intelligence are moulded, in part, by *cultural influences*.
- From the early years of the twentieth century, psychologists developed competing views of the factorial structure of intelligence, which have a continuing influence today.
- Although a factorial theory of intelligence can suggest how human abilities are organised, it cannot explain how they work.
- The analysis of basic components of intelligent activity has highlighted the significance of cognitive speed.
- An alternative account focuses on the efficiency with which those with higher tested intelligence focus their mental efforts, measuring efficiency in terms of glucose metabolism.
- When ideas about intelligence have been applied in education, their influence has been seen as negative in some respects.
- The theory of multiple intelligences has proved popular in educational applications but has also attracted damaging academic criticism.
- Educational psychologists rely on global intelligence scales in their assessment work less than they did in the past.

KEY CONCEPTS AND TERMS

- Intelligence
- Potential
- Cultural influences
- Factorial theories of intelligence

- *g*
- Primary mental abilities
- Speed of information processing

- Multiple intelligences
- Reaction time
- Inspection time
- Intelligence scales

RECOMMENDED FURTHER READING

Journal articles

Adey, P., Csapo, B., Demetriou, A., Hautamäki, J. and Shayer, M. (2007). Can we be intelligent about intelligence? Why education needs the concept of plastic general ability. *Educational Research Review, 2*(2), 75–97.

Deary, I.J. (2012). Intelligence. *Annual Review of Psychology, 63*, 453–82.

Sternberg, R.J. (1999). Successful intelligence: Finding a balance. *Trends in Cognitive Sciences, 3*(11), 436–42.

Books

Cianciolo, A.T. and Sternberg, R.J. (2004). *Intelligence: A brief history*. Oxford, UK: Blackwell.

Flanagan, D.P. and Harrison, P.L. (eds) (2005). *Contemporary Intellectual Assessment: Theories, tests and issues* (2nd edn). New York: Guilford Press (especially chapters 1–8).

SAMPLE ESSAY TITLES

1 'Psychological theories of intelligence reflect the social and cultural values of their society.' Discuss.
2 Evaluate the strengths and weaknesses of factorial theories of intelligence.
3 To what degree do psychological research and theory support the use of the word 'quick' to describe someone who is intelligent?
4 What are the advantages and disadvantages of defining moderate and severe learning difficulties in terms of intelligence?
5 Educational psychologists are reported to have turned away from the use of normative intelligence scales. Evaluate reasons why they might have chosen to do so.

REFERENCES

Adey, P., Csapo, B., Demetriou, A., Hautamäki, J. and Shayer, M. (2007). Can we be intelligent about intelligence? Why education needs the concept of plastic general ability. *Educational Research Review, 2*(2), 75–97.

Alloway, T.P. and Alloway, R.G. (2010). Investigating the predictive roles of working memory and IQ in academic attainment. *Journal of Experimental Child Psychology, 106*, 20–9.

Almeida, L.S., Prieto, M.D., Ferreira, A.I., Bermejo, M.R., Ferrando, M. and Ferrándiz, C. (2010). Intelligence assessment: Gardner multiple intelligence theory as an alternative. *Learning and Individual Differences, 20*(3), 225–30.

Bartholomew, D.J., Deary, I.J. and Lawn, M. (2009). A new lease of life for Thomson's bonds model of intelligence. *Psychological Review, 116*, 567–79.

Blackwell, L.S., Trzesniewski, K.H. and Dweck, C.S. (2007). Implicit theories of intelligence predict achievement across an adolescent transition: A longitudinal study and an intervention. *Child Development, 78*(1), 246–63.

Bozic, N. and Morris, S. (2005). Traumatic brain injury in childhood and adolescence: The role of educational psychology services in promoting effective recovery. *Educational and Child Psychology, 22*(2), 108–20.

Carroll, J.B. (1993). *Human Cognitive Abilities: A survey of factor analytic studies.* New York: Cambridge University Press.

Carroll, J.B. (2005). The three-stratum theory of cognitive abilities. In D.P. Flanagan and P.L. Harrison (eds), *Contemporary Intellectual Assessment: Theories, tests and issues* (2nd edn). New York: Guilford Press, pp. 69–76.

Chabris, C.F. and Hebert, B.M. (2012). Most reported genetic associations with general intelligence are probably false positives. *Psychological Science, 23*(11), 1314–23.

Chen, J.-Q. and Gardner, H. (2005). Assessment based on multiple-intelligences theory. In D.P. Flanagan and P.L. Harrison (eds), *Contemporary Intellectual Assessment: Theories, tests and issues* (2nd edn). New York: Guilford Press, pp. 77–102.

Colom, R., Jung, R.E. and Haier, R.J. (2006). Distributed brain sites for the *g*-factor of intelligence. *NeuroImage, 31*(3), 1359–65.

Deary, I.J. (2012). Intelligence. *Annual Review of Psychology, 63*, 453–82.

Deary, I.J., Penke, L. and Johnson, W. (2010). The neuroscience of human intelligence differences. *Nature Reviews Neuroscience, 11*, 201–11.

Deary, I.J. and Stough, C. (1996). Intelligence and inspection time: Achievements, prospects, and problems. *American Psychologist, 51*, 599–608.

Department for Education (DfE)/Department of Health (DoH) (2014). *Special Educational Needs and Disability Code of Practice: 0 to 25 years.* London: DfE.

Department for Education and Employment (DfEE) (2000). *Educational Psychology Services (England): Current role, good practice and future directions. The Report of the working group.* London: HMSO.

Dickens, W.T. and Flynn, J.R. (2006). Black Americans reduce the racial IQ gap: Evidence from standardization samples. *Psychological Science, 17*(10), 913–20.

Dickson, M.D.L. (1938). *Child Guidance.* London: Sands.

Elliott, J. (2003). Dynamic assessment in educational settings: Realising potential. *Educational Review, 55*(1), 15–32.

Ericsson, K.A. and Charness, N. (1994). Expert performance: Its stricture and acquisition. *American Psychologist, 49*(8), 725–47.

Farrell, P., Dunning, T. and Foley, J. (1989). Methods used by educational psychologists to assess children with learning difficulties. *School Psychology International, 10*, 47–55.

Farrell, P. and Smith, N. (1982). A survey of methods educational psychologists use to assess children with learning difficulties. *Occasional Papers of the Division of Educational and Child Psychology, 6*(2), 31–41.

Farrell, P., Woods, K., Lewis, S., Rooney, S., Squires, G. and O'Connor, M. (2006). *A Review of the Functions and Contribution of Educational Psychologists in England and Wales in Light of 'Every Child Matters: Change for children'.* London: Department for Education and Skills.

Flugel, J. (1947). An inquiry as to popular views on intelligence and related topics. *British Journal of Educational Psychology*, *27*, 140–52.

Flynn, J.R. (1999). Searching for justice: The discovery of IQ gains over time. *American Psychologist*, *54*, 5–20.

Frederickson, N. and Cline, T. (2009). *Special Educational Needs, Inclusion and Diversity. A textbook* (2nd edn). Buckingham, UK: Open University Press.

Freeman, J. (1998). *Educating the Very Able: Current international research*. London: The Stationery Office.

Freeman, L. and Miller, A. (2001). Norm-referenced, criterion-referenced and dynamic assessment: What exactly is the point? *Educational Psychology in Practice*, *17*(1), 37–41.

Gardner, H. (1983). *Frames of Mind: The theory of multiple intelligences*. London: Basic Books.

Gardner, H. (1999). *Intelligence Reframed: Multiple intelligences for the 21st century*. New York: Basic Books.

Gipps, C. and Murphy, P. (1994). *A Fair Test? Assessment, achievement and equity*. Buckingham, UK: Open University Press.

Goleman, D. (1996). *Emotional Intelligence: Why it can matter more than IQ*. London: Bloomsbury.

Haier, R.J. (1993). Cerebral glucose metabolism and intelligence. In P.A. Vernon (ed.), *Biological Approaches to the Study of Human Intelligence*. Norwood, NJ: Ablex, pp. 317–32.

Horn, J.L. and Blankson, N. (2005). Foundations for better understanding of cognitive abilities. In D.P. Flanagan and P.L. Harrison (eds), *Contemporary Intellectual Assessment: Theories, tests and issues* (2nd edn). New York: Guilford Press, pp. 41–68.

Jensen, A.R. (1998). *The g Factor: The science of mental ability*. Westport, CT: Praeger.

Johnson, R.C., McClearn, G.E., Yuen, S., Nagoshi, C.T., Ahern, F.M. and Cole, R.E. (1985). Galton's data a century later. *American Psychologist*, *40*(8), 875–92.

Johnson, W., te Nijenhuis, J. and Bouchard, T.B. (2008). Still just 1 *g*: Consistent results from five test batteries. *Intelligence*, *36*(1), 81–95.

Joseph, L.M., McCachran, M.E. and Naglieri, J.A. (2003). PASS cognitive processes, phonological processes, and basic reading performance for a sample of referred primary-grade children. *Journal of Research in Reading*, *26*, 304–14.

Klein, P. (1997). Multiplying the problems of intelligence by eight: A critique of Gardner's theory. *Canadian Journal of Education*, *22*(4), 377–94.

Lauchlan, F. and Carrigan, D. (2013). *Improving Learning Through Dynamic Assessment*. London: Jessica Kingsley.

Lokke, C., Gersch, I., M'Gadzah, H. and Frederickson, N. (1997). The resurrection of psychometrics: Fact or fiction? *Educational Psychology in Practice*, *12*(4), 222–33.

Lucas, B. and Claxton, G. (2010). *New Kinds of Smart: How the science of learnable intelligence is changing education*. Maidenhead, UK: Open University Press.

Mackintosh, N.J. (2007). Review of Lynn's 'Race differences in intelligence: An evolutionary hypothesis'. *Intelligence*, *35*(1), 94–6.

McMahon, S.D., Rose, D.S. and Parks, M. (2004). Multiple intelligences and reading achievement: An examination of the Teele Inventory of Multiple Intelligences. *Journal of Experimental Education*, *73*(1), 41–52.

Naglieri, J.A. and Das, J.P. (1997). *Cognitive Assessment System*. Itasca, IL: Riverside.

Neubauer, A.C. and Fink, A. (2009). Intelligence and neural efficiency. *Neuroscience & Biobehavioral Reviews*, *33*(7), 1004–23.

O'Connor, T.G., Rutter, M., Beckett, C., Keaveney, L., Kreppner, J. and the English and Romanian Adoptees Study Team (2000). The effects of global severe privation on cognitive competence: Extension and longitudinal follow-up. *Child Development*, *71*, 376–90.

Özdermir, P., Güneysu, S. and Tekkaya, C. (2006). Enhancing learning through multiple intelligences. *Journal of Biological Education*, *40*(2), 74–8.

Porter J. (2005). Severe learning difficulties. In A. Lewis and B. Norwich (eds), *Special Teaching for Special Children: A pedagogy for inclusion?* Milton Keynes, UK: Open University, pp. 53–66.

Rattan, A., Good, C. and Dweck, C.S. (2012). 'It's ok – Not everyone can be good at math': Instructors with an entity theory comfort (and demotivate) students. *Journal of Experimental Social Psychology*, *48*(3), 731–7.

Rattan, A., Savani, K., Naidu, N.V.R. and Dweck, C.S. (2012). Can everyone become highly intelligent? Cultural differences in and societal consequences of beliefs about the universal potential for intelligence. *Journal of Personality and Social Psychology*, *103*(5), 787–803.

Reisman, J.M. (1991). *A History of Clinical Psychology* (2nd edn). New York: Hemisphere.

Roid, G. (2003). *Stanford–Binet Intelligence Scales* (5th edn). Itasca, IL: Riverside.

Rutter, M., Tizard, J. and Whitmore, K. (1970). *Education, Health and Behaviour*. London: Longman.

Sampson, O. (1980). *Child Guidance: Its history, provenance and future*. British Psychological Society Division of Educational and Child Psychology Occasional Papers, Vol 3, No 3. London: British Psychological Society.

Scarr, S. (1984). *Race, Social Class and Individual Differences in IQ*. London: Lawrence Erlbaum.

Shipstone, K. and Burt, S. (1973).Twenty-five years on: A replication of Flugel's (1947) work on lay popular views of intelligence and related topics. *British Journal of Educational Psychology*, *56*, 183–7.

Simonoff, E., Pickles, A., Chadwick, O., Gringras, P., Wood, N., Higgins, S., Maney, J.-A., Karia, N., Iqbal, H. and Moore, A. (2006). The Croydon Assessment of Learning Study: Prevalence and educational identification of mild mental retardation. *Journal of Child Psychology and Psychiatry*, *47*(8), 828–39.

Sternberg, R.J. (1981). Intelligence and nonentrenchment. *Journal of Educational Psychology*, *73*(1), 1–16.

Sternberg, R.J. (2010). WICS: A new model for school psychology. *School Psychology International*, *31*(6), 599–616.

Sternberg, R.J. and Grigorenko, E.L. (2002). The theory of successful intelligence as a basis for gifted education. *Gifted Child Quarterly*, *46*, 265–77.

Summerfield Committee (1968). *Psychologists in Education Services*. London: HMSO.

Sutherland, A.E. (1990). Selection in Northern Ireland: From 1947 Act to 1989 Order. *Research Papers in Education*, *5*(1), 29–48.

Swami, V., Furnham, A., Maakip, I., Ahmad, M.S., Nawi, N., Voo, P.S.K., Christopher, A.N. and Garwood, J. (2008). Beliefs about the meaning and measurement of intelligence: A cross-cultural comparison of American, British and Malaysian undergraduates. *Applied Cognitive Psychology*, *22*, 235–46.

Trzaskowski, M., Shakeshaft, N.G. and Plomin, R. (2013). Intelligence indexes generalist genes for cognitive abilities. *Intelligence*, *41*(5), 560–5.

Turkheimer, E., Haley, A., Waldron, M., D'Onfrio, B.M. and Gottesman, I.I. (2003). Socioeconomic status modified heritability of IQ in young children. *Psychological Science*, *14*(6), 623–8.

Visser, B.A., Ashton, M.C. and Vernon, P.A. (2006). Beyond g: Putting multiple intelligences theory to the test. *Intelligence*, *34*, 487–502.

Wang, X., Georgiou, G. and Das, J.P. (2012). Examining the effects of PASS cognitive processes on Chinese reading accuracy and fluency. *Learning and Individual Differences*, *22*(1), 139–43.

Wasserman, J.D. and Tulsky, D.S. (2005). A history of intelligence assessment. In D.P. Flanagan and P.L. Harrison (eds), *Contemporary Intellectual Assessment: Theories, tests and issues* (2nd edn). New York: Guilford Press, pp. 3–22.

White, J. (2004). *Howard Gardner: The myth of multiple intelligences*. Lecture at the Institute of Education, University of London, 17 November. Available online at http://eprints.ioe.ac.uk/1263/1/WhiteJ2005HowardGardner1.pdf (accessed 21 November 2014).

Woods, K. and Farrell, P. (2006). Approaches to psychological assessment in England and Wales. *School Psychology International*, *27*(4), 387–404.

Yang, S. and Sternberg, R.J. (1997). Taiwanese Chinese people's conceptions of intelligence. *Intelligence*, *25*(1), 21–36.

Ylonen, A. and Norwich, B. (2012). Using lesson study to develop teaching approaches for secondary school pupils with moderate learning difficulties: Teachers' concepts, attitudes and pedagogic strategies. *European Journal of Special Needs Education*, *27*(3), 301–17.

Zigler, E. (1999). The individual with mental retardation as a whole person. In E. Zigler and D. Bennett-Gates (eds), *Personality Development in Individuals with Mental Retardation*. Cambridge, UK: Cambridge University Press, pp. 1–16.

4 Raising educational achievement

What can instructional psychology contribute?

Anthea Gulliford and Andy Miller

CHAPTER SUMMARY

In this chapter, you will learn about various ways that educational psychologists have attempted to employ 'instructional psychology' to help raise educational attainments in schools, especially with pupils whom teachers have traditionally found to be the hardest to teach. We will begin by looking at the different ways that educationalists in general have used the term 'underachievement' and at a range of interventions through which educational psychologists have attempted to help raise the attainments of low-, and underachieving children and young people (CYP). The term 'instructional psychology' is used in various ways. In this chapter, it refers to factors in a young person's learning environment, and particularly to actual teaching styles and methods, such as the use of behavioural objectives, task analysis, direct instruction and precision teaching, as they relate to the learning of core skills. Each of these approaches will be examined, and the basic tenets will be illustrated by case examples that suggest that instructional psychology has a role to play in raising attainment in children. Finally, the results from larger-scale applications of instructional psychology aimed at lower-achieving children across a number of classrooms and schools will be explored, which highlight the potential for this type of instructional psychology to reduce underachievement by supporting the attainments of all learners.

LEARNING OUTCOMES

When you have studied this chapter, you should be able to:

1 explain instructional psychology and the evidence for its efficacy as an approach to teaching, for individuals and groups;
2 explain issues of low educational achievement and the rationale and value of instructional psychology methods for supporting achievement;
3 analyse data recording methods within instructional approaches to literacy skill learning, in order to draw conclusions about teaching effectiveness.

INTRODUCTION

At the heart of the profession of educational psychology is a focus upon the achievements of CYP – the reaching of the learner's potential. This challenge, of promoting attainment, translates into the premise that the task for the EP is to analyse the current status quo and support educational arrangements to be made to facilitate next possible steps for the individual – in whatever domain of development. It is this that arguably positions the profession within the perennial debate around achievement and attainment in schools.

Governments have sought, globally and historically, to raise educational standards in schools and to eradicate a seemingly stubborn 'tail of underachievement' – the phenomenon whereby the lowest achievers in our schools seem to be the hardest to reach in terms of raising their attainments. EPs have, throughout the history of their profession, been active in attempts to rectify this. Although EPs have typically found their work to be focused upon supporting the development and learning of individuals, there has been, too, some focus upon the way in which these elements can be supported through larger-scale interventions to support many pupils. In this way, EPs have been able to demonstrate and argue for the potential contribution of instructional psychology to reducing underachievement.

CONCEPTIONS OF 'UNDERACHIEVEMENT'

The term 'underachievement' has long been found within the everyday discourse in education, although its field of reference and its popularity as an explanatory construct have passed through a number of fashions and phases in the past half-century.

Implicit in this term is the notion of potential: that a learner 'ought' to be achieving better in some way, based upon expectations of them as individuals or as representatives of a particular population (Goodman and Gregg, 2010, offer further discussion of this). Where these expectations derive from is an interesting question and relevant for understanding how EPs have responded to issues of underachievement.

When, historically, the practice of intelligence testing among EPs was at its zenith, the notion of underachievement was applied to circumstances where a child or young person was found to be attaining, in a core academic area, at a level below that which 'might be expected', given their IQ. In the parlance of the time, youngsters identified by such means were often described as 'not reaching their potential'. If the academic area in question was literacy, and it almost always was, then the existence of norm-referenced reading and spelling tests allowed psychologists and others to make precise statements about the extent to which the measure of one differed from the other in terms of the statistical likelihood of the occurrence of that degree of difference. By such means, the extent to which a young person might be deemed to be under-achieving could be stated, not only in terms of the delay in acquiring some academic abilities (e.g. 'three-and-a-half years behind his expected level in reading'), but also in terms of the probability of this occurrence (e.g. 'a disparity of this magnitude or greater is likely to be found in only 1.7 per cent of pupils of his age'). Furthermore, a central ingredient in the diagnosis of such conditions as dyslexia and, later, specific literacy difficulties was usually a discrepancy between some measure of literacy difficulties and an IQ test result. This latter facet of underachievement has been carefully disputed in a detailed debate upon the nature and assessment of literacy difficulties, such that 'discrepancy models' have been effectively discredited (see Stanovitch, 1991; Frederickson and Reason, 1995). This is not the focus here, but it does serve to remind us that attainment in one area of skill may not be reliably predictive of another, bringing some fragility to the notion of underachievement.

The concept of underachievement implies a level of performance that is less than, or *beneath*, that of something else, and the criterion for selecting that comparison has shifted over time. The example above, of literacy, highlights comparison *within* individuals. Other examples have drawn attention to comparison *between* groups. In the early days of the expansion of sociological studies within education, much attention was paid to social class. So, Willis (1977), for example, in a classic ethnographic study, argued that the curriculum in what were then secondary modern schools was designed to meet the political and social need for a large workforce engaged in manual labour. In this sense, it was argued that many working-class youngsters underachieved in comparison with their more advantaged and affluent middle-class counterparts. Other studies have posited an underachievement of girls against boys before 1970 or so, and then, since 1988 or thereabouts, of boys against girls (Marks, 2000) and of children from ethnic minority groups (Gilborn and Mirza, 2000) against white youngsters. This picture is far from homogeneous, however, with variation between differing populations, and the gender gap is larger for some ethnic groups: Bangladeshi, Pakistani and African (Cassen and Kingdon, 2007).

More recently, the data suggests continued concern for the attainments of those from classes with lower socio-economic status. Cassen and Kingdon (2007) noted the over-representation of white working-class children in low-achieving groups and, among those, a high proportion of boys. Echoes of this are found in Ofsted's review of SEN and disability (2010), which noted, not only the over-representation of CYP from disadvantaged backgrounds in SEN populations, but that little had changed in the past 5 years, with differentials to be found in the attainment of this group in comparison with peers at any point in time, and in terms of *rates* of progress over time, leading to ever greater disparities as children progress through the education system after entry at age 5 (Goodman and Gregg, 2010).

By the mid 1990s, the comparison that was galvanising action on the part of the newly elected New Labour government was between British pupils and their counterparts in other countries. In a defining study that brought the term 'the long tail of underachievement' to the fore, Brooks *et al.* (1996) investigated the reading performance of 9-year-olds in Britain and compared these results with those obtained on the same tests, from children of the same age, across twenty-seven countries. They found that the proportion of children in the UK scoring in the upper and middle ranges compared favourably with the highest-attaining countries. The UK, however, was noted to have a greater-than-average proportion of children who achieve poorly. At around the same time, the Third International Mathematics and Science Study reported equally gloomy results for mathematics when compared with forty-five other countries (Beaton *et al.*, 1996). In addition to this tail of underachievement being judged too long, it was also characterised as 'stubborn', as being resistant to modification, leading to concerns that, not only were individual educational achievements under threat, but also the country's very future, in terms of economic competitiveness. This phenomenon, of a higher proportion of lower achievers, has been noted, in a review of international achievement data by Tymms and Merrell (2007), to have been present since the 1950s; to be a relatively consistent phenomenon; and to be associated with the US, Scotland and Singapore, suggesting its occurrence may, in part at least, be associated with the irregular features of the English language, which hamper literacy development. It is also noted by these authors that the average attainments of UK pupils continues to be relatively high in international comparisons, allowing concern to rest, then, upon the proportionate issue of those who do not reach average levels.

In an attempt to rectify this, governments since the 1990s have set targets for children at age 11 years, in terms of levels of attainment on standard assessment tasks allied to the National Curriculum. Through this, not only are individual youngsters who do not meet the 'expected' level for their age group identified as underachieving, but schools themselves can also earn this designation and its attendant negative publicity, if too great a proportion of their students are deemed to be individually underachieving This framework is problematic, of course, as any consideration of statistical principles immediately highlights the fact that the laws of normal distribution will not allow for 'all' pupils to attain an expected level that is based upon an average. Nevertheless, subsequent developments have employed increasingly sophisticated forms of data analysis in order, for instance, to determine the degree of improvement, or 'value added', that might be due to school rather than pupil factors, or to home in more particularly on discrete subgroups of pupils whose scores are relatively depressed (Mansell, 2011). In all these developments though, the central organising principle is that the concept of underachievement is to be understood as a shortfall, whether for the individual or the organisation, against a centrally prescribed expectation.

EDUCATIONAL PSYCHOLOGISTS AND UNDERACHIEVEMENT

The question of the validity of the constructed models of expected achievement is one for review elsewhere. What we can say is that, for practising EPs, the issues associated with underachievement for individuals can be complex.

Historically, underpinning the role of the EP is the task of assessment, which allows those around a struggling learner to come to a better understanding of the child's needs (refer to Chapter 1). Assessments within the statutory framework have allowed for a staged model of assessment and intervention, first by schools, and subsequently by other professionals, including EPs, to support the attainment of a struggling learner. For the neediest learners, unable to respond to the various levels of provision offered to them by schools, a local authority is required to consider assessment and provision for more complex needs. In either case, the intention has been to ensure that, first, a child's needs can be assessed, and, second, that the provision required to meet these could be identified. These activities have been designated as sequential and spiral, contributing to ever-greater understanding of the child.

These processes reflect the way in which SENs have been understood and responded to at a policy level in the UK since the Education Act of 1981. EPs became pivotal in these, with their role in *statutory* assessment sometimes identified by others as their key one (Ashton and Roberts, 2006). Some disappointment has been articulated over the years at the scope within this for the EP to enable the development of interventions to support better achievements by the learner, because of the time spent upon assessment (Leyden, 1999; Ashton and Roberts, 2006; Fallon *et al.*, 2010). In addition, it has often been argued that the statutory SEN frameworks have leaned towards conceptualisations of need that are within child, and potentially deficit based, in contradiction to the constructivist and interactionist models held by the majority of the profession (Moore, 2005). This tension has continued to exist, despite a pivotal call in 1978, by Gillham and colleagues, for greater attention to be paid to the learning environment in promoting benefits for a child. An axiom of the EP profession has long been that, in order to change children, one had to change what had happened to them (Gillham, 1999).

Those interested in raising achievement in schools – policymakers and theorists – attend to many factors, including leadership, organisation, grouping, curriculum, school culture and so forth (Muijs *et al.*, 2004). The need for high-quality instructional practices is noted, although attention often falls upon the generic skills and qualities of the teaching force, or upon features of the learning environment that might impede learning, such as difficult behaviour in the classroom. Instructional psychology, in contrast, draws our focus towards features of the environment that can be manipulated in order to attain appropriate responses by the learner (De Corte, 2000). This leads us to the interest of EPs in instructional psychology.

Instructional psychology in the UK grew through the work of a number of psychologists who began to draw attention to the need to consider the conditions for instruction and learning, challenging dominant thinking about assessment and teaching. In addition to this, a strong evidence base for its use began to emerge in the United States (Gallagher *et al.*, 2006). Proponents of instructional psychology in the UK have argued for its place in shaping curriculum delivery for all children. As Solity and colleagues state, 'the key to ensuring that children make progress is what and how they are taught rather than the availability of additional resources, parental support or one-to-one teaching' (Solity *et al.*, 2000, p. 124). Contentious as elements of this view might be to some, there is evidence from classroom investigations that indicates that simply ensuring the presence of additional help such as teaching assistants cannot be guaranteed per se to enable a struggling learner's progress (Alborz *et al.*, 2009;

Blatchford *et al.*, 2009). Blatchford and colleagues have highlighted how support for struggling learners needs to be very carefully attuned, if it is to have any positive effect (Blatchford *et al.*, 2012). A review of the Pupil Premium, a funding initiative aiming to support the most educationally vulnerable groups, underlines the same point, observing low levels of change in provision for under-attaining pupils, or of outcomes, at this early stage in its inception (Ofsted, 2012). By implication, all these lines of evidence enhance the case for a carefully scaffolded learning environment as being central to a child's progress.

INSTRUCTIONAL PSYCHOLOGY

The term instructional psychology can refer to a broad church of ideas relating to environmental adjustments for the learner, but here it will be used to denote those approaches that aim to mediate a controlled and reduced learning environment that promotes core academic skills. The roots of this form of instructional psychology lie in behavioural psychology, in ideas that point the way to reviewing how the context is adjusted to ensure successful performance by the learner on the task (Lindsley, 1992; Gallagher, 2006; Roberts and Norwich, 2010). Importantly, the place of reinforcement in learning is scrutinised (Skinner, 1954). A key feature of this approach is that the learner's attainment on a task is not only just that: it also becomes the assessment that informs the next presentation of a task, and thus success criteria drive the delivery of a learner's programme.

Within the work of some EPs in the UK, a number of contributory elements of such an instructional psychology – such as behavioural objectives, task analysis, direct instruction and precision teaching – may be found, and the remainder of this chapter examines each of these in greater detail.

Behavioural objectives

Ainscow and Tweddle (1979) called for an approach based on curriculum (or task) analysis and the generation of learning objectives, echoing the work of school psychologists from the US, who had developed educational approaches that incorporated operant conditioning into instructional design. By placing an emphasis on 'behavioural objectives', these authors argued for a much greater focus upon factors over which teachers had some control.

Behavioural objectives have two main characteristics: they contain an action and they are observable. So, 'writes down the numbers 1 to 10 from a model' would meet these criteria, whereas 'knows the sounds of the letters a to j' does not, the latter not being expressed as an observable action. Ainscow and Tweddle argued that a major advantage of behavioural objectives was that teachers who acquired the skills involved in writing these were subsequently far better able to plan their teaching activities with an explicit goal for the learner in mind. Although this may seem rather obvious and simplistic, it should be remembered that the pupils they were specifically concerned with were those who had failed to progress very much with less 'precise' methods, where a reasonable degree of incidental or vicarious learning might have been required. Focus Box 4.1 presents an example of such a pupil.

FOCUS 4.1

Using behavioural objectives with Michael – a case example

Michael was a 13-year-old student in a secondary school who was referred to one of the authors because his parents wanted to know whether he might be better placed in a small unit for young people with dyslexia/specific literacy difficulties. He had been experiencing difficulties with reading and spelling throughout his school career and, upon transfer to secondary schooling, he struggled with the subject-based academic curriculum, especially with homework, despite the best efforts of a skilled special needs support department.

Michael had a statement of SEN that identified his specific literacy difficulties, but he was reluctant to be withdrawn from some lessons into the special needs department, to which he attached great stigma. In conversation, it was apparent that he was an articulate and thoughtful young person, and assessments showed his level of verbal comprehension to lie within the high average range for his age.

When Michael was assessed at age 13 years 2 months (13–2), using the Wechsler Objective Reading Dimensions, he obtained a reading age for reading accuracy of 6–6 and for reading comprehension of 6–3. This test has a basal level of 6–0 for both measures. So, in Figure 4.1, these scores are partially extrapolated back to a chronological age of 6–0, where normally developing youngsters would be predicted to obtain reading ages of around 6–0 for both accuracy and comprehension, indicating just how little reading progress Michael had made in 7 years of schooling.

At around the time of this assessment, Michael's case file was also scrutinised in order to ascertain any types of special provision of teaching approaches that had been applied. These are represented by boxed capital letters and explained in the key.

It was clear that various interventions over a 7-year period had failed to make any substantial impact on his levels of reading and, hence, on Michael's ability to access the wider curriculum.

Consequently, and with the agreement of everybody involved, it was decided to devise a programme based on instructional psychology and on the use of behavioural objectives. A set of resource materials – *Alpha to Omega* – was selected, as this represents a graded sequence of phonic exercises aimed particularly at young people with specific literacy needs. A small book was devised, and on each of the first ten pages was written a behavioural objective, with spaces for a start date and a finish date. So, the very first page contained:

> Task 1: Recite after a model the first 8 letters of the alphabet, A–H (for two days running)
>
> Start date:
>
> Finish date:

The remaining nine pages each contained a behavioural objective, ending with 'Task 10: Recite the 5 vowels'. The tasks were sequenced to include writing tasks as well as reciting.

Michael's teachers were encouraged to use whatever teaching methods they favoured in order to enable Michael to carry out and achieve the objective. It was also explained to Michael that, although some of the early exercises would feel very elementary, they were part of a long sequence that would be approached ten at a time. At the beginning of each daily (or, where possible, twice-daily) teaching session, Michael was *always* shown the current ten pages of objectives, with those already achieved and those still to be worked upon being emphasised. No more than ten objectives were ever set in advance, but, as the teaching progressed, the ever-growing set of those already mastered was always revisited at the beginning of each session.

Michael and his teachers responded positively and persevered with this system for 15 months, with later objectives concerned with writing sentences from dictation, spelling words conforming to specific rules and solving anagrams. After this period, Michael was again tested on the same reading test, and his impressive achievements are also presented in Figure 4.1.

FOCUS 4.1 *continued*

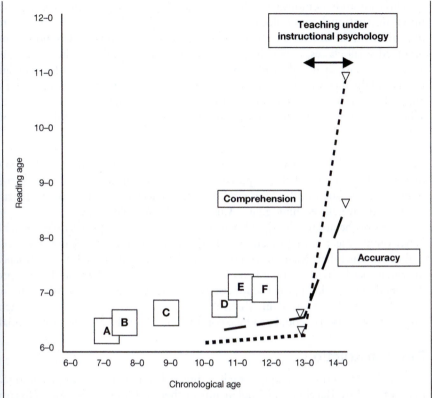

FIGURE 4.1 Michael's reading ages at 13 years 2 months, his extrapolated course of development since 6 years, and the various educational interventions made during this period.

Key: A – Michael is in a class of 32 children with 2 teachers. His parents request 'an assessment' of his abilities at age 7–1 when he is about to transfer to junior school/Key Stage 2; B – Michael is transferred to a 'special teaching facility' based in a local junior school at age 7–9; C – the local authority issues a statement of SEN when Michael is 9–0, and among its recommendations are the development of 'sight vocabulary and phonic skills' and 'a sympathetic approach to self-esteem'; D – a red filter (transparent plastic overlay) is temporarily introduced over reading materials by the school when Michael is aged 11–0 (some suggest this aids reading by reducing glare and/or facilitating visual processing); E – at an annual review of his statement, at age 11–5, his teachers and parents minute that he has 'mood swings' and is 'obstreperous and unco-operative at home and school' and 'appears very depressed'; F – when in secondary school, at age 12–0, it was recorded that Michael and his parents were very concerned about his ability to access and carry out the work required of him at this new phase of schooling.

FOCUS 4.1 *continued*

This case study demonstrates that a 15-month period of teaching based specifically upon instructional psychology principles was able to produce rates of reading improvement far in excess of that gained by following standard SEN procedures that involved small classes, expert help and formal reviews (and red filters). This explicit attention to task-analysed small steps, the fine grain of teaching and learning arrangements and the motivational consequence of unambiguous feedback concerning success enabled Michael to become more settled into his secondary school, to subsequently achieve a number of GCSE passes and, eventually, to enrol for a full-time course in computing at a college of further education.

In Michael's case example, the task (or curriculum) analysis was achieved fairly easily by sequencing the objectives so that they corresponded closely to the *Alpha to Omega* materials. Proponents of these approaches also paid considerable attention to aspects of task analysis, such as the 'step size' between objectives, their correct ordering and the links to overall teaching goals (Ainscow and Tweddle, 1979).

Critics of the approach argued that, if spread across a pupil's whole curriculum, a behavioural-objectives approach would deliver an extremely restricted and excessively dull educational diet. Many learning theorists, too, are interested in the *dynamic* ways in which social interaction mediates learning (Slavin *et al.*, 2009), and the approaches described here could appear minimalist and even, at times, sterile. Advocates, on the other hand, replied that, as in Michael's case study above, a regular approach for a small part of every day could produce considerable and valuable gains in essential skills.

Direct instruction

Direct instruction (DI) is a highly teacher-directed and prescribed approach to teaching first outlined by Bereiter and Englemann in their 1966 book *Teaching Disadvantaged Children in the Preschool*. It is fair to say that, since that time, the approach has generated strong feelings within some in the educational world. For some, DI is seen as overly reductionist, rendering learners into automata who must attend only to specific details of the mechanics of learning. Furthermore, DI appears to leave little room for the learner's own motivations (Kuhn, 2007), to the potential detriment of the process. To counterbalance this, arguments are made that highlight the way in which teaching a skill directly, concisely and without environmental distractions offers the learner a robust and effective opportunity to learn what needs to be learned.

This debate took an uncomfortable turn during the 1980s, when a longitudinal evaluation of differing types of kindergarten (nursery) curriculum was undertaken. Although it appeared to suggest that the DI-based curriculum was associated with later 'delinquency' in its recipients, rebuttals of the study exposed methodological flaws that undermined this claim (see Focus Box 4.2).

In DI approaches, the period of instruction is tightly organised and aims to maximise for students their *academic engaged time*, even if this is to occur for only one or two minutes each day. In order to do this, the teacher employs a pre-prepared script and a set of materials containing a task-analysed sequence of objectives. The teacher's delivery emphasises clarity and lack of ambiguity, building in rhythm, pacing, intonation and pointing. The teaching technique always employs some form of a *model–lead–test* sequence, which has been seen by its critics as potentially robotic, whereas its advocates emphasise the security provided for the learner and the inclusion of *errorless learning*. An example extract is provided in Table 4.1.

Direct instruction and controversy

This report of the High/Scope Preschool Curriculum study traces the effects on young people through age 15 of three well-implemented preschool curriculum models – the High/Scope model, the Distar model, and a model in the nursery school tradition . . . The three preschool curriculum groups differed little in their patterns of IQ and school achievement over time. According to self reports at age 15, the group that had attended the Distar preschool program engaged in twice as many delinquent acts as did the other two curriculum groups, including five times as many acts of property violence. The Distar group also reported relatively poor relations with their families, less participation in sports, fewer school job appointments, and less reaching out to others for help with personal problems. These findings, based on a small sample, are by no means definitive; but they do suggest possible consequences of preschool curriculum models that ought to be considered.

(Schweinhart *et al.*, 1986, p. 15; reproduced with permission from Elsevier)

This conclusion, stated in alarmist terms, has been widely disseminated in the news media. Of course, it is an alarming conclusion – sufficiently alarming that it threatens in one stroke to undo the extensive and well-documented case for the educational benefits of direct instruction. Under close examination of the facts that are provided, however, the damning evidence quickly evaporates . . . In its mythic role, however, [Bereiter's 1966 book with Englemann] has stood for a host of dark forces that many educators imagine to be lurking in the background of early childhood education. Actually reading the book, which very few of the mythmakers appear to have done, would go a long way toward dispelling such phantasms.

(Bereiter, 1986, p. 289 and p. 291; reproduced with permission from Elsevier)

NB: Bereiter's rebuttal attacks the methodology employed by Schweinhart *et al.* (1986), and in particular the use of a self-report approach, which he claims is 'distressingly silent on matters of procedure'. He notes that, for both groups, DI and High/Scope, half of the participants report having been picked up or arrested by police, which suggests, not only that there is no difference between the groups, but that the High/Scope group was not the 'ideal', as supposed, after all. The differences between groups were not statistically significant, and the self-report questionnaire did not include information on female forms of delinquency, and yet 61 per cent of the High/Scope group were female, but only 44 per cent of the DI group. Finally, the study was not conducted 'blind', with participants and researchers being

FOCUS 4.2

FOCUS 4.2 *continued*

aware of the comparison with the High/Scope group. All of these details, it is indicated, significantly undermine the case made by Schweinhart.

Brown (2005) noted problems with attempts to replicate the Schweinhart findings by Cole *et al.* (1993) when employing a more rigorously controlled design, leaving the original claims appearing unreliable based upon design, sampling and calculation issues. Illustrating points raised in Chapter 2 of this volume in terms of close description of method, Brown suggests that the original Schweinhart study may have been founded upon a Type 1 error and draws our attention to the utility of the null hypothesis for intervention research: that is, we do need to understand what has no effect, or what mechanisms we cannot trace, as much as those that do have measurable effects and identifiable mechanisms.

TABLE 4.1 An example of a portion of a 'teaching trial' for single-word recognition

	Teacher	*Pupil*
Introduction	We are going to learn to read this list of words today. I'll go first, then we'll do them together and then you can have a go on your own	
Model	Ready. This word says *house*	
Lead	Let's do it together. Ready. This word says . . . *house*	*House*
Test	Now you try it. This word says . . .	*House*
Correction after test (only if needed)	This word says '*house*'. You say it.	*House*

The teacher adheres very closely to the script, avoiding extra comment and ensuring that a brisk pace and good flow are maintained. Within the approach, teachers' additional utterances, even when intended as helpful or reassuring, are seen as distractions from academic engaged time and interruptions to the learning. Each run through, or 'trial', as above, is completed quickly, with its outcome – either 'correct' or 'correct with correction' – recorded before the next trial is commenced. The correction option ensures errorless learning, in that the student always finishes with a correct response. Sequences of objectives move the learning from these early acquisition skills on to fluency building, using such methods as precision teaching (see below). Within reading, subsequent objectives would also address reading passages of prose, developing phonic skills and the comprehension of passages.

Large-scale evaluation of direct instruction

During the 1960s, the US government undertook a huge initiative – the Headstart Project – that aimed to provide cognitive and affective enrichment to disadvantaged preschoolers in the inner cities. Despite some considerable successes, one disappointing finding was that the gains, the 'head start', made by these young children during this preschool intervention were not maintained through their first few years of formal schooling, with the children slipping back to a level that might have been predicted had no additional help been provided in the first place.

Consequently, a second major initiative – *Project Follow Through*, dubbed at the time the largest educational experiment ever – was funded over a 9-year period and aimed to compare the effects of a range of different educational interventions carried out during the first 3 years of schooling (Carnine, 1979). In total, 75,000 children, spread across 139 sites, were tested in terms of basic academic skills (e.g. word recognition, spelling, maths computation), cognitive skills (e.g. reading with comprehension, maths problem-solving) and affective measures (e.g. self-esteem, degree of taking responsibility for academic successes and failures, etc.).

One of nine different interventions, which ranged from highly teacher-directed approaches such as DI, through to the child-centred and discovery-learning ethos of the then highly fashionable British 'open classroom', was employed in each of the participating institutions, with each supported by a university department sympathetic to the particular approach. Despite considerable difficulties associated with definition, measurement and comparison of diverse interventions, repeated scrutiny of the data identified some consistent patterns in the evidence.

The main findings relevant to the topic of this chapter that emerged from Project Follow Through were as follows:

*   Those approaches based upon DI were the only interventions to produce positive outcomes in basic skills, cognitive skills and affective measures (i.e. outcomes beyond that which would have been predicted had no intervention taken place, and where individual children each provided their own baseline comparison measures).
*   Only four interventions produced positive outcomes in any categories.
*   The more child-centred approaches particularly failed to produce positive measures.

In terms of affective measures, it was particularly surprising to some, both that DI produced positive responses, and that the open classroom failed to do so. A prevalent feeling at the time was that DI might be able to encourage the 'rote learning' of very basic skills, but it would not be able to develop higher-order, cognitive skills or happier, more confident learners. These latter areas were seen as the province of a more child-centred ethos. This finding has been extended by studies that explored the variables influenced by learners under DI, including self-concept (see below).

The pitting of DI against other teaching approaches continued. Swanson (2000, p. 20) captured a major element of this long-running contest as follows: 'There has been some lively debate . . . as to whether instruction should be top–down via emphasising the knowledge base, heuristics and explicit strategies, or a bottom–up emphasis that entails hierarchical instruction at the skill level'. He attempted to summarise and distil the effects of DI by carrying out a meta-analysis of 3,164 studies. The major finding from Swanson's review was that a combined programme of DI and strategy ('top–down', or guidance as) instruction yielded higher effect sizes (0.84) than

DI (0.68) or strategy alone (0.72). The conclusion drawn was that a combined model of DI and strategy instruction can positively influence children with learning difficulties, with regression analysis showing several components (e.g. sequencing, daily testing, segmentation and synthesis) yielding particularly high effect sizes.

Further echoes of the debate regarding teaching approaches persist. An experimental study by Klahr and Nigram (2004) attested to the effectiveness of DI approaches compared with discovery learning in the area of science education, both in terms of learning basic procedures for designing and interpreting simple experiments and with subsequent transfer and application of this basic skill to the more diffuse and authentic context of scientific reasoning. Dean and Kuhn (2007) challenged this, however, with a finding that, over a longer period of time, there were no superior effects of DI, and indeed a 'practice' condition, with no instruction, saw students attaining better overall.

Mayer (2004) helpfully outlined ideas that seek to account for DI's contribution, through explaining a learner's processes when developing new knowledge. Noting *cognitive* rather than *behavioural* activity as central to successful learning, he identified the key events for the learner as: *receiving incoming information, organising it into a coherent structure* and *integrating it with other organised knowledge*, as needed. This model proposes 'incoming information' as the critical element, which DI supports, whereas, in discovery learning, the learner may evade key information, or indeed proceed with the wrong information at the very outset of a task or problem. This modelling of the learning process helps to identify the *mechanisms* through which DI may promote its positive effects.

Haring and Eaton's instructional hierarchy

In the hypothetical DI example above, we imagined a pupil who might be learning to read a set of common words 'by sight' (rather than, say, by phonic analysis). Of course, teachers of young children, especially those with learning difficulties, will point out that these pupils will usually have considerable difficulty in retaining their learning, so that, when returning to the task the next day, or whenever, it is likely that the young person may not be able to read those words, leading either to soul-destroying repetition for the child (and teacher), or to a search for other teaching methods, or to the abandonment of this particular teaching objective. It is in these circumstances that Haring and Eaton's (1978) *instructional hierarchy* can prove a very useful explanatory framework.

Haring and Eaton (1978) proposed five stages of instruction and learning (see Table 4.2). Within this framework, the child who learns something one day and has forgotten it the next – a common cry from teachers of youngsters with learning difficulties – has only reached an acquisition stage for that skill – in our example, the reading of a list of words. His or her learning will not be maintained unless an explicit strategy aimed at ensuring fluency is also devised. This is where precision teaching comes in.

Precision teaching

Precision teaching (PT) was developed by Lindsley (1971), in the US, as a method for improving learners' fluency, making daily assessments of progress and providing immediate feedback to both learners and teachers, and for that reason it is sometimes

TABLE 4.2 After Haring and Eaton's (1978) five stages of instruction and learning

Acquisition	Learners become able to perform a new skill, aiming for *accuracy*
Fluency	The learner becomes able to perform the new skill with both accuracy and *fluency*
Maintenance	Accuracy and fluency are maintained, even in the absence of periods of direct teaching of the skill
Generalisation	Learners are supported to apply the skill across different contexts
Adaptation	Learners are able to apply the skill in new ways, for example solving new problems, with less support

Source: Haring and Eaton, 1978

known as precision monitoring. This allows for close structuring of the skills the learner is to work on, through each step being closely tailored to previous performance. It has been developed as an effective approach, following an enthusiastic take up in the UK by a number of educational psychologists in the West Midlands in the early 1980s (Booth and Jay, 1981; Raybould and Solity, 1982; Williams and Muncey, 1982).

Although Kessissoglou and Farrell pointed out in 1995 that early interest did not seem to have been maintained, at least in publications within the profession, a renaissance was triggered by the British Psychological Society's 1999 working party report *Dyslexia, Literacy and Psychological Assessment*. Among its conclusions was the recommendation that PT (and single-subject experiments) offer 'a set of strategies for carrying out focused assessments of pupil performance over time and for recording progress in a way that facilitates judgements about accuracy and fluency of performance' (British Psychological Society, 1999, p. 55). An important feature of the approach is its brevity: brief, structured teaching (of the teacher's choice) of around 5 minutes is followed by a 1-minute probe, with random presentation of the target items being learned, to assess progress towards success criteria. Focus Box 4.3. presents a case study example.

The y-axes for frequency charts are represented as a semi-logarithmic rather than a linear scale, so that similar rates of progress have the same gradient – for example, doubling a success rate from, say, five to ten correct per minute has the same gradient as doubling the rate from twenty to forty per minute, or any other doubling. Ratio or 'celeration' charts, as they are known, play an important part in allowing students to receive feedback from their performance. This is hypothesised to support, in turn, the growth of task-related self-efficacy associated with PT (Roberts and Norwich, 2010).

In the example in Focus Box 4.3, Ayesha has undertaken three targets. On the first target, for example, she has increased her success rate from fifteen to forty-nine per minute, while simultaneously reducing her errors. Haring and Eaton's hierarchy predicts that the learning will be retained, with her having achieved such fluency, allowing instruction for maintenance and generalisation to be considered, and for new skills to be built upon this foundation.

As we saw above, the contribution of achievement to self-concept was identified in Project Follow Through's examination of another branch of instructional psychology. The growth of self-concept of the learner is explored by Magliaro *et al.*

Using precision teaching with Ayesha – a case example

A PT approach was used by a trainee EP to support a young girl, Ayesha, in Year 1, aged 6 years, with identified literacy needs. Assessment found a need for Ayesha to develop her fluency in reading high-frequency words at sight, to complement her emerging phonological skills. Daily brief teaching interventions were followed by presentation of a timed, 1-minute 'probe sheet' containing the taught words repeated in randomised sequences. Ayesha's correct and incorrect responses were logged on a graph. An *aim rate* for accuracy appropriate to each child is set as part of the intervention, and fresh targets are added as each one is achieved.

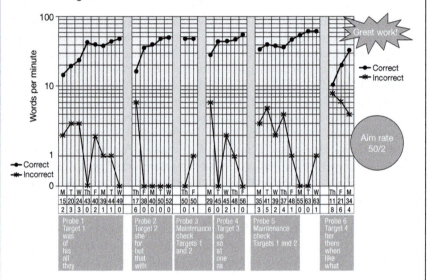

FIGURE 4.2 Ayesha's precision teaching chart

FOCUS 4.3

(2005), who observe that the success orientation of DI, for example, is designed to feed, not only the attainments of the individual, but the *sense* of academic capability. Outside the discussion on instructional psychology, the relationship between academic self-concept and achievement has been fruitfully and extensively debated. Directionality in this relationship is hypothesised (Craven and Marsh, 2008), with academic self-concept being seen as playing a role in attainment (Marsh and Martin, 2010). This notion again gives us insight into the *mechanisms* of instructional psychology, and it is possible to see the potential circularity of success in learning that is likely to be generated through its approaches.

PT continues to be recognised, among educational psychologists, as a potentially powerful, evidenced-based tool (Downer, 2007; Hope, 2013), but one where there is limited take-up in the wider education system (Gallagher, 2006). Although Roberts and Norwich (2010) describe PT successfully employed across groups identified in secondary schools to support reading skills, accounts in the UK typically illustrate its

ACTIVITY 4.1

Using fluency charts to make decisions about teaching

Look at the four fluency charts in Figure 4.3 and attempt to match each of these with a statement from the list of possible interpretations. Then, try to make the further link between each of these and a related teaching implication.

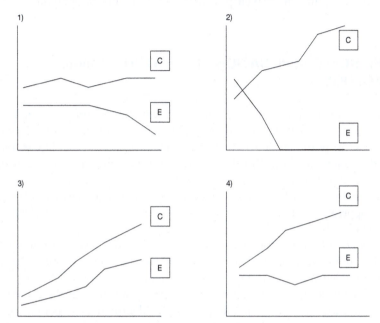

FIGURE 4.3 Fluency charts (C = correct; E = errors)

Possible interpretations
(a) The task is appropriate, learning is taking place, and the error rate has been reduced.
(b) Learning is taking place, but the error rate is not reducing.
(c) Learning is not taking place.
(d) Learning is taking place, but the error rate is increasing.

Teaching implications
(w) Change the emphasis of the teaching to focus specifically on the items leading to errors.
(x) Re-emphasise the need for accuracy and encourage the child to go more slowly for a while.
(y) Move to the next task in the sequence, if the preselected success criterion has been achieved.
(z) Reduce the size of the task, change the teaching method or increase incentives.

value as a targeted intervention to teach specific skills for small numbers of underachieving children, with maths (Chiesa and Robertson, 2000; Gallagher, 2006) or literacy (Reason and Morfidi, 2001; Hughes *et al.*, 2007; Hope, 2013). An increasingly diverse range of accounts now include the use of the approach with young people representing specific populations – for example, those who have autism (Kerr *et al.*, 2003; Beeson, 2013), those who have suffered traumatic brain injuries (Chapman *et al.*, 2005) or looked-after children (Tirapani, 2011). Work to support this latter population exemplifies how well placed the EP is to promote attainment through instructional psychology for young people identified as vulnerable underachievers.

LARGER-SCALE APPLICATIONS OF INSTRUCTIONAL PSYCHOLOGY

In the main, this chapter has concerned itself with interventions carried out with individual pupils, which was where the early activities of instructional psychology enthusiasts were primarily directed, class-based approaches such as Distar not having been widely adopted in the British context. However, the case has also been made for an instructional psychology that attempts to raise the attainments of all children and young people with low achievement levels, whether designated as having SEN or not, by applying psychological principles of teaching, learning and curriculum design across a whole school.

Miller *et al.* (1985) developed a larger-scale system that aimed to train teachers in DI and PT, using teaching methods to address each of Bruner's (1966) three modes in which knowledge is represented – enactive, iconic and symbolic – as well as, at the same time, supporting these teachers as they carried out individualised interventions within their classrooms with pupils previously identified as experiencing serious literacy difficulties. In this way, three EPs were able to support ninety-five children and their teachers across a large geographical area and over a period of a year. Upon evaluation after this period, 84 per cent of participating teachers completed questionnaires that indicated that 289 DI and 187 PT programmes had been successfully completed with these children.

An even larger-scale application can be found in the *Early Reading Research* carried out by Solity *et al.* (2000) in six experimental and six comparison schools, involving a total of 370 children who were followed for 2 years from reception age. The relevant experimental school teachers were trained in distinctive instructional principles to teach their children, 'through distributed rather than massed practice three times a day for ten to fifteen minutes; how to generalise their skills and, through a process known as interleaved learning which minimises forgetting' (Solity *et al.*, 2000, p. 115). Detailed attention was also paid to other aspects in a 'framework for teaching reading' informed by instructional psychology, resulting, after 2 school years, in the experimental-school children outperforming the comparison-school children on all measures of literacy – word reading, comprehension, letter sounds, synthesis, segmentation and spelling – but not rhyming, which was deliberately not taught. Solity *et al.* (2000) also found that their approach had made a significant impact on the learning outcomes of both lower- and higher-achieving pupils and concluded that there are 'alternative ways of making provision for lower achieving pupils than through the legislative and administrative approaches promoted within the field of special education' (Solity *et al.*, 2000, p. 125).

Shapiro and Solity (2008) consolidated the evidence for the place of instructional psychology in whole-class teaching, in a study arguing for the efficacy of whole-class instruction for early readers, as opposed to differential and tailored packages. With an intervention focusing on the phonological skills of children, significant reading gains were made by all, but, in particular, by the *lower* but not *lowest* achievers in a class group. Those who benefited most appeared, in fact, to be those identified, statistically, as the 'underachievers' in population studies. This study illustrated two important features of instructional psychology noted above, *distributed practice* and *interleaved learning*, both of which lend themselves to general classroom teaching. Distributed practice, as noted, supports retention of new material – where the time-lag conditions are right (Seabrook *et al.*, 2005; Cepeda *et al.*, 2009) – and interleaved learning is held to enhance discriminant responding, that is, the capacity of the learning to distinguish similar skills during acquisition (Rohrer, 2012), hypothesised to be an important feature of securing developing knowledge.

This, together with the commentary of Gallagher *et al.* (2006), who review the role of PT in building fluency, offers some illumination of the pathway to reducing underachievement. Slavin *et al.*'s best-evidence review of approaches to promoting early reading (2009) notes that, 'whereas phonics appears necessary in reading instruction, adding a phonics focus is not enough to increase reading achievement', and highlights the need for clear instructional approaches that, 'are characterized by extensive professional development in classroom strategies intended to maximize students' participation and engagement, give them effective metacognitive strategies for comprehending text, and strengthen their phonics skills' (Slavin *et al.*, 2009, p. 1543).

Certainly, evidence suggests that instructional psychology, which asks teachers to set close goals for their students and to guide them in specific instructional ways, can play an effective part in raising achievement. Gallagher and colleagues (2006) go so far as to suggest that it is precisely the development of the dysfluency that contributes to underachievement in schools that instructional psychology, and PT in particular, is effective in tackling.

CONCLUSION

We have seen that teaching approaches that derive from instructional psychology can help to overcome *educational underachievement*, this conclusion being supported by case studies employing single-case designs, as well as larger-scale experimental approaches. These studies can also be seen to address many of the various conceptualisations of underachievement. The implementation of such approaches has, in turn, focused attention upon a range of disparate questions, such as the effectiveness of formal arrangements for addressing SEN, the relationship between basic and higher-order skills and self-esteem, the uneasy perceptions of control and prescription within teaching, assessment of progress and queries about the most productive forms of feedback. Given that instructional psychology impinges on so many educational concerns, it is perhaps not surprising that it has generated its enthusiastic supporters, as well as its sceptical critics, with strong feelings and contentious debate frequently flaring up between these two camps.

SUMMARY OF MAIN ISSUES ADDRESSED IN THIS CHAPTER

- Educational underachievement has been conceptualised in varying ways, including the notions that some individuals do not reach their 'potential', that some groups – girls, boys, members of ethnic minorities – achieve at a lower level than others, that some schools achieve less pupil progress than comparison schools, and that some countries are less successful than others in terms of key academic skills.
- The UK has been found to have a longer tail of underachievement – that is, more young people obtaining low scores in reading and mathematics – than many other countries.
- EPs have a legally prescribed role in contributing help to that minority of low-achieving young people who are seen as having SEN. Some have argued that they can broaden that contribution by drawing on instructional psychology, addressing a far wider group of low achievers. Instructional psychology, under this argument, is seen as the key to ensuring that all children progress.
- Carefully sequenced behavioural objectives can provide motivation and successful learning opportunities.
- Project Follow Through compared the relative effectiveness of nine different teaching approaches with the progress of socially and economically deprived youngsters in the first 3 years of schooling in the US. Direct instruction was found to be the most effective approach in terms of basic skills, cognitive skills and affective measures.
- A five-stage instructional hierarchy developed by Haring and Eaton, with stages of *acquisition, fluency, maintenance, generalisation* and *adaptation*, has helped account for some of the difficulties commonly experienced by slower-learning children, and their teachers.
- Precision-teaching approaches have been promoted in the UK by some EPs and can be used to make daily assessments of learning and to improve learners' fluency levels.
- Some EPs have provided examples of larger-scale applications of successful teaching interventions deriving from instructional psychology.

KEY CONCEPTS AND TERMS

- Educational underachievement
- Instructional psychology
- Learning environment
- Behavioural objectives

- Task analysis
- Direct instruction
- Academic engaged time
- Errorless learning
- Model–lead–test

- Project Follow Through
- Instructional hierarchy
- Precision teaching
- Early Reading Research

RECOMMENDATIONS FOR FURTHER READING

Journal articles

Bereiter, C. (1986). Does Direct Instruction cause delinquency? *Early Childhood Research Quarterly*, *1*, 289–92.

Chapman, S.C., Exing, C.B. and Mozzoni, M.P. (2005). Precision teaching and fluency training across cognitive, physical, and academic tasks in children with traumatic brain injury: A multiple baseline study. *Behavioural Interventions*, *20*(1), 37–49.

Dean, D. and Kuhn, D. (2007). Direct instruction vs. discovery: The long view. *Science Education*, *91*(3), 384–97.

Klahr, D. and Nigram, M. (2004). The equivalence of learning paths in early science instruction: Effects of direct instruction and discovery learning. *Psychological Science*, *15*(10), 661–7.

Solity, J., Deavers, R., Kerfoot, S., Crane, G. and Cannon, K. (2000). The Early Reading Research: The impact of instructional psychology. *Educational Psychology in Practice*, *16*(2), 109–29.

Books and book chapters

Frederickson, N. and Cline, T. (2008). *Special Educational Needs, Inclusion and Diversity. A textbook* (2nd edn). Buckingham, UK: Open University Press.

Swanson, H.L. (2000). What instruction works for students with learning disabilities? Summarizing the results from a meta-analysis of intervention studies. In R. Gersten and E.P. Schiller (eds), *Contemporary Special Education Research: Synthesis of the knowledge base on critical instructional issues*. Mahwah, NJ: Lawrence Erlbaum.

SAMPLE ESSAY TITLES

1 Can instructional psychology help eradicate the long tail of educational underachievement?
2 Instructional psychology encourages teaching approaches that focus on dull rote learning and only the most basic of skills and knowledge. Discuss.
3 How might instructional psychology challenge common conceptualisations of 'special educational needs'?
4 Direct instruction approaches have generated attacks from various educationalists. Why have some educational psychologists persisted in promoting these and other aspects of instructional psychology?

REFERENCES

Ainscow, M. and Tweddle, D.A. (1979). *Preventing Classroom Failure. An objectives approach.* Chichester, UK: John Wiley.

Alborz, A., Pearson, D., Farrell, P. and Howes, A. (2009). The impact of adult support staff on pupils and mainstream schools. Technical report. In *Research Evidence in Education Library.* London: EPPI-Centre, Social Science Research Unit, Institute of Education, University of London.

Ashton, R. and Roberts, E. (2006). What is valuable and unique about the educational psychologist? *Educational Psychology in Practice, 22*(2), 111–23.

Beaton, A.E., Martin, M.O., Mulla, I.V.S., Gonzalez, E.J., Smith, T.A. and Kelly, D.L. (1996). *Science Achievement in the Middle School Years. IEA's third international mathematics and science survey.* Chestnut Hill, MA: TIMSS–Boston College.

Beeson, P. (2013). Investigating this incorporation of precision teaching assessment methods within a structured approach for children with autism. Unpublished DAppEdPsy thesis, University of Nottingham.

Bereiter, C. (1986). Does Direct Instruction cause delinquency? *Early Childhood Research Quarterly, 1*, 289–92.

Bereiter, C. and Engelmann, S. (1966). *Teaching Disadvantaged Children in the Preschool.* Englewood Cliffs, NJ: Prentice-Hall, pp. 48–9.

Blatchford, P., Bassett, P., Brown, P., Martin, C., Russell, A., and Webster, R. (2009). *The Deployment and Impact of Support Staff Project. Research summary. Short summary of the main findings, conclusions and recommendations from the DISS project.* London: Institute of Education, London and DCSF.

Blatchford, P., Webster, R. and Russell, A. (2012). *Challenging the Role and Deployment of Teaching Assistants in Mainstream Schools: The impact on schools. Final report on the Effective Deployment of Teaching Assistants (EDTA) project.* London: Institute of Education.

Booth, S.R. and Jay, M. (1981). The use of precision teaching technology in the work of the educational psychologist. *Journal of the Association of Educational Psychologists, 5*(5), 21–6.

British Psychological Society (1999). *Dyslexia, Literacy and Psychological Assessment. Report of a working party of the Division of Educational and Child Psychology.* Leicester, UK: British Psychological Society.

Brooks, G., Pugh, A.K. and Shagen, I. (1996). *Reading performance at 9*. Slough, UK: National Foundation for Educational Research.

Brown, W.H. (2005). Sometimes the null hypothesis is useful information. *Journal of Early Intervention, 27*(2), 87–91.

Bruner, J.K. (1966). *Towards a Theory of Instruction*. Cambridge, MA: Harvard University Press.

Carnine, D. (1979). Direct instruction: A successful system for educationally high risk children. *Journal of Curriculum Studies, 11*(1), 29–46.

Cassen, R. and Kingdon, G. (2007). *Tackling Low Educational Achievement*. London. Joseph Rowntree Foundation.

Cepeda, N.J., Coburn, N., Rohrer, D., Wixted, J.T., Mozer, M.C. and Pashler, H. (2009). Optimizing distributed practice. *Experimental Psychology (formerly Zeitschrift für Experimentelle Psychologie), 56*(4), 236–46.

Chapman, S.C., Exing, C.B. and Mozzoni, M.P. (2005). Precision teaching and fluency training across cognitive, physical, and academic tasks in children with traumatic brain injury: A multiple baseline study. *Behavioural Interventions, 20*(1), 37–49.

Chiesa, M. and Robertson, A. (2000). Precision teaching and fluency training: Making maths easier for pupils and teachers. *Educational Psychology in Practice, 16*(3), 297–310.

Cole, K.N., Dale, P.S., Mills, P.E. and Jenkins, J.R. (1993). Interaction between early intervention curricula and student characteristics. *Exceptional Children, 60*(1), 17–28.

Craven, R. and Marsh, H.W. (2008). The centrality of the self-concept construct for psychological wellbeing and unlocking human potential: Implications for child and educational psychologists. *Educational and Child Psychology, 25*(2), 104–18.

De Corte, E. (2000). Marrying theory building and the improvement of school practice: A permanent challenge for instructional psychology. *Learning and Instruction, 10*(3), 249–66.

Dean Jr, D. and Kuhn, D. (2007). Direct instruction vs. discovery: The long view. *Science Education, 91*(3), 384–97.

Downer, A.C. (2007). The national literacy strategy sight recognition programme implemented by teaching assistants: A precision teaching approach. *Educational Psychology in Practice, 23*(2), 129–43.

Fallon, K., Woods, K. and Rooney, S. (2010). A discussion of the developing role of educational psychologists within Children's Services. *Educational Psychology in Practice, 26*(1), 1–23.

Frederickson, N. and Reason, R. (1995). Discrepancy definitions of specific learning difficulties. *Educational Psychology in Practice, 10*(4), 195–205.

Gallagher, E. (2006). Improving a mathematical key skill using precision teaching. *Irish Educational Studies, 25*(3), 303–19.

Gallagher, E., Bones, R. and Lombe, J. (2006). Precision teaching and education: Is fluency the missing link between success and failure? *Irish Educational Studies, 25*(1), 93–105.

Gilborn, D. and Mirza, H.S. (2000). *Educational Inequality. Mapping race, class and gender*. London: Ofsted.

Gillham, B. (1999). The writing of *Reconstructing Educational Psychology*. *Educational Psychology in Pratice, 14*(4), 220–1.

Goodman, A. and Gregg, P. (2010). *Poorer Children's Educational Attainment: How important are attitudes and behaviour?* York, UK: Joseph Rowntree Foundation. Available online at www.jrf.org.uk (accessed 23 November 2014).

Haring, N.G. and Eaton, M.D. (1978). Systematic instructional procedures: An instructional hierarchy. In N.G. Haring, T.C. Lovitt, M.D. Eaton and C.L. Hansen (eds), *The Fourth R – Research in the classroom.* Columbus, OH: Charles E. Merrill.

Hope, J. (2013). An evaluation of a direct instruction/precision teaching intervention on the academic self-concept and reading fluency of 'vulnerable' Year 7 pupils. Unpublished DAppEdPsy thesis, University of Nottingham.

Hughes, J.C., Beverley, M. and Whitehead, J. (2007). Using precision teaching to increase the fluency of word reading with problem readers. *European Journal of Behavior Analysis, 8*(2), 221.

Kerr, K., Smyth, P. and McDowell, C. (2003). Precision teaching children with autism: Helping design effective programmes. *Early Child Development and Care, 17*(4), 399–410.

Kessissoglou, S. and Farrell, P. (1995). Whatever happened to precision teaching? *British Journal of Special Education, 22*(2), 60–3.

Klahr, D. and Nigram, M. (2004). The equivalence of learning paths in early science instruction: Effects of direct instruction and discovery learning. *Psychological Science, 15*(10), 661–7.

Kuhn, D. (2007). Is direct instruction an answer to the right question? *Educational Psychologist, 42*(2), 109–13.

Leyden, G. (1999). Time for change: The reformulation of applied psychology for LEAs and schools. *Educational Psychology in Practice, 14*(4), 222–8.

Lindsley, O.R. (1971). Precision teaching in perspective: An interview. *Teaching Exceptional Children, 3*, 114–9.

Lindsley, O.R. (1992). Precision teaching: by teachers for children. *Journal of Applied Behaviour Analysis, 25*(1), 51–7.

Magliaro, S.G., Lockee, B.B. and Burton, J.K. (2005). Direct instruction revisited: A key model for instructional technology. *Educational Technology Research and Development, 53*(4), 41–55.

Mansell, W. (2011). Improving exam results, but to what end? The limitations of New Labour's control mechanism for schools: Assessment-based accountability. *Journal of Educational Administration and History, 43*(4), 291–308.

Marks, J. (2000). *The Betrayed Generations.* London: Centre for Policy Studies.

Marsh, H.W. and Martin, A.J. (2010). Academic self-concept and academic achievement: Relations and causal ordering. *British Journal of Educational Psychology, 81*(1), 59–77.

Mayer, R.E. (2004). Should there be a three-strikes rule against pure discovery learning? *American Psychologist, 59*(1), 14.

Miller, A., Jewell, T., Booth, S. and Robson, D. (1985). Delivering educational programmes to slow learners. *Educational Psychology in Practice, 1*(3), 99–104.

Moore, J. (2005). Recognising and questioning the epistemological basis of educational psychology practice. *Educational Psychology in Practice, 21*(2), 103–16.

Muijs, D., Harris, A., Chapman, C., Stoll, L. and Russ, J. (2004). Improving schools in socioeconomically disadvantaged areas – A review of research evidence. *School Effectiveness and School Improvement, 15*(2), 149–75.

Ofsted (2010). *The Special Educational Needs and Disability Review. A statement is not enough.* Manchester, UK: Ofsted.

Ofsted (2012). *The Pupil Premium. How schools are using the Pupil Premium funding to raise achievement for disadvantaged pupils.* Manchester, UK: Ofsted.

Raybould, E.C. and Solity, J. (1982). Teaching with precision. *Special Education Forward Trends,* 8(2), 9–13.

Reason, R. and Morfidi, E. (2001). Literacy difficulties and single-case experimental design. *Educational Psychology in Practice,* 17(3), 227–44.

Roberts, W. and Norwich, B. (2010). Using precision teaching to enhance the word reading skills and academic self-concept of secondary school students: A role for professional educational psychologists. *Educational Psychology in Practice,* 26(3), 279–98.

Rohrer, D. (2012). Interleaving helps students distinguish among similar concepts. *Educational Psychology Review,* 24(3), 355–67.

Schweinhart, L.L., Weikart, D.P. and Larner, M.B. (1986). Consequences of three preschool curriculum models through age 15. *Early Childhood Research Quarterly,* 1, 15–45.

Seabrook, R., Brown, G.D. and Solity, J.E. (2005). Distributed and massed practice: From laboratory to classroom. *Applied Cognitive Psychology,* 19(1), 107–22.

Shapiro, L.R. and Solity, J. (2008). Delivering phonological and phonics training within whole-class teaching. *British Journal of Educational Psychology,* 78(4), 597–620.

Skinner, B.F. (1954). The science of learning and the art of teaching. *Harvard Educational Review,* 24(2), 86–97.

Slavin, R.E., Lake, C., Chambers, B., Cheung, A. and Davis, S. (2009). Effective reading programs for the elementary grades: A best-evidence synthesis. *Review of Educational Research,* 79(4), 1391–466.

Solity, J., Deavers, R., Kerfoot, S., Crane, G. and Cannon, K. (2000). The Early Reading Research: The impact of instructional psychology. *Educational Psychology in Practice,* 16(2), 109–29.

Stanovich, K. (1991). Discrepancy definitions of reading disability: Has intelligence led us astray? *Reading Research Quarterly,* 26, 7–29.

Swanson, H.L. (2000). What instruction works for students with learning disabilities? Summarizing the results from a meta-analysis of intervention studies. In R. Gersten and E.P. Schiller (eds), *Contemporary Special Education Research: Synthesis of the knowledge base on critical instructional issues.* Mahwah, NJ: Lawrence Erlbaum.

Tirapani, E.-L. (2011). The impact of an evidence-based literacy intervention upon the wellbeing, resilience and academic self-concept of children in care. Unpublished DAppEdPsy thesis, University of Nottingham.

Tymms, P. and Merrell, C. (2007). *Standards and Quality in English Primary Schools Over Time: The national evidence. Evidence to the Primary Review.* Cambridge, UK: University of Cambridge.

Williams, H. and Muncey, J. (1982). Precision teaching before behavioural objectives. *Journal of the Association of Educational Psychologists,* 5(8), 40–2.

Willis, P. (1977). *Learning to Labour. How working-class kids get working class jobs.* New York: Columbia University Press.

5 Inclusion for children with special educational needs

How can psychology help?

Nathan Lambert and Norah Frederickson

CHAPTER SUMMARY

This chapter will examine some of the complexities and controversies surrounding the prevailing international policy of inclusion. *Though inclusion in fact pertains to* all *students, the focus here will be upon the inclusion of children with* special educational needs (SEN). *Definitions of inclusion will be explored, the history of inclusive education will be outlined, and current practice will be described. Research into the efficacy of inclusion, typified by investigations comparing mainstream placements with segregated 'special' schooling, will be considered. Discussion will illustrate the range of methodological challenges encountered in research of this type and the need for more varied methodological approaches in future research. Further discussion will examine how psychological theory has been conscripted to support arguments on both sides of the inclusion debate, and will consider the contribution that psychological theory has made, and could make, to this area of social policy and educational psychology practice.*

When you have studied this chapter, you should be able to:

1   critically evaluate the arguments that are made for and against inclusion and identify their sociopolitical or scientific bases;
2   discuss the research evidence on the efficacy of inclusion, its methodological limitations and the methods that can be used to collate and appraise this evidence;
3   describe the different strands of psychological theory that have contributed to research on the social outcomes of inclusion;
4   describe the wider relevance of psychological theory to inclusive practice in education.

WHAT IS INCLUSION?

The broadest definition of inclusion is that it involves maximising the participation of all learners in *mainstream* community schools, regardless of ability, gender, language, ethnicity, economic status, social class, care status, religion, disability or sexual orientation. At the heart of inclusive education is the development of policies, curricula, cultures and practices that ensure diverse learning needs can be met, whatever the origin or nature of those needs, in mainstream educational settings (British Psychological Society, 2002; UNESCO, 2009). Although it is clear from such a definition that inclusion in fact pertains to all students, the focus here – as in the inclusion literature itself – is on the inclusion of children with SEN.

THE HISTORY OF INCLUSION IN EDUCATION

The establishment of Thomas Braidwood's Academy for the Deaf in 1760 represented the beginning of more than two centuries of steady expansion for 'special schooling', across the UK, that, by the early 1980s, saw almost 2 per cent of the UK school-age population – essentially, those whose development was considered in some way atypical – being taught in non-mainstream *special schools*, away from their typically developing peers. This policy of segregated provision, intended to enable and educate children previously thought to be uneducable, became the subject of significant debate from the 1960s onwards, however, notably within the movement for comprehensive schooling (Norwich, 2008) and within the context of the civil rights movement (Hodkinson, 2010). The debate reached a critical point in 1978 with the publication of the influential Warnock Report on educational provision for 'handicapped children and young people' (DES, 1978), which led to the adoption throughout UK education of a policy of *integration*. According to the 1981 Education Act, children with SEN were in future to be integrated in mainstream schools, as long as they could receive the educational provision they required, their parents were supportive of such a placement, their integration did not lead to the education of others being disrupted, and the arrangements were consistent with the efficient use of resources.

With nearly a decade of integration to reflect upon, the late 1980s and early 1990s saw further debate regarding the efficacy of integration. A distinction emerged between integration (also referred to in the US as *mainstreaming*) and the notion of inclusion: where integration had tended to be seen in terms of the *pupils* adapting, or else receiving additional support so as to be able to 'fit in' with existing mainstream education, those promoting inclusion placed greater emphasis on the need for *schools* to adapt, so as to be better placed to meet the needs of *all* pupils. Essentially, with inclusion:

> It is not the child who is included but the school and the teaching which are inclusive. The special needs are therefore no longer those of the child, but those of the school, and thus go beyond the limits of integration.
>
> (Thomazet, 2009, p. 553)

As Lindsay (2007) has noted, this important conceptual distinction is not always clear in practice. Indeed, it is often difficult to judge just how inclusive a particular arrangement is, with many pupils who have been described as being included actually receiving their education through a *combination* of segregational, integrational and inclusive practice. As one way of accounting for this problem, Norwich (2008) has suggested considering *inclusivity* as a continuum, as set out in Figure 5.1.

Most separate:

- Full time residential provision

- Full time day special school

- Part time special – part time mainstream

- Full time special unit within mainstream school

- Part time special unit within mainstream school, part time ordinary class

- Full time ordinary class within mainstream school with some withdrawal and some in-class support

- Full time ordinary class within mainstream school with some in-class support

- Full time in ordinary class

Most included

FIGURE 5.1 Continuum of special education provision

Source: Norwich, 2008. ©2008 Brahm Norwich journal compilation, ©2008 NASEN. Reproduced with permission

THE CURRENT PICTURE

Over the past 20 years, inclusion has been embraced by many countries as a key educational policy. The Salamanca Statement, which was signed by the representatives of ninety-two countries, called on governments 'to adopt the principle of inclusive education, enrolling all children in regular schools unless there are compelling reasons for doing otherwise' (UNESCO, 1994, p. 8). 'Inclusion and participation', it was stated, 'are essential to human dignity and to the enjoyment and exercise of human rights' (UNESCO, 1994, p. 18). National legislation in many countries, including the US (IDEA, 1997) and the UK (DfES, 2001), subsequently promoted inclusive education for pupils who have SEN or disabilities.

The UK Special Educational Needs and Disability Act of 2001 stated that children who have significant additional needs (currently identified through a *Statement of Special Educational Needs* or an *Education, Health and Care (EHC) Plan*) must be educated in a mainstream school, unless this would be incompatible with parental wishes or with the provision of efficient education for other children (DfES, 2001, Section 324), this requirement being repeated in the more recent Children and Families Act (2014).The impact of such legislation on practice, however, is perhaps not as apparent as one might expect. Considering the period from 1983 to 2001, Norwich (2008) identifies a decrease in the percentage of children being taught in special schools, from 1.87 per cent to 1.30 per cent, and reports that, between 2001 and 2008, the percentage of children being taught in special settings remained at around the 1.2–1.3 per cent level.

Significantly, it has also been argued (e.g. Lloyd, 2008; Greenstein, 2013) that, despite all of the attention on inclusive education over recent decades, educational policy has generally failed to recognise or address 'the inherent injustice of an education system where the curriculum continues to be exclusive and to emphasise narrow academic content, and where the measurement of success and achievement is concerned with attaining a set of norm-related standards' (Lloyd, 2008, p. 234). Essentially, in the absence of significant changes to schools and schooling in general, practice that is often referred to as *inclusion* remains, in many cases, more akin to *integration*.

The political debate around inclusive education remains very much alive, with questions being raised over recent years regarding the ability of mainstream schools to meet the needs of pupils with SEN. In 2011, the UK Department for Education (DfE) published a Green Paper entitled *Support and Aspiration: A new approach to special educational needs*, in which it stated its intention to 'remove the bias towards inclusion' and to 'prevent the unnecessary closure of special schools' (DfE, 2011, p. 5). The DfE has also recently sought to update the 2001 *Code of Practice* on the identification and assessment of special educational needs (DfES, 2001), the document to which all relevant bodies must have regard when making decisions relating to the educational placement of children with SEN. A number of extracts from the new code are set out below and usefully illustrate the complex picture of inclusive education today:

> The majority of children and young people with SEN will have their needs met within local mainstream early years providers, schools or colleges.
>
> (DfE, 2013, Section 7.1, p. 92)

There may be a range of reasons why it may not always be possible to take reasonable steps to prevent a mainstream place from being incompatible with the efficient education of others; for example, where [a pupil's] behaviour systematically, persistently or significantly threatens the safety and/or impedes the learning of others.

(DfE, 2013, Section 7.11, p. 114)

Alongside the general principle of inclusion parents of children with an EHC plan and young people with such a plan have the right to seek a place at a special school ... Parents and young people should have a choice of education settings.

(DfE, 2013, Section 6.8, p. 87)

INCLUSION AND THE EDUCATIONAL PSYCHOLOGIST

The issue of inclusion is understandably one that has a high profile in the work of educational psychologists. Much of the work is carried out at an individual-child level, in terms of consulting with parents and teachers, advising the local authority and supporting schools in developing skills and strategies to meet a broader range of needs. Statements of Special Educational Needs and EHC Plans are produced by means of a statutorily regulated, multi-agency assessment, to which an educational psychologist must contribute their advice. Educational psychologists are also involved with the development, research and evaluation of inclusive initiatives, where they may, for example, work to support the broader school community to change culture, improve systems or reconsider curricula (e.g. Hick, 2005; Hodson *et al.*, 2005; Frederickson *et al.*, 2007). (For further consideration of how psychology can usefully contribute to inclusive education, see Activity Box 5.2.)

SHOULD CHILDREN WITH SEN BE EDUCATED IN MAINSTREAM SCHOOLS?

Jacob's teachers in Activity Box 5.1 have some doubts that he should be educated in a mainstream school, but his parents, and Jacob himself, are committed to this. Whereas his teachers focus on actual or possible outcomes (academic progress, language and communication development), his parents focus on aspirational outcomes, such as being part of his family and local community. Fundamental differences in view are also apparent in the debates between researchers. Lindsay (2003) provides a review of one key aspect of such debates, considering, on the one hand, the view that the efficacy of inclusive education in achieving improved outcomes for children with SEN is a justifiable area for scientific enquiry, while exploring, on the other hand, the position that the adoption of inclusion as a public policy is properly regarded as a matter of rights and morality, to which evaluations of efficacy are largely irrelevant. In fact, there are problems with both the 'rights' position *and* with efficacy research.

Farrell (2000) illustrates some of the dilemmas that may occur when different sets of rights conflict:

ACTIVITY 5.1

Case study

Read the following case study and decide, on the basis of the debate highlighted above, *how* inclusive Jacob's educational provision is.

Jacob is a 9-year-old boy who has Down's Syndrome. He has attended his local primary school since the age of 4. He spent 2 years in the reception class, which means he is now in Year 4, 1 year behind his chronological peers. His parents are committed to him receiving his education in his local mainstream school, which his brother also attends.

Jacob's language development is delayed, and he currently employs Makaton signing to support his communication. He is able to read basic text and write simple sentences. Each morning, for literacy and numeracy lessons, he joins the whole class for the introductory aspect of the lesson and is then withdrawn to work in a quiet room with one other child, with close support from a learning support assistant (LSA). For afternoon sessions, he works in the classroom with LSA support. He has his own learning programmes in everything except project work and PE/games and generally completes different work from the rest of the class.

Jacob has developed a close friendship with one other child, who also has significant SEN, and considers himself friends with a number of other children in the class, joining in with games at playtimes and lunchtimes. He favours games of physical play and sometimes becomes frustrated when others don't want to play his favourite games. His teachers have reported that, over the past few years, as playground interactions have become less physical and more verbal in nature, Jacob's social circle appears to have narrowed.

Jacob has always said he enjoys school and remains keen to attend. More recently, however, he has made a number of comments indicating that he feels he is 'stupid' and has begun to display behaviour that suggests he may be frustrated by some of the challenges of school work.

Jacob's teachers fear that he will not be able to make a successful transition to secondary school. In particular, they fear that the increasingly challenging work will make it even more difficult for Jacob to engage meaningfully in group learning experiences, and that his need for an individualised curriculum means that most of his learning will eventually take place outside the classroom. They are concerned that his language and communication skills are not developing as quickly as they would like. They feel that his needs might be best met through placement in a school for children with moderate learning difficulties.

Jacob's parents feel that the challenges of mainstream education have increased over the years and will increase further still in secondary school. They are keen, however, that he remains in his current placement at least until secondary transfer. Jacob has indicated that he wishes to remain in his current class, with his friends.

A parent may feel that their child has a right to be educated in a mainstream school but an objective assessment of the child might indicate that his/her rights to a good education could only be met in a special school. Whose rights should take preference in cases like this, the parents or the child? In addition, what if placing a child with SEN in a mainstream school seriously disrupts the education of the other pupils? Surely they have a right to a good education as well?

(Farrell, 2000, p. 155)

Strong advocates of the 'rights' position also recognise such dilemmas:

There are also situations in which some choose exclusion – the deaf community comes to mind immediately. Few would argue against their right to choose to be educated together in a school other than their local neighborhood one, despite concerns that segregation may serve to perpetuate the prejudices that make separate schooling desirable in the first place. To argue categorically against the right to make such choices can therefore be seen as an arrogant denial of another's fundamental right to self-determination.

(Gallagher, 2001, p. 638)

The problems with research in this area, and in particular empirical efficacy research, are also substantial and well documented (Madden and Slavin, 1983; Siegel, 1996; Lindsay, 2007) (see Chapter 2 for further discussion of the many challenges presented by 'real world research'). Particular challenges include:

* *Difficulties specifying the independent variable*: The inclusivity of placements is often difficult to ascertain and can certainly vary greatly. Indeed, some practices that are evaluated as inclusion are, in many cases, more akin to integration.
* *Poor matching of participants across groups*: There are often systematic differences between 'included' and 'special school' groups, such that those in the latter group typically have a range of additional problems, rendering group-based experimental design studies particularly challenging.
* *Different objectives across settings*: There are often differences between the curriculum being followed in various settings, typically with greater emphasis being placed on academic subjects in mainstream settings and on self-help and social education in special schools and classes.
* *Different resources across settings*: There are often also differences between the qualifications and experience of teachers in mainstream and special placements, and between the resources available within those settings.

RESEARCH INVESTIGATING OUTCOMES FOR CHILDREN WITH SEN

Methodological problems notwithstanding, most reviews of efficacy research over the last three decades have reached fairly similar conclusions. Early narrative reviews highlighted the inconclusive nature of the evidence, but tended to come down marginally in favour of integration/inclusion, with some qualifications. Madden and Slavin

(1983), for example, concluded that there appeared to be some advantage to integrated placements in relation to both academic and social progress, but only if a suitable individualised or differentiated educational programme was offered. Hegarty (1993) argued that it was difficult to justify maintaining segregated provision if it was no better.

During the 1980s and 1990s, a number of *meta-analyses* were also conducted. These more structured approaches aimed to reduce the possibility of reviewer bias by using statistical summary techniques to explore the numerical results of the reviewed studies. Baker *et al.* (1994–5) summarised three such studies (see Table 5.1). *Effect sizes* were calculated to provide a measure of the strength of the findings that was relatively independent of different study sample sizes. The positive effect sizes reported indicated a small-to-moderate benefit of inclusion for both academic and social outcomes.

Odom *et al.* (2004) conducted a systematic review of articles in peer-reviewed journals and data-based chapters, published between 1990 and 2002, on 3–5-year-olds with disabilities and their typically developing peers in inclusive classroom-based settings. The results were reported using a theoretically based structure capable of accommodating both scientific and social policy issues, Bronfenbrenner's *bioecological model* (Bronfenbrenner and Morris, 2006). The nested systems within which children are thought to develop were mapped on to particular areas of the research literature as follows:

- biosystem: child characteristics;
- microsystem: classroom practices;
- mesosystem: interactions among participants (family members, multiprofessional teams);
- exosystem: social policy;
- macrosystem: cultural and societal values;
- chronosystem: changes in variables over time.

Conclusions from research considering child characteristics (biosystem) and classroom practices (microsystem) were similar to those drawn through the meta-analyses described above. Overall, a range of positive developmental and behavioural outcomes were identified for children in inclusive settings, although children with SEN were not as socially integrated as their typically developing peers.

In another study, Lindsay (2007) reported a target journal review of inclusion efficacy studies published between 2000 and 2005. Eight journals in the field of SEN

TABLE 5.1 Results of meta-analyses on effects of inclusive placement

Author(s)	Carlberg and Kavale	Wang and Baker	Baker
Year published	1980	1985–6	1994
Time period	Pre-1980	1975–84	1983–92
Number of studies	50	11	13
Academic effect size	0.15	0.44	0.08
Social effect size	0.11	0.11	0.28

Source: Baker *et al.*, 1994. Reproduced with permission

were targeted, and 1,373 papers were considered. Of these, only 1 per cent were found to address efficacy issues, either comparing the performance of children with SEN in special and mainstream settings or comparing the performance of children with SEN in mainstream settings with typically developing schoolmates. As with the pre-2000 evidence, the weight of evidence from this review was marginally positive overall. The review concludes that there is a need to research more thoroughly mediators and moderators, in particular those drawn from psychological theory, that support optimal education for children with SEN.

Similar conclusions have emerged from a number of reviews that have focused on social and affective outcomes of inclusion. Interest in these areas has been particularly strong because of predictions, which claimed a basis in psychological theory, that inclusion could be expected to increase social interaction, peer acceptance and positive social behaviour of children with SEN. Initial findings failed to support these expectations and showed that children with SEN were less socially accepted and more rejected by their mainstream classmates. This led some authors to pose the question, 'Is integrating the handicapped psychologically defensible?' (Stobart, 1986), and others to express concern that placement of children with SEN in mainstream schools without appropriate preparation constituted 'misguided mainstreaming' (Gresham, 1982).

Gresham and MacMillan (1997) conducted a review of the social competence and affective functioning of children with high-incidence SEN (e.g. 'moderate learning difficulties', behavioural difficulties, attention deficit hyperactivity disorder (ADHD) and dyslexia) and concluded that the research on the social position of children with moderate SEN was very clear. Compared with their mainstream classmates, they were more poorly accepted, more often rejected and had lower levels of social skills and higher levels of problem behaviours. Findings in the affective area of *self-concepts* were, however, less clear. Some studies reported lower self-concepts for children with SEN, whereas some reported higher self-concepts, and still others failed to find any differences between pupils with SEN and their peers. Drawing on social comparison theory, it was found that much of the research could be interpreted by considering the social group with which children were comparing themselves in different situations. A child's self-concept was usually higher when it was assessed in a special education classroom than when it was assessed in a mainstream classroom, where the achievement of the other children was higher.

Nowicki and Sandieson (2002) also reported some clear findings regarding children's attitudes towards those with intellectual and physical difficulties, following a meta-analysis of articles published between 1990 and 2000. Overall, children without disabilities were preferred to children with either physical or intellectual disabilities; however, inclusive classrooms had a medium-sized effect on facilitating positive attitudes. No consistent effect of type of disability was identified, although there were indications that context–disability interactions might have been operating to shape attitudes. For example, Tripp *et al.* (1995) found that attitudes towards hypothetical children with physical difficulties, assessed by questionnaire during a PE class, were more favourable in non-inclusive classes. By contrast, attitudes to children with learning difficulties did not differ between inclusive and non-inclusive PE classes. In apparent contradiction to *contact theory*, discussed below, the experience of contact with children who have physical difficulties in these PE lessons appeared to have had a negative impact.

More recently, focusing on four key aspects of social participation (*friendships/ relationships, contacts/interactions, students' social self-perception* and *acceptance by classmates*), Koster *et al.* (2010) reported that, compared with students without SEN, students with SEN appeared less well accepted and had significantly fewer friends, fewer interactions with classmates and more interactions with the teacher. They reported, however, that the social self-perception of both groups of students was not significantly different, and that, 'a comparison between students with different categories of disability regarding the four themes of social participation revealed no significant differences' (Koster *et al.*, 2010, p. 59).

RESEARCH INVESTIGATING OUTCOMES *FOR THE CLASSMATES* OF CHILDREN WITH SEN

The effect of the inclusion of children with SEN on classmates *without* SEN has also been an important focus for enquiry over recent years, and research in this area similarly suggests inclusion to have a 'neutral to positive' effect.

Reporting on research utilising the National Pupil Database (which brings together the attainment scores and other education-relevant statistics, including SEN and school setting, of 500,000 UK pupils), Dyson *et al.* (2004) reported that there was no real evidence of a relationship between the inclusivity of a local authority and overall pupil attainment across that local authority, or between the inclusivity of a school and overall pupil attainment within that school. Other factors – socio-economic status, gender, ethnicity and home language – appeared to be much more significant than 'inclusivity' in their impact on pupil attainment. In a subsequent review of twenty-six (predominantly North American) studies considering the effect of increasingly inclusive classrooms on children without SEN, Kalambouka *et al.* (2005) stated that 23 per cent of reported outcomes indicated positive academic and social outcomes for children without SEN, 53 per cent indicated a neutral impact, 10 per cent indicated a mixed impact, and only 15 per cent indicated a negative impact – outcomes being more positive on academic as opposed to social measures.

Ruijs and Peetsma (2009) reviewed literature considering the effects of inclusion on both students *with* and *without* SEN, in terms of both cognitive development and socio-emotional effects. Again, they reported neutral-to-positive effects of inclusive education, concluding that, 'the academic achievement of students with and without special educational needs seems to be comparable to non-inclusive classes or even better in inclusive classes', although 'there may be some differential effects for high- and low-achieving students without special educational needs' (Ruijs and Peetsma, 2009, p. 67). Congruent with previous findings, they also concluded that, with regard to social effects, 'children with special educational needs seem to have a less favourable social position than children without special educational needs' (Ruijs and Peetsma, 2009, p. 67). This research, in fact, reflects much earlier findings, for example Staub and Peck (1994), who reviewed North American studies of the effect of increasingly inclusive classrooms on children without additional needs and concluded that none of the studies found a deceleration of academic progress for the students without SEN: children did not 'pick up' undesirable behaviour, and teacher time was not reduced for children without additional needs.

RESEARCH INVESTIGATING TEACHER ATTITUDES

The importance of teachers' attitudes to the success of inclusion has been increasingly recognised over recent years (e.g. Norwich, 1994; Avramidis and Norwich, 2002; Blecker and Boakes, 2010) and has become another area of interest for researchers. Humphrey and Symes (2013), for example, surveyed fifty-three teachers across eleven secondary schools in the north west of England, ascertaining their perspectives on the inclusion of children with autistic spectrum disorder (ASD) in mainstream secondary schools. They reported finding generally positive attitudes, with senior managers and SEN coordinators (teachers with a special responsibility for, and generally greater experience of, working with children with SEN) reporting greater *self-efficacy* in coping with challenging ASD-related behaviour than other school staff. Larger-scale studies, however, and particularly those wider in scope, have reported less positive findings. De Boer *et al.* (2011, p. 331), in a review of twenty-six international studies investigating *primary*-school teachers' attitudes to inclusion, reported that, 'the majority of teachers hold neutral or negative attitudes towards the inclusion of pupils with special needs in regular primary education' and that, 'no studies reported clear positive results'. Teachers tended to report lacking the competence and confidence to teach children with SEN. Interestingly, the less teaching experience the teachers had, the more positive their view of inclusion tended to be, though the more experience they had of teaching children with SEN specifically, the more positive their view of inclusion. Teachers were reportedly most negative regarding the inclusion of children with learning and behavioural difficulties, and were most positive regarding the inclusion of children with physical and sensory difficulties (De Boer *et al.*, 2011).

As a consequence of such findings, there is now a growing argument for teacher attitudes towards inclusion to be addressed more directly through initial teaching training programmes (e.g. Florian *et al.*, 2010; Forlin, 2010) and increasing examples of developing practice in this field. Killoran *et al.* (2013), for example, reported a positive change in the attitudes of trainee teachers towards inclusion as a result of a pre-service inclusive education course. Interestingly, it has also been argued that teacher attitudes, and more specifically the *teacher–pupil relationship*, can have a significant impact on the social acceptance of children with SEN among their peers (Humphrey and Symes, 2011). Significantly, Robertson *et al.* (2003) reported that the more negative a teacher's relationship with a child with SEN, the less likely it is that the child will be socially accepted by their peers.

HOW CAN PSYCHOLOGICAL THEORY CONTRIBUTE?

It appears, as Lindsay (2007) argues, that more detailed consideration of the contribution of psychological theory would be of value in developing optimal educational experiences for children with SEN. Indeed, psychological theory arguably has a particularly important part to play in the development of optimal inclusive cultures and environments wherein children and young people will be genuinely *socially* included. In this section, we will examine four psychological theories that have been applied to understanding and changing children's attitudes and behaviour towards peers who have SEN:

- theory of planned behaviour;
- contact theory;
- labelling/attribution theory;
- social exchange theory.

Theory of planned behaviour and contact theory

According to the *theory of planned behaviour* (Ajzen, 1991), there are three major influences on behaviour, such as positive interaction with classmates with SEN (see Figure 5.2): one's *attitude toward the behaviour* (one's own positive or negative view of the behaviour), the *subjective norm* (one's perception of the views of other significant people, e.g. parents, teachers, friends) and perceived behavioural control (self-efficacy in relation to the behaviour). These three factors combine to account for the strength of the intention to perform the behaviour in question, which is the major determinant of whether the behaviour is actually carried out. In addition, actual behavioural control may directly impact on ability to carry out the behaviour. To the extent that children are aware of the barriers to carrying out the behaviour, the measure of perceived behavioural control can serve as a proxy for actual control, and this is represented by the dotted line in Figure 5.2. For example, a child may have difficulty carrying out their

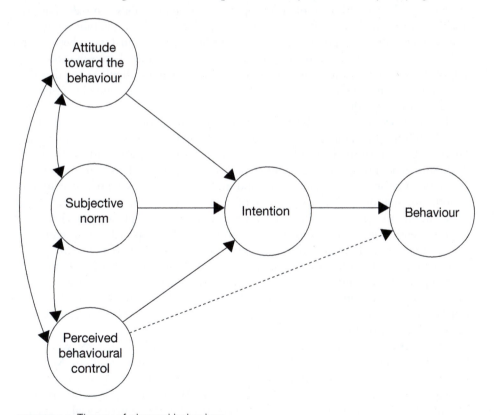

FIGURE 5.2 Theory of planned behaviour

Source: Ajzen, 1991. Reprinted with permission of Elsevier

intention to interact with a classmate with SEN because of organisational arrangements in the classroom, such as teacher-determined groupings. This theory suggests that both attitudes towards classmates with SEN and the balance of environmental facilitators and barriers will be important determinants of behaviour towards children with SEN, and that intervention efforts are likely to need to address both aspects.

A small number of studies have used the theory of planned behaviour to investigate the attitudes and behaviour of children towards peers with SEN in mainstream schools. Consistent with the theory, Roberts and Lindsell (1997) found that 8–12-year-old children's attitudes towards peers with physical disabilities strongly predicted their intentions to interact positively with them. Additionally, children's attitudes correlated significantly with those of their teachers and mothers (the subjective norm). Roberts and Smith (1999) found that children's attitudes towards peers with physical disabilities and their perceived behavioural control were significant predictors of their behavioural intentions to interact with and befriend such peers. In addition, intentions predicted the amount of time children reported spending with their classmates with physical disabilities in the classroom and playground.

Contact theory was identified by Stobart (1986) as one of the theories that, at an early stage, had been 'conscripted to handle the psychological implications of the policy of inclusion' (Stobart, 1986, p. 1). The original theory holds that interaction between groups can change attitudes of in-group members (e.g. pupils who do not have disabilities) towards out-group members (e.g. pupils who have disabilities) and can reduce stereotyping and prejudice if four conditions are met: equal status between the groups in the contact situation, common goals, no competition between groups, and authority's sanction of the contact (Allport, 1954). It is not difficult to see that these conditions are unlikely to have been met in the PE classes in the study by Tripp *et al.* (1995), described earlier.

Both contact theory and the theory of planned behaviour were used by Marom *et al.* (2007) in designing an intervention for children aged 10–12 years intended to improve disability-related attitudes and self-efficacy for interacting with children with disabilities. The intervention was a direct-contact programme between students with disabilities who attended special schools and students without disabilities who attended mainstream schools. A control group of students who were not subject to the intervention was also recruited. The intervention had two phases: (1) children in the intervention group received specific information from special-school staff about the disabilities of the students they were going to meet, together with general information about people with disabilities; (2) children met and interacted directly with pupils with disabilities via joint, non-competitive activities such as music, art and social games. The meetings were held weekly to fortnightly throughout 1 school year. Improvements in attitudes and specific self-efficacy were found for the intervention, but not the control group.

A number of other studies that have drawn on contact theory (e.g. Newberry and Parish, 1987; Maras and Brown, 1996) have also reported positive findings. Maras and Brown (1996), for example, reported that children from a mainstream primary school who were involved in an integration programme with children from a school for children with severe learning disabilities (SLD) showed more positive social orientation towards the pupils with SLD over time, whereas the control group showed little change. However, there are also some less positive findings. Maras and Brown (2000) did not find attitudes to pupils with SEN to be significantly more positive in schools where various kinds of integration were occurring than in control schools that did not have integrated provision. The authors raise questions about the extent to which the contact in some of these schools met Allport's (1954) conditions for success, given large class sizes and limited use by teachers of cooperative learning activities. Nonetheless, this study set out to investigate generalisation of effects from contact with one or more members of an out group to the whole group. Two contrasting models were tested:

1   The *decategorisation model* (Brewer and Miller, 1984) holds that generalisation will be facilitated by a focus on enabling in-group members to get to know out-group members as individuals and minimising the salience of category distinctions.
2   The *'intergroup' contact model* (Hewstone and Brown, 1986) holds that generalisation will be facilitated by a focus on maintaining the salience of 'in-group' and 'out-group' boundaries and emphasising the typicality of the 'out-group' members met, so that attitudes will readily transfer to those not met.

Maras and Brown (2000) selected schools operating integration approaches that related to the two models of contact:

1   where children with SEN were not clearly identified by the schools to their mainstream peers as being members of a wider group;
2   where children with SEN were clearly identified by the schools as members of a group of similar others who were taught separately for all or part of the time. In addition, mainstream children were given information about the children with SEN and how to interact with them.

Children in the intergroup-contact-model schools were found to have more sharply differentiated attitudes across groups and relatively less positive attitudes to children with than without SEN. The hypothesis that the intergroup contact model would facilitate generalisation, however, received support from the finding of correlations between sociometric preferences for known and unknown peers with SEN that were stronger in the categorised than in the decategorised schools.

The intergroup contact model also proved more effective than the decategorisation model in an 'extended contact', as opposed to an actual contact intervention (Cameron and Rutland, 2006). The *extended contact effect*, or 'indirect cross friendship hypothesis', suggests that vicarious experiences of friendship – for example, *knowledge of* in-group members being friends with out-group members – might be effective in reducing prejudice. The intervention was designed for 5–10-year-olds in British primary schools. Once a week, for 6 weeks, stories were read about friendships between non-disabled and disabled children and discussed in small groups. In some stories, the protagonist's disability-category membership was de-emphasised, and their individual attributes were highlighted (decategorisation model); in other stories, category membership was emphasised, and the child's typicality was highlighted (intergroup contact model). In this study, intended behaviour showed positive change in both conditions, and attitudes also showed change in the intergroup condition.

Cameron *et al.* (2011) have subsequently taken the idea of 'extended contact' one step further, investigating the effects of '*imagined contact*' – the 'mental simulation of social interaction with a member or members of an outgroup category' (Crisp *et al.*, 2008, p. 8). It was hypothesised that a child imagining themselves interacting positively with an out-group member would activate feelings similar to those experienced in real-life intergroup interactions, and that the effects of such imagined contact might, therefore, be similar to those of 'direct' or 'extended' contact. The 'imagined contact' in the study of Cameron *et al.* (2011) involved children (aged 5–10 years) being given a picture of a park setting, pictures of park-related objects and photographs of an in-group (non-disabled) child and an out-group (disabled) child. They were asked to imagine themselves in the place of the in-group (non-disabled) child depicted in the photograph and to spend 3 minutes using the photographs and pictures to help them imagine that they were in the park having fun, playing with a disabled friend. Compared with a control group, the children who had engaged in imagined contact subsequently showed reduced intergroup bias in their general attitude and in their ratings of warmth and competence. For the youngest of the children (5–6 years old), imagined contact also led to more positive intended friendship behaviour towards disabled children, though this wasn't apparent in older children (7–10 years), suggesting that imagined contact might be of most benefit to younger children, possibly as they tend to have less out-group experience.

The implications of such findings for practice are significant, with *extended* and *imagined* contact having useful advantages over *direct* contact. For example, extended and imagined contact might avoid negative affect, such as any anxiety elicited by direct contact, and could be particularly useful in preparation for direct contact, prior to the arrival of a child with SEN in a particular mainstream class. Extended and imagined contact might also be especially useful where there is very little opportunity for direct contact, Cameron *et al.* (2011) suggesting that this is particularly advantageous, as it is in low-diversity contexts that intergroup bias is most likely to form and go unchallenged.

Labelling and attribution theory

The implications of recent research on the contact hypothesis would seem to be that more positive attitudes towards children who have SEN can be fostered if their 'special' category membership is clearly apparent to other children. This appears contradictory to the critiques of labelling that played an important role in advocating integration. Dunn argued that labels such as 'mentally retarded', in common use then, served as a 'destructive, self-fulfilling prophecy' (Dunn, 1968, p. 8); however, even research on labelling has consistently shown that peer-group attitudes are more influenced by a child's behaviour than by a categorical label. For example, videotapes of children engaging in positive or negative behaviours were shown to 8–12-year-old viewers, half of whom were told that the child was in a 'special class for the retarded' (Van Bourgondien, 1987). The child's social behaviours, but not the label, had a significant effect on the viewers' attitudes towards them.

More recently, the attitudes and behavioural intentions of 11–12-year-old children towards hypothetical peers described as having ADHD were assessed through response to vignettes (Law *et al.*, 2007). Attitudes towards the characters in the vignettes were found to be mainly negative, and there was a significant relationship between attitudes and willingness to engage in social, academic and physical activities, suggesting that the behaviour of children with ADHD could lead to substantial exclusion by classmates. Diagnostic/psychiatric labels, however, had no additional influence upon attitudes or behavioural intentions.

There is some evidence that a categorical label may sometimes have a protective effect, in terms of helping to ameliorate negative attitudes held by mainstream peers towards children with SEN who exhibit poor social behaviour. Bak and Siperstein (1986), for example, reported on a study in which 9–12-year-old children viewed a video of a child reading. Conditions varied in terms of whether the child was labelled 'mentally retarded' and whether they were depicted as socially withdrawn or aggressive. Assessment of the viewers' attitudes suggested that the label had a protective effect, in that attitudes were less negative with the label when the child was withdrawn; however, this did not hold when the behaviour exhibited was aggressive, when only a weak effect was apparent.

Attribution theory (Weiner, 1985) has proved useful in examining the relationship between perceived deviance and negative peer reactions. A key concept is perception of responsibility. A negative or an unexpected event triggers attributional processes in a search for explanation. Someone who is perceived to be responsible (for example, someone who fails an exam because they don't bother studying) is likely to elicit anger from other people, whereas a person who is not held responsible (someone who fails an exam because they have been ill) is likely to evoke sympathy. Juvonen (1991) suggested that reactions to 'deviant' or different individuals are amenable to attributional analyses, as encounters with such individuals may be regarded as negative or non-normal events that elicit a search for explanation.

Sigelman and Begley (1987) investigated links between the personal controllability of problems and peers' evaluations of blame among 5–6-year-old and 8–9-year-old children. They were told about peers who were either in a wheelchair, obese, learning disabled or aggressive and were either given no causal information or given information about the cause (controllable or uncontrollable) of each problem. Children in both age groups were responsive to the causal information provided and assigned blame in proportion to ascribed responsibility. When causal information was lacking, the children tended to hold all but the child in the wheelchair responsible, although, with age, increasing emphasis was placed on external causes.

The idea that children spontaneously identify 'deviance' among peers and attribute responsibility in ways that lead to particular affective reactions and accepting or rejecting behaviour was investigated by Juvonen (1991). Twelve-year-olds were asked to identify classmates they considered different from themselves and describe how they were different. They also completed a sociometric measure assessing peer acceptance and rejection. Six categories of deviance were identified: rule breaking (including aggression), social image (including bragging), activity level, low achievement, social withdrawal and physical condition. The more children perceived a classmate as different, the more likely they were to reject that classmate. Juvonen (1991) also investigated mediating processes, both in judgements of hypothetical children and judgements of actual classmates. In both cases, perceptions of responsibility for the deviance predicted interpersonal affect (anger and sympathy) and how liked or disliked the 'deviant' child was. These, in turn, predicted social consequences, such as rejection and social support.

Social exchange theory

We have seen from research on attribution theory that non-normative behaviour may receive a more supportive response from classmates where the perpetrator is identified as having SEN or other 'non-blameworthy' difficulties. Comparable findings have been obtained from research on social exchange in children's interpersonal relationships. Social exchange theory (Thibaut and Kelley, 1959; Kelley and Thibaut, 1978) holds that desire for affiliation with others relates to the sum of the perceived costs and benefits of interacting with them, set against some minimum level of expectation – the comparison level. The comparison level may be different for children who have SEN.

A number of studies have found that different behavioural norms are associated with peer-group acceptance and rejection for children who have SEN to those for their mainstream school classmates (Taylor *et al.*, 1987; Roberts and Zubrick, 1992; Nabuzoka and Smith, 1993; Frederickson and Furnham, 2004). The majority of children who were rejected by classmates scored high on costly social behaviours (e.g. aggression) and low on beneficial social behaviours (e.g. cooperation) (Newcomb *et al.*, 1993). The opposite pattern of scores – high on beneficial and low on costly behaviours – was found for well-accepted children. By contrast, children with SEN who were rejected did not show a symmetrical pattern: they had low scores on beneficial behaviours, but did not have high scores on costly behaviours (Frederickson and Furnham, 1998). Asymmetry was also apparent when high acceptance was differentiated from average acceptance. For children with SEN, beneficial behaviours were not characteristic of good peer acceptance, only low levels of costly behaviours.

These findings can be considered in terms of the distinction drawn between *exchange relationships* and *communal relationships* (Clark and Mills, 1979, 1993). The symmetrical behavioural assessments received from classmates by normally developing children are consistent with the application of exchange-relationship norms. The asymmetrical assessments received by children with SEN suggest a special responsiveness to their social needs, consistent with the application of asymmetrical communal norms (Clark and Mills, 1993). Many case studies of relationships between children with SEN and their typically developing classmates also support this conceptualisation. For example, 'Although there is undeniable warmth between the children, most of the comments and nonverbal interactions reflect a helper–helpee relationship, not a reciprocal friendship' (Van der Klift and Kunc, 2002, p. 22), and, 'The interactions, although tending to be highly positive, had the feel of a parental type of role on the part of the children without disabilities' (Evans *et al.*, 1998, p. 134).

In an experimental test of these ideas, Frederickson and Simmonds (2008) investigated the way in which children, aged 8–9 years and 10–11 years, distributed rewards, jointly earned for work done, with classmates who were acquaintances of children with SEN. Among the older, but not the younger, children, findings supported the characterisation of relationships with acquaintances as exchange relationships and those with children who have SEN as asymmetrical, communal relationships.

Social exchange theory can also predict features of the social environment likely to affect intention to interact with classmates who have SEN. For example, Frederickson and Furnham (1998) predicted that the costs, as opposed to benefits, of interaction would be higher in classes that are less cohesive. They also hypothesised that, in classes where mainstream peers perceive their work to be difficult, perceived similarities with children who have SEN will be increased, and the relative costs of working with them will be reduced. In line with these predictions, high levels of classroom cohesiveness (in addition to low levels of disruptive behaviour) were found to be associated with

ACTIVITY 5.2

How else might psychological theory usefully contribute to inclusive education?

In this chapter, the focus has been on how psychological theory and research contribute to our understanding of children's and young people's *social* inclusion in schools – how theories help us understand and influence children's attitudes and behaviour towards peers with SEN. There are, however, many other ways in which psychology can contribute to inclusive education. The job of an educational psychologist is essentially to draw on psychology to promote positive outcomes in education. Consider, then, the psychological domains that form the basis of the work of educational psychologists:

- *Behavioural psychology/learning theory* helps us to understand the effect of context and environment on learning, as well as how one might manipulate these aspects to *optimise* learning.
- *Cognitive psychology* helps us to understand internal mental processes (for example, how people perceive, remember, speak, solve problems) that are of fundamental importance to the development of effective teaching and intervention programmes.
- *Developmental psychology* has furthered understanding of the systematic psychological changes that occur over the course of a life span and informs, in particular, the assessment of children's abilities and needs.
- *Social psychology* helps us to understand how people's thoughts, feelings and behaviours are influenced by the presence of others.
- *Instructional psychology* is concerned with identifying optimal methods of instruction.
- *Cognitive behavioural approaches* concern therapeutic approaches based upon a combination of behavioural and cognitive theory that encourage the questioning of existing cognitions so as to promote new ways of behaving and reacting.
- *Systems psychology and organisational psychology* concern behaviour within complex systems and organisations, both having particular relevance for those intent on making educational organisations – for example, classrooms, schools and local authorities – both more effective and more *inclusive*.

With these psychological domains in mind, what other aspects of educational psychology discussed in this book might be considered to be important for the development of inclusive education?

peer acceptance towards children with SEN. On the other hand, rejection of this group was lower, both when they were rated by peers as 'cooperative' and where the majority of children in the class found the work difficult. This again points to the importance of classroom ethos.

The influence of school-ethos factors on pupils' attitudes to peers with SEN was also investigated by McDougall *et al.* (2004). They found that positive student relationships at the school level and a school goal task structure that promoted learning and understanding for all, rather than social comparison and competition among students, had significant associations with positive attitudes. They suggest that school-wide, ecologically based initiatives aimed at modifying the environment to create a supportive school should be an important element of any effort to enhance attitudes towards students with disabilities.

INCLUSION: IMPLICATIONS FROM PSYCHOLOGICAL THEORY AND RESEARCH

In this section, we have reviewed a number of strands of psychological theory that have been applied in investigating and endeavouring to enhance inclusive practice. There are two consistent findings. First, that aspects of the school social environment can have a predictable and important influence on pupils' attitudes, intentions and actions. Second, for many children with SEN in many school contexts, clearly acknowledging differences, as well as what they have in common with their classmates, appears more likely to facilitate their inclusion than appearing not to recognise or address the differences that exist. This may appear counter-intuitive to some in the field of education; however, it has long been known that, even at relatively young ages, children notice and react to atypical behaviours in other children (Coie and Pennington, 1976; Maas *et al.*, 1978). Rather than classmates being left to make their own (often rather negative) attributions, more positive outcomes are likely to result if adults provide advance information, ongoing explanations and appropriately structured and supported opportunities for contact.

SUMMARY OF MAIN ISSUES ADDRESSED IN THIS CHAPTER

- Inclusion involves providing education in mainstream schools for all children and contrasts with the provision of separate special schools or classes for children with SEN. There remains much debate about the nature of inclusive education.
- The role of scientific research in shaping the social policy of inclusion is disputed. Neither rights considerations nor research evidence are clear cut. Conflicting rights can create ethical dilemmas, and methodological problems with the research evidence can render clear conclusions elusive.
- Reviews of efficacy research using different methodologies have generally identified a marginal advantage of inclusive placements for academic and social outcomes. However, the position of children with SEN on measures of social and affective adjustment is less positive than for their classmates who do not have SEN.

- Four strands of psychological theory addressing aspects of social perception and attribution, interpersonal relationships and group relations were identified, and their contribution to promoting the social inclusion of children with SEN was examined.

KEY CONCEPTS AND TERMS

- Inclusion
- Integration
- Mainstreaming
- Special educational needs
- Meta-analysis
- Effect size
- Bioecological model
- Self-concept

- Subjective norm
- Theory of planned behaviour
- Contact theory
- Self-efficacy
- Decategorisation model
- Intergroup contact model

- Extended contact effect
- Imagined contact effect
- Attribution theory
- Communal relationship
- Exchange relationship

RECOMMENDATIONS FOR FURTHER READING

Journal articles

Cameron, L., Rutland, A., Turner, R., Holman-Nicolas, R. and Powell, C. (2011). Changing attitudes with a little imagination: Imagined contact effects on young children's intergroup bias. *Anales de Psicologia*, 27(3), 708–17.

De Boer, A., Pijl, S.J. and Minnaert, A. (2011). Regular primary schoolteachers' attitudes towards inclusive education: A review of the literature. *International Journal of Inclusive Education*, 15(3), 331–53.

Frederickson, N., Simmonds, E., Evans, L. and Soulsby, C. (2007). Assessing social and affective outcomes of inclusion. *British Journal of Special Education*, 34(2), 105–15.

Gresham, F.M. and MacMillan, D.L. (1997). Social competence and affective characteristics of students with mild disabilities. *Review of Educational Research*, 67, 377–415.

Hodkinson, A. (2010). Inclusive and special education in the English educational system: Historical perspectives, recent developments and future challenges. *British Journal of Special Education*, 37(2), 61–7.

Lindsay, G. (2003). Inclusive education: A critical perspective. *British Journal of Special Education*, 30, 3–12.

Lindsay, G. (2007). Educational psychology and the effectiveness of inclusive education/ mainstreaming. *British Journal of Educational Psychology*, 77, 1–24.

Marom, M., Cohen, D. and Naon, D. (2007). Changing disability-related attitudes and self-efficacy of Israeli children via the Partners to Inclusion Programme. *International Journal of Disability, Development and Education*, 54(1), 113–27.

Norwich, B. (2008). What future for special schools and inclusion? Conceptual and professional perspectives. *British Journal of Special Education, 35*(3), 136–43.

Odom, S.L., Vitztum, J., Wolery, R., Lieber, J., Sandall, S., Hanson, M.J., Beckman, P., Schwartz, I. and Horn, E. (2004). Preschool inclusion in the United States: A review of research from an ecological systems perspective. *Journal of Research in Special Educational Needs, 4*(1), 17–49.

Siegel, B. (1996). Is the emperor wearing clothes? Social policy and the empirical support for full inclusion of children with disabilities in the preschool and early elementary grades. *Social Policy Report, Society for Research in Child Development, X*(2 and 3), 2–17.

Book

Frederickson, N. and Cline, T. (2008). *Special Educational Needs, Inclusion and Diversity. A textbook* (2nd edn). Buckingham, UK: Open University Press.

SAMPLE ESSAY TITLES

1 What are the implications from psychological theory and research for the design of programmes to promote the social inclusion of pupils with SEN?
2 Is labelling always a bad thing? Discuss with reference to the inclusion of children who have SEN.
3 The conditions set by contact theory cannot realistically be met in mainstream schools for most children with severe SEN. Discuss.

REFERENCES

Ajzen, I. (1991). The theory of planned behavior. *Organizational Behavior and Human Decision Processes, 50*, 179–211.

Allport, G.W. (1954). *The Nature of Prejudice.* Oxford, UK: Addison-Wesley.

Avramidis, E. and Norwich, B. (2002). Teachers' attitudes towards integration/inclusion: A review of the literature. *European Journal of Special Needs Education, 17*(2), 129–47.

Bak, J.J. and Siperstein, G.N. (1986). Protective effects of the label 'mentally retarded' on children's attitudes toward mentally retarded peers. *American Journal of Mental Deficiency, 91*(1), 95–7.

Baker, E.T.,Wang, M.C. and Walberg, H.J. (1994–5). The effects of inclusion on learning. *Educational Leadership, 52*, 33–5.

Blecker, N.S. and Boakes, N.J. (2010). Creating a learning environment for all children: Are teachers able and willing? *International Journal of Inclusive Education, 14*(5), 435–47.

Brewer, M. and Miller, N. (1984). Beyond the contact hypothesis: Theoretical perspectives on desegregation. In N. Miller and M. Brewer (eds), *Groups in Conflict.* New York: Academic Press, pp. 281–302.

British Psychological Society (2002). *Division of Educational and Child Psychology (DECP) Professional Practice Guidelines/Inclusive Education Position Paper*. Leicester, UK: British Psychological Society.

Bronfenbrenner, U. and Morris, P.A. (2006). The bio-ecological model of human development. In R.M. Learner and W. Damon (eds), *Handbook of Child Psychology (6th edn): Vol 1, Theoretical Models of Human Development*. Hoboken, NJ: John Wiley, pp. 793–828.

Cameron, L. and Rutland, A. (2006). Extending contact through story reading in school: Reducing children's prejudice towards the disabled. *Journal of Social Issues, 62*(3), 469–88.

Cameron, L., Rutland, A., Turner, R., Holman-Nicolas, R. and Powell, C. (2011). Changing attitudes with a little imagination: Imagined contact effects on young children's intergroup bias. *Anales de Psicologia, 27*(3), 708–17.

Clark, M.S. and Mills, J. (1979). Interpersonal attraction in exchange and communal relationships. *Journal of Personality and Social Psychology, 37*, 12–24.

Clark, M.S. and Mills, J. (1993). The difference between communal and exchange relationships. *Personality and Social Psychology Bulletin, 19*, 684–91.

Coie, J.D. and Pennington, B.E. (1976). Children's perceptions of deviance and disorder. *Child Development, 47*, 407–13.

Crisp, R.J., Stathi, S., Turner, R.N. and Husnu, S. (2008). Imagined intergroup contact: Theory, paradigm and practice. *Social and Personality Psychology Compass, 2*, 1–18.

De Boer, A., Pijl, S.J. and Minnaert, A. (2011). Regular primary schoolteachers' attitudes towards inclusive education: A review of the literature. *International Journal of Inclusive Education, 15*(3), 331–53.

Department for Education (DfE) (2011). *Support and Aspiration: A new approach to special educational needs and disability – A consultation* (Ref CM 8027). London: HMSO. Available online at www.education.gov.uk/publications/standard/publicationdetail/page1/cm% 208027 (accessed 30 November 2014).

Department for Education (DfE) (2013). *Draft Special Educational Needs (SEN) Code of Practice: For 0 to 25 years – Statutory guidance for organisations who work with and support children and young people with SEN*. Available online at www.education.gov.uk/consultations/ downloadableDocs/Draft%20SEN%20Code%20of%20Practice.pdf (accessed 24 November 2014).

Department for Education and Science (DES) (1978). *Special Educational Needs (The Warnock Report)*. London: HMSO.

Department for Education and Skills (DfES) (2001). *Special Educational Needs Code of Practice*. London: HMSO.

Dunn, L.M. (1968). Special education for the mildly retarded – Is much of it justifiable? *Exceptional Children, 35*, 5–22.

Dyson, A., Farrell, P., Polat, F., Hutcheson, G. and Gallannaugh, F. (2004). *Inclusion and Pupil Achievement: Department for Education and Skills (Research Report No 578)*. Available online at http://webarchive.nationalarchives.gov.uk/20130401151715/www.education.gov.uk/ publications/eOrderingDownload/RR578.pdf (accessed 24 November 2014).

Education Act (1981). *Education Act* (c. 60). London: HMSO. Available online at www. educationengland.org.uk/documents/acts/1981-education-act.pdf (accessed 24 November 2014).

Evans, I.M., Goldberg-Arnold, J.S. and Dickson, J.K. (1998). Children's perceptions of equity in peer interactions. In L.H. Meyer, H.-S. Park, M. Grenot-Scheyer, I.S. Schwartz and B. Harry (eds), *Making Friends: The influences of culture and development*. Baltimore, MD: Paul H. Brooks, pp. 133–47.

Farrell, P. (2000). The impact of research on developments in inclusive education. *International Journal of Inclusive Education*, 4(2), 153–62.

Florian, L., Young, K. and Rouse, M. (2010). Preparing teachers for inclusive and diverse educational environments: Studying curricular reform in an initial teacher education course. *International Journal of Inclusive Education*, 14(7), 709–22.

Forlin, C. (2010). Teacher education reform for enhancing teachers' preparedness for inclusion. *International Journal of Inclusive Education*, 14(7), 649–53.

Frederickson, N. and Furnham, A. (2004). The relationship between sociometric status and peer assessed behavioural characteristics of included pupils who have moderate learning difficulties and their classroom peers. *British Journal of Educational Psychology*, 74(3), 391–410.

Frederickson, N. and Simmonds, E. (2008). Special needs, relationship type and distributive justice norms in early and later years of middle childhood. *Social Development*, 17(4), 1056–73.

Frederickson, N., Simmonds, E., Evans, L. and Soulsby, C. (2007). Assessing social and affective outcomes of inclusion. *British Journal of Special Education*, 34(2), 105–15.

Frederickson, N.L. and Furnham, A.F. (1998). Sociometric status group classification of mainstreamed children who have moderate learning difficulties: An investigation of personal and environmental factors. *Journal of Educational Psychology*, 90(4), 772–83.

Gallagher, D.J. (2001). Neutrality as a moral standpoint, conceptual confusion and the full inclusion debate. *Disability in Society*, 16(5), 637–54.

Greenstein, A. (2013). Is this inclusion? Lessons from a very 'special' unit. *International Journal of Inclusive Education*, 18(4), 379–91.

Gresham, F.M. (1982). Misguided mainstreaming: The case for social skills training with handicapped children. *Exceptional Children*, 48, 422–33.

Gresham, F.M. and MacMillan, D.L. (1997). Social competence and affective characteristics of students with mild disabilities. *Review of Educational Research*, 67, 377–415.

Hegarty, S. (1993). Reviewing the literature on integration. *European Journal of Special Needs Education*, 8, 194–200.

Hewstone, M. and Brown, R.J. (1986). Contact is not enough: An intergroup perspective on the contact hypothesis. In M. Hewstone and R. Brown (eds), *Contact and Conflict in Intergroup Encounters*. Oxford, UK: Blackwell, pp. 1–44.

Hick, P. (2005). Supporting the development of more inclusive practices using the index for inclusion. *Educational Psychology in Practice*, 21(2), 117–22.

Hodkinson, A. (2010). Inclusive and special education in the English educational system: Historical perspectives, recent developments and future challenges. *British Journal of Special Education*, 37(2), 61–7.

Hodson, P., Baddeley, A., Laycock, S. and Williams, S. (2005). Helping secondary schools to be more inclusive of Year 7 pupils with SEN. *Educational Psychology in Practice*, 21(1), 53–67.

Humphrey, N. and Symes, W. (2011). Peer interaction patterns among adolescents with autistic spectrum disorders (ASDs) in mainstream secondary schools. *Autism: An International Journal of Research and Practice*, 15, 397–419.

Humphrey, N. and Symes, W. (2013). Inclusive education for pupils with autistic spectrum disorders in secondary mainstream schools: Teacher attitudes, experience and knowledge. *International Journal of Inclusive Education*, 17(1), 32–46.

Individuals with Disabilities Education Act (IDEA) (1997). 20 US Congress. Chapter 33, Sections 1400–1491.

Juvonen, J. (1991). Deviance, perceived responsibility, and negative peer reactions. *Developmental Psychology*, 27(4), 672–81.

Kalambouka, A., Farrell, P., Dyson, A. and Kaplan, I. (2005). *The Impact of Population Inclusivity in Schools on Student Outcomes*. Research Evidence in Education Library. London: EPPI-Centre Social Science Research Unit, Insitute of Education, University of London. Available online at http://eppi.ioe.ac.uk/cms/LinkClick.aspx?fileticket=xRK8efFm_jk%3D&tabid=749&mid=1738 (accessed 24 November 2014).

Kelley, H.H. and Thibaut, J. (1978). *Interpersonal Relations: A theory of interdependence*. New York: Wiley.

Killoran, I., Woronko, D. and Zaretsky, H. (2013). Exploring preservice teachers' attitudes towards inclusion. *International Journal of Inclusive Education*. DOI: 10.1080/13603116.2013.784367

Koster, M., Pijl, S.J., Nakken, H. and Van Houten, E. (2010). Social participation of students with special needs in regular primary education in the Netherlands. *International Journal of Disability, Development and Education*, 57(I), 59–75.

Law, G.U., Sinclair, S. and Fraser, N. (2007). Children's attitudes and behavioural intentions towards a peer with symptoms of ADHD: Does the addition of a diagnostic label make a difference? *Journal of Child Health Care*, 11(2), 98–111.

Lindsay, G. (2003). Inclusive education: A critical perspective. *British Journal of Special Education*, 30, 3–12.

Lindsay, G. (2007). Educational psychology and the effectiveness of inclusive education/mainstreaming. *British Journal of Educational Psychology*, 77, 1–24.

Lloyd, C. (2008). Removing barriers to achievement: A strategy for inclusion or exclusion? *International Journal of Inclusive Education*, 12(2), 221–36.

Maas, E., Marecek, J. and Travers, J.R. (1978). Children's conceptions of disordered behavior. *Child Development*, 49, 146–54.

McDougall, J., De Witt, D.J., King, G., Miller L.T. and Killip, S. (2004). High-school aged youths' attitudes towards their peers with disabilities: The role of school and student interpersonal factors. *International Journal of Disability, Development and Education*, 51(3), 287–313.

Madden, N.A. and Slavin, R.E. (1983). Mainstreaming students with mild handicaps: Academic and social outcomes. *Review of Educational Research*, 53, 519–69.

Maras, P. and Brown, R.J. (1996). Effect of contact on children's attitudes to disability: A longitudinal study. *Journal of Applied Social Psychology*, 26, 2113–34.

Maras, P. and Brown, R.J. (2000). Effects of different forms of school contact on children's attitudes toward disabled and non-disabled peers. *British Journal of Educational Psychology*, *70*, 337–51.

Marom, M., Cohen, D. and Naon, D. (2007). Changing disability-related attitudes and self-efficacy of Israeli children via the Partners to Inclusion Programme. *International Journal of Disability, Development and Education*, *54*(1), 113–27.

Nabuzoka, D. and Smith, P.K. (1993). Sociometric status and social behaviour of children with and without learning difficulties. *Journal of Child Psychology and Psychiatry*, *34*(8), 1435–48.

Newberry, M.K. and Parish, T.S. (1987). Enhancement of attitudes toward handicapped children through social interactions. *The Journal of Social Psychology*, *127*, 59–62.

Newcomb, A.F., Bukowski, W.M. and Pattee, L. (1993). Children's peer relations: A meta-analytic review of popular, rejected, neglected, controversial and average sociometric status. *Psychological Bulletin*, *113*(1), 99–128.

Norwich, B. (1994). The relationship between attitudes to the integration of children with special educational needs and wider socio-political views: A US–English comparison. *European Journal of Special Needs Education*, *9*, 91–106.

Norwich, B. (2008). What future for special schools and inclusion? Conceptual and professional perspectives. *British Journal of Special Education*, *35*(3), 136–43.

Nowicki, E.A. and Sandieson, R. (2002). A meta-analysis of children's attitudes toward individuals with intellectual and physical disabilities. *International Journal of Disability, Development and Education*, *49*, 243–66.

Odom, S.L., Vitztum, J., Wolery, R., Lieber, J., Sandall, S., Hanson, M.J., Beckman, P., Schwartz, I. and Horn, E. (2004). Preschool inclusion in the United States: A review of research from an ecological systems perspective. *Journal of Research in Special Educational Needs*, *4*(1), 17–49.

Roberts, C. and Zubrick, S. (1992). Factors influencing the social status of children with mild academic disabilities in regular classrooms. *Exceptional Children*, *59*, 192–202.

Roberts, C.M. and Lindsell, J.S. (1997). Children's attitudes and behavioural intentions toward peers with disabilities. *International Journal of Disability, Development and Education*, *44*, 133–45.

Roberts, C.M. and Smith, P.R. (1999). Attitudes and behaviour of children towards peers with disabilities. *International Journal of Disability, Development and Education*, *46*(1), 35–50.

Robertson, K., Chamberlain, B. and Kasari, C. (2003). General education teachers' relationships with included students with autism. *Journal of Autism and Developmental Disorders*, *33*(2), 123–30.

Ruijs, N.M. and Peetsma, T.T.D. (2009). Effects of inclusion on students with and without special educational needs reviewed. *Educational Research Review*, *4*(2), 67–79.

Siegel, B. (1996). Is the emperor wearing clothes? Social policy and the empirical support for full inclusion of children with disabilities in the preschool and early elementary grades. *Social Policy Report, Society for Research in Child Development*, *X*(2 and 3), 2–17.

Sigelman, C.K. and Begley, N.L. (1987). The early development of reactions to peers with controllable and uncontrollable problems. *Journal of Paediatric Psychology*, *12*(1), 99–115.

Staub, D. and Peck, C.A. (1994). What are the outcomes for nondisabled students? *The Inclusive School*, *52*(4), 36–40.

Stobart, G. (1986). Is integrating the handicapped psychologically defensible? *Bulletin of the British Psychological Society*, *39*, 1–3.

Taylor, A.R., Asher, S.R. and Williams, G.A. (1987). The social adaptation of mainstreamed mildly retarded children. *Child Development*, *58*, 1321–34.

Thibaut, J.W. and Kelley, H.H. (1959). *The Social Psychology of Groups*. New York: Wiley.

Thomazet, S. (2009). From integration to inclusive education: Does changing the terms improve practice? *International Journal of Inclusive Education*, *13*(6), 553–63.

Tripp, A., French, R. and Sherrill, C. (1995). Contact theory and attitudes of children in physical education programs toward peers with disabilities. *Applied Physical Activity Quarterly*, *12*, 323–32.

United Nations Educational, Scientific and Cultural Organisation (UNESCO) (1994). *The Salamanca Statement and Framework for Action on Special Educational Needs*. Paris: UNESCO. Available online at www.unesco.org/education/pdf/SALAMA_E.PDF (accessed 24 November 2014).

United Nations Educational, Scientific and Cultural Organisation (UNESCO) (2009). *Policy Guidelines on Inclusion in Education*. Paris: UNESCO. Available online at http://unesdoc. unesco.org/images/0017/001778/177849e.pdf (accessed 24 November 2014).

Van Bourgondien, M.E. (1987). Children's responses to retarded peers as a function of social behaviour, labeling and age. *Exceptional Children*, *53*(5), 432–9.

Van der Klift, E. and Kunc, N. (2002). Beyond benevolence. In J.S. Thousand, R.A. Villa and I. Nevins (eds), *Creativity and Collaborative Learning. A practical guide to empowering students and teachers*. Baltimore, MD: Brookes, pp. 391–401.

Weiner, B. (1985). An attributional theory of achievement motivation and emotion. *Psychological Review*, *92*, 548–73.

6 Effective communication in school

Do teachers and students talk the same language?

Tony Cline

CHAPTER SUMMARY

The effective use of language is fundamental to school learning, but the language of school is very different from the language that many children acquire within their families. That difference is experienced in an extreme form by children whose family speak a different language at home from the main language of instruction at school. But even children in a majority language community have to learn to vary their use of language in different environments. This chapter will review how monolingual children learn to communicate in infancy and will examine how the language they learn at that stage differs from the language that they will later need at school. Do differences between home talk and classroom talk *inhibit students' engagement with the curriculum? In the final section of the chapter, we will see how ideas from* sociocultural theory, *based on the work of* Vygotsky, *have been applied to help teachers overcome these challenges. The chapter will include an illustration of how educational psychologists have drawn on research findings in this field to provide support in schools.*

LEARNING OUTCOMES

When you have studied this chapter, you should be able to:

1 describe key features of the development of children's language and other modes of communication before they start school;
2 evaluate the claim that some children find school learning more difficult because the language and *communication skills* they have learned at home have not prepared them well for the demands that are made at school;
3 analyse key features of different forms of classroom talk, employing a well-researched sociocultural approach.

ACTIVITY 6.1

Laurie Lee, the writer, described his first day at school in his autobiography, *Cider with Rosie*, and recalled that his teacher told him to 'Wait there for the present'. 'He went home at the end of the day bitterly disillusioned because he was not given one' (Perera, 1981, p. 4).

In a nursery school in London, a teacher was talking to a 4-year-old girl whose mother, she knew, was from America.

Teacher: Were you born in America? [No reply.] Or were you born in
            England? Do you know?
Child: I was . . . I was born in my mummy's tummy.

(Tizard and Hughes, 1984, p. 207)

A 9-year-old Portuguese child who had recently arrived in the United States was struggling to finish copying a homework assignment from the board when the teacher started erasing it. 'Stop it!', called the child emphatically, using a phrase she had learned from her classmates in the playground. The teacher looked surprised (Menyuk and Brisk, 2005, p. 87).

The actor, Stephen Fry, recalled going up to his older brother, Roger, at his new prep school and calling him by his name. He was told off for doing so. He should call his brother 'Bro'. Only surnames were used: Roger was Fry, R.M., and Stephen was Fry, S.J. (Fry, 1997, p. 2).

When Harry Potter met his future friend, Ron Weasley, on the train going to Hogwarts School at the beginning of his first term there, he tried to explain that he had grown up in an ordinary Muggle family and felt quite ignorant about everything to do with wizardry. He had not known anything about being a wizard or about his parents or about Voldemort. When he used the taboo name, his new friend Ron gasped. He was shocked and a little impressed (Rowling, 1997).

In each of those episodes, a child misunderstood something or made what counted as a mistake. Can you explain exactly what the problem was in each example and how it occurred? What does your analysis tell you about the challenges children face when they move from the *language environment* of their home to a different setting, such as the language environment of a school?

THE EARLY DEVELOPMENT OF LANGUAGE AND COMMUNICATION SKILLS

The initial experiences that lay the foundations for language development

The main questions addressed in this chapter concern how children use the language and communication skills that they have developed in early childhood once they start school. In order to tackle these questions, it is necessary to review key features of preschool language development. The foundations are laid from the very beginning. If infants are given a choice, shortly after birth, between listening to speech sounds and non-speech sounds that are equally complex, they show a preference for the speech sounds. Initially, that preference applies equally to human vocalisations and to the vocalisations of female rhesus monkeys, but, by the age of 3 months, human speech was shown, in one study, to be preferred to rhesus vocalisations (Vouloumanos et al., 2010). At the outset, infants produce sounds that simply relate to their physical state – reflexive vocalisations such as crying and sneezing. However, within 2 months, they move on to squealing, growling, cooing and gurgling, producing sounds that express a wider range of moods and needs (Oller et al., 2013). This activity evolves through experimenting with sounds, playing with their vocal tract and producing squeals, hoots and some vowel-like sounds. As they experience others' attunement and reactions to them and eventually observe their caregivers' modelling of effective communication, infants are stimulated towards the development of language themselves.

There is a good deal of evidence that the basic structures of this development are built into humans' genetic make-up. Those structures are stimulated by caregivers' behaviour – the constant use of the names of objects that an infant can see or hear and the verbal description of actions and events as they are happening in the infant's vicinity. When the child makes clear what they want, by pointing or looking or touching, they are reinforced by obtaining gratification and receiving others' attention. As they hear more and more talk from their family, they begin to babble selectively, making increasing use of the sounds that characterise the languages of those who speak to them. Eventually, they acquire the languages, dialects and accents that they hear around them. The roots of effective communication are simple and adaptable (Gervain and Mehler, 2010).

In trying to understand how these early developments lay the foundation for effective communication in school, it is helpful to consider the ideas about language development associated with the sociocultural theory of Lev Vygotsky. He tried to show how the culture in which a person is brought up influences the course of their development. He used the term culture broadly, to describe the customs of a particular people at a particular time – the learned traditions and aspects of lifestyle that are shared by members of a society, including their habitual ways of thinking, feeling and behaving. Speech was seen as having the role of containing and transmitting culture, as language stores social experience from the past and makes it available to others in the future. Through language, a person can be, not only an active agent who is immersed in what they are doing at this moment, but also 'a reflexive agent' who is distanced from their immediate context (Valsiner, 2000).

Culture has a material aspect in the environment and the objects that people create, and also a symbolic (or semiotic) aspect in the language that they use to describe these things to others. Vygotsky saw culture as having a key formative role in development, as it is transmitted both through social interaction and through speech. Thus, he envisaged the development of language as forming the basis for the development of thinking. The foundation of that process is an infant's social interaction with those around them. This is expressed in what he called 'the general, genetic law of cultural development':

> All the basic forms of the adult's verbal social interaction with the child later become mental functions . . . Any function in the child's cultural development appears twice, or on two planes. First it appears on the social plane and then on the psychological plane. First it appears between people, as an interpsychological category and then within the child, as an intrapsychological category.
>
> (Vygotsky, 1978, p. 73)

There is little direct empirical evidence for this theoretical construction of how the process might operate, but it has had a great deal of influence. We will discuss later in the chapter ways in which researchers with a background in education and psychology have suggested that teachers can draw on Vygotskian ideas to help pupils overcome the challenges that they face in effective classroom communication. One aspect of those challenges is that the initial experiences that provide the foundations of language development vary greatly between children. In many parts of the world, children are exposed to more than one language during their early years and grow up as bilingual speakers. It is estimated that between a half and two-thirds of the world's population are bilingual or multilingual (Baker, 2011), but that is not a universal experience, and some countries, such as England, have, until relatively recently, been mainly monolingual.

Even within the same language or dialect, there may be differences in *socio-economic status* (SES) or ethnic background that correlate with variations in children's language experiences at home. For example, when Hart and Risley (1992) made regular observations for a period of just over 2 years in the homes of forty families in a Midwestern city in the United States, they found marked differences in the frequency of different kinds of utterance by parents in high- and low-SES homes. In the families with lower SES, a substantial proportion (up to 20 per cent) of parent utterances to children functioned to prohibit the children's activities within the home, whereas discouraging prohibitions of that kind were rarely heard in families with higher SES. Instead, the children in higher-SES families were more likely to hear questions (up to 45 per cent of parent utterances) and more frequent repetitions and elaborations of their own topics (up to 5 per cent of parent utterances). Similar findings on SES group differences in the use of language by parents to their children have been reported in other countries, including the UK, and have led to the use of such terms as 'verbal deprivation' to explain weaker school performance in children from lower-SES backgrounds. There is international evidence that, by school entry, there are substantial SES differences in overall language development (e.g. McIntosh *et al.*, 2007).

Such differences in the outcome of early parenting do not appear to be simply the result of differences in the amount and type of talk between parents and children at home, as Hart and Risley's study suggested. In addition, more subtle factors may have an influence. For example, Raviv *et al.* (2004) studied 1,016 families and analysed the relationship between parenting behaviours and 3-year-olds' scores on scales of expressive language, receptive language and the ability to understand basic verbal concepts. The hierarchical regression analyses that they conducted indicated that measures of 'maternal sensitivity' (assessed on the basis of observations of a mother–child play session conducted in their laboratory) and 'cognitive stimulation' (assessed on the basis of an interview and home observations) mediated the relationship between SES and the language outcome measures.

Thus SES may not be adequate as an explanatory variable. Advances in both science and practice may depend on a closer analysis of the processes that directly influence young children's language development, which may or may not be associated with SES. Weisleder and Fernald (2013) collected audio recordings of parent–infant interactions at home, through the day, in Spanish-speaking families of low SES in the New York area. They were surprised to discover differences between families in the amount of child-directed speech that were almost as large as those differences reported by Hart and Risley (1992) across a wide SES range. Where Hart and Risley found that some families in different social groups talked with their children twenty times as much as others, Weisleder and Fernald found an eighteenfold difference in caregiver talk to infants within their more demographically homogeneous sample. They noted that the differences in parental engagement that they observed were not correlated with factors linked to SES, such as maternal education, and concluded that, 'although variability in parenting behaviors is consistently linked to factors related to SES, there is also considerable variability in parental verbal engagement that is independent of social class' (p. 2150). In a longitudinal study in the west of England, Roulstone *et al.* (2011) showed that what they termed 'the communication environment' during a child's early years had an impact on early language development and performance on school entry that was independent of social background. The key features of this communication environment included a score for the mother's parenting, which took into account a range of activities and interactions with the child, her perceived feelings of being supported, and the resources available to them.

Nonverbal communication and pragmatic skills

When young children speak their first word, most parents celebrate what they see as an important milestone in development. Doherty-Sneddon (2003) has pointed out that they tend not to recognise key milestones in *nonverbal communication* in the same way: 'We seldom hear parents report when their children first began pointing to ask for something, or when they first used an action like flapping their hands to represent a bird' (p. 9). She argues that people underestimate the importance of such steps in the development of children's overall communicative competence. Just as infants are attuned to recognise and seek out speech sounds, they are also sensitive to some forms of nonverbal communication, such as smiling and pointing.

This ability to read the nonverbal signals communicated by those around them is mirrored by an ability to develop the use of many forms of nonverbal communication themselves. Young children learn to direct their eye gaze at what they want others to know they are interested in. They also develop increasingly sophisticated ways of communicating their feelings and desires through facial expressions. They learn the conventional meanings that different hand gestures have in their society, so that they can convey agreement or dissent with their hands alone. They learn to illustrate their speech with gestures, to support the message they want to put over, for example by drawing a visual picture in the air, or pointing at something while talking about it, or beating out the rhythm of their speech to emphasise particular words as they are spoken. The linking of nonverbal and verbal communication in this way fosters effective language learning (Goldin-Meadow *et al.*, 2007). Eventually, they can draw on the full range of their communication resources, nonverbal and verbal, to understand others and to convey their own meaning and intentions. What they do not learn at this stage are the conventions of communication that hold sway at school. The foundations are laid, but the specific expectations of teachers and peers in that setting will be learned later.

In order to be a competent user of a language, a child must develop knowledge of, and skills in using, its structure and key components:

- its sound system (phonology), for example which sounds normally occur in words and which do not;
- its structural rules at the level of the word (morphology), for example how the form of a noun changes when it is plural ('dogs' as opposed to 'dog' in English);
- the ways in which words may be combined together to form sentences (syntax), for example the rule that states that the object of a verb comes after the verb in English ('The dog gnawed the bone', rather than 'The bone gnawed the dog');
- the ways in which words and sentences convey meaning (semantics), for example the link between the word 'dog' and the 'meaning' of the word, 'a four-legged, domesticated animal of a particular type'.

It is not enough, however, to have a grasp of the key components of a language. In addition, a person who is to use the language effectively for the purposes of

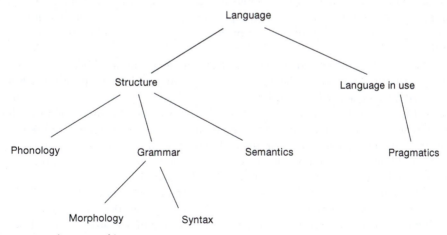

FIGURE 6.1 Aspects of language

Source: Adapted from D. Crystal (1988). *Introduction to Language Pathology*. Reproduced with permission of John Wiley

communication with others needs to know *how* it is used; they require *pragmatic skills.* For example, they need to appreciate and follow the conventions of turn taking in conversation, and they need to understand when a change in the tone of a person's voice means that a question is really a command, for example when a child's mother says, 'Aren't your toys in an awful mess?'

Pragmatic rules may vary between social and ethnic groups within a society, as well as between societies. For many children, the move from home to nursery or school is made more challenging because the pragmatic rules they have learned at home lead them to misinterpret communications from others in the new setting, or to communicate a meaning they do not intend. They may fail to make eye contact when it is expected and thus give the inaccurate impression of being sullen and unwilling to talk. Like the Portuguese girl who was quoted in Activity Box 6.1, they may put requests in a direct way ('I want . . .'), when an indirect form is considered more polite and respectful ('Can I have . . .'). Like Harry Potter, they may unselfconsciously use a word or name that is normally considered taboo in their new environment.

ENTERING THE NEW LANGUAGE ENVIRONMENTS OF NURSERY AND SCHOOL

Conversations between adults and children

When children leave the domestic environments of early childcare for the larger-scale, more institutional settings of nursery or school, new language demands are made of them. They encounter a wider range of different people, from a greater variety of speech backgrounds, they are involved in a new set of social routines requiring different types of language, and they must learn to use the *vocabulary* and syntactical forms associated with the demands of school subjects. They bring multifaceted communication skills to these new challenges. However, a child is unlikely to achieve their full potential for communicating with others unless the people they are talking to are able to play an active role in interpreting, repairing and augmenting what they are trying to say. This can be a key role of staff in the early years in schooling (Dockrell *et al.*, 2012).

Many teachers believe that the key determining factor in children's success in negotiating the linguistic challenges at school lies in preschool preparation at home. For example, a teacher from Bridgend in South Wales responded to a survey on the subject by suggesting: 'Often parents do not know any songs or rhymes and have little idea of how to talk to and play with their children' (Basic Skills Agency, 2003, p. 18). At the same time, there have been research reports focusing on nurseries and schools that would not make comfortable reading for teachers who attribute the problems to children's language environment at home. Observational research in the past has sometimes indicated that early years settings may stimulate less extensive and less wide-ranging talk in young children, from all backgrounds, than they use when at home with their parents. For example, a study of a small group of 4-year-old girls in London in the 1980s indicated that they had relatively few encounters with adults in the child-centred play environment of their nursery schools and classes. The most common theme of their brief conversations with staff was their own play, in contrast to the much greater variety of topics that were touched on in the course of everyday conversations at home. The staff asked them many questions about what they were doing, questions that they answered briefly or not at all. Beyond that, 'they rarely asked the staff questions of their own, or made the kind of spontaneous remarks that keep a conversation going' (Tizard and Hughes, 1984, p. 198).

Findings of this kind led to serious efforts to improve communication practices in early years settings. However, more recent studies have shown that early years staff have very often continued to manage their daily conversations with children in ways that are unlikely to foster rich language development. For example, Siraj-Blatchford *et al.* (2002) conducted extensive classroom observation in twelve early years settings that had been selected as exemplars of good practice. Out of 1,967 questions that staff asked children during their recordings, 60.8 per cent were unclassified, 34.1 per cent were closed questions, and only 5.1 per cent were open questions. The researchers pointed out that open-ended questioning is more likely to provide significant

Key features of the language-learning environment at school

During an ambitious research programme that was established partly as a response to the government review that is described on the next page, Dockrell *et al.* (2012) developed an evidence-based instrument for observing the ways in which individual classrooms support communication. They identified three main areas that were highlighted in the research literature and were, therefore, included as dimensions in their observation tool:

- *Language Learning Environment – the physical environment and learning context.* This dimension lists what is available within the environment. Many of the items are semi-permanent features of the classroom reflecting the infrastructure to support language learning or aspects refer to how the teacher manages the learning environment.
- *Language Learning Opportunities – the structured opportunities to support children's language development.* This dimension is indicative of the opportunities for language learning that are available in the classroom such as group work.
- *Language Learning Interactions – the ways in which adults in the setting talk with children.* This includes techniques used by adults to acknowledge the children's needs (such as getting down to the child's level, pacing language used, confirming contributions), to support them in developing their language skills (such as labelling, using appropriate open-ended questions), to encourage non-verbal communication (such as praising good listening skills), to direct language learning (such as commenting), and to model language responses (such as scripting).

(Dockrell *et al.*, 2012, p. 20)

FOCUS 6.1

encouragement for children to take the initiative in a conversation and to stimulate sustained, shared thinking (p. 55). When Bilton (2012) observed children and adults in the external play areas of four early years settings more recently, she found a similar pattern of interaction: there were more than twice as many conversational initiatives from adults that centred on domestic matters as there were initiatives that might lead to extended conversation, for example through 'why'/'how'/'what' questions. There is some survey evidence that the initial training of teachers and other staff who work in early years settings in England may not prepare them adequately in the area of speech and language development (Mroz, 2006). The report of a project by a group of educational psychologists working in London has suggested that brief in-school training at a later stage of their career may not be enough to change established poor practice in staff questioning in the classroom (Bickford-Smith *et al.*, 2005). Widespread concern about such matters led to the establishment of a government review of services for children and young people (0–19) with speech, language and communication needs, led by John Bercow, which recommended that, 'speech, language and communication and Speech, Language and Communication Needs (should be) a core requirement or unit at the appropriate level in all qualifications for the children's workforce' (DCSF, 2008, p. 9).

Bridging the gap between home and school

Bridging the gap between home and school is a major challenge for all those involved – children, parents and teachers. Children's play sometimes focuses on bridging a specific gap that is relevant to this chapter – the language gap between school and home. A key feature of nurseries and other early years settings is the provision for free play, where children can participate in activities that represent lifelike situations, such as cooking and cleaning a 'house' or driving a 'car'. When they play a role in these situations, children often imitate the more mature language they have heard from adults engaging in those activities. They not only practise the kind of language that accompanies these activities, but also further their knowledge of how to participate in different kinds of conversation (Menyuk and Brisk, 2005, Chapter 4).

The learning process extends beyond the school when they take school language home, while playing 'school' in the home setting. Children import the vocabulary, syntax and tone of their classroom when playing the role of teacher with younger siblings at home. For example, Gregory (2005) presents an excerpt from a maths 'lesson' in which 11-year-old Wahida took the role of teacher and her 8-year-old sister Sayeda was pupil. Sayeda had solved one problem successfully.

> Wahida: So, I'm going to put some sums on the board for you, OK? Ready?
> Sayeda: Yes.
> Wahida: The first sum's going to be – OK Sayeda do you remember to write the date first?
> Sayeda: Yes, Miss.
> Wahida: Well done! Now I'm going to write the sums. The first sum is 30 × 5 equals? If you want to do lattice, you can. Or you can do your own way, you can or you can do in your mind, but I would love to see some working out.

Gregory points out that Wahida models her use of language on that of her teacher, both in her choice of lesson-related words and in the way that she structures her speech, for example referring to her requirements using indirect rather than direct speech (that she 'would love to see some working out') (2005, p. 228). Sayeda cooperates readily and also adopts the conventions of school speech. When psychologists highlight the gap between the language of home and the language of school in some social groups, they often focus on the language models provided by parents. Gregory argues that 'playful talk' provides a bridge between the two domains, and she has shown that siblings and grandparents may play a role in such talk, as well as parents.

THE IMPACT OF SCHOOLING ON CHILDREN'S LANGUAGE

Key features of language development in the middle years of childhood

Attending school on a full-time basis leads to a significant increase in the range of sources of input to children's language learning. Their vocabulary and what they try to say encompass new kinds of abstraction and ambiguity. During this developmental stage, there are also dramatic developments in their pragmatic competence, as they become more able to take the perspectives of other people with whom they are talking. These major trends are summarised in Table 6.1.

The central process is the growth of vocabulary. This can be thought of as a step-by-step process in which each exposure to a word helps a child to deepen and broaden

TABLE 6.1 Critical processes in early and later language development

	Young children	School-age children and adolescents
Types of input	Learn language through listening and watching	Learn language through listening, watching *and* reading
Level of awareness	Absorb language unselfconsciously from those around them	Often learn through reflecting on and analysing language as an entity in itself, influenced by increasing metalinguistic awareness
Level of abstraction	Add words to their vocabulary that generally have concrete referents (e.g. traffic lights, Peugeot, motorway)	Also add words to their vocabulary that represent abstract concepts (e.g. welfare, relevance, democracy) and words or phrases that are interpreted metaphorically (e.g. 'skeleton in the closet')
Level of ambiguity	Tend to interpret what they hear literally	Appreciate and come to enjoy word play in puns, riddles, jokes and advertisements
Awareness of the perspectives of others	Adjust their linguistic style to the person they are speaking to, only to a limited extent	Are increasingly aware of the thoughts, feelings and needs of whomever they are speaking to and adjust the content and style of their speech accordingly

Source: Adapted from Nippold, 1998, pp. 4–6

their understanding of what the word means and how it is used. Researchers seeking to assess vocabulary development have distinguished three levels of mastery:

1   the *receptive* level of word knowledge, which can be tested by showing a child a page of four different pictures and asking them, for example, to 'point to *veranda*';
2   the *contextual* level of word knowledge, which can be tested by asking a child to describe a context in which the word might be used, for example with the question, 'When is a time that you would be *quivering*?';
3   the *expressive* level of word knowledge, which can be tested by asking a child to define a word with no further clarification, for example, 'Tell me what the word *saunter* means' (Pullen *et al.*, 2010).

As the child's vocabulary grows, the structural features of their speech change. They speak in longer and more complex sentences, and they use the morphological options in the language more extensively, for instance adding prefixes and suffixes to familiar words, such as *displeased* and *excitement*. Their increasing literacy skills transform the range of language to which they are exposed and make available to them models and sources that encompass specialist vocabulary and formal syntax outside the scope of everyday conversation. When they come across unfamiliar words in a story, they soon add them to their growing lexicon. They themselves learn to tell a story (employing narrative skills) and to explain concepts (employing expository skills). These modes of discourse are quite distinct: narratives focus on people, their actions and motivations, and describe the unfolding of events over time, whereas expository texts focus on concepts and issues and explain ideas, claims and arguments in terms of the logical interrelations among them (Berman and Nir-Sagiv, 2007, pp. 79–80). In a study of written texts produced by native English speakers of different ages, Berman and Nir-Sagiv showed that young people use more advanced vocabulary and grammar in expository texts than in narrative texts, and that they learn to organise the telling of a story by middle childhood, but do not generally master the construction of an expository text until adolescence.

Reviewing the rules of classroom talk

What is the best way of running a whole-class discussion so that all the children articulate their ideas about the topic that is being discussed? Traditionally, the teacher stands at the front of the classroom and asks a series of questions. Pupils who know the answer to a question put up their hands, and the teacher chooses one of them to tell the class what they think the answer is. It has recently been suggested that this practice is unhelpful. It is a well-established way of managing a lesson, and almost all of us will have experienced it as pupils. What can possibly be wrong with it? Critics have highlighted many limitations:

1   Some children who know the answer will not put up their hands, for fear that they will look foolish if they are wrong or that they will be labelled as 'geeks' or 'swots' if they are right.
2   Some who do not know the answer will put their hands up eagerly anyway, because they cannot bear to be left out.

3   The procedure may be undermined by teacher bias that leads to children from particular groups rarely being given the chance to contribute.
4   The exercise addresses only the teacher's agenda and risks overlooking important questions and concerns that some children have.
5   If a substantial proportion of the teacher's questions are closed questions (and they rarely ask open-ended questions), the children will be given limited practice in articulating more complex ideas on the topic. With a closed question, the task may simply become guessing what the teacher has in mind.

There are many alternative ways for a teacher to manage classroom discussion that can overcome these problems. Detailed observations have shown that a successful teacher can build on opportunities that arise over time, in a series of lessons, to help children develop a fuller understanding of complex ideas and the words that express them. For example, Twiner et al. (2014) studied class discussions during eight history lessons on the topic of the Great Fire of London with a class of 6–7-year-old pupils. Their analysis, among other things, illustrates the gradual evolution of the full and accurate use by one girl, Lior, of the word 'firebreak'. The teacher created learning situations (such as asking the children to write a diary as though they had been an eye witness at the time). However, the teacher's intended and planned interactions were shown not to be the only factor in the children's acquisition of an understanding of the events and the vocabulary to describe them. In addition, it was important that the teacher was able to respond to the children's interpretations (and misinterpretations) of what they learned, taking what they said seriously and involving them as active agents in their learning. There were 'intended' trajectories in the way they made words make meaning (i.e. intended by the teacher), and there were also 'instantiated' trajectories (their actual interpretations of what they heard and saw, which were often not exactly what the teacher had planned). For example, Lior empathised with the people whose houses were pulled down to create firebreaks. 'Where could they live?' she asked. The teacher was sufficiently responsive to the pupils for them to be reassured that, 'their concerns about the human dimension of the historical dilemmas are valid' and thus enable them to engage with the larger questions of public policy that were the focus of the official history curriculum (Twiner et al., 2014, p. 99).

Teachers' strategies for ensuring the active participation of all pupils in classroom talk often involve some form of discussion in pairs or small groups, which is sometimes followed by plenary discussion with the whole class or by a presentation of each group's conclusions to their peers, or some combination of these. But it would be wrong to assume that discussion in small groups necessarily leads to children practising worthwhile communication skills. They may often be unclear about what exactly they are expected to do, and they may have little idea of what would constitute a good, effective discussion. After all, for many of them, school will be the only place where they experience such discussions. Focus Box 6.2 presents an extract illustrating the kind of unproductive talk that can result, if a group of 9–10-year-old children are set a discussion task, with little training or preparation. This extract was collected by Mercer et al. (2004) as part of a larger-scale study. It was recorded by a group who were working through a computer-based task on the soundproofing qualities of various materials.

Transcript 1: Control school group who are working on 'Keep it quiet'

Hannah:	(*reads from screen*) Keep it Quiet. Which material is the best insulation? Click 'measure' to take a sound reading. Does the pitch make a difference?
Darryl:	No we don't want clothes. See what one it is then. (*Points to screen*)
Hannah:	No it's cloth.
Darryl:	Oh it's cloth.
Hannah:	Go down. This is better when Stephanie's in our group.
Darryl:	Metal?
Hannah:	Right try it.
Deborah:	Try what? That?
Hannah:	Try 'glass'.
Darryl:	Yeah.
Deborah:	No one.
Hannah:	Now.
Darryl:	(*interrupts*) Measure.
Hannah:	Now measure. Hold. (*Turns volume control dial below screen*)
Darryl:	Results, notes.
Hannah:	Results. We need to go on a different one now. Results.
Darryl:	Yeah, you need to go there so you can write everything down.
Hannah:	I'm not writing.

(Mercer *et al.*, 2004, pp. 368–9)

Focus Box 6.3 presents an extract from the discussion of a group who had received training, designed by Mercer and his colleagues, on the basis of sociocultural principles that had been derived initially from Vygotsky's theoretical ideas on the development of language and cognition.

FOCUS 6.3

Transcript 2: Target school group who are working on 'Blocking out light'

Ross:	OK. (*reads from screen*) Talk together about a plan to test all the different types of paper.
Alana:	Dijek, how much did you think it would be for tissue paper?
Dijek:	At least ten because tissue paper is thin. Tissue paper can wear out and you can see through, other people in the way, and light can shine in it.
Alana:	OK. Thanks.
Alana:	(to Ross) Why do you think it?
Ross:	Because I tested it before!
Alana:	No, Ross, what did you think? How much did you think? Tissue paper. How much tissue paper did you think it would be to block out the light?
Ross:	At first I thought it would be five, but second –
Alana:	Why did you think that?
Ross:	Because when it was in the overhead projector you could see a little bit of it, but not all of it, so I thought it would be like, five to block out the light.
Alana:	That's a good reason. I thought, I thought it would be between five and seven because, I thought it would be between five and seven because normally when you're at home if you lay it on top, with one sheet you can see through but if you lay on about five or six pieces on top you can't see through. So that's why I was thinking about five or six.

(Mercer *et al.*, 2004, p. 369)

One of the team's training strategies was to ask pupils to draw up a set of 'ground rules' for making effective, productive discussion happen during a joint activity. Here is one example developed by a group of trainee teachers:

- Seek contributions from all group members, ensuring that everyone has a chance to speak.
- Actively listen and stay involved.
- Be positive and open to new ideas.
- Question others about their ideas.
- Respect and value other people's opinions and feelings.
- Explain your ideas concisely but clearly.
- Give clear reasons for your opinions, and expect them from others.

- Challenge and discuss points if you disagree.
- In case of alternative proposals, decide together which is supported by the best reasons.
- Keep to the subject.
- Be ready to compromise and reach agreement if possible (Mercer, 2005, p. 19).

ACTIVITY 6.2

Distinguishing between different types of classroom talk

Mercer and his colleagues suggested that the extract in Focus Box 6.2 exemplifies a type of group exchange that they called *disputational talk*, and that the one in Focus Box 6.3 could be described as *exploratory talk*. The second of these extracts was recorded in a school where they had introduced a training programme to help the children learn 'Thinking Together'. You will not be surprised that they considered the second extract educationally more valuable than the first, and that they thought it showed higher-order communication skills.

1 Can you identify what specific differences there are in the use of language between the two groups?
2 The extracts that are given here show only the language the children used, and not their nonverbal communication. If a video had been available, what characteristics would you expect to find in the nonverbal behaviour and pragmatic skills displayed in each group?

When you have arrived at an answer to the first question, you may like to examine Mercer's own account of differences between 'disputational talk' and 'exploratory talk', which is summarised in the Appendix to this chapter. How far has your analysis of these extracts identified the points he highlighted?

The programmes of study for English in the revised National Curriculum stipulate that children in primary schools should be taught to:

- listen and respond appropriately to adults and their peers;
- ask relevant questions to extend their understanding and knowledge;
- use relevant strategies to build their vocabulary;
- articulate and justify answers, arguments and opinions;
- give well-structured descriptions, explanations and narratives for different purposes, including for expressing feelings;
- maintain attention and participate actively in collaborative conversations, staying on topic and initiating and responding to comments;
- use spoken language to develop understanding through speculating, hypothesising, imagining and exploring ideas;
- speak audibly and fluently with an increasing command of Standard English;

- participate in discussions, presentations, performances, role-play, improvisations and debates;
- gain, maintain and monitor the interest of the listener(s);
- consider and evaluate different viewpoints, attending to and building on the contributions of others;
- select and use appropriate registers for effective communication (DfE, 2013, p. 7).

The research programme undertaken by Mercer's team suggests one way in which educational psychology can help teachers to achieve these objectives. He has argued that it is because some children do not gain access to the use of language for sustained, shared reasoning at home that an explicit and structured intervention is required to enable all pupils to benefit from these approaches at school (Mercer, 2005).

SUMMARY OF MAIN ISSUES ADDRESSED IN THIS CHAPTER

- The chapter began by outlining some key features of early language development: infants' early sensitivity to the speech sounds they hear, their experimentation with producing their own sounds and the stimulation provided by caregivers.
- The ideas about language development associated with the sociocultural theory of Lev Vygotsky may be helpful in trying to understand how these early developments lay the foundation for effective communication in school.
- Nonverbal communication skills and pragmatic skills are crucial aspects of the overall communicative competence that children must develop. Their importance to effective communication has sometimes been underestimated in the past.
- For many children the move from home to nursery or school is made more challenging because the pragmatic rules they have learned at home lead them to misinterpret communications from others in the new setting, or to communicate a meaning themselves that they do not intend.
- When children leave the domestic environments of early childcare for the larger-scale, more institutional settings of nursery or school, new language demands are made of them. They bring multifaceted communication skills to these new challenges, but many still benefit less than they could initially, because of a mismatch between their language skill and the demands made of them.
- This mismatch is blamed by many teachers on poor preparation at home during the preschool years. At the same time, research in nurseries and schools has suggested that the environment they provide is not always as stimulating for children's language development as it could be.
- Whatever the limitations of either environment, however, there are continuing impressive advances in language development during the middle years of childhood – in vocabulary and range, syntactical complexity and pragmatic competence.
- Psychology has been successfully applied to improving the strategies that are used to plan and manage discussion in the classroom. The aim was to draw on principles derived from Vygotsky's sociocultural theory in order to help children move from 'disputational talk' to 'exploratory talk' when working in groups.

KEY CONCEPTS AND TERMS

- Classroom talk
- Communication skills
- Deprivation
- Disputational talk
- Exploratory talk
- Language environment
- Nonverbal communication
- Pragmatic skills
- Sociocultural theory
- Socio-economic status
- Vocabulary
- Vygotsky

RECOMMENDATIONS FOR FURTHER READING

Journal articles

Gervain, J. and Mehler, J. (2010). Speech perception and language acquisition in the first year of life. *Annual Review of Psychology, 61*, 191–218.

Mercer, N., Dawes, L., Wegerif, R. and Sams, C. (2004). Reasoning as a scientist: Ways of helping children to use language to learn science. *British Educational Research Journal, 30*(3), 359–77.

Twiner, A., Littleton, K., Coffin, C. and Whitelock, D. (2014). Meaning making as an interactional accomplishment: A temporal analysis of intentionality and improvisation in classroom dialogue. *International Journal of Educational Research, 63*, 94–106.

Books and longer research reports

Menyuk, P. and Brisk, M.E. (2005). *Language Development and Education: Children with varying language experience.* New York: Palgrave Macmillan.

Mercer, N. and Littleton, K. (2007). *Dialogue and the Development of Children's Thinking.* London: Routledge.

Roulstone, S., Law, J., Rush, R., Clegg, J. and Peters, T. (2011). *Investigating the Role of Language in Children's Early Educational Outcomes.* London: Department for Education, and Bristol: University of the West of England. Available online at www.gov.uk/government/uploads/system/uploads/attachment_data/file/181549/DFE-RR134.pdf (accessed 17 January 2014).

SAMPLE ESSAY TITLES

1 Many teachers think that their pupils lack the language skills they require when they start school. How would you account for this?
2 'Teachers and children talk a different language.' Discuss.
3 What contribution can psychology make to helping teachers foster children's language development in the classroom?

APPENDIX

Mercer and his colleagues (Mercer *et al.*, 2004; Mercer, 2005; Mercer and Littleton, 2007) differentiated between three types of talk in classroom groups, two of which are exemplified in Focus Boxes 6.2 and 6.3.

Talk of a mainly 'disputational' type, they thought, has these features:

- It is not usually associated with processes of joint reasoning and knowledge construction.
- Although the children interact a good deal, they think on their own, rather than developing ideas and reasoning jointly.
- They tend to be defensive and competitive.
- They show off with information and ideas or withhold them, but do not often share them.
- There are often what the research called 'tit-for-tat "yes it is", "no it isn't" patterns of assertion and counter-assertion'.
- They pass negative judgements on each other's contribution.
- They squabble and bicker, rather than pursuing a reasoned argument.

This is to be differentiated from 'cumulative talk', which has these features:

- Ideas and information are shared, and joint decisions are made.
- Participants rarely challenge each other's arguments or ask for evidence or offer constructive criticism of what someone else has said.
- There appears to be solidarity and trust among group members, and they draw on each other's ideas, but typically only by repeating or confirming them, rather than building on them and taking the argument further.

Note that cumulative talk is not illustrated with an extract here.

The features of 'exploratory talk' are as follows:

- Group members work together and show 'a joint, coordinated form of co-reasoning in language with speakers sharing knowledge, challenging ideas, evaluating evidence and considering options in a reasoned and equitable way'.
- Ideas and reasoning are put before the rest of the group in an explicit form that others can understand and evaluate.
- Peers compare possible explanations and seek to agree on the best reasoning possible with the information they have available.
- There is conflict, but it is constructive. It is clear that the group's aim is to achieve a consensus.
- 'Everyone is free to express their views and . . . the most reasonable views gain acceptance.'

(Adapted from Mercer and Littleton, 2007, pp. 62–3)

REFERENCES

Baker, C. (2011). *Foundations of Bilingual Education and Bilingualism* (5th edn). Clevedon, UK: Multilingual Matters.

Basic Skills Agency (2003). *Survey into Young Children's Skills on Entry into Education.* London: Basic Skills Agency.

Berman, R.A. and Nir-Sagiv, B. (2007). Comparing narrative and expository text construction across adolescence: A developmental paradox. *Discourse Processes, 43*(2), 79–120.

Bickford-Smith, A., Wijayatilake, L. and Woods, G. (2005). Evaluating the effectiveness of an early years language intervention. *Educational Psychology in Practice, 21*(3), 161–73.

Bilton, H. (2012). The type and frequency of interactions that occur between staff and children outside in Early Years Foundation Stage settings during a fixed playtime period when there are tricycles available. *European Early Childhood Education Research Journal, 20*(3), 403–21.

Department for Children, Schools and Families (DCSF) (2008). *The Bercow Report: A review of services for children and young people (0–19) with speech, language and communication needs.* Nottingham, UK: DCSF Publications.

Department for Education (DfE) (2013). *National Curriculum English Programmes of Study.* Available online at www.gov.uk/government/publications/national-curriculum-in-england-english-programmes-of-study (accessed 25 November 2014).

Dockrell, J., Ricketts, J. and Lindsay, G. (2012). *Understanding Speech, Language and Communication Needs: Profiles of need and provision* (Ref DfE- RR247). London: DfE.

Doherty-Sneddon, G. (2003). *Children's Unspoken Language.* London: Jessica Kingsley.

Fry, S. (1997). *Moab is My Washpot: An autobiography.* London: Random House.

Gervain, J. and Mehler, J. (2010). Speech perception and language acquisition in the first year of life. *Annual Review of Psychology, 61,* 191–218.

Goldin-Meadow, S., Goodrich, W., Sauer, E. and Iverson, J.M. (2007). Young children use their hands to tell their mothers what to say. *Developmental Science, 10,* 778–85.

Gregory, E. (2005). Playful talk: The interspace between home and school discourse. *Early Years, 25*(3), 223–36.

Hart, B. and Risley, T.R. (1992). American parenting of language-learning children: Persisting differences in family-child interactions observed in natural home environments. *Developmental Psychology, 28*(6), 1096–105.

McIntosh, B., Crosbie, S., Holm, A., Dodd, B. and Thomas, S. (2007). Enhancing the phonological awareness and language skills of socially disadvantaged preschoolers: An interdisciplinary programme. *Child Language Teaching and Therapy, 23*(3), 267–86.

Menyuk, P. and Brisk, M.E. (2005). *Language Development and Education: Children with varying language experience.* New York: Palgrave Macmillan.

Mercer, N. (2005). Thinking together. *NALDIC Quarterly, 2*(3), 18–22.

Mercer, N., Dawes, L., Wegerif, R. and Sams, C. (2004). Reasoning as a scientist: Ways of helping children to use language to learn science. *British Educational Research Journal, 30* (3), 359–77.

Mercer, N. and Littleton, K. (2007). *Dialogue and the Development of Children's Thinking*. London: Routledge.

Mroz, M. (2006). Teaching in the Foundation Stage: How current systems support teachers' knowledge and understanding of children's speech and language. *International Journal of Early Years Education*, *14*(1), 45–61.

Nippold, M.A. (1998). *Later Language Development: The school-age and adolescent years* (2nd edn). Austin, TX: Pro-Ed.

Oller, D.K., Buder, E.H., Ramsdell, H.L., Warlaumont, A.S., Chorna, L. and Bakeman R. (2013). Functional flexibility of infant vocalization and the emergence of language. *Proceedings of the National Academy of Sciences*, *110*(16), 6318–23.

Perera, K. (1981). *Children's Writing and Reading: Analysing classroom language*. Oxford, UK: Blackwell.

Pullen, P.C., Tuckwiller, E.D., Konold, T.R., Maynard, K.L. and Coyne, M.D. (2010). A tiered intervention model for early vocabulary instruction: The effects of tiered instruction for young students at risk for reading disability. *Learning Disabilities Research*, *25*(3), 110–23.

Raviv, T., Kessenich, M. and Morrison, F.J. (2004). A mediational model of the association between socioeconomic status and three-year-old language abilities: The role of parenting factors. *Early Childhood Research Quarterly*, *19*, 528–47.

Roulstone, S., Law, J., Rush, R., Clegg, J. and Peters, T. (2011). *Investigating the Role of Language in Children's Early Educational Outcomes*. London: Department for Education, and Bristol: University of the West of England. Available online at www.gov.uk/government/uploads/system/uploads/attachment_data/file/181549/DFE-RR134.pdf (accessed 17 January 2014).

Rowling, J.K. (1997). *Harry Potter and the Philosopher's Stone*. London: Bloomsbury.

Siraj-Blatchford, I., Sylva, K., Muttock, K., Gilden, R. and Bell, D. (2002). *Researching Effective Pedagogy in the Early Years* (DfES Ref RR356). London: DfES.

Tizard, B. and Hughes, M. (1984). *Young Children Learning: Talking and thinking at home and at school*. London: Fontana.

Twiner, A., Littleton, K., Coffin, C. and Whitelock, D. (2014). Meaning making as an interactional accomplishment: A temporal analysis of intentionality and improvisation in classroom dialogue. *International Journal of Educational Research*, *63*, 94–106.

Valsiner, J. (2000). *Culture and Human Development: An introduction*. London: SAGE.

Vouloumanos, A., Hauser, M.D., Werker, J.F. and Martin, A. (2010). The tuning of human neonates' preference for speech. *Child Development*, *81*(2), 517–27.

Vygotsky, L.S. (1978). *Mind in Society: The development of higher psychological processes*. Cambridge, MA: Harvard University Press.

Weisleder, A. and Fernald, A. (2013). Talking to children matters: Early language experience strengthens processing and builds vocabulary. *Psychological Science*, *24*(11), 2143–52.

7 Can we cure dyslexia?

Ben Hayes and Norah Frederickson

CHAPTER SUMMARY

A number of controversies surround the concept of dyslexia. *McGuinness (2004, p. 2) writes that:*

> The source of English children's difficulties in learning to read and spell is the English spelling system and the way it is taught. [Cross-cultural] comparisons provide irrefutable evidence that a biological theory of 'dyslexia', a deficit presumed to be a property of the child, is untenable, ruling out the popular 'phonological deficit theory' of dyslexia . . . English-speaking children have trouble learning to read and spell because of our complex spelling code and because of current teaching methods, not because of aberrant genes.

By contrast, Vellutino et al. *(2004, p. 25) concluded that, 'results obtained in genetic, neuroanatomical and psycho-physiological studies' support the view that dyslexia involves 'basic cognitive deficits of biological origin'.*

More recently, Elliott and Grigorenko (2014) reviewed the 'dyslexia debate' in some detail and argued that, 'The term "dyslexia" has surely outgrown its conceptual and diagnostic usefulness' (p. 176). What dyslexia is and what causes it are the first two controversies that will be explored in this chapter.

Another controversy relates to what schools and teachers can do to support children who find reading and spelling difficult to learn. Some describe dyslexia as a lifelong condition, where those who have dyslexia will need to learn to cope with the long-term effects of their condition (Firth et al., *2013). Others argue that children who have dyslexia can recover the skills they need for reading and spelling, if they get the right support: 'There is good evidence to show that phonological-based interventions are effective in ameliorating dyslexic difficulties' (Duff and Clarke, 2011, p. 9).*

In this chapter, we will examine these areas of controversy. First, we investigate definitions of dyslexia and review the evidence on different theories about the causes of dyslexia. The chapter then explores how reading is taught, how effective interventions have been in helping children learn to read when they have difficulty, and the extent to which dyslexia can be overcome using the right teaching approaches.

LEARNING OUTCOMES

When you have studied this chapter, you should be able to:

1 evaluate the advantages and disadvantages of different approaches to the definition of dyslexia;
2 identify similarities and differences between different theories of dyslexia and evaluate their utility, both in explaining findings from group studies and in describing the problems faced by particular individuals;
3 describe the principal approaches to the teaching of reading and their underpinnings in psychological theory and research;
4 evaluate the extent to which children with reading difficulties can recover from the difficulties they have when effective interventions are used.

WHAT IS DYSLEXIA?

Dyslexia is derived from Greek and translates as 'difficulty with words'. It is a term that has wide public recognition and lacks the stigma associated with many learning difficulties. In a journal editorial introducing research looking at how concepts of dyslexia have changed over time, Snowling (2012, p. e2) notes that, 'The science of dyslexia is well advanced', and that views on dyslexia are converging. However, definitions of dyslexia have changed a great deal over time, competing definitions have sometimes stood in stark contrast to each other, and there is certainly not universal consensus, even today.

ACTIVITY 7.1

1 Read the following definitions of dyslexia and identify what they have in common.
2 Decide to what extent they use exclusionary criteria (say what dyslexia is not) or inclusionary criteria (say what dyslexia is).
3 What would be the implications of these different approaches for teachers and educational psychologists in identifying and assessing children with dyslexia?

- Definition A: A disorder manifested by difficulty in learning to read, despite conventional instruction, adequate intelligence and sociocultural opportunity.

> It depends on fundamental cognitive disabilities that are frequently of constitutional origin (World Federation of Neurology, 1968, in Critchley and Critchley, 1978).
>
> - Definition B: 'Dyslexia is evident when accurate and fluent word reading and/or spelling is learned very incompletely or with great difficulty. This focuses on literacy learning at the "word level" and implies that the problem is severe and persistent despite appropriate learning opportunities. It provides the basis for a staged process of assessment through teaching' (British Psychological Society, 1999, p. 18).
> - Definition C: 'Dyslexia is a learning difficulty that primarily affects the skills involved in accurate and fluent word reading and spelling. Characteristic features of dyslexia are difficulties in phonological awareness, verbal memory and verbal processing speed. Dyslexia occurs across the range of intellectual abilities. It is best thought of as a continuum, not a distinct category, and there are no clear cut-off points' (Rose, 2009, p. 10).

Definition B differs from the other two in that it is descriptive, with no explanatory elements. This accords with arguments made by some (e.g. Tonnessen, 1997) that identifying characteristics should be differentiated from causal factors, and the latter should be excluded from definitions of dyslexia. This is considered desirable in order to provide a common basis for identifying a population on which various scientific explanatory models could be tested. However, definitions of dyslexia are not only used to select participants for psychological research. A major reason for the controversy surrounding definitions of dyslexia has been their use in conferring eligibility for special educational resources.

Definition C makes reference to specific explanatory elements, such as *phonological* awareness. It also contrasts with Definition A by explicitly ruling out the need for 'adequate intelligence' as being a factor that should be considered.

Until the turn of the century, variants of Definition A had been either explicitly or implicitly incorporated in special education assessment policy and practice, both in the UK (Frederickson and Reason, 1995) and the US (Gresham, 2002). Identification had, in effect, come to depend on the demonstration of a sufficiently large discrepancy between the child's scores on an intelligence test and a reading test. This *IQ–achievement* discrepancy approach to defining dyslexia, apparently based on the assumption that intelligence defines potential for reading attainment, has attracted increasing criticism. It was an issue hotly debated by educational psychologists in the UK (Frederickson and Reason, 1995; Ashton, 1996; Solity, 1996).

It has been demonstrated that children with low IQs can have good word-reading skills, so undermining the assumption on which the IQ–achievement discrepancy approach is based (Siegel, 1992). Stuebing *et al.* (2002) conducted a meta-analysis of forty-six studies to assess the validity of classifying poor readers as those who demonstrated an IQ–achievement discrepancy (and qualified for special help) and those who did not. They concluded that large overlaps between the two groups and negligible-to-small differences found on variables closely related to the reading process seriously questioned the validity of the approach. In addition, the utility, and indeed equity, of the approach have been challenged by findings that poor readers with and without a discrepancy do not differ in their *response to intervention* (RTI) (Stage *et al.*, 2003).

Response to intervention

The degree of response a child's reading difficulties show to a properly delivered, evidence-based intervention has been advocated, in place of an IQ–achievement discrepancy, as a qualification criterion for special educational provision (Gresham, 2002; Vaughn and Fuchs, 2003). Although conventional instruction and adequate social and cultural opportunity are also listed in Definition A, alongside adequate intelligence, little attention was previously paid to their systematic assessment. Clay (1987) convincingly argued that virtually all studies of reading difficulties failed to control for the potentially confounding effects of inadequate instruction or prereading experience, which could mimic the effects of organically based *learning disabilities*. This has continued to be a problem with the literature on dyslexia, until more recently, when emphasis has been placed on study selection criteria that include failure to respond adequately to interventions validated as effective for most children of comparable age/stage of reading development (see Vellutino *et al.*, 2004). Such studies, which will be discussed in more detail later in the chapter, have indicated that the ease with which children's reading difficulties can be remediated is unrelated to IQ, and that the use of IQ scores is counter-indicated as a selection criterion in scientific studies of the biologically based cognitive deficits in dyslexia.

These developments in the field have far-reaching implications for research and practice. Compared with administering tests of intelligence and reading to calculate a discrepancy, considerably greater time and cost are involved in obtaining a sample for a research study by first running an intervention programme to select non–responders. Despite the additional time needed, RTI selection criteria have become a good practice standard for identifying participants in research (Duff, 2008). For practitioners also, there have been pressures for change. The US Department of Education, Office of Special Education Programs (2002) recommended the elimination of discrepancy criteria from identification of learning disabilities and the use instead of RTI approaches, using interventions that are supported by research.

In November 2013, *The Psychologist* journal reported on a talk given by Margaret Snowling (Jarrett, 2013; see Focus Box 7.1).

Although there are a range of views on what underlies the sometimes persistent difficulties that children have with reading, Snowling has argued that there are increasingly areas of agreement. The evidence that these difficulties are not a diagnosis but are a continuum also leads many educational psychologists to see the term 'dyslexia' itself as redundant. For simplicity's sake, we continue to use it here, mindful of Snowling's points. Alongside views on what these difficulties are, there are many questions about *why* they occur, or why 'dyslexia' exists, if you choose to use the term. So, what are the risk factors that might cause dyslexia? It is to this question that we now turn.

The way the term 'dyslexia' is bandied around in the popular press, you get the sense that it's a precise diagnosis, something you either have or you don't. Answering questions at the end of her joint British Psychological Society/British Academy lecture, BPS Fellow Professor Margaret Snowling exposed this as a myth. 'Dyslexia is just another name for poor reading', she said. 'Where you put the cut off between dyslexia and normal reading has to be agreed within your education system, your school – it could be a national policy, a policy within a local authority – there isn't any gold standard.'

There may not be universal agreement on where to draw the line, but research into developmental dyslexia has come a long way since the first case was described by a British GP as 'word-blindness' in 1896. Such early accounts, Snowling explained, suffered from referral bias – the deficits had to be severe enough that a child wound up in a doctor's clinic. Back then the condition also tended to be seen as specific and perceptual, so that it became the domain of 'eye doctors'.

Our understanding of dyslexia – nowadays recognised as a 'neurodevelopmental disorder' affecting the ability to read and spell – was placed on surer footing by a seminal paper published in the mid-1970s. Snowling explained how Michael Rutter and William Yule's epidemiological work on the Isle of Wight led them to distinguish between children who read poorly relative to their IQ (they called this 'specific reading retardation') and those who read poorly for their age ('general reading backwardness'). This research made an important contribution, Snowling said, because it showed that both groups of children experienced language delays and deficits that pre-dated their reading problems.

Today there are several agreed-upon facts about dyslexia, Snowling continued. It runs in families; it's associated with a phonological deficit (i.e. a difficulty translating letters into sounds); and it can manifest in various ways behaviourally. 'The contemporary view', said Snowling, 'is that dyslexia is not a diagnosis, rather it's a dimensional disorder. Many people have dyslexia and it will vary from mild to severe. It occurs in individuals with all levels of intellectual ability, and it's associated with multiple risk factors, not a single cause.'

(Jarrett, 2013, p. 788; reprinted with permission of the British Psychological Society)

WHAT CAUSES DYSLEXIA?

Early researchers in the field characterised dyslexia as a visual processing problem: 'congenital word blindness' (Hinshelwood, 1900) or 'strephosymbolia' (twisted symbols; Orton, 1925). Orton considered delayed establishment of hemispheric dominance responsible for failure to supress mirror-image alternatives, leading to confusions of 'b' and 'd', 'saw' and 'was', etc. These ideas held sway until the 1970s–1980s, when careful experimental work showed that verbal mediation was implicated in the apparent visual difficulties (Vellutino, 1987). Instead, it was suggested that dyslexia was a subtle language difficulty that appeared to involve difficulties with phonemic segmentation and phonological coding (representing and accessing the sound of a word as an aid to memory). It is argued that children with dyslexia form mental representations of the sounds of language that are poorly specified or 'fuzzy', which makes it difficult to develop an awareness of the internal sound structure of words and to learn letter–sound relationships (Snowling, 2000).

This understanding of dyslexia has since become established as pre-eminent. From a review of research on dyslexia over the previous four decades, Vellutino *et al.* (2004, p. 2) conclude:

> The evidence suggests that inadequate facility in word identification due, in most cases, to more basic deficits in alphabetic coding is the basic cause of difficulties in learning to read. We next discuss hypothesised deficiencies in reading related cognitive abilities as underlying causes of deficiencies in component reading skills. The evidence in these areas suggests that, in most cases, phonological skills deficiencies associated with phonological coding deficits are the probable causes of the disorder rather than visual, semantic, or syntactic deficits, although reading difficulties in some children may be associated with general language deficits.

Almost identical conclusions are drawn by Ramus *et al.* (2006, p. 27):

> At the proximal level, almost everybody agrees that a phonological deficit is the direct underlying cause of most cases of dyslexia. ... At the distal level, the question is whether the phonological deficit is primary, or whether it is secondary to other cognitive, sensory or motor deficits. We argue that our results and the literature are consistent with the former, i.e. with the theory of a primary, specific phonological deficit.

The distinction between the *proximal* and *distal* levels is illustrated in Figure 7.1, which uses the causal modelling framework (Morton, 2004) to depict the primary phonological theory of dyslexia.

The *causal modelling framework* uses three levels of description to represent possible explanations of developmental problems: the biological, the cognitive and the behavioural. In addition, environmental factors can exert an influence at all three levels. Arrows are used to indicate hypothesised causal chains, and, in Figure 7.1, it can be seen that reading difficulties are hypothesised to be caused by a phonological deficit that disrupts the establishment of *grapheme–phoneme (letter–sound) correspondences*. However, in this case, at a more distant level of explanation, the hypothesised cognitive-level difficulty links to an abnormality at the brain level in left perisylvian

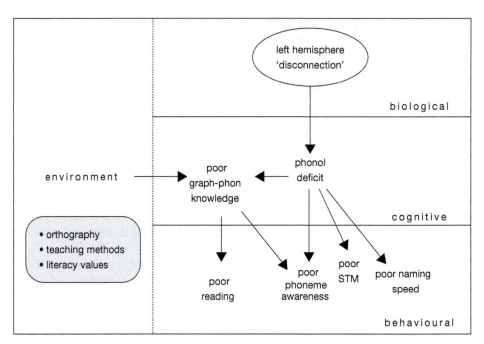

FIGURE 7.1 A causal model of dyslexia as the result of a phonological deficit

Source: Frith, 1999. ©John Wiley. Reproduced with permission

areas involved in phonology (Ramus, 2004). Other theories posit other distal causes. In the *cerebellar theory* of dyslexia (Nicolson and Fawcett, 1990), at a distal level, the deficit in fluent automatic phonological skills is hypothesised to be caused by a timing/ sequence deficit resulting from a cerebellar abnormality.

White *et al.* (2006) tested the cerebellar and pure phonological hypotheses along with two further hypotheses:

- the *temporal processing* hypothesis (Tallal, 2004), which proposes a deficit in the processing of rapidly changing stimuli that impairs the ability to make fine discriminations between phonemes;
- the magnocellular hypothesis (Stein and Talcott, 1999), which proposes a deficit in the suppression of visual traces, so that images of words persist for too long and exert partial masking effects.

Children with dyslexia and controls, aged 8–12 years, were compared on a range of measures, and the clustering of difficulties was examined for individual children. The article is followed by four commentaries, some from proponents of the theories challenged by the findings. Both methodology and interpretations are challenged in the commentaries, which are subsequently responded to by the authors of the original paper. The sequence of papers relating to the White *et al.* (2006) study offer an interesting demonstration of critical analysis and argument by leading researchers in the field.

White *et al.* (2006) report multiple-case-study analysis as well as a between-group analysis. This is of particular interest, given the challenges for educational psychologists of using findings from group studies to inform their work with individual children, which was highlighted as a theme in Chapter 1. Despite the weight of evidence supporting the phonological deficit approach, a sizeable minority of the children with dyslexia in the White *et al.* (2006) study did not have a significant phonological deficit. Many of the children in that study had received specialist phonologically based intervention, which is likely to have improved their phonological skills. Phonological difficulties are usually found to be more prevalent (around 80 per cent) among children identified by educational psychologists as having specific reading difficulty/dyslexia, but who have not received specialist intervention (Frederickson and Frith, 1998). This reminds us that psychologists need to be aware of other possible causes of dyslexia, if they are to be effective in working with the 20 per cent of children who do not show phonological impairments.

Genes and biology

Other biological-level information and hypotheses that can be recorded in the causal modelling framework include sensory or genetic factors. From their review of genetic research in dyslexia, Pennington and Olson (2005) note that there is a strong tendency for dyslexia to be inherited. Grigorenko (2012) notes that about twenty different gene areas might be involved in reading difficulties, some areas or 'loci' involving hundreds of specific genes. Although some progress has been made in identifying the actual gene variants involved, Grigorenko notes some caveats. Genetic variation is weaker in early childhood, and the association becomes stronger throughout life, and the association between reading and the genome appears to be stronger for people who find reading difficult. In addition, 'there is tremendous variation in how genetic factors manifest themselves in different languages in which reading is acquired' (Grigorenko, 2012, p. 175).

Smith (2011) notes that, although specific gene *mutations* that could cause dyslexia have not been found, it is the processes that regulate gene *expression* that are most likely to influence the biological aspects of language-processing and reading difficulties. Smith argues that these regulatory processes are likely to be key, and that these processes are *epigenetic*, rather than genetic. The distinction has great significance: a genetic mutation can be passed down from generation to generation. Even if you change your life in a way that compensates for (or even overcomes) the difficulty the mutation might have given you, the same mutation is passed down in the genetic code to your children, and they will experience the same effect. However, an epigenetic process will influence how genes are expressed in biology. If people live in a way that means that the effect the gene has is changed, then they can affect the impact the gene has on their biology. Crucially, however, this epigenetic difference can then be passed on to subsequent generations, changing the expression of the gene in their biology. Carey (2011) gives the example of the transgenerational inheritance effects of malnutrition, seen in the Dutch Winter Hunger of 1944, to explain how acquired characteristics can be passed down from generation to generation, in mechanisms where the genetic code is not altered, but the way it is expressed is. Individuals who were prenatally exposed to famine during the Dutch Hunger Winter in 1944–5 had, six decades later, less DNA methylation in some genes compared with their unexposed, same-sex siblings. The environmental impact of the famine had altered how their genes were expressed in that generation and the next. This same mechanism, Smith argues, underpins trans-generational inheritance in language processes and associated reading skills.

So, can transgenerational inheritance of literacy difficulties be changed? Can children born into families where epigenetic processes might be making it harder to learn to read change the pathway that they are following? Snowling *et al.* (2007) followed 'at-risk' children born in families with a history of dyslexia. The children had been studied longitudinally from the age of 3 years onwards and were seen again at age 12–13 years. Almost half the sample was classified as having significant reading and spelling problems (and emotional difficulties), and even those who did not meet the classification criteria did not read fluently. There was evidence of enduring literacy difficulties, with no evidence of catching up with normally achieving controls between the ages of 8 and 13. Although the at-risk children, with and without significant literacy problems, did not differ on measures of their family literacy environment, those who had significant problems read less themselves.

The causes of reading difficulties can be explored using the causal modelling framework, and, as research progresses, an increasingly refined picture emerges. New ways of understanding how the environment can affect our gene expression and transgenerational inheritance can potentially offer greater insights into why reading difficulties can persist.

Can teaching methods cause dyslexia?

McGuinness (1997, p. 122) describes dyslexia as, 'a label applied to children who are so confused by their poor reading instruction that they can't overcome it without special help', adding, 'nor do so-called dyslexic children have any more trouble learning to read than other children if they are taught with an appropriate method'. At the environmental level in Figure 7.1, 'teaching methods' are certainly shown as a possible influence. To what extent can it be said that methods of teaching reading cause dyslexia?

Vellutino and Fletcher (2005) argue that, because the acquisition of important reading subskills, such as phonological awareness and letter–sound correspondences, can be dependent on the type of teaching approach received (Foorman *et al.*, 1998), it is important to establish that there has been adequate instruction before assuming the cause of early reading difficulties is biological. Indeed, Vellutino *et al.* (1996) reported findings that suggest that most early reading difficulties are related to deficiencies in early literacy experience and/or teaching and concluded that these are often a primary cause. They followed children longitudinally from 5 to 9 years of age. At age 6–7 years, subsamples of poor and normal readers were selected and randomly assigned to either a tutored group or a non-tutored, 'contrast' group. Children in the tutored group were given daily tutoring (30 minutes per day) for between two and three school terms, depending on progress. Children in the non-tutored group received the normal special needs support available in their school.

At the start of the programme, 9 per cent of 6–7-year-olds were found to have a reading test score below the fifteenth percentile and a significant IQ–achievement discrepancy. After a term and a half of individual tutoring for half an hour per day, only 1 per cent remained below the fifteenth percentile (with a further 2 per cent below the thirtieth percentile). Results on a battery of tests were interpreted as indicating

METHOD 7.1

Neuroscience and reading interventions: connecting brain and behaviour

Some studies with children have shown differences in measures of brain functioning between dyslexic and normally developing readers that ameliorate with improvements in word reading following intervention. For example, initial differences between normally developing readers and those with dyslexia were established by Simos *et al.* (2000). They used *magnetic source imaging*, which detects changes in magnetic fields surrounding neuronal electrical discharges, to describe the following sequence of activation when normally developing children read: occipital areas that support primary visual processing, followed by basal temporal areas in both hemispheres, followed by three areas in the left temporal and parietal areas of the left hemisphere (the superior temporal gyrus, Wernicke's area and the angular gyrus). By contrast, in children with dyslexia, in this final stage these areas are activated, but in the right rather than the left hemisphere. It is unclear whether this different pattern reflects compensatory processing.

In a further study (Simos *et al.*, 2002), when eight children with severe dyslexia, aged 7–17 years, were given intensive (10 hours per week over 8 weeks) phonologically based instruction, reading-accuracy scores rose into the average range, and there was a significant increase in left-hemisphere activation of those areas typically activated in normally developing readers. Consistent with the greater resistance to intervention of reading fluency, delays were apparent in these left-hemisphere responses.

A further study provided evidence that normalising changes in brain activity and adequate RTI were linked, but also that resistance to evidence-supported intervention was reflected in patterns of brain activity. Simos *et al.* (2007) monitored spatiotemporal profiles of brain activity in 6–8-year-old children with dyslexia during a two-stage intensive intervention delivered to pairs of pupils. Stage 1 focused on phonological decoding skills for 8 weeks (2 × 50-minute sessions per day), and Stage 2 focused on rapid word recognition ability for a further 8 weeks (1 hour per day). The fifteen children in this study had previously been identified as inadequate responders to reading instruction that was effective for most participants.

Clinically significant improvement in reading-standard scores was noted in eight children, who also showed 'normalizing' changes in their spatiotemporal profiles of regional brain activity (increased duration of activity in the left temporoparietal region and a shift in the relative timing of activity in temporoparietal and inferior frontal regions). Seven children who demonstrated 'compensatory' changes in brain activity (increased duration of activity in the right temporoparietal region and frontal areas, bilaterally) did not show an adequate RTI. A control group of normally developing readers did not show systematic changes in brain activity during the study, which suggests that the changes observed were associated with the special programme and were not simply the result of developmental changes or of normal classroom teaching.

that continuing reading difficulties were due primarily to basic deficits in phonological skills. IQ scores did not distinguish between poor readers who were easy and difficult to remediate, whereas phonological skills (e.g. phoneme segmentation, rapid naming) did distinguish between and within these groups. Method Box 7.1 shows that there is now evidence of the impact of such interventions at the biological level.

The instruction received is one important environmental influence on dyslexia; the orthography of the language in which instruction occurs is another. Alphabetic writing systems demand high levels of phonological skills. Writing systems that do not use small speech sounds as the basis for written symbols, but instead use syllables, whole words or meanings, should present fewer difficulties for individuals with phonological problems. This is illustrated by the case study presented by Wydell and Butterworth (1999) of a dyslexic boy, bilingual in English and Japanese, who only showed reading and writing difficulties in English.

Alphabetic languages vary in the transparency of their orthographies (the consistency with which the written symbols map on to sounds). English is notoriously inconsistent, and Seymour et al. (2003) found that the rate of literacy-skills acquisition relates to the consistency of the orthography of the language. Correspondingly, Caravolas (2005) reviewed studies showing that children with dyslexia typically experience milder difficulties, in particular with reading accuracy relative to reading fluency and spelling, and suggested that this reflected the lower levels of demand placed on phonological skills. Research study selection criteria for dyslexia in more *transparent orthographies* tend to centre on speed and fluency rather than error rate. Goswami (2005) has suggested that the failure of most studies to find differences between the efficacy of large- versus small-unit *phonics* instruction may reflect relative advantages of each instructional approach in dealing with the inconsistency of English and cautioned that generalisation of research findings in English to other languages may not be valid.

Vellutino et al. (2004) describe dyslexia as a 'complex condition that depends on the dynamic interaction between certain innate susceptibilities as well as the home and school environments on the one hand, and the cultures in which children learn to read on the other' (p. 18). They note that some transparent orthographies may aid learning to the point where the underlying difficulty is hidden, whereas others, such as English, may aggravate the problem. There are clear parallels with reading instruction. It is possible to argue both that inadequate instruction or other experiential factors are responsible for the problems of many poor readers and that biological factors are important. This reflects developing understanding of the ways in which brain and environment interact in the process of learning to read.

CAN DYSLEXIA BE CURED?

At the start of this chapter, it was noted that Duff and Clarke (2011) have concluded that the difficulties dyslexic individuals face can be 'ameliorated'. We have also reviewed neurological evidence from Simos and colleagues indicating that dyslexic children's brain function can be 'normalised' through intensive intervention. In the remainder of the chapter, we will now turn our attention more fully to the question of intervention and to what extent we now know how to 'cure' children who are described as having dyslexia. The section begins by analysing the debates that have existed about how reading should be taught, before focusing specifically on interventions for children who have persistent difficulties learning literacy.

What is the best way to learn to read and write?

Some time ago, Goodman (1967) and Smith (1978) popularised a 'whole-language' approach, where the emphasis is placed on contextual knowledge, using syntactic or semantic cues to identify a word, rather than features of the printed word. Here, reading was conceived of as a 'psycholinguistic guessing game', where features of a printed word were not seen as a primary source of hypotheses about its identity, but were used to test hypotheses generated from the grammatical context and the meaning of the passage. Even as a model of skilled reading, the assumptions of the 'psycholinguistic guessing game' approach were quickly found to lack empirical support. Skilled adult readers were only able to predict 25 per cent of the words in connected prose, and prediction took longer than just looking at the word (Gough *et al.*, 1981). Reading for meaning proved to be dependent on good word-decoding skills, rather than the other way round (see Adams and Bruck, 1993).

A further assumption of the approach was that children and adults employ the same processes when reading, processes that utilise the neurological mechanisms underpinning spoken language. It was argued that, through exposure to print and the use of semantic and syntactic cues in the context of meaningful stories, children would develop the knowledge required to decode print, with minimal explicit teaching of letter–sound correspondences. These assumptions have been questioned from a cognitive neuroscience perspective:

> Language is a human instinct, but written language is not. Language is found in all societies, present and past. . . . All healthy children master their own language without lessons or corrections. When children are thrown together without a usable language, they invent one of their own. Compare all this with writing. Writing systems have been invented a small number of times in history. . . . Until recently, most children never learned to read or write; even with today's universal education, many children struggle and fail. A group of children is no more likely to invent an alphabet than it is to invent the internal combustion engine. Children are wired for sound, but print is an optional accessory that must be painstakingly bolted on. This basic fact about human nature should be the starting point for any discussion of how to teach our children to read and write.
>
> (Pinker, 1997)

The set of problems facing children learning to read are summarised by Snow and Juel (2005, p. 501):

> the problem of the alphabetic principle, which requires learning how to segment speech into sounds represented by graphemes; the problem of English orthography, which requires going beyond simple phoneme–grapheme links to represent the morphemic, historical and etymological information preserved in the writing system; and the problem of comprehension which requires building a representation of textual and situational information.

All of the major theories of reading development represent the solution of the first two of these problems as key achievements needed to move between qualitatively different stages or phases in the acquisition of word-recognition skill (see Table 7.1). *Logographic* strategies involve the use of distinctive visual or contextual features to recognise words, alphabetic strategies focus on sound–spelling rules, and *orthographic* strategies focus on larger spelling patterns, especially morphemic units (as in 'sign', 'signal', 'signify').

The focus on sub-lexical (e.g. letter, syllable) elements apparent in the theories of early reading development in Table 7.1 parallels the findings of all the recent reviews and meta-analyses of the effectiveness of different methods for teaching reading. These have highlighted a need for explicit and systematic teaching of letter–sound correspondences in reading, alongside a focus on reading for meaning (Snow and Juel, 2005). This has been interpreted by some as permissive of a haphazard eclecticism in selecting methods of teaching reading, an interpretation specifically denounced in the preface to at least one US report, which has stressed that an integrated, coherent approach to literacy development is needed (National Reading Council, 1998).

A similar approach was taken in the UK when a National Curriculum was introduced in 1989. The reading process was conceptualised as involving four strategies or 'searchlights' – sources of knowledge readers use to 'illuminate' their processing: phonic (sounds and spelling) knowledge, grammatical knowledge, word recognition and graphic knowledge, and knowledge of context. However, reports from inspectors indicated that the statutory phonic component of the programme was often a neglected or weak feature of the teaching. As a result, a *National Literacy Strategy* was introduced in the UK in 1998. This strategy provided detailed guidance on how to teach phonics.

TABLE 7.1 A schematic summary of different stage/phase theories of learning to read

Proponents	Chall (1983)	Frith (1985)	Ehri (2002)	Stuart and Coltheart (1988)	Seymour and Duncan (2001)
Number of developmental periods	5	3	4	2	4
1 Pre-reading	Stage 0: Letters/Book exposure	Logographic	Pre-alphabetic		Pre-literacy
2 Early reading	Memory and contextual guessing		Partial alphabetic	Partial orthographic	Dual foundation
3 Decoding	Stage 1: Decoding, attending to letters/sounds	Alphabetic	Full alphabetic	Complete orthographic	Alphabetic
					Logographic
4 Fluent reading	Stage 2: Fluency, consolidation	Orthographic	Consolidated alphabetic Automaticity		Orthographic Morphographic

Source: Adapted from Ehri, 2005. ©John Wiley. Reproduced with permission

Rose (2006) revised the content of the literacy curriculum and moved away from the 'searchlights' model of reading in favour of the 'simple' view of reading (Gough and Tunmer, 1986), where reading is seen as the product of single-word decoding and language comprehension. It was recommended that high-quality, systematic phonic work should be taught as the prime approach to decoding (reading) and encoding (spelling) words. What is more, a particular approach to teaching phonics, synthetic phonics, was endorsed.

The synthetic phonics approach is defined by Torgerson *et al.* (2006) as focusing on the phonemes associated with particular graphemes, which are pronounced in isolation and blended together (synthesised). For example, children are taught to take a single-syllable word such as *cat* apart into its three letters, pronounce a phoneme for each letter in turn, /k, æ, t/, and blend the phonemes together to form a word. Synthetic phonics is contrasted with analytic phonics, in which children analyse whole words to identify the common phoneme in a set of words. For example, teacher and pupils discuss how the following words are alike: *pat, park, push* and *pen*.

The Rose report (2006) has been criticised for basing the recommendation of synthetic phonics on insufficient evidence, for example by Wyse and Styles (2007), who cite the findings of systematic reviews from the US and the UK in support of their criticisms. In the US, the National Reading Panel (2000) did not find evidence that teaching programmes focused on small units in words (phonemes) were any more effective than those focusing on larger units ('onset–rime', e.g. *sh-op, st-op, dr-op*), or that synthetic approaches focused on blending were more effective than analytic approaches focused on word families. In the UK, Torgersen *et al.* (2006) concluded that the weight of evidence was weak (only three randomised controlled trials were located), and no statistically significant difference in effectiveness was found between synthetic and analytic phonics instruction.

Since then, Johnston *et al.* (2012) have published further data for children who were 6 years into their reading instruction in school and either following a synthetic or an analytic approach. The results highlight the benefits that synthetic phonics can have for word reading, spelling and reading comprehension, and that there may be particular benefits for boys.

Other research has revealed further complications. Stasio *et al.* (2012) undertook a randomised controlled trial that discovered advantages for analytic phonics for particular groups. The authors conclude that:

> In summary, the present findings of this study mark a contribution to knowledge by suggesting, we think for the first time, that early analytic phonics interventions might have greater long-term effects when delivered in pre-formal school education to children from low-SES backgrounds who often had English as an additional language. More research using true experimental designs (and ultimately, systematic review) is needed to explore the differences between the two intervention methods over longer periods of time using larger representative samples of children to drive evidence-based policy.
>
> (Stasio *et al.*, 2012, p. 82)

Do the same conclusions apply to young children at risk for reading failure?

A study by Hatcher *et al.* (2004) suggests that they may not. Reception-year children (aged 4–5 years) were divided into four matched groups and randomly assigned to one of three experimental teaching conditions (delivered to groups of 10–15 children for three 10-minute sessions per week):

- reading with rhyme;
- reading with phoneme;
- reading with rhyme and phoneme;
- reading (control condition where children were taught as a class, in groups and as individuals).

In each experimental condition, there was a strong phonic component, and the same amount of time was devoted to reading instruction. For normally developing children, no differential effects of the different teaching programmes were found. However, for children identified as being at risk of reading failure, training in phoneme skills resulted in greater gains in phoneme awareness and in reading skills. These findings suggest that any reading programme that contains a highly structured phonic component is sufficient for most 4–5-year-old children to learn to read effectively, but, for young children at risk of reading delay, additional training in phoneme awareness and linking phonemes with letters is required.

What intervention strategies are effective for children with dyslexia?

Compared with children who learn to read with ease, children who experience difficulties learning to read appear to need instruction that is more explicit, more intensive and more supportive, in terms both of motivating encouragement and cognitive structuring or scaffolding (Torgesen, 2002, 2005). Supportive evidence from a study by Torgesen *et al.* (2001) is summarised in Figure 7.2. In this study, two interventions were implemented with 9–10-year-old children who had been receiving special education services for dyslexia for at least 16 months and whose reading attainments were at a 5–6-year age equivalent level. The children were randomly allocated to one of the interventions that provided *supportive* and *explicit* teaching on phomemic awareness and phonemic-based decoding strategies. The interventions, auditory discrimination in depth and embedded phonics, differed in the proportion of time spent focusing on activities using single words (85 per cent versus 20 per cent), on building fluency with high-frequency words (10 per cent versus 30 per cent), and reading words in meaningful context with teacher support (5 per cent versus 50 per cent). The interventions were both *intensive*, providing 67.5 hours of individual teaching in two 50-minute sessions each day for around 8 weeks.

From Figure 7.2, it can be seen that the programmes had very similar effects, producing large and lasting gains in reading attainment. The scores shown are standard scores that have a mean of 100 and standard deviation of 15 and allow a child's performance to be compared with others of their age. At the start of the study, the children

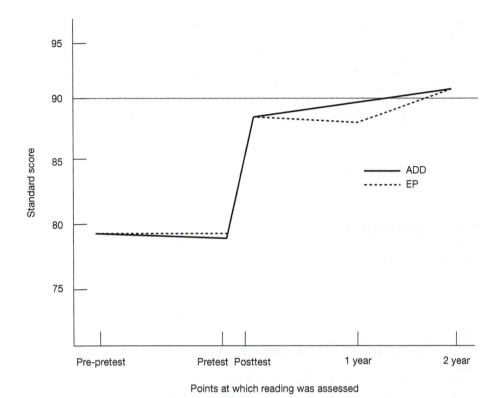

FIGURE 7.2 Standard reading scores before, during and after 67.5 hours of intensive intervention

Notes: ADD = auditory discrimination in depth; EP = embedded phonics

Source: Torgesen *et al.*, 2001, p. 26; ©SAGE. Reproduced with permission

were scoring below 80 on average, placing them in the bottom 7 per cent of the population. This was despite having received special education services for the previous 16 months, during which they had made some improvements in their reading performance, so that they had not fallen any further behind, but neither had they 'caught up' at all. Following the 8-week intervention, the children were scoring close to 90 on average, a score that placed them above 30 per cent of children of their age, so that they had caught up significantly with others of their age and were performing in the lower part of the average range (defined as within one standard deviation of the mean). An important caveat is that these are group averages, the interventions were not equally successful with all children. In addition, despite improvements in reading accuracy, reading fluency remained substantially below average, a common finding from intervention programmes for children described as having dyslexia (Torgesen, 2005).

What about changes at the biological level?

Earlier in the chapter, a series of studies by Simos and colleagues were presented to illustrate how methodological developments have changed the way we can investigate responses to intervention. In fact, these studies represent only a fraction of the work that has been conducted in this area. Molfese (2012) reviews the results of eight different neuroimaging studies published between 2002 and 2008. These studies used either functional magnetic resonance imaging (fMRI) or magnetoencephalography (MEG) to generate images of brain function before and after instruction. The instructional programmes varied from 28 hours to 670 hours, but all studies showed patterns of 'normalization'. Molfese concludes that, 'both MEG and fMRI [studies show] consistent findings that adequate RTI is accompanied by in most cases normalization in the brain of children with reading disability to more closely resemble the brain activation profiles of typically developing children.' Although 'most cases' is very encouraging, a proportion of children in these studies, 0.5–1 per cent, did not respond.

FACT AND OPINION

The debate about how to help children who struggle with literacy can involve many different claims and opinions; see Focus Box 7.2.

FOCUS 7.2

Extract from How to cure dyslexia

Sam Blumenthal, writing in the *New American*, describes an experience he had teaching a student who had been taught to read using a look–say method. He describes how the student misread words and how he found reading so difficult that he never read for pleasure. Sam describes the teaching approaches that he used. These focused on spotting the errors he was making and splitting words into sections, building phonemic awareness.

> It took about a year, but after it was done, he had become a good phonetic reader and a lover of books. So I knew that dyslexia could be cured long before the neuroscientists discovered the plasticity of the brain. It takes time and effort, but it can be done.
>
> (Sam Blumenfeld, *The New American*, 2012,
> www.thenewamerican.com/reviews/opinion/item/
> 10919-how-to-cure-dyslexia)

ACTIVITY 7.2

Read Focus Box 7.2. The claims made are based on the personal experience of a tutor who saw change in students he worked with. Consider the research presented in this chapter and make a note of key evidence that you might draw on when answering the following questions:

- Sam claims that the 'look–say' method of teaching was at the root of his student's difficulties. What evidence is there that such an ineffective teaching approach can cause dyslexia?
- Sam claims that, after about a year of teaching, his student's dyslexia was cured. What evidence is there from the research reviewed in this chapter for how long it might take to gain effective reading skills, given the right intervention?

SUMMARY OF MAIN ISSUES ADDRESSED IN THIS CHAPTER

- The definition of dyslexia remains controversial. Central issues are: the use of exclusionary or inclusionary criteria and the use of explanatory, as well as descriptive, elements.
- The IQ–achievement discrepancy approach to defining dyslexia, which was formerly influential in both research and practice, has been challenged on the grounds of validity, equity and utility. It is now recommended that response-to-intervention criteria are used instead in sample selection for research and decisions about eligibility for special provision.
- The overwhelming weight of evidence supports the phonological deficit theory of dyslexia. However, all children with reading problems do not show phonological impairments, and other hypotheses for the difficulties experienced must be considered in these cases.
- There has been hot debate over the best method for teaching reading. Psychological theory and research have supported explicit teaching of phonics for all children in the early stages of learning to read. For children at risk of reading failure and those with dyslexia, there is evidence that teaching needs to be more explicit, intensive and supportively structured.
- Intensive phonologically based intervention can produce significant improvements in the reading and related cognitive processes (notably phonological skills) of children with dyslexia. Findings from neuroscientific studies show that differences between the brain function of children with dyslexia and that of normally developing readers can also be normalised by this kind of educational intervention.
- Epigenetic influences on dyslexia may underlie strong transgenerational inheritance and familial incidence. Environmental influences on the nature of the problems with

reading that will be experienced include the language of instruction, as well as the nature of the instruction received. It is concluded that dyslexia results from complex interactions between biologically based cognitive abilities and environmental demands and supports.

KEY CONCEPTS AND TERMS

- Dyslexia
- Learning disabilities
- IQ–achievement discrepancy
- Response to intervention
- National Literacy Strategy
- Phonics: synthetic

- and analytic
- Grapheme–phoneme correspondences
- Logographic
- Orthographic
- Phonological
- Magnetic source imaging
- Proximal

- Distal
- Causal modelling framework
- Epigenetics
- Cerebellar theory
- Temporal processing
- Transparent orthographies

RECOMMENDATIONS FOR FURTHER READING

Journal articles

Duff, F.J. and Clarke, P. (2011). Practitioner review: Reading disorders: What are the effective interventions and how should they be implemented and evaluated? *Journal of Child Psychology and Psychiatry, 52*(1), 3–12.

Frith, U. (1999). Paradoxes in the definition of dyslexia. *Dyslexia, 5*, 192–214.

Snowling, M.J. (2012). Changing concepts of dyslexia: Nature, treatment and comorbidity. *Journal of Child Psychology and Psychiatry, 53*(9), e1–e3.

Vellutino, F.R., Fletcher, J.M., Snowling, M.J. and Scanlon, D.M. (2004). Specific reading disability (dyslexia): What have we learned in the past four decades? *Journal of Child Psychology and Psychiatry, 45*(1), 2–40.

Books and book chapters

Breznitz, Z., Rubinsten, O., Molfese, V. and Molfese, D. (2012). *Reading, Writing, Mathematics and the Developing Brain: Listening to many voices.* New York: Springer.

Elliott, J. and Grigorenko, E. (2014). *The Dyslexia Debate.* Cambridge, UK: Cambridge University Press.

Torgesen, J.K. (2005). Recent discoveries on remedial interventions for children with dyslexia. In M.J. Snowling and C. Hulme (eds), *The Science of Reading: A handbook.* Oxford, UK: Blackwell.

SAMPLE ESSAY TITLES

1 Evaluate the strengths and weaknesses of two definitions of dyslexia.
2 Poor reading instruction is the main cause of dyslexia, and good reading instruction is the most effective cure. Discuss.
3 Evaluate the claim that science has discovered how to overcome dyslexia, and therefore all children should be able to read if taught properly.
4 To what extent can dyslexia be seen as a language difficulty?
5 Discuss to what extent it is possible for children to recover from dyslexia if they have the right help.

REFERENCES

Adams, M.J. and Bruck, M. (1993). Word recognition: The interface of educational policies and scientific research. *Reading and Writing: An Interdisciplinary Journal, 5*, 113–39.

Ashton, C. (1996). In defence of discrepancy definitions of specific learning difficulties. *Educational Psychology in Practice, 12*(3), 131–40.

British Psychological Society (1999). *Dyslexia, Literacy and Psychological Assessment* (Report of a Working Party of the Division of Educational and Child Psychology). Leicester, UK: British Psychological Society.

Caravolas, M. (2005). The nature and causes of dyslexia in different languages. In M.J. Snowling and C. Hulme (eds), *The Science of Reading: A handbook*. Oxford, UK: Blackwell.

Carey, N. (2011). *The Epigenetics Revolution*. London: Icon.

Chall, J.S. (1983). *Learning to Read. The great debate* (2nd edn). Fort Worth, TX: Harcourt Brace College.

Clay, M. (1987). Learning to be learning disabled. *New Zealand Journal of Educational Studies, 22*, 155–73.

Critchley, M. and Critchley, E.A. (1978). *Dyslexia Defined*. London: Heinemann Medical.

Duff, F.J. (2008). Defining reading disorders and evaluating reading interventions: Perspectives from the response to intervention model. *Educational and Child Psychology, 25*, 31–6.

Duff, F.J. and Clarke, P. (2011). Practitioner review: Reading disorders: What are the effective interventions and how should they be implemented and evaluated? *Journal of Child Psychology and Psychiatry, 52*(1), 3–12.

Ehri, L.C. (2002). Faces of acquisition in learning to read words and implications for teaching. *British Journal of Educational Psychology: Monograph Series, 1*, 7–28.

Ehri, L.C. (2005). Development of sight word reading: Phases and findings. In M.J. Snowling and C. Hulme (eds), *The Science of Reading: A handbook*. Oxford, UK: Blackwell.

Elliott, J. and Grigorenko, E. (2014). *The Dyslexia Debate*. Cambridge, UK: Cambridge University Press.

Firth, N., Frydenberg, E., Steeg, C. and Bond, L. (2013). Coping successfully with dyslexia: An initial study of an inclusive school-based resilience programme. *Dyslexia, 19*(2), 113–30.

Foorman, B.R., Francis, D.J., Fletcher, J.M., Schatschneider, C. and Mehta, P. (1998). The role of instruction in learning to read: Preventing reading failure in at-risk children. *Journal of Educational Psychology, 90,* 37–55.

Frederickson, N. and Frith, U. (1998). Identifying dyslexia in bilingual children: A phonological approach within inner London Sylheti speakers. *Dyslexia, 4,* 119–31.

Frederickson, N. and Reason, R. (1995). Discrepancy definitions of specific learning difficulties. *Educational Psychology in Practice, 10*(4), 195–205.

Frith, U. (1985). Beneath the surface of developmental dyslexia. In K.E. Patterson, J.C. Marshall and M. Coltheart (eds), *Surface Dyslexia: Neuro-psychological and cognitive studies of phonological reading.* London: Erlbaum, pp. 301–30.

Frith, U. (1999). Paradoxes in the definition of dyslexia. *Dyslexia, 5,* 192–214.

Goodman, K.S. (1967). Reading: A psycho-linguistic guessing game. *Journal of the Reading Specialist, 6,* 126–35.

Goswami, U. (2005). Synthetic phonics and learning to read: A cross-language perspective. *Educational Psychology in Practice, 21*(4), 273–82.

Gough, P.B., Alford, J.A. and Holley-Wilcox, P. (1981). Words and contexts. In O.J.L. Tzeng and H. Singer (eds), *Perceptions of Print: Reading research in experimental psychology.* Hillsdale, NJ: Erlbaum, pp. 85–102.

Gough, P.B. and Tunmer, W.E. (1986). Decoding, reading and reading disability. *Remedial and Special Education, 7,* 6–10.

Gresham, F.M. (2002). Responsiveness to intervention: An alternative approach to the identification of learning disabilities. In R. Bradley, L. Danielson and D.P. Hallahan (eds), *Identification of Learning Disabilities: Researched practice.* Mahwah, NJ: Erlbaum.

Grigorenko, E. (2012). Genetic sciences for developmentalists: An example of reading ability and disability. In S. Sala and M. Anderson, *Neuroscience in Education: The good the bad and the ugly.* Oxford, UK: Oxford University Press.

Hatcher, P.J., Hulme, C. and Snowling, M.J. (2004). Explicit phoneme training combined with phonic reading instruction helps young children at risk of reading failure. *Journal of Child Psychology and Psychiatry, 45*(2), 338–58.

Hinshelwood, J. (1900). Congenital word blindness. *Lancet, 1,* 1506–8.

Jarrett, C. (2013). Untangling dyslexia. *The Psychologist, 26*(11), 788–9.

Johnston, R., McGeowan, S. and Watson, J. (2012). Long-term effects of synthetic versus analytic phonics teaching on the reading and spelling ability of 10 year old boys and girls. *Reading and Writing, 25,* 1136–384.

McGuinness, D. (1997). *Why Children Can't Read and What We Can Do About It.* London: Penguin.

McGuinness, D. (2004). *Early Reading Instruction. What science really tells us about how to teach reading.* Hong Kong: Bradford.

Molfese, P. (2012). Imaging studies of reading disabilities in children. In Z. Breznitz, O. Rubinsten, V. Molfese and D. Molfese (eds), *Reading, Writing, Mathematics and the Developing Brain: Listening to many voices.* New York: Springer.

Morton, J. (2004). *Understanding Developmental Disorders: A causal modelling approach.* Oxford, UK: Blackwell.

National Reading Council (1998). *Preventing Reading Difficulties in Young Children.* C.E. Snow, M.S. Burns and P. Griffin (eds). Washington, DC: National Academy.

National Reading Panel (2000). *Teaching Children to Read: An evidence-based assessment of the scientific research literature on reading and its implications for reading instruction.* Washington, DC: National Institute for Child Health and Human Development.

Nicolson, R. and Fawcett, A. (1990). Automaticity: A new framework for dyslexia research? *Cognition, 35,* 159–82.

Orton, S.T. (1925). 'Word-blindness' in school children. *Archives of Neurology and Psychiatry, 14,* 581–615.

Pennington, B.F. and Olson, R.K. (2005). Genetics of dyslexia. In M.J. Snowling and C. Hulme (eds), *The Science of Reading: A handbook.* Oxford, UK: Blackwell.

Pinker, S. (1997). Foreword. In D. McGuinness, *Why Our Children Can't Read and What We Can Do About It: A scientific revolution in reading.* London: Penguin Education.

Ramus, F. (2004). Neurobiology of dyslexia: A reinterpretation of the data. *Trends in Neurosciences, 27*(12), 720–6.

Ramus, F., White, S. and Frith, U. (2006). Weighing the evidence between competing theories of dyslexia. *Developmental Science, 9*(3), 265–9.

Rose, J. (2006). *Independent Review of the Teaching of Early Reading.* London: DfES Publications.

Rose, J. (2009). *Identifying and Teaching Children and Young People with Dyslexia and Literacy Difficulties.* Nottingham, UK: DCFS.

Seymour, P.H.K., Aro, M. and Erskine, J.M. (2003). Foundation literacy acquisition in European orthographies. *British Journal of Psychology, 94,* 143–74.

Seymour, P.H.K. and Duncan, L.G. (2001). Learning to read in English. *Psychology: The Journal of the Hellenic Psychological Society, 8,* 281–99.

Siegel, L.S. (1992). An evaluation of the discrepancy definition of dyslexia. *Journal of Learning Disabilities, 25,* 616–29.

Simos, P.G., Breier, J.I., Fletcher, J.M., Bergman, E. and Papanicolau, A.C. (2000). Cerebral mechanisms involved in word reading in dyslexic children. *Cerebral Cortex, 10,* 809–16.

Simos, P.G., Fletcher, J.M., Bergman, E., Breier, J.I., Foorman, B.R., Castillo, E.M., Fitzgerald, M. and Papanicolau, A.C. (2002). Dyslexia-specific brain activation profile becomes normal following successful remedial training. *Neurology, 58,* 1203–13.

Simos, P.G., Fletcher, J.M., Sarkari, S., Billingsley, R.L., Denton, C. and Papanicolaou, A.C. (2007). Altering the brain circuits for reading through intervention: A magnetic source imaging study. *Neuropsychology, 21*(4), 485–96.

Smith, F. (1978). *Understanding Reading: A psycho-linguistic analysis of reading and learning to read* (2nd edn). New York: Holt, Rinehart & Winston.

Smith, S. (2011). Approach to epigenetic analysis in language disorders. *Journal of Neuro-developmental Disorders, 3,* 356–64.

Snow, C.E. and Juel, C. (2005). Teaching children to read: What do we know about how to do it? In M.J. Snowling and C. Hulme (eds), *The Science of Reading: A handbook.* Malden, MA: Blackwell Publishing, pp. 501–20.

Snowling, M.J. (2000). *Dyslexia* (2nd edn). Oxford, UK: Blackwell.

Snowling, M.J. (2012). Changing concepts of dyslexia: Nature, treatment and comorbidity. *Journal of Child Psychology and Psychiatry, 53*(9), e1–e3.

Snowling, M.J., Muter, B. and Carroll, J. (2007). Children at family risk of dyslexia: A follow up in early adolescence. *Journal of Child Psychology & Psychiatry, 48*(6), 609–18.

Solity, J. (1996). Discrepancy definitions of dyslexia: An assessment through teaching approach. *Educational Psychology in Practice, 12*(3), 141–51.

Stage, S.A., Abbott, R.D., Jenkins, J.R. and Berninger, V.W. (2003). Predicting response to early reading intervention from verbal IQ, reading-related language abilities, attention ratings and verbal IQ–word reading discrepancy: Failure to validate discrepancy method. *Journal of Learning Disabilities, 36*(1), 24–33.

Stasio, M., Savage, R. and Abrami, P. (2012). A follow-up study of the ABRACADABRA web-based literacy intervention in Grade 1. *Journal of Research in Reading, 35*(1), 69–86.

Stein, J. and Talcott, J. (1999). Impaired neuronal timing in developmental dyslexia – The magnocellular hypothesis. *Dyslexia, 5*, 59–77.

Stuart, M. and Coltheart, M. (1988). Does reading develop in a sequence of stages? *Cognition, 30*, 139–81.

Stuebing, K.K., Fletcher, J.M., LeDoux, J.M., Lyon, G.R., Shaywitz, S.E. and Shaywitz, B.A. (2002). Validity of IQ–discrepancy classifications of reading disabilities: A meta-analysis. *American Educational Research Journal, 39*, 469–518.

Tallal, P. (2004). Improving language and literacy is a matter of time. *Nature Reviews Neuroscience, 5*, 721–8.

Tonnessen, F.E. (1997). How can we best define dyslexia? *Dyslexia, 3*, 78–92.

Torgerson, C.J., Brooks, G. and Hall, J. (2006). *A Systematic Review of the Research Literature on the Use of Phonics in the Teaching of Reading and Spelling*. Nottingham, UK: DfES.

Torgesen, J.K. (2002). The prevention of reading difficulties. *Journal of School Psychology, 40*(1), 7–26.

Torgesen, J.K. (2005). Recent discoveries on remedial interventions for children with dyslexia. In M.J. Snowling and C. Hulme (eds), *The Science of Reading: A handbook*. Oxford, UK: Blackwell.

Torgesen, J.K., Alexander, A.W., Wagner, R.K., Rashotte, C.A., Voller, K., Conway, T. (2001). Intensive remedial instruction for children with severe reading disabilities: Immediate and long term outcomes from two instructional approaches. *Journal of Learning Disabilities, 34*, 33–58.

US Department of Education, Office of Special Education Programs (2002). *Specific Learning Disabilities: Finding common ground*. Washington, DC: Author.

Vaughn, S. and Fuchs, L.S. (2003). Redefining learning disabilities as inadequate response to instruction: The promise and potential problems. *Learning Disabilities Research and Practice, 18*(3), 137–46.

Vellutino, F.R. (1987). Dyslexia. *Scientific American, 256*(3), 34–41.

Vellutino, F.R. and Fletcher, J.M. (2005). Developmental dyslexia. In M.J. Snowling and C. Hulme (eds), *The Science of Reading: A handbook*. Oxford, UK: Blackwell.

Vellutino, F.R., Fletcher, J.M., Snowling, M.J. and Scanlon, D.M. (2004). Specific reading disability (dyslexia): What have we learned in the past four decades? *Journal of Child Psychology and Psychiatry, 45*(1), 2–40.

Vellutino, F.R., Scanlon, D.M., Sipay, E., Small, S., Pratt, A., Chen, R. and Denckla, M.B. (1996). Cognitive profiles of difficult-to-remediate and readily-remediated poor readers: Early intervention as a vehicle for distinguishing between cognitive and experiential deficits as basic causes of specific reading disability. *Journal of Educational Psychology, 88*, 601–38.

White, S., Milne, E., Rosen, S., Hansen, P., Swettenham, J., Frith, U. and Ramus, F. (2006). The role of sensory motor impairments in dyslexia: A multiple case study of dyslexic children. *Developmental Science, 9*(3), 237–69.

Wydell, T.N. and Butterworth, B. (1999). A case study of an English–Japanese bilingual with monolingual dyslexia. *Cognition, 70*, 273–305.

Wyse, D. and Styles, M. (2007). Synthetic phonics and the teaching of reading: The debate surrounding England's 'Rose Report'. *Literacy, 41*(1), 35–42.

8 Why does mathematics make so many people fearful?

Tony Cline

CHAPTER SUMMARY

In this chapter, you will consider how mathematics as a subject differs from other subjects in the school curriculum and will reflect on why that makes it intimidating for many students. We will examine the impact of maths anxiety on learning and will outline how mathematical thinking and mathematical practices develop through childhood. We will also examine how they are affected by cultural and linguistic diversity.

LEARNING OUTCOMES

When you have studied this chapter, you should be able to:

1   identify key features of mathematics that lead to many people experiencing it as challenging;
2   evaluate different accounts of how maths anxiety is thought to develop and how it may be addressed;
3   outline key features of the development of mathematical thinking and mathematical practices during childhood;
4   explain the significance that children's cultural and language background may have for their learning of mathematics and the development of any anxiety they may feel about mathematics.

THE CHALLENGES OF MATHEMATICS

ACTIVITY 8.1

Which of the sentences below best describe school mathematics as you experienced it when you were at school and as you think of it now?

(a) You need to learn a set of rules and procedures based on rules.

(b) There is a fixed body of knowledge that cannot be questioned.

(c) You learn through a variety of lively activities.

(d) You sometimes get messy.

(e) You are often asked a closed question and need to find the correct answer.

(f) You have time to speculate and time to discuss important ideas.

(g) It makes you more creative.

(h) The teacher often works at a fast pace.

(i) It makes you feel that you are being tested and judged.

(j) It exercises your imagination.

(k) It develops your empathy for other people who are different from yourself.

(l) It makes you look around you with fresh eyes.

(m) It makes you think logically.

(n) There are lots of tricks you have to learn for how to do things.

(o) Everyone in the class has an opinion, and every opinion counts.

(p) You learn how to ask questions.

(q) You learn to look at a situation from different perspectives.

(r) It is efficient and requires you to be efficient.

(s) You have to be neat in the way that you work, or you will make mistakes.

Examine the statements in the box that are shown against the letters that are found in the words 'mathematics' and 'number'. These have been identified by Trujillo and Hadfield (1999) and Bibby (2002) as characterising many people's image of maths lessons at school. The statements that are linked to other letters of the alphabet indicate reactions that are less often associated with mathematics in the literature.

Mathematical knowledge and mathematical reasoning are key tools that we use when thinking about how the world around us is organised. A person who is confident in the use of mathematics can deal with questions about quantity, about spatial and structural relationships, and about measurement and time. So, mathematical thinking is fundamental to other subjects, both in the sciences and the humanities. As a school subject, mathematics is important, a 'core' subject in the curriculum. At the same time, it relies on the use of abstract concepts and rigorous logical reasoning. Its language is precise and has no redundancy. Each element in mathematical knowledge is related to every other element, and many of those elements can only be understood by following the sequence of assumptions behind them. So, mathematics is not only important, it is also difficult. Perhaps that is why many people find it intimidating, and some become anxious about mathematics tasks that they associate with school.

'Maths anxiety' may involve 'a feeling of panic, helplessness, paralysis and mental disorganization that arises among some people when they are required to solve a mathematical problem' and is likely to lead to negative attitudes towards any tasks that require the management of numbers (Núñez-Peña et al., 2013, p. 36). A start has been made on investigating the neuropsychological footprint of these feelings and perceptions. In a functional MRI study of a group of 7–9-year-old children, Young et al. (2012) showed that maths anxiety was associated with hyperactivity in the right amygdala regions of the brain that are important for processing negative emotions. Importantly, they also found that maths anxiety was associated with reduced activity in those prefrontal cortical regions that are thought to be involved in mathematical reasoning. A similar fMRI study of undergraduate students by Lyons and Beilock (2012) differentiated brain activity during a period when participants were anticipating a mathematics task from activity during the task itself. They found that students who had scored high on a maths anxiety scale showed heightened activity in the expected cortical regions when they received a cue that led them to expect a maths task rather than a language task. This change occurred before they embarked on the task itself.

Recent research has confirmed earlier studies that showed that maths anxiety has a narrow focus. For example, Wu et al. (2012) reported that, in the same group of children, maths anxiety was correlated with maths-attainment scores independently of a score for *general trait anxiety* and was not correlated with reading-attainment scores. It is possible to break down the general construct of maths anxiety into more tightly defined components. For example, Gierl and Bisanz (1995) differentiated between *mathematics test anxiety* ('feelings of nervousness associated with past, present and future mathematical testing situations') and *mathematics problem-solving anxiety* ('feelings of nervousness associated with situations both in and out of school that require students to solve math problems and use the solutions in some way'). On the basis of a factor analysis of a newly developed maths anxiety scale, Wu et al. (2012) identified two principal components – a factor related to numerical concepts, which they called numerical processing anxiety, and another related to situations involving the execution of maths, which they called situational and performance anxiety.

But what are the initial causes of the problem? Hypotheses about the causes and development of maths anxiety have tended to focus on neuropsychological vulnerability, cognitive factors (such as mismatched learning styles), personality factors (such as general self-esteem) and environmental factors (such as negative school experiences). Many adults trace their negative feelings about maths back to their own schooldays. In this context, it is salutary to bear in mind that the people studied by Trujillo and Hadfield (1999) and Bibby (2002), whose attributions were paraphrased in Activity Box 8.1 at the beginning of the chapter, were primary school teachers or trainee teachers. What kinds of message about mathematics as a school subject will they have communicated to their pupils? It has been suggested that teachers who have negative beliefs about mathematics may lay the foundation for a response of learned helplessness from their pupils. For example, Uusimaki and Nason (2004) interviewed a sample of eighteen pre-service trainee primary school teachers in Eastern Australia who had expressed anxiety about maths in a large-scale survey questionnaire. Two-thirds of this group traced their negative beliefs about the subject back to their experience of it as children in primary school. Beilock *et al.* (2010) presented some tentative evidence that teachers' feelings about mathematics may have a particularly strong impact on pupils of the same gender. (See the discussion of gender and maths anxiety in the section, 'Cognitive abilities associated with proficiency in mathematics', below.) It is necessary at this point to review what is known about some key processes in the development of mathematical thinking and mathematical practices through childhood. We will consider that topic before returning to the question of how people's anxieties and negative beliefs about mathematics can best be addressed.

THE DEVELOPMENT OF MATHEMATICAL THINKING AND MATHEMATICAL PRACTICES THROUGH CHILDHOOD

Teaching methods that risk creating maths anxiety and teaching methods that may foster 'mathematical resilience'

The language of mathematics involves symbols and diagrams that can be interpreted only by those who understand the conventions that govern them. When the symbols and conventions are fully understood, together with the concepts that underpin them, information can be manipulated and communicated in a form that is concise, simple and transparent. All too often, however, pupils learn the symbols that are used in mathematics and the procedures for manipulating them, but do not develop an understanding of what the symbols mean, or why the procedures work. A child in this position might successfully use a carefully learned 'rule' to find the answer (198) to the sum:

$$792 \div 4 = ?$$

However, they might complete the sum solely by knowing how to 'carry over' the remainder after dividing 7 in the hundreds column by 4, without understanding what transformation occurs when the remainder (3 × 100) is converted to a number (3) in the tens column. The effects of that lack of understanding may be seen in various ways: the child may make uncorrected errors that seem obviously mistaken to anyone who is following the logic of what is being done, and the child may be unable to apply the procedure for dividing large amounts to new numbers, or to numbers in a different pattern, or to numbers that are embedded in a word problem, such as:

If a team of four people won £792 in the Lottery and divided it equally among them, how much would be given to each person?

Procedural knowledge (knowing *how*) involves knowing the written language of mathematics (the system of symbols used to represent numbers such as '151' and mathematical operations such as '+' or '÷') and also the step-by-step prescriptions for manipulating numbers (such as rules and algorithms for addition and division). *Conceptual understanding* (knowing *why*) involves such processes as insight, discovery and the integration of different pieces of information (Baroody, 2003, Figure 1.2). This distinction between 'procedural knowledge' and 'conceptual understanding' has been very influential in mathematics education, and the terminology used to describe it has frequently changed. For example, Skemp (1976) outlined the differences he saw between 'relational understanding' ('knowing both what to do and why') and 'instrumental understanding' (which involves applying 'rules without reasons').

It has gradually become clear that this way of describing forms of mathematical knowledge does not offer a sound foundation for analysing what is known about children's learning processes. First, children often invent their own procedures, and a successful procedure needs at least some conceptual basis or underpinning. Second, some learning of new procedures is not driven by conceptual knowledge alone, but instead draws directly on procedural instruction or procedural analogies. Baroody, in Baroody and Dowker (2003, p. 26), described a framework comprising four aspects of proficiency in mathematics that is seen as providing a more adequate conceptualisation of what children need to learn:

- *Conceptual understanding* . . . comprehension of maths concepts, operations, and relations.
- *Computational fluency* . . . skill in computing efficiently (quickly and accurately), appropriately, and flexibly.
- *Strategic mathematical thinking* . . . the ability to formulate, represent and solve mathematical problems ('strategic competence') and the capacity for logical thought, reflection, explanation and justification ('adaptive reasoning').
- *Productive disposition* . . . a habitual inclination to see mathematics as sensible, useful and worthwhile, coupled with a belief in diligence and one's efficacy.

Baroody argued that all of these elements are required for children to be effective in making use of their mathematical knowledge and to *want* to use it. He emphasised that the definition given here of computational fluency implies an expertise that is adaptive and is not just capable of being applied in a routine way to familiar problems. Those who study statistics as part of a course in psychology may like to reflect on how far their recent experience in this area of applied mathematics confirms or challenges Baroody's ideas.

Although there was no encouragement for this in the new National Curriculum that was introduced in England and Wales in 1988, many schools continued to employ a narrow and tightly structured approach to mathematics teaching within the framework of that curriculum (Boaler, 1998). If teachers value procedural knowledge above everything else (as they did, for example, in England in the nineteenth and early twentieth centuries), they tend to adopt repetitive drill methods based on behavioural principles such as associative learning. It is assumed that these methods will help students develop a confident grasp of the methods of calculation that they are required to learn. However, Boaler's evaluation demonstrated that pupils taught through a repetitive 'drill' strategy disliked the subject more and were less able to apply their procedural knowledge to unfamiliar situations than pupils taught through what she described as a more open system.

What do these ideas and findings about the goals and outcomes of mathematics education have to do with maths anxiety? The connection is through the impact of the methods of teaching associated with different goals. Research into the impact of different methods of teaching is a difficult and controversial area of research in educational psychology. However, the study by Newstead (1998) that is featured in Method Box 8.1 illustrates the contribution that such research can make when the technical challenges that it presents are successfully overcome. Even so, there are always limitations to the generalisability of such findings. Newstead acknowledged that larger

METHOD 8.1

Newstead (1998) studied maths anxiety in a sample of 9–11-year-old pupils who were taught maths through *'traditional' or 'alternative' approaches*, in five mixed-sex primary schools in a 'relatively rural environment in the UK'. In a 'traditional' approach, the pupils were taught standard, pencil-and-paper methods of computation through teacher demonstration followed by individual practice. The pupils had to practise and master the calculation methods first, before they applied them to everyday situations in word sums. In Newstead's definition of an 'alternative' approach, on the other hand, 'pupils use and discuss their own strategies for solving word sums, which are used as the principal vehicle for learning. Solving non-routine problems and discussing strategies in small groups are of primary importance' (p. 58). Careful checks were made to confirm whether or not each teacher was employing one of these approaches. The sample comprised fifty-eight pupils learning mathematics through 'alternative' methods with two teachers, and 113 pupils learning the subject from four teachers through 'traditional' methods.

Each pupil was given a questionnaire about maths anxiety. To illustrate the content of the questionnaire, the items that elicited the most anxious responses involved the teacher asking the pupil questions and division with big numbers, whereas the items that elicited the least anxious responses involved everyday situations such as deciding which cool drink is cheaper in a shop and working out what time it would be 25 minutes from now.

A factor analysis of the scores on this questionnaire indicated that two meaningful factors could be extracted from the results – a factor that was mainly concerned with doing actual sums and working with numbers (e.g. adding 97 + 45 on paper, working out the change from £5 after spending £3.87) and a factor that covered more social or public aspects of doing mathematics (e.g. the teacher asking questions about how much one knows about maths, having a classmate finish first). (You will note that these are comparable to the factors identified by Wu *et al.* (2012) that were described earlier in the chapter.) There were no significant differences between age groups or between boys and girls on the overall anxiety score in Newstead's sample, but pupils taught through a traditional approach showed significantly higher anxiety overall than those taught through an alternative approach. When the factor profile was examined, it was found that the traditionally taught group had significantly higher scores than the alternative group on the social anxiety factor, but not on the general sum/number factor.

samples than she had had would be needed in order to demonstrate clearer evidence of the relationship between teaching approach and types of anxiety. She also emphasised that her findings apply to young children, and that the picture may be quite different with other age groups. For example, although a traditional approach appeared to exacerbate anxiety in children within the age group she studied, it may help to reduce maths anxiety in college students who have developed their negative feelings about maths when they were younger. Nonetheless, alongside Boaler's (1998) evidence, her work suggests that one element in a strategy to reduce the development of maths anxiety at school may be to review teaching methods and, in particular, to emphasise a broad range of learning goals in the subject, along the lines of Baroody's (2003) framework.

The title of this chapter and a good deal of the content up to this point have been quite negative. We have concentrated on things that go wrong and tried to analyse how that happens. A promising alternative perspective is to study what can go right and focus on the *positive* aspects of psychology. Johnston-Wilder and Lee (2010) came to this view from listening to stories from people who exhibited mathematics phobia and reading the related literature. The more they did so, they wrote, 'the more that it appeared to us that the way that mathematics is often taught in English mathematics classrooms is an unwitting form of cognitive abuse' (pp. 2–3). They developed a construct that they sought to contrast with maths anxiety – the idea of *mathematical resilience*. Working in one school, they aimed to develop strategies that would encourage learners to approach mathematics with a positive mindset. Building mathematical resilience, they said, would mean that:

> [Pupils] will persevere when faced with difficulties, will work collaboratively with their peers, will have the language skills needed to express their understandings or lack of it and will have a growth theory of learning, that is they will know that the more they work at mathematics the more successful they will be.
>
> (Johnston-Wilder and Lee, 2010, p. 3)

The notion of a growth theory of learning is associated with an influential analysis of learning motivation that discriminates between people who have different mindsets about the learning process. Those with an 'incremental theory' mindset tend to believe that their own abilities are malleable and can increase and can be controlled, whereas

TABLE 8.1 What is the mindset for learning of a student with an entity or an incremental implicit theory of intelligence?

	Entity theory	Incremental theory
What are the student's main goals?	To appear clever	To learn successfully
What value does the student place on effort and help and strategies?	A higher value	A lower value
How does the student typically respond to challenge?	Tends to give up easily	Tends to keep trying and work harder
How do their attainments change when they face difficulty?	They typically remain low or deteriorate	Their attainments typically improve

Source: Adapted from Yeager and Dweck, 2012

those who have an 'entity theory' mindset tend to believe that such characteristics in themselves are fixed by their heredity or biology and cannot be changed (Yeager and Dweck, 2012). (See the discussion in Chapter 4 of the relationship between self-concept and attainment.)

In a subsequent paper, Lee and Johnston-Wilder (2013) described how they recruited and trained pupils, from the full range of maths ability sets in a girls' secondary school, to act as 'ambassadors' in their school. The training workshops were designed to introduce the pupils to different ways in which mathematics can be learned and to enable them to become coresearchers in discovering the opinions of their peers concerning learning mathematics. This project was planned, in part, as an exploration of how researchers and teachers can draw on *pupil voice* in school improvement. It was not thought sufficient simply to ask for pupils' suggestions about how maths might be taught more effectively. For them to develop ideas that would go beyond extensions and elaborations of how they were already being taught, they needed to be exposed to other ways of doing things, to learn the impressions of their fellow pupils and to feel authorised to act in an unfamiliar role. Activity Box 8.2 outlines some of the methods of teaching that Johnston-Wilder and Lee described or used in these two studies and invites you to reflect on their likely impact.

ACTIVITY 8.2

Teaching methods, maths anxiety and maths resilience

The lists of maths learning activities below are taken from Johnston-Wilder and Lee (2010) and Lee and Johnston-Wilder (2013) and have been divided into a set that the authors thought to be more likely to generate maths anxiety and a set they appear to have designed to foster mathematical resilience. Can you identify the key features of each activity that might lead a researcher to place them in one category or the other?

Activities thought more likely to generate maths anxiety

- Perform a task rapidly that requires feats of memory.
- Memorise formulae without understanding what they mean.
- Listen to the teacher explain a single isolated technique of calculation and then complete exercises practising the technique that are designed to help you to remember how and when to use it.

Activities thought more likely to foster maths resilience

- Use *people maths*, where a group has to represent mathematical ideas using their own bodies, for example being asked to envision their shoulders and body as axes and to make straight-line graphs using their arms.
- Make a mathematics trail around the school by spotting mathematical ideas in the buildings and writing out a trail for other groups to follow.
- Create a PowerPoint presentation about an aspect of mathematics of their choice that they found difficult.

Cognitive processing and maths anxiety

Cognitive psychology offers a quite different approach to studying maths anxiety. Ashcraft *et al.* (1998) showed that students with high scores for maths anxiety obtained lower scores on a maths achievement test. However, when they analysed the results for the achievement test in greater detail, they found that there were no maths-anxiety effects in the easier section of the test, which comprised arithmetic problems with whole numbers. Anxiety effects were only found when the items became more difficult (e.g. with mixed fractions such as 'ten and a quarter plus seven and two thirds'). In other studies, the team highlighted a particular difference between groups with high and low maths anxiety: those in the 'high' group took a much longer time to complete somewhat difficult arithmetic problems. 'Our interpretation was that carrying, or any procedural aspect of arithmetic, might place a heavy demand on *working memory* (WM), the system for conscious, effortful mental processing' (Ashcraft, 2002, p. 183). Their key theoretical reference point was processing efficiency theory (Eysenck and Calvo, 1992). This states that anxiety disrupts the performance of a task, because those who experience it give attention to their intrusive thoughts and feelings rather than to the task they are supposed to be completing. These *intrusive thoughts* impact on their effectiveness in maths to the degree that the maths task depends on WM. They concluded that this might explain why participants with high anxiety do as well as less anxious individuals on simple maths tasks but show a marked decrement in performance with more difficult items.

Subsequent research has elaborated this theoretical account further. In a study of 5–8-year-olds, Ramirez *et al.* (2013) found that not all their participants showed the expected relationship between high maths anxiety and a decrement in performance on the more difficult items in a maths test. This relationship was present among children who had relatively high scores on a test of WM, but not among those with relatively low WM scores. The authors highlighted the position of children with good WM who rely on the direct retrieval of remembered maths facts, as opposed to finger counting when solving maths problems. It is these children, they suggested, whose performance is likely to be affected when maths anxiety causes a depletion of the cognitive resources available to support maths: 'Low-WM children's math achievement may remain relatively unaffected by math anxiety precisely because they use less sophisticated (and less WM-demanding) problem-solving strategies' (p. 196).

Cognitive abilities associated with proficiency in mathematics

In this section, we move from analysing the processes that affect a successful outcome in learning to an approach that derives from a quite different tradition of psychological research – the *psychometric analysis* of cognitive abilities. The key questions that are asked are:

- What cognitive abilities are required for effective mathematical thinking?
- How do these abilities support the performance of mathematical tasks? (Carroll, 1996).

In Activity Box 8.3, consider which of the abilities listed in the top half of the box are likely to be involved when a person solves the problems that are listed in the bottom half.

ACTIVITY 8.3

Here is a list of some of the cognitive abilities that have been associated with proficiency in mathematics (Carroll, 1996; Hegarty and Kozhevnikov, 1999; Baroody, 2003):

(a) oral language comprehension – the ability to understand short sentences in real-life contexts;
(b) pictorial imagery – the ability to construct vivid and detailed visual images;
(c) procedural knowledge relating to the manipulation of numbers;
(d) reading comprehension – the ability to answer questions about the meaning and implications of short pieces of text;
(e) reading decoding – the ability to read aloud short passages of text fluently and accurately;
(f) schematic imagery – the ability to represent the spatial relationships between objects and imagine spatial transformations;
(g) long-term verbal memory – the ability to retain linguistic information over time.

Examine the list of mathematics problems given below, which are all taken from the original framework for the National Numeracy Framework in England, where they illustrated the outcomes expected of pupils aged 8–11 (DfEE, 1999). Which of the abilities (a)–(g) do you think is likely to be involved when a person solves each of these problems?

1 The perimeter of a square is 274 cm. What is the length of each side?
2 Every day a machine makes 100,000 paper clips, which go into boxes. A full box has 120 paper clips. How many full boxes can be made from 100,000 paper clips?
3 Calculate 24% of 525.
4 Find two consecutive numbers with a product of 182.
5 (i) △   (ii)   △   (iii)   △ △
           △ △ △   △ △ △ △ △
   The triangles represent counters that make up a number sequence. Calculate how many counters there will be in the sixth number and in the twentieth number, and write a formula for the number of counters in the nth number in the sequence.
6 Count all the rectangles in this diagram:

We expect that you will decide, as you examine the question carefully, that most of the skills and abilities that are listed in the top half of the box are required for all of the six tasks, to a greater or lesser degree. However, there are probably one (or perhaps two) items that you will have decided are not important for those tasks. The first item that is not needed is pictorial imagery – the ability to construct visual images. Hegarty and Kozhevnikov (1999) showed that this was used less than schematic imagery by 11–13-year-old boys solving maths problems – a result that was subsequently replicated with a sample of students of the same age in the USA, including a group with learning disabilities (van Garderen and Montague, 2003).

Perhaps one reason why some people do less well in school mathematics and are more anxious about it is that their profile of cognitive abilities has strengths in areas that do not contribute significantly to maths performance and weaknesses in areas that are psychometrically crucial for it. This idea has been used to explain group differences such as those between males and females. It used to be claimed that males do consistently better than females in mathematics, but that is not the case (Gallagher and Kaufmann, 2005; Lindberg et al., 2010). However, there are aspects of the subject where they do have greater success. For example, boys and men obtain higher scores than girls and women on some spatial tests, such as a test of the ability to visualise shapes and motion in three dimensions – an ability that is crucial to some forms of mathematical problem solving. Maloney et al. (2012) presented evidence that sex differences in maths anxiety may be due in part to sex differences in spatial ability. Two groups of adults completed questionnaires assessing their level of maths anxiety and their aptitude and preference for processing spatial configurations and schematic images. The results indicated that controlling for spatial ability eliminated the sex differences in maths anxiety.

Steele (1997) has argued that the 'underperformance' of girls and women in what is treated by society as a traditionally male domain is due to 'stereotype threat'. Where negative stereotypes about a group are widely held, members of the group can fear being reduced to that stereotype. 'For those who identify with the domain to which the stereotype is relevant, this predicament can be self-threatening' (Steele, 1997, p. 614). Thus, although most students will experience some anxiety when taking a maths test, those who belong to groups with a negative stereotype will feel that more acutely, because they will anticipate the possibility of confirming the *negative group stereotype*. Steele argued that that could increase their anxiety, with the effect of making them do less well than they might otherwise have.

Other researchers have challenged the assertion that women are more anxious about mathematics than men. For example, Ashcraft (2002) suggested that an artefact might have influenced the survey findings: women are more willing to disclose personal attitudes generally, so that men who are equally anxious about the subject may not so readily acknowledge it in a survey. Perhaps, too, any *gender differences* in reactions to mathematics reflect more general gender differences in interests in dealing with people and living things (believed to be stronger in women) and interests in dealing with abstractions and non-living things (believed to be stronger in men). (Compare with Baron-Cohen's empathising/systematising theory of autism, which is outlined in Chapter 9 on autism.) Jacobs et al. (2005) showed that parental beliefs and attitudes may be a factor in sex differences in interest in mathematics. But is this because the parents are reacting to different interests shown by girls and boys, or are they themselves behaving in a way that leads to these group differences? The data that they report do not make it possible to decide between these alternative possible explanations. It is clear that the overall picture is very complicated, and a psychometric analysis of group differences in mathematics abilities on its own offers only a partial account of these phenomena. If we are to fully understand maths anxiety, we need to appreciate how social expectations and conventions influence the way maths is perceived by different groups in society.

MATHEMATICS IN ITS CULTURAL CONTEXT

Mathematics is often seen as a universal language, because it follows standard structural rules and refers to universal concepts in abstract terms. However, as we have seen, it is not possible to ignore the fact that mathematics is learned and practised in social settings. The ways in which people represent mathematical problems and the procedures that they use to tackle them will differ from one cultural context to another. For example, imagine that two baskets each contain three chickens. A primary-school child in the UK would probably use their knowledge of the multiplication tables to calculate that there are six chickens altogether. In a classic study, Gay and Cole (1967) asked a sample of members of the Kpelle, an indigenous group in Liberia, about this. They reported that the participants 'would either count 3 two times on their fingers or make two groups of three pebbles and count them' (Nunes, 2004, p. 13). A series of studies in different countries followed, demonstrating that young people could carry out complex mathematical tasks in an everyday context, employing local methods that did not reflect what they were taught in school. Examples included children in Brazil calculating change in a street market (Nunes, Scliemann and Carraher 1993) and the size of an irregular sugar cane field (Abreu, 1995).

Home mathematics and school mathematics

In a multicultural society, children are likely to be exposed to different versions of mathematics as they move between home and school. How they negotiate the transition from one to another will be influenced by how their parents and teachers represent the value of each version. Thus Abreu and Cline (2003) reported that some immigrant parents taught their children multiplication tables by rote at home, at a time when they were not being taught them in this way at school. The parents felt that, otherwise, their children would not be on the same wavelength as cousins and other members of the extended family 'back home'. Children may become anxious about *school maths* when they perceive a large gap between what is represented as *maths at home* and what they are required to learn at school. Thus, in the same study, Kashif (aged 7), who was born in this country to parents who had come here from Pakistan, was described by his teacher as lacking confidence in the subject, in spite of receiving a good deal of help at home. During an interview with Kashif, it became clear that he did not think his mother or sister did maths 'properly', that is in the same way as the teacher, and an interview with his parents indicated that they did not appreciate that requiring him to learn different procedures for addition and subtraction might cause confusion. Meanwhile, his teacher acknowledged that she had not 'really met

Kashif's mum'. The poor communication between the various people in this situation appeared to be a crucial factor in maintaining Kashif's low confidence in maths (Abreu, Cline and Shamsi, 2002, pp. 135–8: Case Study 1). School inspectors have suggested that family learning initiatives that help parents to understand the culture of the classroom and the way their children are being taught can have a positive impact on performance (Ofsted, 2009), and specific local initiatives of this kind have been developed to meet the needs of parents from minority language communities (Driver, 2010).

Comparative studies of mathematics learning across cultures and across languages

A series of international studies of attainment in mathematics have shown substantial differences between the standards achieved by children in different countries, with children in some Asian countries (specifically China, Japan and Korea) consistently outperforming children from the US, the UK and western Europe (Jerrim and Choi, 2014). There are many possible cultural and social factors in these national differences, including, for example, variation in teaching methods and teaching time, as well as home–school support.

One explanation that has stimulated a good deal of research interest focuses on differences in the way numbers are expressed in different languages. Researchers suggested that many problems arise in some Western languages because of the irregular way in which the decimal system is represented in words (e.g. 'eleven' and 'twelve' in English, compared with what is translated as 'ten one' and 'ten two' in Chinese and Japanese). Miura (1987) and others showed that children in countries where the language represented the number system transparently were particularly advantaged in tasks that involved judgements about place value. However, it is difficult to disentangle this factor from others when comparisons are made between diverse countries such as China and the US.

Dowker et al. (2008) attempted to reduce the likelihood of other factors affecting the outcome by investigating arithmetic performance and the understanding of two-digit numbers in primary-school children from different home-language backgrounds within a single society – children from Welsh- and English-speaking families in south Wales in the first study, and children from Tamil- and English-speaking families in London and Oxford in the second study. Welsh has a much more regular and consistent way of representing the number system than English, and Tamil is more consistent than English and less consistent than Welsh. Their findings suggested that the counting system can have some influence on arithmetical performance, even when other educational factors are controlled, but its impact is limited to quite specific activities, such as reading and comparing two-digit numbers. They concluded that differences in language cannot, on their own, account for large-scale, global, cross-national differences in arithmetic.

It can be assumed that the cultural and other factors that affect other aspects of mathematics will also have an influence on maths anxiety. For example, substantial differences in mathematical practices between home and school or the relative transparency and consistency of the linguistic system for representing numbers might each be expected to have an impact. The Programme for International Student Assessment's 2012 survey of 15-year-olds in over sixty countries provided preliminary evidence to support this (OECD, 2013). Internationally, the problem of maths anxiety remains serious as students approach the end of their schooling: 30 per cent reported that they feel helpless when doing mathematics problems (25 per cent of boys and 35 per cent of girls). At the individual-student level and at the country level, higher scores for maths anxiety were correlated with lower scores for maths performance. 'On average across OECD countries, greater mathematics anxiety is associated with a decrease in performance of 34 score points – or the equivalent of almost an additional year of school' (p. 94). These stark findings emphasise the need for further research that will enable us to better understand how the processes that influence maths anxiety operate differentially across cultures and languages.

CONCLUSION: ADDRESSING THE PROBLEM OF MATHS ANXIETY

If maths anxiety is understood as a personal phobia, it is likely that the treatment will be a psychologically based intervention with the individual who is anxious, such as systematic desensitisation. However, if it is considered that anxieties develop because of the way the subject is taught or the way in which language represents the number system, or if anxieties are associated with only some aspects of the subject and not others, it seems possible to address the problem, not by pathologising the individual learner and intervening with them personally, but by adjusting how the subject is taught or presented to them. As in some other chapters in this book, this one has started with a problem that appears to be located at the individual level and has shown how the perspective of educational psychology now broadens out from that level and takes full account of the intellectual, social and cultural context in which the individual encounters mathematics. However, a full account of the problem will not only adopt that broader perspective: it will also focus on the level of cognitive processing. As we saw in the section on 'Cognitive processing and maths anxiety', adjusting the burden that a mathematics task places on working memory can reduce the impact of maths anxiety on performance.

SUMMARY OF MAIN ISSUES ADDRESSED IN THIS CHAPTER

- Many people find mathematics intimidating at school, and some become anxious about it.
- Research on the causes and development of maths anxiety has drawn on a range of methods of enquiry from education, psychology and neuroscience.
- One element in a strategy to reduce the development of maths anxiety at school may be to review teaching methods.
- There is evidence that anxiety disrupts cognitive processing in more difficult maths tasks more than it does in easier tasks. This may be because intrusive thoughts impact on anxious participants' effectiveness in maths to the degree that the maths task depends on working memory.
- A psychometric analysis of group differences in mathematics abilities on its own offers only a partial account of these differences.

- As the complex relationship between gender and maths anxiety illustrates, a full account of maths anxiety must take account of the influence of social expectations and conventions on the ways in which maths is perceived by different groups in society.
- Mathematics is often seen as a universal language because it follows standard structural rules and refers to universal concepts in abstract terms. However, it is important to take account of the different ways in which people represent mathematical problems and the procedures that they use to tackle them in different cultural contexts.
- In a multicultural society, children may be exposed to different versions of mathematics as they move between home and school and may become anxious about school maths when they perceive a large gap between what is represented as maths at home and what they are required to learn at school.
- Research has not confirmed suggestions that international differences in standards of attainment in maths may be caused by differences in the way that the number system is represented in different languages.
- Thus, the perspective of educational psychology on maths anxiety takes account, not only of patterns of cognitive processing at the individual level, but also of the intellectual, social and cultural contexts in which the individual encounters mathematics.

KEY CONCEPTS AND TERMS

- Maths anxiety
- General (trait) anxiety
- Teacher anxiety
- Conceptual understanding and procedural knowledge in mathematics
- Traditional and alternative approaches to teaching maths
- Intrusive thoughts
- Working memory
- Psychometric analysis
- Mathematical resilience
- Negative group stereotype
- Gender differences
- Differences between 'home maths' and 'school maths'
- Number languages
- Multilevel explanations of maths anxiety

RECOMMENDATIONS FOR FURTHER READING

Journal articles

Ashcraft, M.H. (2002). Math anxiety: Personal, educational, and cognitive consequences. *Current Directions in Psychological Science*, *11*(5), 181–5.

Maloney, E.A., Schaeffer, M.W. and Beilock, S.L. (2013). Mathematics anxiety and stereotype threat: Shared mechanisms, negative consequences and promising interventions. *Research in Mathematics Education*, *15*(2), 115–28.

Yeager, D.S. and Dweck, C.S. (2012). Mindsets that promote resilience: When students believe that personal characteristics can be developed. *Educational Psychologist*, *47*(4), 302–14.

Books

Boaler, J. (2009). *The Elephant in the Classroom: Helping children learn and love maths.* London: Souvenir.

Baroody, A.J. and Dowker, A. (eds) (2003). *The Development of Arithmetic Concepts and Skills: Constructing adaptive expertise.* London: Lawrence Erlbaum.

SAMPLE ESSAY TITLES

1 The head of the maths department in a large secondary school has asked your advice as a psychologist on how to reduce the incidence of anxiety in maths lessons. Outline the advice you would give her and explain your reasons for it.
2 What part does anxiety play in gender differences in mathematics attainment at school?
3 What psychological processes appear to be involved when anxiety disrupts mathematics performance?
4 What would you expect to be the implications for educational psychologists of cultural variation in mathematical language and practices?

REFERENCES

Abreu, G. de (1995). Understanding how children experience the relationship between home and school mathematics. *Mind, Culture and Activity: An International Journal*, *2*(2), 119–42.

Abreu, G. de and Cline, T. (2003). Schooled mathematics and cultural knowledge. *Pedagogy, Culture and Society*, *11*(1), 11–30.

Abreu, G. de, Cline, T. and Shamsi, A. (2002). Exploring ways parents participate in their children's school mathematical learning: Case studies in multiethnic primary schools. In G. de Abreu, A.J. Bishop and N.C. Presmeg (eds), *Transitions Between Contexts of Mathematical Practices*. Dordrecht, Netherlands: Kluwer Academic, pp. 123–48.

Ashcraft, M.H. (2002). Math anxiety: Personal, educational, and cognitive consequences. *Current Directions in Psychological Science, 11*(5), 181–5.

Ashcraft, M.H., Kirk, E.P. and Hopko, D. (1998). On the cognitive consequences of mathematics anxiety. In C. Donlan (ed.), *The Development of Mathematical Skills*. Hove, UK: Psychology Press, pp. 175–96.

Baroody, A.J. (2003). The development of adaptive expertise and flexibility: The integration of conceptual and procedural knowledge. In A.J. Baroody and A. Dowker (eds), *The Development of Arithmetic Concepts and Skills: Constructing adaptive expertise*. London: Lawrence Erlbaum, pp. 1–32.

Baroody, A.J. and Dowker, A. (eds) (2003). *The Development of Arithmetic Concepts and Skills: Constructing adaptive expertise*. London: Lawrence Erlbaum Associates.

Beilock, S.L., Gunderson, E.A., Ramirez, G. and Levine, S.C. (2010). Female teachers' math anxiety affects girls' math achievement. *Proceedings of the National Academy of Sciences of the United States of America, 107*(5), 1860–3.

Bibby, T. (2002). Shame: An emotional response to doing mathematics as an adult and a teacher. *British Educational Research Journal, 28*(5), 705–21.

Boaler, J. (1998). Open and closed mathematics: Student experiences and understandings. *Journal for Research in Mathematics Education, 29*(1), 41–62.

Carroll, J.B. (1996). Mathematical abilities: Some results from factor analysis. In R.J. Sternberg and T. Ben-Zeev (eds), *The Nature of Mathematical Thinking*. Mahwah, NJ: Lawrence Erlbaum, pp. 3–26.

Department for Education and Employment (DfEE) (1999). *The National Numeracy Strategy: Framework for teaching mathematics from Reception to Year 6*. London: DfEE.

Dowker, A., Bala, S. and Lloyd, D. (2008). Linguistic influences on mathematical development: How important is the transparency of the counting system? *Philosophical Psychology, 21*(4), 523–38.

Driver, C. (2010). Family learning in mathematics. *NALDIC Quarterly, 7*(4), 7–8.

Eysenck, M.W. and Calvo, M.G. (1992). Anxiety and performance: The processing efficiency theory. *Cognition and Emotion, 6*, 409–34.

Gallagher, A.M. and Kaufmann, J.C. (eds) (2005). *Gender Differences in Mathematics: An integrative psychological approach*. Cambridge, UK: Cambridge University Press.

Gay, J. and Cole, M. (1967). *The New Mathematics and an Old Culture*. New York: Holt, Rinehart & Winston.

Gierl, M.J. and Bisanz, J. (1995). Anxieties and attitudes related to mathematics in grades 3 and 6. *Journal of Experimental Education, 63*, 139–58.

Hegarty, M. and Kozhevnikov, M. (1999). Types of visual–spatial representations and mathematical problem solving. *Journal of Educational Psychology, 91*(4), 684–9.

Jacobs, J.E., Davis-Kean, P., Bleeker, M., Eccles, J.S. and Malachuk, O. (2005). 'I can, but I don't want to': The impact of parents, interests, and activities on gender differences in math. In A.M. Gallagher and J.C. Kaufmann (eds), *Gender Differences in Mathematics: An integrative psychological approach*. Cambridge, UK: Cambridge University Press, pp. 246–63.

Jerrim, J. and Choi, Á. (2014). The mathematics skills of school children: How does England compare to the high-performing East Asian jurisdictions? *Journal of Education Policy*, *19*(3), 349–76.

Johnston-Wilder, S. and Lee, C. (2010). Developing mathematical resilience. Paper presented at BERA Annual Conference 1–4 September, University of Warwick.

Lee, C. and Johnston-Wilder, S. (2013). Learning mathematics – Letting the pupils have their say. *Educational Studies in Mathematics*, *83*, 163–80.

Lindberg, S.M., Hyde, J.S., Petersen, J.L. and Linn, M.C. (2010). New trends in gender and mathematics performance: A meta-analysis. *Psychological Bulletin*, *136*(6), 1123–35.

Lyons, I.M. and Beilock, S.L. (2012). Mathematics anxiety: Separating the math from the anxiety. *Cerebral Cortex*, *22*, 2102–10.

Maloney, E.A., Waechter, S., Risko, E.F. and Fugelsang, J.A. (2012). Reducing the sex difference in math anxiety: The role of spatial processing ability. *Learning and Individual Differences*, *22*(3), 380–4.

Miura, I.T. (1987). Mathematics achievement as a function of language. *Journal of Educational Psychology*, *79*(1), 79–82.

Newstead, K. (1998). Aspects of children's mathematics anxiety. *Educational Studies in Mathematics*, *36*(1), 53–71.

Nunes, T. (2004). *Teaching Mathematics to Deaf Children*. London: Whurr.

Nunes, T., Scliemann, A.D. and Carraher, D.W. (1993). *Street Mathematics and School Mathematics*. New York: Cambridge University Press.

Núñez-Peña, M.I., Suárez-Pellicioni, M. and Bono, R. (2013). Effects of math anxiety on student success in higher education. *International Journal of Educational Research*, *58*, 36–43.

OECD (2013). Mathematics self-beliefs and participation in mathematics-related activities. In *PISA Results. Vol 3: Ready to learn*. Paris: OECD, Chap 4, pp. 79–104. Available online at www.oecd.org/pisa/keyfindings/PISA2012-Vol3-Chap4.pdf (accessed 21 March 2013).

Ofsted (2009). *Family Learning: An evaluation of the benefits of family learning for participants, their families and the wider community* (Report ref 080265). London: Office for Standards in Education, Children's Services and Skills.

Ramirez, G., Gunderson, E.A., Levine, S.C. and Beilock, S.L. (2013). Math anxiety, working memory, and math achievement in early elementary school. *Journal of Cognition and Development*, *14*(2), 187–202.

Skemp, R.R. (1976). Relational understanding and instrumental understanding. *Mathematics Teaching*, *77*, 20–6.

Steele, C. (1997). A threat in the air: How stereotypes shape intellectual identity and performance. *American Psychologist*, *52*, 613–29.

Trujillo, K.M. and Hadfield, O.D. (1999). Tracing the roots of mathematics anxiety through in-depth interviews with pre-service elementary teachers. *College Student Journal*, *33*(2), 219–32.

Uusimaki, L. and Nason, R. (2004). Causes underlying pre-service teachers' negative beliefs and anxieties about mathematics. *Proceedings of 28th Conference of the International Group for the Psychology of Mathematics Education*, *4*, 369–76. Available online at www.emis.de/proceedings/PME28 (accessed 5 October 2006).

van Garderen, D. and Montague, M. (2003). Visual–spatial representation, mathematical problem solving and students of varying abilities. *Learning Disabilities Research and Practice*, *18*(4), 246–54.

Wu, S.S., Barth, M., Amin, H., Malcarne, V. and Menon, V. (2012). Math anxiety in second and third graders and its relation to mathematics achievement. *Frontiers in Psychology*, *3*(162), 1–11.

Yeager, D.S. and Dweck, C.S. (2012). Mindsets that promote resilience: When students believe that personal characteristics can be developed. *Educational Psychologist*, *47*(4), 302–14.

Young, C.B., Wu, S.S. and Menon, V. (2012). The neurodevelopmental basis of math anxiety. *Psychological Science*, *23*(5), 492–501.

III | Social, emotional and behavioural issues in school

9 Educating children with autism

What use are psychological theory and research?

Susan Birch and Norah Frederickson

CHAPTER SUMMARY

In this chapter, you will learn about some of the challenges teachers face in educating children with autism. We begin by asking 'What is autism?', describing and illustrating key characteristics of autism and discussing associated difficulties and strengths. We then consider what is currently known about what causes autism, looking briefly at some controversies surrounding prevalence and diagnosis in particular. Recognising the crucial explanatory role of cognitive-level explanations in autism, three prominent cognitive theories of autism are reviewed: theory of mind, executive dysfunction and central coherence. Finally, we examine the significant role that psychological theory and research have played in developing approaches to the education of children who have autism. Two distinct strands of influence are identified, one that draws on behavioural psychology and takes no specific account of diagnostic features of autism, and one that draws directly on cognitive theories of autism. Examples of associated intervention programmes are described, together with ethical and methodological issues relating to their implementation and evaluation.

LEARNING OUTCOMES

When you have studied this chapter, you should be able to:

1 describe the triad of impairments that characterise *autism spectrum disorders*;
2 explain the principal cognitive theories of autism and the research designs that have been used to investigate them;
3 evaluate the theoretical and research bases of educational approaches for children with autism spectrum disorders.

WHAT IS AUTISM?

Autism was first described by Kanner, an American psychiatrist, in 1943, through the presentation of a number of case studies of children who shared certain characteristics: 'autistic aloneness' and 'desire for sameness'. In addition, Kanner identified 'islets of ability' in some of these children, such as phenomenal memory for poems or names and precise recall of complex patterns. The difficulties experienced by children with autism were systematically investigated across a whole population of children by Wing and Gould (1979) and characterised as a 'triad of impairments': in reciprocal social interaction, verbal and nonverbal communication, and imagination. The major international diagnostic classification systems, *DSM-IV-TR* (American Psychiatric Association, 2000) and *ICD-10* (World Health Organisation, 1995), identified the following diagnostic indicators for autism:

1   Qualitative abnormalities in reciprocal social interaction:
    (a) inadequate use of nonverbal behaviours to regulate social interaction;
    (b) failure to develop age-appropriate peer relationships;
    (c) lack of social or emotional reciprocity;
    (d) little sharing of enjoyment, achievement or interests with others.
2   Qualitative abnormalities in communication:
    (a) delayed or absent development of language;
    (b) difficulty initiating or sustaining conversation;
    (c) repetitive, unusual or stereotyped use of language;
    (d) lack of age-appropriate pretend or socially imitative play.
3   Restricted, repetitive behaviours, activities or interests:
    (a) interests that are extremely narrow, intense or unusual;
    (b) unreasonable insistence on sameness and following specific routines or rituals;
    (c) stereotyped and repetitive motor mannerisms;
    (d) preoccupation with parts of objects.

Since the 1990s, the classification systems also applied these criteria in defining *Asperger syndrome*, a disorder named after the Austrian paediatrician who first described it in 1944. As with autism, abnormalities in social interaction and restricted, repetitive behaviours were present. However, a diagnosis of Asperger syndrome did not require that the child showed early abnormalities in communication. More recently, the validity of drawing a categorical distinction between Asperger syndrome and high-functioning autism has increasingly been questioned. As they grow older, children with these diagnoses become increasingly difficult to distinguish on the basis of their behaviour, their performance on neuropsychological assessments and the educational outcomes they achieve (Ozonoff and Griffith, 2000; Ozonoff *et al.*, 2000). Accordingly, a dimensional approach involving a continuum of 'autistic propensity' (Rutter, 1999) gained acceptance, and the term '*autistic spectrum disorders*' (ASD) was introduced.

Indeed, *DSM-5* (the latest revision of the *Diagnostic and Statistical Manual of Mental Disorders*; American Psychiatric Association, 2013), published after more than a decade of work, recognises the spectrum nature of ASD and introduces one umbrella disorder 'Autism Spectrum Disorder', subsuming the four separate disorders that were included in *DSM-IV-TR* (autism, Asperger syndrome, pervasive disorder of childhood (not otherwise specified) and childhood disintegrative disorder). ASD is described in *DSM-5* in terms of two domains of behaviour: difficulties in social communication and social interaction, and unusually restricted repetitive behaviours and interests. A new diagnosis, social (pragmatic) communication disorder, has now been introduced for individuals who present with 'a persistent difficulty with verbal and nonverbal communication that cannot be explained by low cognitive ability' (American Psychiatric Association, 2013, SCD factsheet), but without the restricted, repetitive pattern of behaviour, interests or activities that is needed for a diagnosis of ASD.

The new diagnostic criteria are, therefore, likely to lead to significant changes for both practitioners and for researchers working with individuals with ASD and their families. Lai *et al.* (2013) discuss that studies so far seem to indicate that the new criteria have better specificity (so fewer 'false positives'), but reduced sensitivity, particularly for older children, adolescents and adults without significant learning difficulties and for those who previously may have received a diagnosis of Asperger syndrome. They suggest that people fitting these descriptors may be less likely to be diagnosed with autism than previously. The potential impact for individuals and their families, for real-life settings supporting them and for professional practice remains to be seen. In terms of future research, Lai *et al.* (2013) discuss whether the introduction of specifiers and subgroups might be needed, given the heterogeneous nature of ASD, and they highlight the ideas of Geschwind and Levitt (2007, in Lai *et al.*, 2013), 'that there are "many autisms", with partially distinct etiologies, nested within the umbrella term of ASD' (p. 2).

AUTISM: OTHER DIFFICULTIES AND STRENGTHS

Many early studies conducted with children with diagnoses of ASD reported that approximately 75 per cent of children with ASD also had moderate or severe learning difficulties (IQ scores below 70). However, more recent population studies have reported much lower percentages, with only around half of children diagnosed with an ASD having this level of learning difficulties. For example, in their sample of 156 children with ASD, Charman *et al.* (2011) identified that only 55.2 per cent of children had an IQ below 70 (i.e. 69 or below). Of the total sample, 25.4 per cent were of average intelligence, and 2.7 per cent were of above-average intelligence. Given the sampling procedure that was used in this study, the authors also suggest that the estimate of 45 per cent of children having an IQ of 70 or above should be viewed as a minimum estimate. The change in the proportion of children with ASD also found to have severe learning difficulties is thought to be partly due to the widening of diagnostic criteria to include more children who are more able.

Similarly, earlier views suggesting that children with ASD have a higher performance IQ (PIQ) than verbal IQ (VIQ) have also been re-examined. Charman *et al.* (2011) found that the majority of children with an ASD diagnosis, in a smaller sample of 127 children who were able to complete ten WISC-III-UK subtests, did not show a clinically significant level of discrepancy between PIQ and VIQ. However, for the minority who did show a discrepancy, then there was a higher proportion of children where PIQ was greater than VIQ, than where VIQ was greater than PIQ. Around 10 per cent of children with ASD also show some special talents. These 'savant' skills may

ACTIVITY 9.1

Interview with class teacher of Alex, aged 6 years, 6 months

Read the following description of Alex and identify which of the indicators of ASD are present. Make a note of the evidence in support of each of your diagnostic decisions. Would Alex have been given the same diagnosis under *DSM-IV-TR* as under *DSM-5*? Make a note also of any other behaviours the class teacher identifies as unusual that are not listed in the diagnostic indicators.

Alex has a wide vocabulary. However his use of language tends to focus on factual information and areas of special interest, the grammar and syntax being reminiscent of stilted adult language rather than that of a young boy. He does not take turns well in conversation, tending to speak on his own terms about subjects of interest to him, usually dinosaurs or buses – he knows all the bus routes and route numbers in his area. He does not respond well to group directions, he does not understand in the same way as other children, he takes things more literally. For example, if you say 'sit down', he will sit down where he is. You need to say 'go to table 4 and sit down on a chair'.

His social interactions are on his own terms. Sometimes he's oblivious to the other children, and then at other times he wants to have some kind of interaction but the interaction is totally inappropriate, so if he's sitting on the floor he will grab another child and pull the child to him, so that that child is sitting near him because that's the way he sees having a friend sitting by him. He will also grab equipment he wants rather than ask for it. If he wants another child's attention he will grab them and physically try to get them to do as he wants, rather than talk to them. He can become distressed if others do not conform to his expectations or understand what he wants.

Alex finds PE difficult and can become particularly challenging in his behaviour, shrieking and screaming so that he has to be taken out of the hall. In the classroom he will only do a written task if he can do it on a whiteboard, he will not use a pencil and write on paper. He'll start the task and the first sentence will be one that he's been asked to do and then it will deteriorate and he'll just end up writing lists, such as the names of the children in his class, bus numbers or the names of countries. He likes all sorts of lists, particularly the names of people, so he can tell you the full name of every child in the class, and some of the children have got four or five names, and the spelling will be correct – this is really amazing!

(Adapted from Dunsmuir and Frederickson, 2005)

be in a range of areas, such as drawing, playing an instrument, calculating or being able to give the day of the week for any date in the calendar (Hermelin, 2001). Most significantly, perhaps, for educational psychologists, however, was the finding in Charman *et al.*'s study (2011) that overall adaptive outcome (as assessed by the Vineland adaptive behaviour scale – a measure of how a child is perceived to function) was significantly lower than IQ – most notably in the high-IQ groups, and that children with ASD were most behind their same-age peers in the area of daily living skills, suggesting that children's 'ability to cope in the everyday world . . . can be considerably impaired even for the most "high functioning" individual' (p. 625).

Unusual sensory responses have frequently been reported in children with ASD (Baranek *et al.*, 2014). These may include hypo- or hypersensitivity, unusual responses to sensory stimuli of various kinds, preoccupations with the sensory features of objects, or perceptual processing problems. Although there are individual differences, auditory processing problems are often noted, whereas visual–spatial processing tends to be identified as an area of relative strength. There are conflicting reports on the extent of motor-skills difficulties in ASD, and it is likely that considerable variability exists. It is suggested also that, in some cases, motor planning deficits, involving motivational aspects or slower movement preparation, may be mistaken for general clumsiness.

WHAT CAUSES AUTISM?

It is now well established that autism is a neurodevelopmental disorder with a biological basis in which genetic factors are strongly implicated (Medical Research Council, 2001). Heritability estimates greater than 0.90 have been obtained from twin studies where concordance rates of 60 per cent for monozygotic (or identical) twins compared with 5 per cent for dizygotic (or fraternal) pairs are reported. Ronald and Hoekstra (2011) reviewed more than thirty twin studies published in the previous decade, focusing on children and young people with ASDs and autistic traits. They report the findings of three more recent twin studies in which median values for concordance of 88 per cent for monozygotic and 31 per cent for dizygotic twin pairs in a broader ASD group were reported.

Rutter (2013) also draws attention to the conclusive findings of recent research that autism is multifactorial in nature and that, 'there must be non-genetic risk factors that are causally implicated' (p. 1753). Environmental influences have been identified as being potentially important, possibly acting through an interaction with genetic susceptibility involving several different genes, leading to a complex set of aetiological processes (Ronald and Hoekstra, 2011), triggering ASD or affecting the severity of its manifestation. Rutter (2013) suggests, on the basis of recent studies, that environmental risk factors are likely to involve physical causes during the prenatal or early postnatal periods. Research has also focused on whether the triad of impairments in autism have a shared causal pathway and are influenced by the same genetic and environmental factors, or whether they are, in fact, independent (the 'fractionable-triad approach'; for an introduction, see Happé and Ronald, 2008; Brunsdon and Happé, 2014; Rutter, 2014).

One puzzle is the rapid increase in prevalence that has been reported, as this would not be expected in a biologically based disorder that is strongly genetically influenced.

This does not appear to be explained solely by the introduction of broader classification criteria. For example, an occurrence rate of 4–5 per 10,000 was reported for strictly defined autism by Wing and Gould in 1979, whereas Baird *et al.*, in 2006, reported the prevalence of strictly defined autism as 39 per 10,000, with 116 per 10,000 for all ASDs. Similarly, Elsabbagh *et al.*'s systematic review (2012) compared prevalence estimates from studies from northern European countries, published between 1966 and 1999 (range 1.9–72.6 per 10,000), with those obtained in studies published since 2000 (range 7.2–116.2 per 10,000). A clear increase in prevalence is, thus, noted in both comparisons. It has been argued that, in addition to broader classification systems, increased awareness among practitioners, better identification and more sensitive assessment instruments could be contributory factors (Wing and Potter, 2002).

Although prevalence has increased overall, patterns across samples are consistent in indicating a biological and strongly genetic basis. For example, prevalence does not differ significantly between different geographical locations, ethnic groups or socio-economic status levels (Elsabbagh *et al.*, 2012). A consistent finding is that ASD is more common in males, with a ratio of 4:1 for 'classic autism' and a much higher ratio for Asperger syndrome. Baron-Cohen *et al.* (2011) explore possible reasons for this, including the difficulty diagnosing ASD in females who present with a different or subtler profile, which is not recognised with current assessment tools and procedures. They also explore biological reasons, for example that ASD features are an over-expression of features of the psychological and physiological attributes of the male brain. Baron-Cohen *et al.* (2011) also suggest that ASD in females could be underdiagnosed, as females may be more motivated and skilled at behaving in a way that masks their difficulties (e.g. through imitating others), and so are more able to conform socially.

Another area of research focuses on the recognition that autistic traits are found in the general population and have been found to be continuously distributed, throughout the normal range and to the clinical extreme (e.g. Hoekstra *et al.*, 2008). The term 'broader autistic phenotype' (Sucksmith *et al.*, 2011) has been used to describe a pattern of skills often found in relatives of people with autism, but at a subclinical level. These include patterns of social skills, communication traits and personality features. Sucksmith *et al.* conclude that, 'studies on the Broader Autistic Phenotype will continue to offer valuable insights by bringing researchers closer to the genetic aetiology and neurobiological pathways underlying autism' (2011, p. 382), as well as supporting the development of interventions to improve the skills of parents of children with ASD, with the aim of then providing, for example, improved social and communicative environments for the children.

CAUSATION AND COGNITION

So far, we have considered the behaviours that lead to a diagnosis of autism and some possible biological causes in terms of changes to brain structure and function resulting from more fundamental biological (genetic) influences and from possible environmental influences. Morton (2004) highlighted that cognitive variables have a crucial explanatory role in autism and other developmental disorders, mediating between the biological and behavioural levels of explanation. Currently, there are three prominent cognitive theories of autism, involving theory of mind (ToM), executive dysfunction and central coherence.

Theory of mind

Baron-Cohen *et al.* (1985) suggested that many of the characteristics of autism stem from an impairment in the ability to 'mind-read' or attribute mental states to other people in order to predict their behaviour. This *mentalising* ability allows immediate implicit attribution of beliefs and motives to others. In order to test children's understanding of others' beliefs about a situation, as distinct from their understanding of the physical situation as such, Wimmer and Perner (1983) developed a method for inducing *false* beliefs. In their investigations of the development of ToM in young children, they found that, from about 4 years of age, children were able to understand that others could have a false belief and to use that understanding to predict their behaviour. Baron-Cohen *et al.* adapted Wimmer and Perner's method in the Sally–Anne experiment described in Method Box 9.1, which you should read now.

The interpretation of *false-belief-task* failure by children with ASD has been subjected to considerable investigation. If you look at the diagnostic criteria for autism at the start of the chapter, you might wonder whether high-functioning children with autism who lack age-appropriate pretend play might fail the Sally–Anne task when asked to attribute mental states to two plastic dolls, but not if real people were involved. This possibility was tested by Leslie and Frith (1988) in a scenario that involved two adults. One hid a coin and then left the room, and the other moved the coin in a conspiratorial manner and hid it elsewhere. In this experiment, 70 per cent of the children with autism said that, when the first adult returned, they would look in the new location for the coin. When asked questions, the children with autism incorrectly answered that the first adult would think and know that the coin was in the new location, even though they correctly answered that the first adult had not seen the coin moved.

Many subsequent studies have confirmed that children with autism experience disproportionate difficulties with mentalising (see Frith, 2003). However, they can handle false representations of the physical world. When a scene is photographed (e.g. a bedroom, where a cat is sitting on a chair) and then rearranged (the cat is moved from the chair to the bed), children with autism have no relative difficulty in correctly identifying where the cat will be in the photograph (Leslie and Thaiss, 1992). Deficits have also been identified in the first year of life in areas regarded as precursors to the abilities needed to pass false-belief tasks and use language effectively for communication. These include imitation (Rogers and Pennington, 1991) and joint attention (Mundy *et al.*, 1990), where a young child will follow their mother's eye gaze and 'read' her expression of pleasure or apprehension when deciding whether to approach an unfamiliar object or person. Young children may also engage others in joint attention when they point to 'show' objects to them. Children with autism tend not to engage in this proto-declarative pointing, although they engage in instrumental pointing when they want an object. More recent studies (e.g. Apicella *et al.*, 2013) have also begun to look at the development of reciprocity in early infancy and, using analysis of family movies, they suggest that, not only do infants later diagnosed with autism show less motor activity and reduced vocalisations compared with typically developing infants,

METHOD 9.1

The Sally–Anne false-belief task

FIGURE 9.1 The Sally–Anne false-belief task

Source: Frith, 2003. ©Wiley-Blackwell. Reproduced with permission

In the Sally–Anne experiment, two dolls are used to act out the story shown above. Children who are able to mentalise will say that, when Sally comes back from her walk, she will look in the basket for her marble, because they will understand that she has not seen Anne move it and so will still believe that it is there. Children who are unable to understand that others have different beliefs from themselves will say that Sally will look in the box, because that is where they know it is.

Three groups of children, all with a mental age above 3 years, took part in the Baron-Cohen *et al.* experiment (1985): children with autism, children with Down's syndrome and normally developing children. Most of the children with autism answered incorrectly, whereas most of the children in the other two groups gave the right answer. The inclusion in the study of a group of children with Down's syndrome showed that the failure on this task of children with autism could not be attributed to their learning difficulties more generally. In addition, all children correctly answered two control questions, 'Where is the marble really?' and 'Where was the marble in the beginning?', demonstrating understanding of the change in the physical location of the marble during the story.

(From Frith, 2003)

but that the caregivers subsequently showed shorter periods of involvement with the infants and less 'affectionate touch'. Hence, they suggest that, from a very early age, the patterns of interaction between an infant later diagnosed with ASD and their caregivers may subtly influence the development of reciprocal relationships, an important precursor for effective communication and social interaction.

However, not all children with autism fail ToM tests, and their relative difficulties on tasks that involve mentalising tend to diminish with age. Happé (1995) conducted a meta-analysis that showed that most normally developing children passed false-belief tests such as the Sally–Anne task by age 5 years. The majority of children with learning difficulties were able to pass these tests when they had achieved a mental age of 5 years. By contrast, the majority of children with autism did not pass until they had a mental age of 10 years. Even for those children with autism who eventually succeed with simple mentalising tasks such as the Sally–Anne task, more complex tasks can continue to present difficulties.

Brain imaging studies conducted with adults who have high-functioning autism indicate differences from normal control adults in the pattern of brain activation elicited by tasks involving mentalising. It is now accepted that some individuals with autism can compensate to some extent for the lack of an inbuilt mentalising mechanism by learning alternative strategies, for example applying explicit procedures and rules.

Frith (2012) highlights more recent work that has investigated ToM further through adapting the Sally–Anne task so that it can be used nonverbally to explore the social impairments of very young infants, through studying either prolonged looking or anticipatory eye movements (Onishi and Baillargeon, 2005; Southgate *et al.*, 2007). Research has suggested that very young nonverbal infants can indeed mentalise. However, adults with autism who could pass the standard ToM task failed to show anticipatory eye gaze in this implicit test, as non-autistic adults would. Frith goes on to suggest, then, that, although many adults with autism can learn strategies to compensate for difficulties in mentalising, it is the 'early-appearing, implicit form of ToM that points to a core problem in autism' (Frith, 2012, p. 2085).

Executive dysfunctions

The absence of an inbuilt mentalising mechanism, 'mind-blindness', can account for many of the impairments in reciprocal social interaction and communication that are characteristic of autism. However, restricted, repetitive behaviours, activities or interests cannot be explained by delayed or absent mentalising abilities. It had been proposed that impairments in executive function (EF) underlie these characteristics of children with autism (Ozonoff, 1997). Executive functions refer to the abilities needed to prepare for and carry out complex behaviour. These include planning, prioritising, monitoring several tasks and switching between them, inhibiting inappropriate impulsive actions, generating novel approaches to a situation and weighing conse-quences for alternative course of actions. A common feature of executive-function behaviours is the ability to disengage from the immediate environment or external context and direct behaviour instead by mental/internal processes (Shallice, 1988).

Although executive dysfunctions are not unique to children with autism, they are very often present. Children with autism typically score well below age norms on tests of EF such as the Wisconsin card-sorting test. On this test, children are initially asked to sort cards and are given feedback on whether they are sorting correctly according to an undisclosed rule (e.g. number, shape, colour). Once the child has achieved ten correct card sorts, the sorting rule is suddenly changed, without comment. The number of perseverative responses is noted, that is responses that use the old sorting rule, despite feedback that it is wrong. The lack of higher-order executive control can feasibly account for the repetitive actions of many children with autism and their difficulty in behaving flexibly and generating novel approaches.

Hughes (2011) presents a review of the research around the development of EFs, including in relation to research around autism. She highlights, not only the evidence for associations between impaired inhibitory control and high-level repetitive behaviours, but also that there is evidence suggesting that deficits in pretend play may also link with EF theories, reflecting an impairment in the ability to generalise, rather than in the ability to have an understanding of mental states (Jarrold *et al.*, 2010, cited by Hughes, 2011). She also cites the work of Pellicano (2010), exploring the importance of early EF skills in the developmental trajectory of ToM skills in children with autism. Hughes goes on to suggest that considering associations between EF and ToM in children with autism will lead to a more refined theoretical understanding.

In considering hypotheses around the 'fractionation of autism', Brunsdon and Happé (2014) highlight that existing evidence appears to suggest 'significant relations' between ToM and EF (p. 26) in terms of performance on cognitive tasks. In their review, they also consider evidence put forward by White (2013, in Brunsdon and Happé, 2014) for the opposite position to that of Pellicano (2010, in Hughes, 2011), whereby it is in fact mentalising difficulties that underlie the weaker performance of children with ASD on EF tasks through a difficulty in 'inferring implicit information', for example in respect of having an understanding of an experimenter's expectations about a task.

Central coherence

Neither executive dysfunctions nor mentalising deficits can easily account for special abilities or 'savant' skills shown by some children with autism, sometimes despite very low scores overall on tests of general intellectual functioning. Frith (1989) proposed that this can be explained by impaired central coherence. In normally developing individuals, there is an in-built propensity to integrate information, form coherence over a wide range of stimuli and generalise over as wide a range of contexts as possible. People will automatically seek to make 'sense' from perceiving connections and meaningful links from meaningless materials.

Frith (1989) suggested that, in children with autism, this capacity for coherence is diminished, and that this is sometimes relatively advantageous. For example, Shah and Frith (1993) sought to explain why children with autism tend to show relatively better performance on the block-design subtest of the Weschler intelligence scale for children. This involves assembling four or nine cubes so that the top surfaces match a printed pattern. It was found that segmenting the pattern into single cube components greatly helped both normally developing children and those with learning disabilities. However, the performance of children with autism did not improve, suggesting that they were already well able to overcome the strong drive to cohesion experienced by the other children.

Happé *et al.* (2001) suggest that, although mean scores on tests of central coherence will be lower in people with autism than in those without, central coherence may be a cognitive or information processing style that varies in the normal population and among people with autism. Using laboratory tasks such as the embedded-figures task (which involves detecting a hidden figure within a larger meaningful line drawing; see Figure 9.2), they found a higher rate of weak central coherence in parents of boys who have autism than in parents of normally developing boys or of boys with dyslexia. There were parallel differences in everyday life, for example involving special interests, attention to detail, insistence on routines and intolerance of change (Briskman *et al.*, 2001).

Baron-Cohen (2002) has reported similar patterns of findings, although the labelling of the hypothesised cognitive styles involved is slightly different. Baron-Cohen distinguishes a *systematising* from an *empathising* information processing style and defines these in terms of orientation to, and understanding of, physical as opposed to psychological information about the world. Systematising is defined as 'a drive to understand and derive rules about a system' (Grove *et al.*, 2013, p. 601) that is thought to enable individuals to predict how a system may behave and, hence, to have a sense

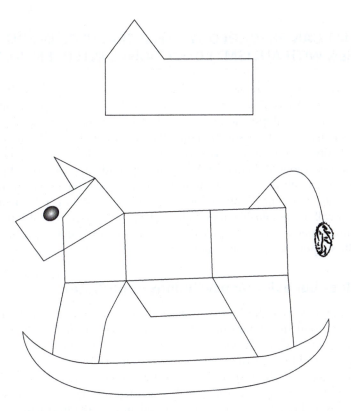

FIGURE 9.2 Sample item from the children's embedded-figures test: 'house' embedded in 'rocking horse'

Source: Witkins *et al.*, 1971. Reproduced with permission

of control over that system. As these styles are often held to be characteristic of males and females, respectively, this idea has been referred to as the extreme male brain theory of autism. Although supporting data for this theory are perhaps limited (Volkmar et al., 2004), it has attracted considerable popular press coverage and is often misrepresented as holding that all men are autistic!

Charman et al. (2011) suggest that it is increasingly recognised that no one cognitive theory of autism provides adequate explanation of the heterogeneity of behavioural presentations of people with ASD, and, hence, research is increasingly aiming to explain a particular behaviour seen in people with ASD, rather than to provide one unifying theory for the spectrum of difficulties experienced. Ronald and Hoekstra (2011) suggested, on the basis of their review of twin studies, that causal explanations for the 'three core sets of symptoms that define ASD . . . should be sought for each group separately, rather than for autism as a whole' (p. 265; see also Happé and Ronald, 2008; Brunsdon and Happé, 2014). Frith (2012) reflects on the progress made in autism research since cognitive studies of autism began in the 1960s, but, despite this, she highlights that there is still a long way to go, particularly in relation to our understanding of educational interventions.

SO, WHAT CAN PSYCHOLOGY OFFER TEACHERS IN EDUCATING CHILDREN WITH AUTISM? EDUCATIONAL INTERVENTIONS

Psychological theory and research have had a very significant impact on the education of children with ASD. Two distinct strands of influence can be identified. The first draws on behavioural psychology and takes no account either of diagnosis or characteristic features of autism. By contrast, the second draws directly on cognitive theories of autism. Revisiting Chapters 1 and 2, you will see how an understanding of relevant psychological theory for ASD can help guide the educational psychologist, both in terms of informed assessment and also in developing a case formulation and, hence, designing an intervention for an individual child in a particular context. Similarly, it will prove valuable in providing advice to settings or local authorities about the potential effectiveness of applied interventions for children with ASD (what empirically supported treatments are there?).

What does behavioural psychology contribute?

Developed by Lovaas in the 1960s, the *applied behavioural analysis* (ABA) approach was successful in producing empirically validated improvements in language, learning and social behaviour of children with ASD, where previous approaches had failed. The approach involved highly structured operant learning techniques, such as discrete trial training and task analysis. Task analysis was used on complex behaviour to develop a sequence of discrete responses that could be trained through a series of drills. A drill typically consisted of a trainer-provided antecedent (e.g. the instruction 'sit down'), a response from the child and a consequence rewarding a correct response (tangible reinforcers such as small bites of food or play with a favourite toy were often used initially, but paired with verbal praise so that the tangible reward could gradually be faded). Emphasis was placed on providing physical or verbal prompts to maximise successful performance and on shaping desired behaviour through rewarding successive approximations. An incorrect response might be ignored, or the child might be told 'no'.

Designed for children aged 2–4 years, ABA programmes of this kind are carried out at home on a one-to-one basis with the child, by trained parents or other personnel. Because of their understanding of behavioural principles, psychology students are often encouraged to apply for training and part-time positions as ABA therapists. The programmes are intensive: initial studies indicated 40 hours per week as desirable, whereas later studies reported 27 hours per week, over a period of 3 years, together with planned integration experiences in a nursery school in the second and third year, where taught skills could be generalised. Although criticised for placing unrealistic demands on parents, initial efficacy research highlighted the importance of programme intensity. Lovaas (1987) reported that children with ASD who received ABA for 40 hours a week achieved significantly better outcomes than either those who received 10 hours a week or those who received a different, nonspecified treatment. A follow-up study suggested that there was good maintenance of treatment effects (McEachin et al., 1993).

However, a number of controversies have surrounded the Lovaas approach and its evaluation. One, relating to the use of *punishment* when the approach was first introduced is considered in Ethics Box 9.1. The other that will be considered here is the strong claim by Lovaas that some 40 per cent of children achieve normal functioning as a result of the programme, and that this 'recovery' from autism calls into question the existence of a neurological disorder. A number of methodological critiques of the evaluative research by Lovaas and his colleagues have been published (Schopler et al., 1989; Rutter, 1996; Gresham and MacMillan, 1997b). Gresham and MacMillan (1997a) challenged the criteria used to judge normal functioning (IQ and educational placement), on the basis that these are gross measures that do not necessarily reflect improvements in the characteristic areas of difficulty in autism. In addition, they may reflect the operation of other, uncontrolled factors; for example, educational placement will be heavily influenced by the policy of individual school districts. Gresham and MacMillan (1997a) also raised concerns about participant selection and representativeness, substantial differences across groups in the time periods between assessments, the matching of the groups and the absence of random assignment. The issue of random assignment was addressed in two replication studies (Smith et al., 1997, 2000). The replications did not find gains in language and IQ of the same magnitude as in the original study. Also, lower gains were found where children met the full criteria for autism, as opposed to occupying positions on the spectrum where fewer difficulties are experienced. However, available group data supported the conclusion that there is an overall enhancement of developmental rate where children receive an ABA programme for 27 hour or more per week, from appropriately trained and supervised personnel (Mastergeorge et al., 2003). More recent reviews of the evidence for early intensive behavioural intervention (EIBI) suggest that EIBI is effective for supporting children with autism on a range of outcomes, for some, but not all children (e.g. Eldevick et al., 2009; Howlin et al., 2009; Warren et al., 2011).

When first introduced, aversive consequences were employed in the ABA programmes pioneered by Lovaas with children who have ASD. These generally consisted of a shouted 'No!' or a slap on the leg. Lovaas and his colleagues did conduct one laboratory study that used electric cattle prods to shape the social behaviour of children with ASD (Lovaas *et al.*, 1965), but there is no indication that such strategies were ever advocated to parents or nurseries! It appears that the aversives that were advocated were considered to have an important effect in achieving desired outcomes for the children: 'Introduction of contingent aversives resulted in a sudden and stable reduction in the inappropriate behaviors and a sudden and stable increase in appropriate behaviors' (Lovaas, 1987, p. 7).

Aversives are no longer used in ABA programmes because of changes in ethical and legal frameworks, which are illustrated by the following extracts. Read these and consider whether the use of physical punishment could ever be justified. What arguments could be made, both for and against? Is there additional research evidence you would want to have in making your decision? Do you consider research evidence relevant in resolving ethical dilemmas?

UN Convention on the Rights of the Child
Article 37
States Parties shall ensure that:
(a) No child shall be subjected to torture or other cruel, inhuman or degrading treatment or punishment.

(Unicef, 1989)

British Psychological Society Code of Ethics and Conduct
3.1 Standard of General Responsibility
Psychologists should:
(i) Avoid harming clients, but take into account that the interests of different clients may conflict. The psychologist will need to weigh these interests and the potential harm caused by alternative courses of action or inaction.

(British Psychological Society, 2009)

The Health and Care Professions Council: Standards of conduct, performance and ethics
Standard 1: You must act in the best interests of service users
You must not do anything, or allow someone else to do anything that you have good reason to believe will put the health, safety or wellbeing of a service user in danger. This includes both your own actions and those of other people. You should take appropriate action to protect the rights of children and vulnerable adults if you believe they are at risk, including following national and local policies.

(Health and Care Professions Council, 2012)

ETHICS 9.1

What does cognitive psychology contribute?

The second strand of psychological theory and research that has been influential in the education of children with ASD is that relating to cognitive theories of autism. Explanations of these theories and their implications for adapting classroom environments and teaching strategies now feature prominently in preparing teachers to work with children who have ASD (Jordan, 1999; Warwickshire County Council, 2005). Although implications of problems with EFs and central coherence receive discussion, these are often already to be found in educational approaches for children with ASD. For example, the treatment and education of autistic and communication handicapped children approach (TEACCH; Schopler and Mesibov, 1995), which was originally developed in 1972, uses a highly structured, visually based approach in organising the classroom environment and learning materials. Key features of the approach include: explicit prompts, signals to initiate as well as to finish activities, reminder notes, a transparently structured environment, use of visual timetables setting out sequences of activities across a whole day or week, and advance preparation for any changes in routine. Hence, although derived from a study of the behaviour of children with ASD in different types of environment, rather than directly from cognitive theories of autism, the key features of the approach are likely to be of great help to people with executive dysfunctions or weak central coherence (Tutt *et al.*, 2006). *TEACCH* strategies have not only been used in home- and school-based settings, but they have also been adapted for use in a range of other settings, including in early intervention programmes, residential programmes, social groups, individual and group counselling sessions, medical, dental and therapy appointments, and sheltered employment sites (Mesibov and Shea, 2011).

By contrast, the research on a ToM deficit in autism has changed practitioners' perspectives on the social problems experienced by children with ASD and led to the development of new intervention approaches. A number of programmes have been developed to teach the perspective-taking or 'mind-reading' skills involved (e.g. Howlin *et al.*, 1999). Although it is generally found that children with ASD can be trained to perform successfully in the teaching sessions, they do not generalise the learning to other contexts or apply the strategies in conversation and other social situations.

Ozonoff and Miller (1995) used a control-group design with small numbers of 11–16-year-olds with ASD and normal intelligence. They provided explicit and systematic instruction in the underlying social–cognitive principles necessary to infer the mental states of others and, in addition, taught specific interactional and conversational skills. They found significant improvement in false-belief-task performance by the treatment group, but not the control group. However, there was no generalisation to naturalistic contexts and no change in teacher and parent reports of social behaviour.

Hadwin *et al.* (1996, 1997) focused on the teaching of important general principles, for example perception causes knowledge: a person will know x if they see or hear about it – Little Red Riding Hood doesn't know the wolf is in her grandmother's house because she didn't see him go there. Thirty children with ASD aged 4–13 years received intensive training involving many examples and different approaches (e.g. picture stories, puppet stories, role-play). The results showed that it was possible to teach children with ASD to pass tasks that assess mental-state understanding. However, there was no evidence of positive effects on spontaneous pretend play or conversational skills, leading the authors to conclude that the children appeared to be passing tasks by learning specific rules to apply, rather than developing any genuine understanding of the concepts involved.

Hoddenbach et al. (2012) provide an overview of more recent studies exploring the effectiveness of social-skills interventions focusing specifically on ToM (e.g. Fisher and Happé, 2005; Begeer et al., 2011, in Hoddenbach et al., 2012). In line with the findings above, they suggest that, although interventions appear to have an impact on ToM understanding, there appears to be little impact on aspects of everyday functioning relating to social behaviours, as assessed by teachers or parents.

In contrast to attempts to teach ToM abilities, the Social Stories™ approach, developed by Carol Gray (Gray, 1998; Howley and Arnold, 2005), draws on psychological theory and research in ToM and central coherence in providing compensatory information to assist individuals with ASD make sense of specific social situations. Specially constructed, short personalised stories, usually written by teachers, speech therapists and parents, are used to teach children with autism how to manage their own behaviour during a social situation that they may find challenging or confusing. The stories are designed to provide 'missing information' about the perspectives of others, relevant social cues and expected social behaviour, in a clear description of where the activity will take place, when it will occur, who will be participating, and what will happen.

Reviews of research on the effectiveness of *social stories* (Ali and Frederickson, 2006; Reynhout and Carter, 2006; Rust and Smith, 2006) have concluded that the approach shows promise. However, a number of methodological issues have been raised, including inadequate participant description in some reports, the relatively modest extent of some of the changes in targeted behaviours, the frequent use of other interventions alongside social stories and the predominant use of *single-case experimental designs*. Single-case experimental designs (as reviewed in Chapter 2) have particular strengths, both in their use by scientist–practitioners to develop the evidence base for practice (Barker et al., 2002) and in research areas where there are small samples and substantial participant heterogeneity. However, they also have weaknesses in terms of the adequacy of controls available for threats to internal validity, such as maturation, placebo effects or experimenter artefacts (Rosnow and Rosenthal, 2005).

More recently, Karkhaneh et al. (2010) carried out a systematic review that aimed to build on previous reviews through focusing on randomised controlled trials or controlled clinical trials evaluating a social story intervention versus any other intervention for individuals with ASD. Six studies were identified (all dissertations produced in the US between 2002 and 2006), with participants aged between 4 and 14 years, targeting game-playing skills, prosocial behaviours, emotion recognition or social skills. Although they noted the small sample sizes and poor methodological quality of all of the included studies, they concluded that, in line with previous reviews, the social stories interventions appeared to support short-term improvements in social functioning among school-aged high-functioning children with autism. Five of the studies showed benefits across a range of outcomes, including social interaction, story comprehension, generalised social comprehension, facial emotion learning and labelling, social skills, aggressive behaviour and communication skills. Although recognising the positive shift in the quality of methodologies used in evaluating the effectiveness of these interventions, Karkhaneh *et al.* do go on to note the need for further research that incorporates more rigorous designs and investigates aspects such as generalisation and long-term maintenance of intervention effects and critical components of the implementation of the social stories approach.

Comparative intervention studies

A question that arises regularly for practising EPs is whether one intervention for ASD is 'better than another' – for example, whether ABA is a more effective (and cost-effective) intervention for young children with ASD than provision in a nursery setting. A literature search will identify many studies reviewing interventions and comparing one with another. One example is a study by Magiati *et al.* (2007) that reported a 2-year follow-up study of forty-four children between the ages of 22 and 54 months, with a diagnosis of autism, who received at least 15 hours weekly of specialist intervention, either community implemented, home-based EIBI or specialist nursery provision. The nurseries used a range of approaches within the setting, including TEACCH-based approaches (Schopler, 1997) and the picture exchange communication system (Bondy and Frost, 1994). They describe how the EIBI children received significantly more hours of intervention and followed more special dietary and other biological interventions and alternative treatments (with the exception of extracurricular educational interventions) than the nursery group. From the detail given, cost-wise, the ABA approaches appear, over the whole sample, to have been on average marginally cheaper than the specialist nursery provision. They found that the two interventions produced comparable results, with both groups showing improvements in raw scores across a range of functioning over time, but little improvement on standardised scores. Children with higher cognitive and language functioning tended to make more progress, regardless of which intervention they received, but age at intake and intensity of the treatment did not appear to be related to child outcomes.

The authors conclude that there is a need to improve and increase autism-specific, school-based provision, and that no one intervention appears universally to be more effective for ASD than any other, but that there may be common elements underlying many ASD interventions that are effective in supporting children's development. Educational psychologists designing and delivering interventions for children with autism should take into account the range of possible interventions available, including their theoretical basis and efficacy research, and provision should be carefully tailored to each individual child's needs and context, with careful monitoring of progress incorporated.

SUMMARY OF MAIN ISSUES ADDRESSED IN THIS CHAPTER

- The key behavioural features of ASD can be conceptualised as a triad of impairments: in reciprocal social interaction, verbal and nonverbal communication, and imagination.
- Children with ASD may also have learning difficulties and hyper- or hyposensitivity to sensory stimuli. However, relative strengths in visuo-spatial processing and reasoning skills are also apparent, and around 10 per cent have special talents or 'savant' skills.

- Autism is a neurodevelopmental disorder with a biological basis in which genetic factors are strongly implicated. Recent increases in prevalence rates appear primarily attributable to diagnostic practices.
- There are three dominant cognitive theories of autism:
  - Theory of mind proposes a core deficit in the ability to 'mind-read' or attribute mental states to other people. False-belief tasks have been an important source of supportive evidence. This theory can account for many of the impairments in reciprocal social interaction and communication in autism.
  - Executive functions are needed to prepare for and carry out complex behaviours such as planning, prioritising, switching between tasks, inhibiting inappropriate impulsive actions and generating novel approaches. Impairments in executive functions could account for the restricted, repetitive behaviours, activities or interests found in autism.
  - Weak central coherence, a reduced drive to make meaning and an increased focus on parts rather than wholes, is seen as one end of a dimension. The theory helps to explain some areas of relative strength in ASD, such as performance on visuo-spatial analysis tasks.
- Psychological theory and research have had a significant impact on the education of children with ASD in two ways:
  - through the application of applied behavioural analysis in programmes such as that developed by Lovaas;
  - through the application of cognitive theories of autism programmes that have been developed to teach 'mind-reading' skills and to develop compensatory strategies, such as social stories.

KEY CONCEPTS AND TERMS

- Autism
- Asperger syndrome
- Autistic/autism spectrum disorders (ASDs)
- Prevalence
- Theory of mind

- Mentalising
- False-belief task
- Executive dysfunction
- Central coherence
- Applied behavioural analysis

- Punishment
- TEACCH
- Social stories
- Single-case experimental designs

RECOMMENDATIONS FOR FURTHER READING

Journal articles

Brunsdon, V.E.A. and Happé, F. (2014). Exploring the 'fractionation' of autism at the cognitive level. *Autism, 18*(1), 17–30.

Frith, U. (2012). Why we need cognitive explanations of autism. The 38th Sir Frederick Bartlett Lecture. *The Quarterly Journal of Experimental Psychology, 65*(11), 2073–92.

Karkhaneh, M., Clark, B., Ospina, M.B., Seida, J.C., Smith, V. and Hartling, L. (2010). Social Stories™ to improve social skills in children with autism spectrum disorder: A systematic review. *Autism, 14*(6), 641–62.

Rutter, M. (2013). Changing concepts and findings on autism. *Journal of Autism and Developmental Disorders, 43*(8), 1749–57.

Rutter, M.L. (2011). Progress in understanding autism: 2007–2010. *Journal of Autism and Developmental Disorders, 41*(4), 395–404.

Sucksmith, E., Roth, I. and Hoekstra, R.A. (2011). Autistic traits below the clinical threshold: Re-examining the broader autism phenotype in the 21st century. *Neuropsychology Review, 21*(4), 360–89.

Tutt, R., Powell, S. and Thornton, M. (2006). Educational approaches in autism: What we know about what we do. *Educational Psychology in Practice, 22*, 69–81.

Wing, L. and Potter, D. (2002). The epidemiology of autism: Is the prevalence rising? *Mental Retardation and Developmental Disabilities Research Reviews, 8*, 151–61.

Books

Frith, U. (2003). *Autism: Explaining the enigma* (2nd edn). Oxford, UK: Blackwell.

National Research Council (2001). *Educating Children with Autism*. Washington, DC: National Academy Press.

SAMPLE ESSAY TITLES

1 To what extent can a 'theory of mind' deficit account for the triad of impairments in autism?
2 Design an evidence-based intervention programme for Alex (Activity Box 9.1), justifying the approaches you decide to include with reference to relevant literature.
3 Evaluate the strengths and weaknesses of research evidence on the use of social stories with children who have ASD.
4 You have been asked to give a talk to sixth-form volunteers on 'Supporting children with ASD in school: Key insights from psychology'. Explain what you will include in your talk and why.

REFERENCES

Ali, S. and Frederickson, N. (2006). Investigating the evidence base of social stories. *Educational Psychology in Practice, 22*(4), 355–77.

American Psychiatric Association (2000). *Diagnostic and Statistical Manual of Mental Disorder, Fourth Edition, Text Revision (DSM-IV-TR)*. Washington, DC: American Psychiatric Publishing.

American Psychiatric Association (2013). *Diagnostic and Statistical Manual of Mental Disorder* (5th edn) (*DSM-5*). Washington, DC: American Psychiatric Publishing.

Apicella, F., Chericoni, N., Costanzo, V., Baldini, S., Billeci, L., Cohen, D. and Muratori, F. (2013). Reciprocity in interaction: A window on the first year of life in autism. *Autism Research and Treatment*, 1–12. Available online at http://dx.doi.org/10.1155/2013/705895 (accessed 26 November 2014).

Baird, G., Simonoff, E., Pickles, A., Chandler, S., Loucas, T., Meldrum, D. and Charman, T. (2006). Prevalence of disorder orders of the Autistic Spectrum in a population cohort of children in South Thames: The special needs and Autism project (SNAP). *Lancet, 368*, 210–15.

Baranek, G.T., Little, L.M., Parham, D., Ausderau, K.K. and Sabatos-Devito, M.G. (2014). Sensory features in autism spectrum disorders. In *Handbook of Autism and Pervasive Developmental Disorders*, Hoboken, NJ: Wiley, pp. 378–408.

Barker, C., Pistrang, N. and Elliott, R. (2002). *Research Methods in Clinical Psychology: An introduction for students and practitioners* (2nd edn). London: Wiley.

Baron-Cohen, S. (2002). The extreme male brain theory of autism. *Trends in Cognitive Science, 6*(6), 248–54.

Baron-Cohen, S., Leslie, A.M. and Frith, U. (1985). Does the autistic child have a 'theory of mind'? *Cognition, 4*, 37–46.

Baron-Cohen, S., Lombardo, M.V., Auyeung, B., Ashwin, E., Chakrabarti, B. and Knickmeyer, R. (2011). Why are autism spectrum conditions more prevalent in males? *PLoS Biology, 9*(6), e1001081.

Begeer, S., Gevers, C., Clifford, P., Verhoeve, M., Kat, K., Hoddenbach, E. and Boer, F. (2011). Theory of mind training in children with autism: A randomized controlled trial. *Journal of Autism and Developmental Disorders, 41*(8), 997–1006.

Bondy, A.S. and Frost, L.A. (1994). *PECS: The Picture Exchange Communication System training manual*. Cherry Hill, NJ: Pyramid Educational Consultants.

Briskman, J., Happé, F. and Frith, U. (2001). Exploring the cognitive phenotype of autism: Weak 'central coherence' of parents and siblings of children with autism II. Real life skills and preferences. *Journal of Child Psychology & Psychiatry, 42*, 309–16.

British Psychological Society (2009). *Code of Ethics and Conduct*. Leicester, UK: British Psychological Society.

Brunsdon, V.E.A. and Happé, F. (2014). Exploring the 'fractionation' of autism at the cognitive level. *Autism, 18*(1), 17–30.

Charman, T., Pickles, A., Simonoff, E., Chandler, S., Loucas, T. and Baird, G. (2011). IQ in children with autism spectrum disorders: Data from the Special Needs and Autism Project (SNAP). *Psychological Medicine, 41*(3), 619.

Dunsmuir, S. and Frederickson, N. (eds) (2005). *Autistic Spectrum Disorders* [CD]. London: Educational Psychology Publishing, University College London.

Eldevick, S., Hastings, R.P., Hughes, J.C., Jahr, E., Eikeseth, S. and Cross S. (2009). Meta-analysis of early intensive behavioral intervention for children with autism. *Journal of Clinical Child and Adolescent Psychology*, *38*, 439–50.

Elsabbagh, M., Divan, G., Koh, Y.J., Kim, Y.S., Kauchali, S., Marcín, C. and Fombonne, E. (2012). Global prevalence of autism and other pervasive developmental disorders. *Autism Research*, *5*(3), 160–79.

Frith, U. (1989). *Autism: Explaining the enigma*. Oxford, UK: Blackwell.

Frith, U. (2003). *Autism: Explaining the enigma* (2nd edn). Oxford, UK: Blackwell.

Frith, U. (2012). Why we need cognitive explanations of autism. The 38th Sir Frederick Bartlett Lecture. *The Quarterly Journal of Experimental Psychology*, *65*(11), 2073–92.

Gray, C.A. (1998). Social stories and comic strip conversations with students with Asperger's syndrome and high functioning autism. In E. Schloper and G.B. Mesibov (eds), *Asperger's Syndrome or High Functioning Autism? Current issues in autism*. New York: Plenum Press, pp. 167–98.

Gresham, F.M. and MacMillan, D.L. (1997a). Autistic recovery? An analysis and critique of the empirical evidence on the early intervention project. *Behavioral Disorders*, *22*(4), 185–201.

Gresham, F.M. and MacMillan, D.L. (1997b). Denial and defensiveness in the place of fact and reason: Rejoinder to Smith and Lovaas. *Behavioral Disorders*, *22*(4), 219–30.

Grove, R., Baillie, A., Allison, C., Baron-Cohen, S. and Hoekstra, R.A. (2013). Empathizing, systemizing, and autistic traits: Latent structure in individuals with autism, their parents, and general population controls. *Journal of Abnormal Psychology*, *122*(2), 600–9.

Hadwin, J., Baron-Cohen, S., Howlin, P. and Hill, K. (1996). Can children with autism be taught concepts of emotion, belief and pretence? *Development and Psychopathology*, *8*(2), 345–65.

Hadwin, J., Baron-Cohen, S., Howlin, P. and Hill, K. (1997). Does teaching theory of mind have an effect on the ability to develop conversation in children with autism? *Journal of Autism and Developmental Disorders*, *27*(5), 519–37.

Happé, F. (1995). The role of age and verbal ability in the theory of mind task performance of subjects with autism. *Child Development*, *66*, 843–55.

Happé, F., Briskman, J. and Frith, U. (2001). Exploring the cognitive phenotype of autism: Weak 'central coherence' in parents and siblings of children with autism. One experimental test. *Journal of Child Psychology and Psychiatry*, *42*, 299–307.

Happé, F. and Ronald, A. (2008). The 'fractionable autism triad': A review of evidence from behavioural, genetic, cognitive and neural research. *Neuropsychological Review*, *18*, 287–304.

Health and Care Professions Council (HCPC) (2012). *Standards of Conduct, Performance and Ethics*. London: HCPC.

Hermelin, B. (2001). *Bright Splinters of the Mind. A personal story of research with autistic savants*. London: Jessica Kingsley.

Hoddenbach, E., Clifford, P., Gevers, C., Clauser, C., Boer, F., Koot, H.M. and Begeer, S.M. (2012). Individual differences in the efficacy of a short Theory of Mind intervention for children with autism: A randomized controlled trial. Available online at www.trialsjournal. com/content/13/1/206 (accessed 27 April 2014).

Hoekstra, R.A., Bartels, M., Cath, D.C. and Boomsma, D.I. (2008). Factor structure, reliability and criterion validity of the Autism-Spectrum Quotient (AQ): A study in Dutch population and patient groups. *Journal of Autism and Developmental Disorders, 38*(8), 1555–66.

Howley, M. and Arnold, E. (2005). *Revealing the Hidden Social Code.* London: Jessica Kingsley.

Howlin, P., Baron-Cohen, S. and Hadwin, J. (1999). *Teaching Children with Autism to Mind-Read: A practical guide for teachers and parents.* London: Wiley.

Howlin, P., Magiati, I. and Charman, T. (2009). Systematic review of early intensive behavioral interventions for children with autism. *Journal Information, 114*(1), 23–41.

Hughes, C. (2011). Changes and challenges in 20 years of research into the development of executive functions. *Infant and Child Development, 20*(3), 251–71.

Jordan, R. (1999). *Autistic Spectrum Disorders: An introductory handbook for practitioners.* London: David Fulton.

Karkhaneh, M., Clark, B., Ospina, M.B., Seida, J.C., Smith, V. and Hartling, L. (2010). Social Stories™ to improve social skills in children with autism spectrum disorder: A systematic review. *Autism, 14*(6), 641–62.

Lai, M.C., Lombardo, M.V., Chakrabarti, B. and Baron-Cohen, S. (2013). Subgrouping the autism 'spectrum'. *PLOS Biology, 11*(4), e1001544.

Leslie, A. and Frith, U. (1988). Autistic children's understanding of seeing, knowing and believing. *British Journal of Developmental Psychology, 6*, 316–24.

Leslie, A. and Thaiss, L. (1992). Domain specificity in conceptual development: Evidence from autism. *Cognition, 43*, 467–79.

Lovaas, O.I. (1987). Behavioural treatment and normal intellectual and educational functioning in autistic children. *Journal of Consulting and Clinical Psychology, 55*, 3–9.

Lovaas, O.I., Schaeffer, B. and Simmons, J.Q. (1965). Building social behaviour in autistic children by use of electric shock. *Journal of Experimental Research and Personality, 1*(2), 99–109.

Magiati, I., Charman, T. and Howlin, P. (2007). A two-year prospective follow-up study of community-based early intensive behavioural intervention and specialist nursery provision for children with autism spectrum disorders. *Journal of Child Psychology and Psychiatry, 48*(8), 803–12.

Mastergeorge, A.M., Rogers, S.J., Corbett, B.A. and Solomon, M. (2003). Non medical interventions for autistic spectrum disorders. In S. Ozonoff, S.J. Rogers and R.L. Hendren (eds), *Autistic Spectrum Disorders: A research review for practitioners.* Washington, DC: American Psychiatric Publishing, 133–60.

McEachin, J., Smith, T. and Lovaas, O.I. (1993). Long-term outcome for children with autism who received early intensive behavioral treatment. *American Journal of Mental Retardation, 97*(4), 359–72.

Medical Research Council (MRC) (2001). *MRC Review of Autism Research Epidemiology and Causes.* London: Medical Research Council.

Mesibov, G.B. and Shea, V. (2011). TEACCH. In J.S. Kreutzer, J. DeLuca and B. Caplan (eds), *Encyclopaedia of Clinical Neuropsychology.* Springer: New York, pp. 2472–7.

Morton, J. (2004). *Understanding Developmental Disorders: A causal modelling approach*. Oxford, UK: Blackwell.

Mundy, P., Sigman, M. and Kasari, C. (1990). A longitudinal study of joint tension and language development in autistic children. *Journal of Autism and Developmental Disorders, 20*, 115–28.

Onishi, K.H. and Baillargeon, R. (2005). Do 15-month-old infants understand false beliefs? *Science, 308*(5719), 255–58.

Ozonoff, S. (1997). Components of executive function deficits in autism and other disorders. In J. Russell (ed.), *Autism as an Executive Disorder*. Oxford, UK: Oxford University Press, pp. 179–211.

Ozonoff, S. and Griffith, E.M. (2000). Neuropsychological functioning and the external validity of Asperger syndrome. In A. Klin, F. Volkmar and S.S. Sparrow (eds), *Asperger Syndrome*. New York: Guilford Press, pp. 72–96.

Ozonoff, S. and Miller, J.N. (1995). Teaching theory of mind: A new approach to social skills training for individuals with autism. *Journal of Autism and Development Disorders, 25*(4), 415–33.

Ozonoff, S., South, M. and Miller, J.N. (2000). DSM-IV-defined Asperger syndrome: Cognitive, behavioral and early history differentiation from high functioning autism. *Autism, 4*, 29–46.

Reynhout, G. and Carter, M. (2006). Social Stories™ for children with disabilities. *Journal of Autism and Developmental Disorders, 36*(4), 445–69.

Rogers, S.J. and Pennington, B.F. (1991). A theoretical approach to the deficits in infantile autism. *Development and Psychopathology, 3*, 137–62.

Ronald, A. and Hoekstra, R.A. (2011). Autism spectrum disorders and autistic traits: A decade of new twin studies. *American Journal of Medical Genetics Part B: Neuropsychiatric Genetics, 156*(3), 255–74.

Rosnow, R.L. and Rosenthal, R. (2005). *Beginning Behavioral Research: A conceptual primer* (5th edn). New York: Pearson/Prentice Hall.

Rust, J. and Smith, A. (2006). How should the effectiveness of social stories to modify the behaviour of children on the autistic spectrum be tested? Lessons from the literature. *Autism, 10*(2), 125–38.

Rutter, M. (1996). Autism research: Prospects and priorities. *Journal of Autism and Developmental Disorders, 26*(2), 257–75.

Rutter, M. (1999). Autism: Two-way interplay between research and clinical work. *Journal of Child Psychology and Psychiatry, 40*, 169–88.

Rutter, M. (2013). Changing concepts and findings on autism. *Journal of Autism and Developmental Disorders, 43*(8), 1749–57.

Rutter, M. (2014). Addressing the issue of fractionation in autism spectrum disorder: A commentary on Brunsdon and Happé, Frazier *et al.*, Hobson and Mandy *et al*. *Autism, 18*(1), 55–7.

Schopler, E. (1997). Implementation of TEACCH philosophy. *Handbook of Autism and Pervasive Developmental Disorders, 2*, 767–95.

Schopler, E. and Mesibov, G. (1995). *Learning and Cognition in Autism*. New York: Plenum Press.

Schopler, E., Short, B. and Mesibov, G. (1989). Relation of behavioral treatment to normal functioning: Comment on Lovaas. *Journal of Consulting and Clinical Psychology, 57,* 162–4.

Shah, A. and Frith, U. (1993). Why do autistic individuals show superior performance on the block design task? *Journal of Child Psychology and Psychiatry, 34*(8), 1351–64.

Shallice, T. (1988). *From Neuropsychology to Mental Structure.* Cambridge, UK: Cambridge University Press.

Smith, T., Eikeseth, S., Klevstrand, M. and Lovaas, O.I. (1997). Intensive behavioural treatment for pre-schoolers with severe mental retardation and pervasive developmental disorder. *American Journal of Mental Retardation, 102,* 238–49.

Smith, T., Groen, A.D. and Wynn, J.W. (2000). Randomised trial of intensive early intervention for children with Pervasive Developmental Disorder. *American Journal of Mental Retardation, 105,* 269–85.

Southgate, V., Senju, A. and Csibra, G. (2007). Action anticipation through attribution of false belief by 2-year-olds. *Psychological Science, 18*(7), 587–92.

Sucksmith, E., Roth, I. and Hoekstra, R.A. (2011). Autistic traits below the clinical threshold: Re-examining the broader autism phenotype in the 21st century. *Neuropsychology Review, 21*(4), 360–89.

Tutt, R., Powell, S. and Thornton, M. (2006). Educational approaches in autism: What we know about what we do. *Educational Psychology in Practice, 22,* 69–81.

Unicef (1989). *Convention on the Rights of the Child.* London: Unicef UK. Available online at www.unicef.org.uk/Documents/Publication-pdfs/UNCRC_PRESS200910web.pdf (accessed 2 December 2014).

Volkmar, F.R., Lord, C., Bailey, A., Schultz, R.T. and Klin, A. (2004). Autism and pervasive developmental disorders. *Journal of Child Psychology and Psychiatry, 45,* 135–70.

Warren, Z., McPheeters, M.L., Sathe, N., Foss-Feig, J.H., Glasser, A. and Veenstra-VanderWeele, J. (2011). A systematic review of early intensive intervention for autism spectrum disorders. *Pediatrics, 127*(5), e1303–11.

Warwickshire County Council (2005). *An ASD Tool Kit for Teachers.* Warwick, UK: Warwickshire County Council.

Wimmer, H. and Perner, J. (1983). Beliefs about beliefs: Representations and constraining function of wrong beliefs in young childrens' understanding of deception. *Cognition, 13,* 103–28.

Wing, L. and Gould, J. (1979). Severe impairments of social interaction and associated abnormalities in children: Epidemiology and classification. *Journal of Autism and Developmental Disorders, 9,* 11–29.

Wing, L. and Potter, D. (2002). The epidemiology of autism: Is the prevalence rising? *Mental Retardation and Developmental Disabilities Research Reviews, 8,* 151–61.

Witkins, H., Oltman, P., Raskin, E. and Karp, S. (1971). *A Manual for Embedded Figures Test, Children's Embedded Figures Test & Group Embedded Figures Test.* Palo Alto, CA: Consulting Psychologists Press.

World Health Organisation (1995). *International Classification of Disability – Version 10 (ICD-10).* Geneva: WHO.

10 Managing classroom behaviour

Perspectives from psychology

Anthea Gulliford and Andy Miller

CHAPTER SUMMARY

In this chapter, a number of psychological perspectives on difficult classroom behaviour – including behavioural, cognitive *and* psychodynamic *– will be reviewed. We shall explore how such perspectives can help us to understand difficult behaviour, and how they inform, at various levels, interventions aimed at achieving calm and positive learning environments for all children, including the most vulnerable.* Ecological systems theories *are noted to help in guiding* individual, class *and* whole-school *approaches, and a distinction will be drawn between* reactive *and* preventive *approaches. The contribution of* applied behaviour analysis *to understanding difficult behaviour will be discussed in some depth. Turning to various* cognitive approaches, *studies of the* causal attributions *of teachers, parents and pupils about behaviour will then be considered. Finally, consideration will be given to the way in which psychodynamic insights can inform understanding of, and interventions for, managing classroom behaviour. Case studies illustrating the ways in which educational psychologists intervene with casework involving difficult behaviour will highlight the importance of problem formulation when supporting individual pupils displaying challenging behaviour.*

LEARNING OUTCOMES

When you have studied this chapter, you should be able to:

1 identify differing perspectives upon understanding and intervening with classroom behaviour, including the implications of ecological systems theories for approaching behaviour management in schools;
2 explain the key principles of applied behaviour analysis (ABA);
3 explain what ABA has taught us about preventive, class and whole-school approaches to behaviour management;
4 explain causal attributions and their potential to support the practice of applied psychologists working with challenging behaviour;
5 identify the similarities and contradictions between the causal attributions of students, teachers and parents in how they make sense of the causes of challenging behaviour in schools and classrooms;
6 outline how psychodynamic approaches such as *attachment theory* can contribute to the development of positive school climates and well-being in young people.

INTRODUCTION

Managing everyday classroom behaviour, whether classed as difficult or not, is undoubtedly a challenge for all teachers, whatever the collective or individual features of the children they are working with. As well-ordered classrooms are understood to be an essential part of a young person's learning environment, the focus falls, from all quarters (politicians, policymakers, parents, teachers), upon the question of how best to promote and maintain good order.

Difficult behaviour in schools is by no means a new phenomenon, despite the best attempts of the media to persuade us of the constant worsening of behaviour in schools. Although there is some evidence to suggest that the incidence of extreme disruption by more needy and challenging pupils is currently a higher concern, overall, general standards of classroom behaviour appear to be improving (Apter *et al.*, 2010). A consistent finding, when the views of teachers are systematically solicited, is that the *most* difficult aspect of classroom behaviour for teachers is that of persistent, low-level disruption, such as talking out of turn and hindering other children. Results from research carried out for the Elton Report, published in 1989, show a remarkable similarity to those cited by the Chief Inspector for Schools below:

> Few teachers in our survey reported physical aggression towards themselves. Most of these did not rate it as the most difficult behaviour with which they had to deal. Teachers in our survey were most concerned about the cumulative effects of disruption to their lessons caused by relatively trivial but persistent misbehaviour.
> (DfES, 1989)

The most common forms of misbehaviour are incessant chatter, calling out, inattention and other forms of nuisance that irritate staff and interrupt learning.

(Ofsted, 2005)

RESPONDING TO THE ISSUE OF BEHAVIOUR

Many policy responses associated with managing difficult behaviour in schools are formulated in terms of a language of *discipline and control*. In contrast, psychology – although holding the same goal of achieving order and containment for all – offers a different terminology. Applied psychology aims to identify fruitful pathways through which to both *understand* and *intervene with* difficult behaviour and offers a range of perspectives, and theoretical and practical evidence, to guide interventions that seek to *promote positive learning environments for all*.

The temptation is to see difficult classroom behaviour as a discrete and categorical concern, but, of course, for each scenario, the interplay of factors and perceptions of those involved is complex. Among these elements, the role of the instructional context is particularly significant, with many young people who show difficult behaviour in school being those who experience some form of difficulty with the curriculum. Halonen *et al.* (2006), for example, illustrate the cumulative interrelationship between reading delay and externalising difficulties – for example, challenging behaviour in the classroom. It is important for the practitioner not to treat such data deterministically when considering the needs of a young person they are working with, but to bear such factors in mind as potential influences, as illustrated in the problem-solving example of Chapter 1 in this volume.

In addition to the problem-solving frameworks seen in Chapter 1, ecological systems theories help to address such complexities. Bronfenbrenner's model (Bronfenbrenner and Morris, 2006), as explored in Chapters 4 and 11, delineates the systems between which a child moves, and interactions within and between them, allowing us to capture those multiple influences. Of significance here is the way in which the conceptualisation of schools can be supported by ecological systems insights. A systems view of behavioural management interventions allows us to distinguish between interventions focused on the *individual* child, or on *groups* (classes), or on the *whole school* – with differential effects of such attention. This, in turn, draws us towards another important distinction, that of *reactive* versus *preventive* approaches, where the former, responding to established problems, can be seen as less efficient in terms of support time and demands, but where the latter are, perhaps, initially less appealing to school staff, who have many other demands to focus upon. This point is also illustrated in Chapter 11, in relation to bullying.

PSYCHOLOGICAL PERSPECTIVES ON DIFFICULT BEHAVIOUR IN SCHOOLS

For applied psychologists, there are a number of key domains that have particular relevance to the issue of difficult behaviour. The contribution of behavioural theories through ABA will be explored first, followed by consideration of cognitive and psychodynamic perspectives.

BEHAVIOURAL PERSPECTIVES

In the chronology of approaches to understanding classroom behaviour, behavioural approaches, founded upon the work of Skinner (1953), inevitably played a fundamental role.

Behavioural psychology focuses on the contingencies between behaviour and its environment, leading to an analysis of context and interactions, the *antecedents* and *consequences* to behaviour, and potentially to carefully designed interventions. This paradigm assumed prominence during the first half of the twentieth century, but, by the mid 1960s, and in the light of cognitive psychology's emergence, its predominance as a theoretical standpoint within psychology was arguably on the wane. Despite this decline, a proliferation of behavioural procedures linked to problems of children in clinical settings and, ultimately, classrooms was seen during the 1960s (Landrum and Kauffman, 2006), with the growth of ABA being particularly notable.

ABA was described as being characterised by:

> systematic efforts to change socially important behaviours in positive ways through the application of behavioural principles, with strict reliance on the frequent, repeated assessment of observable and measurable behaviour [and with] the goal of establishing a functional relationship between independent and dependent variables.
>
> (Landrum and Kauffman, 2006, p. 53)

ABA draws upon three key principles from *operant conditioning*:

- a concern with *clearly defined* and *observable behaviour*, rather than assumed personality characteristics or motivations of pupils;
- the careful collection and *recording of data*;
- a focus on *settings* in which behaviour occurs and the signals or triggers that may act as antecedents to the behaviour, as well as the consequences that follow the behaviour.

In terms of evidence concerning behavioural psychology and individuals, a seminal (American) study by Madsen *et al.* (1968) was significant in its focus upon remediating the behaviour of three specific individuals (two primary-aged and one at kindergarten). The youngest child showed high levels of difficult and challenging behaviour, for example pushing, hitting, grabbing objects or swearing. Nine categories of inappropriate behaviour were devised with class teachers (including gross motor activity, object noise, disturbance of others' property, contact, verbalisation, turning around, other mouthing objects and isolate play), and one category of appropriate behaviour. Two observers were trained over a 2-week period to make precise records of the pupils' behaviour in the classroom (keeping a record of five 10-second intervals in every minute, over a 20-minute period, on three occasions each week).

The study's aim was to investigate the effects on pupils' classroom behaviour of teachers varying their use of praise, ignoring and the explaining of *rules*. For the first intervention phase, the teachers were asked to aim for at least four to six repetitions of the *rules* each day, at times other than when somebody had misbehaved, these rules being no more than five or six in number, short and to the point, and framed in a positive rather than a negative form (for example, 'sit quietly while working', rather than 'don't talk to your neighbours').

The second phase involved the teacher *ignoring inappropriate behaviour*, unless this was leading to a pupil being hurt. The purpose was to test the possibility that inappropriate behaviour was being strengthened in some cases ('reinforced') by the attention paid to it by the teachers, even though they intended this attention to act as a punishment. The teachers in the study found this a particularly difficult strategy to implement and sustain as an intervention on its own.

The third phase, the *praise* condition, was framed as 'catching the child being good'. The teachers were asked to give praise, attention or smiles when the pupil was doing what was expected during the particular class in question. The teachers were also encouraged to 'shape by successive approximation', starting by giving praise and attention to the first signs of appropriate behaviour and building towards greater goals. Emphasis was to be placed on positive and helpful social behaviour and following group rules.

The rules and the ignoring phases on their own produced little change from the baseline condition, but the combination of *rules, praise and ignoring* proved highly effective in reducing inappropriate behaviour. This pioneering study illustrates the genesis of some of the fundamental features of the use of ABA approaches in classroom settings. 'Rules, praise, ignore' has emerged as a successful strategy and continues to be promoted (Gable *et al.*, 2009).

ABA STRATEGY

LaVigna (2000) reviewed three basic ABA strategies:

- *Differential reinforcement of alternative response*: most typically, these strategies reward a student for 'being good', defined in some behavioural sense. This would be seen as a response that was a preferable alternative to whatever was causing the initial concern.
- *Differential reinforcement of the omission of a response*: in common parlance, this rewards a student for not committing some specified misbehaviour.
- *Differential reinforcement of lower rates of responding*: this rewards students for being 'naughty' less and less often.

In reviewing the evidence, LaVigna (2000) concludes that the differential reinforcement of the omission of a response is generally the most effective strategy for classroom settings. However, because of its negative formulation, in terms of the omission of something, it was recommended that such a strategy should always be accompanied by a direct teaching programme to teach the child positive alternatives to the problem behaviour in question.

A word about 'rewards'

Positive reinforcement in the form of praise from teachers was a distinctive feature of the Madsen *et al.* study (1968), and rewards of various types have been incorporated

| Material | Symbolic | Activity | Social | Intrinsic |
| (e.g. food) | (e.g. smiley faces) | (e.g. game) | (e.g. praise) | |

FIGURE 10.1 The spectrum of classroom-based reinforcers

Source: Adapted from Goodwin and Coates, 1976

into ABA studies and interventions ever since. However, Goodwin and Coates (1976) provided a useful corrective to the uncritical application of rewards, pointing out that the goal of any intervention in an educational setting should be for the young person to experience the particular behaviours and accomplishments being encouraged as *intrinsically motivating* in themselves.

Social reinforcement such as teacher praise or peer encouragement should only be necessary in circumstances where the student's skills level and accomplishment are not of a high enough standard for them to yet be a reinforcer in themselves. Similarly, Goodwin and Coates argue that interventions should only employ *reinforcers* further to the left in Figure 10.1 if praise and encouragement are not powerful enough to increase a desired behaviour. In such circumstances, guiding principles would be to move only as far to the left as is necessary for increasing this behaviour, to always pair material, activity or symbolic reinforcement with praise and intrinsically motivating and interesting tasks, and to plan for progression to the right as it becomes possible to do so, phasing out these explicit and contrived reinforcers.

An extensive literature on the differential effects of praise highlights the ways in which praise can focus upon performance or behaviour (e.g. Mueller and Dweck, 1998). Following a comprehensive review of the literature, Henderlong and Lepper (2002, p. 774) concluded that praise in itself may serve either to 'undermine, enhance or have no effect on children's motivation'. They identify the perception of the *sincerity* with which praise is used as being particularly beneficial to intrinsic motivation and also single out attribution to controllable causes, the promotion of autonomy and the avoidance of over-reliance on social comparisons as other features strongly contributing to positive effects of praise upon outcomes for students. It is helpful, here, to consider the work of Ryan and Deci, who propose, through self-determination theory, the significance of intrinsic motivation (Ryan and Deci, 2000) for the individual. Fulfilment of needs in *autonomy*, *competence* and *relatedness* bring greatest self-determination, or self-efficacy. Praise, here, can become demotivating, through undermining *intrinsic* motivation and leaving the learner externally manipulated (Deci *et al.*, 2001).

A word about 'punishments'

Sanctions or punishments, although not present in the original studies of Madsen *et al.*, soon became associated, in the public mind at least, with the practice of 'behaviour modification' and were a feature of many supposed ABA interventions (see Chapter 9). This was despite the bad name brought upon behaviour modification approaches through the scandal of the 'pin-down' episode in residential settings homes of Staffordshire in the UK in 1980s, which illustrated the potential terrible effects of poorly ingested behavioural psychology used by carers. Children were subject to punishment-based approaches, involving significant deprivation and degradation (Levy and Kahan, 1991).

Behavioural psychology, however, identifies that punishment is problematic for a number of reasons, not least because it risks *reinforcing* the specific behaviour it aims to eliminate (for example, through inadvertently rewarding it). Kearney (2007) notes that punishment risks, first, merely *suppressing* behaviours (by implication, failing to generate new, more adaptive ones) and, second, being *overly specific* and having effects upon the behaviour only in the presence of the aversive consequences. So, for example, imagine the scenario where a young person who persistently calls out in class is either sent out of class (*inadvertent reward*), or, perhaps, given a detention, when in fact the behaviour was driven by work-related anxiety, which surfaces in subsequent lessons (*supressing behaviour*), or is dealt with by reprimands from a passing senior manager in the school, but continues in the behaviour once the usual, newly qualified teacher resumes control (*temporary suppression*). Punishment, in these examples, risks teaching the young person a yet more complex and subtle set of difficult-to-manage behaviours (Kearney, 2007), doing little to support long-term behaviour change.

In addition to the guiding principles from behavioural psychology, there is an evidence base that shows the deleterious effects of a negative, sanctions-based approach in schools. Sugai and Horner (2002) identified that the retreat to punitive approaches in schools, characterised by restatements of rules associated with linked threats of punishment, is indeed highly likely to *increase* the rates of the very undesirable behaviours it aims to diminish, in addition to creating a climate that distracts from the instructional focus that a school is primarily aiming to promote. Nagging repetition and threats are teacher behaviours that are likely to escalate the behaviours that they aim to reduce (Gable *et al.*, 2009).

A final comment regarding punishment concerns one extreme form of sanction in the education system, *exclusion*, which results in the removal of a young person from the educational site, temporarily or permanently. Evidence consistently shows how this strategy can be applied without prior recourse to positive interventions by educational organisations (Maag, 2012). There is also concerning evidence of the disproportionate application of this strategy to children and young people who belong to certain communities; that the boys of black families are noticeably over-represented in the exclusion data (DFE, 2012) has, for example, provoked much discussion over the years (Parsons, 2005). As removing the child permanently from the classroom has enormous long-term social consequences for the individual, community and society, this phenomenon is an illustration of how psychology and social policy often have a unique interface; psychology has a role to play in the promotion of equality and in the promotion of environments that can support all children in attaining their potential.

Validity

Questions have been raised over the years regarding the ecological validity of some measures used in ABA. Early misgivings were voiced most vividly by Winnet and Winkler (1972), who saw many early American behavioural approaches as encouraging pupils to 'be still, be quiet, be docile'. McNamara and Harrop (1981) argued for more socially useful outcomes, and, in a review of quality indicators for single-subject investigations Horner and colleagues noted the importance of the *social validity* of the target behaviour for a child (Horner *et al.*, 2005). This refers to the perceived *utility* and *relevance* of the target behaviour – for example, how acceptable, relevant or useful it may be for a young person showing difficulties in interpersonal relating to be rewarded for sitting still in their chair. Behavioural psychology has had to defend itself against the charge of reductionism, too, and the risks of appearing to focus upon the *external* life of the individual, at the expense of other relevant factors for behaviour change.

Subsequent studies have become far more driven by the recognition that pupils who succeeded at conventionally valued school activities were likely, as a result, to identify more closely with the aims of the school and receive more naturally occurring praise and encouragement for their efforts. A creative example was provided by Burland (1979), who described work in a school for pupils with emotional and behavioural difficulties in which behavioural principles were rigorously but creatively employed to teach pupils a range of social and leisure skills – everything from juggling to riding unicycles.

FROM CONSEQUENCES TO ANTECEDENTS: A FOCUS UPON THE ENVIRONMENT

Two of the early British proponents of ABA, Harrop and McNamara (1979), made the point that those involved in supporting challenging situations had to ask whether the curriculum within the classroom where the difficult behaviour was manifest should be altered to meet the pupils' interests and aptitudes, before a fuller behavioural intervention was embarked upon, and this leads us to the consideration of the *antecedents* to behaviour and its contexts.

Behavioural psychology, of course, depends upon observational methods, and studies of *classroom interactions* over the years have been fruitful, despite the difficulties involved in assuring the reliability and validity of the data (Harrop and Swinson, 2007).

Studies have reviewed the relative rates of academic-related (low) and behaviour-related (high) verbal feedback typically found, the relationship between teacher positive feedback and rates of on-task behaviour (Swinson and Knight, 2007), for example, and the effects upon the academic self-concept of 8–9-year-olds of *specific praise* (positive effects) versus *positive praise* (no effect) (Chalk and Bizo, 2004). Most recently, in a national, large-scale study, Apter and colleagues noted the positive nature of verbal feedback to pupils by teachers in proportion to that witnessed in previous studies (Apter *et al.*, 2010). Positive correlations between on-task behaviour and teachers' positive academic comments and higher levels of verbal teacher feedback in national strategy lessons (literacy and numeracy) were also noted. Helping teachers to respond to these data is a potential role for psychologists, usually through consultative practice, although Rathel *et al.* (2013) report the use of emailed performance feedback to teachers enhancing the rates of positive praise from teachers, with effects identified in this single-case experimental design study upon the performance of individual, indicative pupils.

Considering the effects of classroom layout, Wheldall *et al.* (1981) carried out an experiment with two classes of 10- and 11-year-olds. The amount of 'on-task' behaviour was recorded over a 2-week period while the children were seated around tables, the measurements then being repeated for a further 2 weeks while the children were seated in rows. Examination of the data revealed that the rows condition had the greatest effect on the children with low initial on-task behaviour, the very pupils for whom behavioural interventions might more usually have been devised. This strand of research interest still finds expression in publications such as that by Hastings and Wood (2002).

Studies have offered cumulative insights into evidence-based strategies for effective *classroom management*. An early experimental validation of the behavioural approach's positive contribution to *management of a whole class* was provided by Tsoi and Yule (1976), who used extra break time as a reinforcer. Two types of strategy were each shown to be effective, one where the behaviour of a single child formed the basis for reinforcement for all the class, and one in which changes in the behaviour of the whole class were required. Subsequently, Merrett and Wheldall (1978) evaluated the effective combination of a '*rules, ignore and praise*' approach with a 'timer game', and Rennie (1980) demonstrated the positive outcomes achieved by other game strategies, all with whole classes. Williams (2012) illustrated the ABA underpinnings and positive effects of a differential reinforcement of alternative behaviour strategy, 'fair pairs', where three-part praise (*pupil name, clear praise, statement of specific behaviour*) is delivered to differentially reinforce the desired behaviour. Gable *et al.* (2009), reviewing the evidence for ABA, highlight the acceptance of the following, among other features, in good classroom management:

- the use of a limited number of classroom rules, with specific, brief, clear teacher instruction upon these;
- enforcing rules through 'precision requests' – which can be helpful, as compliance with rules and disruption co-vary: 'Daniel, we have to close our books, now. You do it too please' [teacher waits];
- rules that aim to build positive expectations in a classroom, with a positive *cohesion function*;
- praise that is contingent and behaviour specific: 'Jo, I like the way you are waiting quietly';
- planned (safe) ignoring of undesirable behaviour, within reason.

FROM REACTIVE STRATEGIES TO PREVENTATIVE APPROACHES

Clunies-Ross *et al.* (2008) observed that *reactive* strategies for behaviour management in the classroom (that is, responding to already occurring behaviour) can be associated with elevated teacher stress. There is also evidence that a greater focus upon *preventive* programmes is likely to correlate with increased prosocial behavioural skills in students. As well as whole-class approaches being a means of capitalising upon the potential of behavioural approaches, a parallel drive among psychologists and others has been towards the *prevention* of classroom difficulties through various teacher training and school policy development initiatives.

In 1986, an innovatory set of training materials, *Preventative Approaches to Disruption* (Chisholm *et al.*, 1986), drawing upon Kounin's (1970) studies of classroom management as well as the ABA research literature, was devised by a group of educational psychologists. In another influential set of resource materials, *Building a Better Behaved*

School, Galvin *et al.* (1990) combined a similar breadth of research studies with extensive professional experience of working in schools, drawing specific attention to the crucial importance of establishing clear and mutually agreed policies within schools for encouraging positive pupil behaviour.

A further approach to classroom management, delivered as a package through accredited workshops, is *assertive discipline*, developed by Canter and Canter (1976). Although these materials originally concentrated heavily on systems of rewards and punishments allied to clear statements of classroom rules, subsequent revisions (Canter and Canter, 1992) have placed a greater emphasis on students' self-regulation and the underlying rationales for classroom rules. Some have noted the lack of clear, or any, reliable evidence regarding this approach, however (Brophy, 2006; Maag, 2012), as well as the exclusionary risks of an 'obedience' model (Maag, 2012), where the primary goals of approaches to behaviour management should be positive behaviour management *with* inclusion.

APPLICATIONS OF BEHAVIOURAL APPROACHES IN EDUCATIONAL PROVISION, POLICY AND LEGISLATION

ABA, particularly in the US, has continued to move forward. For some, it has evolved as positive behaviour support or positive behaviour intervention support, reflecting the encompassing of a greater breadth of focus than simply the extinction of undesirable behaviours, or behavioural contingencies or the promotion of positive behaviours (LaVigna and Willis, 2012), aiming for a more holistic view of the young person's development and functioning overall. The broader term aims to understand behaviours of focus in the more holistic context of an individual's life, and to ensure ecological and social validity, that is, seeing the broader end-point of intervention as positive social functioning, rather than simply compliance with small behavioural targets. Professionals should be aiming to enhance the prosocial strengths of the individual, as they naturally occur in their social context, and making environmental adaptations that will reduce the negative ones (Dunlap *et al.*, 2014; Marchant *et al.*, 2012).

Elsewhere, the term functional behaviour analysis (FBA) captures the helpful methods through which applied psychologists can employ behavioural psychology to analyse the *function* and *features* of behaviour, in order to intervene with it (O'Neill and Stephenson, 2010; Allday *et al.*, 2011). These latter authors proffer reminders of the utility of FBA at the various levels of focus in behaviour management: whole school, class or group, and individual. FBA is seen as so effective in addressing complex behaviour in the individual that it is enshrined in federal law in the US as the response needed for any young person exhibiting significant behavioural difficulties (O'Neill and Stephenson, 2010), although the practical and conceptual complexities of administering robust FBA mean that practice may vary (Mathews *et al.*, 2013).

In mainstream schools in the UK, FBA, anecdotally, retains a profile of use in the casework practice of educational psychologists (see Eccles and Pitchford, 1997, for an example), and it certainly has a strong resonance with the ethical and ecological underpinnings to the professional practice of educational psychology.

There is evidence, too, of the environmental applications of behavioural psychology (Williams, 2012), and many educational psychologists report using more diffuse approaches that evidently have underpinnings in behavioural psychology (Hart, 2010). General practices in education appear to have changed from an initial wariness towards ABA in the early 1970s to a situation where, nowadays, some of the 'blunter' aspects of the approach, if not perhaps some of the finer and more crucial details, are to be found in a range of educational policy and legislation. Talk of targets, rewards, sanctions and rules pervades strategies and plans and was to be found in, for example, pastoral support programmes (DfEE, 1999), home–school agreements (DfEE, 2000) and the special educational needs *Code of Practice* (DfES, 2001). Central government (DfES, 2007) previously cited the Elton Report (DfES, 1989) as the source for its claim that an effective classroom management policy is one that reflects a ratio of five rewards to every sanction. Currently, a checklist form of guidance on behaviour in schools

ACTIVITY 10.1

Table 10.1 offers some examples of school-based practices. Note down your comments upon the extent to which they meet the key principles of behavioural psychology as set out above.

TABLE 10.1 School-based practices

Red class, Year 3 pupils	Can you identify (a) any footprints of behavioural psychology and (b) any suggested amendments?
1. Pupils' names are listed on a chart at the front of the class, and stars are given by the teacher during the course of the week	
2. Pupils in the class have a shared reward system, whereby they can earn marbles in a jar during the course of the week for being good	
3. If sufficient marbles are earned, such that the jar become full, pupils can earn 'golden time' on Friday afternoon	
4. If the jar is not filled by Friday afternoon, the teacher empties it and begins the exercise again on Monday morning the following week	
5. Pupils have home–school diaries, and at the front of these is written a clear message for them and their parents: 'If you are trying your best, you are doing well ☺'	
6. A passing visitor to the school during the week hears the teacher state the following: 'James, I like the way you are helping Zoe'	
7. The headteacher, passing in the corridor later in the day, hears the teacher say: 'How many times do I have to tell you? Stop behaving in this silly way!'	

(DFE, 2011) seems to contain some residual elements of behavioural psychology for effective classroom management. However, Yeager and Walton (2011), in a review of the powerful effects of brief psychosocial interventions upon pupil academic attainment, comment upon the need for *theoretical* and *contextual expertise*, and show how small adjustments in previously successful interventions hold the potential, not just to undermine the original purposes, but to lead to *negative* effects for pupils. They discourage a 'checklist' approach, seeing it as potentially overlooking the key theoretical elements for success. A parallel phenomenon might be argued regarding behavioural interventions. A phenomenon familiar to many practising psychologists is that of encountering traces of behavioural psychology in its various diluted incarnations in classrooms, accompanied by lack of apparent effect at best, or, at worst, achieving the opposite of the intended effects.

FROM A FOCUS SOLELY ON BEHAVIOUR TO THE INCLUSION OF COGNITION AND AFFECT

A theoretical challenge to behavioural approaches came from the evidence offered by early studies into the effects of 'self-recording', that is, the monitoring of behaviour by the student themselves, often in relation to a pre-agreed contract or goal. An investigation of a 13-year-old boy's on-task behaviour during a self-recording intervention showed a significant change from the baseline period to the intervention period (Merrett and Blundell, 1982). This, together with other developments in the wider field of psychology, indicated the need to consider the perceptions and formulations of the individual regarding their experience when intervening with behaviour; in other words, the need to acknowledge the role of cognition.

COGNITIVE PERSPECTIVES AND THEIR APPLICATIONS

Cognitive perspectives upon difficult behaviour identify the behaviour as the external manifestation of internal processes that may be driven in part by maladaptive cognitions, or cognitions that have adapted to difficult psychosocial circumstances for that individual, but do not easily allow for further adaptation in the classroom. These insights may offer an applied psychologist pathways forward, for example, through approaches to cognitive restructuring of perceptions with a young person, with their teachers or parents, through either explicit, formalised approaches (Rait *et al.*, 2010), or through less-explicit, informal approaches. *Cognitive behaviour therapy* (CBT) is particularly concerned with thoughts implicated in selective attention and in irrational beliefs in the form of 'negative automatic thoughts'. Interventions, often conceived of as experiments in *doing* and/or *construing* things differently, are drawn up to address unhelpful thoughts and beliefs (Greig, 2007; Fuggle *et al.*, 2013). Various studies indicate the utility of these ideas for group-based work in schools (Squires 2001, 2010; Ruttledge and Petrides, 2012; Squires and Caddick, 2012).

A number of specific cognitive theories are relevant to the question of intervening with difficult behaviour. Social information processing theory, for example, has been influential. Behaviour difficulties in the form of aggressive acts towards peers have been linked to '*hostile attribution of intent*'. De Castro et al. (2002) conducted a meta-analysis of forty-one studies with 6,017 participants and found a robust significant association between children's hostile attribution of intent towards peers and their aggressive behaviour. They summarise the well-accepted hypothesis that:

> Well-known risk factors for the development of aggressive behaviour problems, such as rejection by peers ... and harsh parenting ... predispose children to attribute hostile intent, particularly if their cognitive capacities to process these experiences are limited ... Hostile attributions of intent, in turn, are believed to cause aggressive behaviour, instigate more problematic social interactions, and thereby limit non-aggressive interactions that could provide opportunities to learn prosocial behaviours ... Thus, it is suggested that hostile attribution may be a key element in the development and persistence of behaviour problems over time.
>
> (p. 916)

This perspective can allow exploration at the individual level or inform classroom or group interventions. Cole et al. (2012) supply an example, in a cognitive behavioural (CB)-based intervention, to reduce anger-related difficulties, underpinned by insights around the hostile attributional biases of the young people. This study, as with others, noted the importance of aiming to *increase self-regulation* in children through CB-based work.

A role for developmental cognitive neuroscience, too, has been explored by Frederickson *et al.* (2013), who identified the positive effects of an intervention for children with significant social, emotional and behavioural needs. The intervention drew upon recent studies from cognitive neuroscience that explore the relationship between fMRI studies and behavioural traits. Various studies cited by the authors identify links between physiological development and *traits* such as callous–unemotional traits (Viding and Blair, 2005) or *behaviours* such as reactive aggression or emotional regulation (Sterzer and Stadler, 2009). Frederickson and colleagues found tentative evidence of change and positive response to the programme designed with the connections between these elements in mind, potentially illustrating a new paradigm needing further exploration in remediating difficult behaviour: conjoining developmental cognitive neuroscience with applied study of behaviour change.

PERSONAL CONSTRUCT PSYCHOLOGY

For many educational psychologists, the core of their professional role is informed by the repositioning of the student experience, to ensure that 'pupil voice' contributes to the formulations and interventions around them (Harding and Atkinson, 2009; Swinson, 2010), and this can be a very significant activity for children and young people experiencing difficult adjustment in school. Cognitive paradigms lend themselves to this work.

Investigations of cognition in individuals have, for many educational psychologists, been informed by Personal Construct Psychology (PCP) (Fransella, 2003). This influential theory, devised by George Kelly (Kelly, 1963), puts forward a theory of personal construing that, at its heart, is interested in the unique patterns of construing for each individual (Fransella, 2003; Bannister and Fransella, 2013). Kelly stressed the bonded nature of emotion to cognition, and it can, therefore, be helpful where a practitioner aims to understand the holistic worldview of an individual. The ideas from PCP have led to many psychologists promoting the theoretical framework as one that might support assessment work with young people experiencing difficulties in school and that might, therefore, inform interventions (e.g. Hardman, 2001). More detailed examples of the uses of PCP can be found in the work of Ravenette (1997), who developed creative techniques to elicit the narratives forming a young person's perspective that can help identify key *elements* of their world and, in turn, their bipolar constructs (Bannister and Fransella, 1986). Gaining insight into these allows for review and exploration of the construing systems of the young person, with a view to adaptation and mediation of these through their permeability to new information. Cognitive theories have shown how distortions of the available evidence – for example, attributions of hostile intent – are powerful and self-perpetuating, and PCP can assist through allowing expansion of information. PCP is distinctive within cognitive approaches in positioning itself primarily as a constructivist approach, with insights gained by a practitioner being those that are informed by the construing of the practitioner him- or herself (Fransella, 2005). Events are fundamentally interpreted and constructed by those who perceive them. Case Study 10.1 offers an example of individual practitioner work illustrating this, and its connections to supporting a case of challenging behaviour.

CASE STUDY 10.1 A YOUNG PERSON IN A PUPIL REFERRAL UNIT

Austin is 15 years and 6 months old and in Year 11. He has been permanently excluded from his mainstream school and now attends an 'alternative' educational provision, where he receives instruction on core subjects, English, maths and science, together with some technology programmes. He hopes to become a mechanic and to gain an apprenticeship in the future.

Although he attended well during Year 10, his attendance has become partial, and his mentor is concerned and confused as to why Austin is no longer attending. Whereas previously Austin's relationships with his peers were positive, it seems now that there are some sporadic difficulties and instances of challenging behaviour.

In discussion with Austin, an educational psychologist notes the following:

- He has been spending time at home with his older brother, who is not in employment.
- Austin's mother and brother both drink during the evenings, and Austin has begun to join them.
- Austin says that he does want to become a mechanic.

Austin talked to the educational psychologist about his wider family members and identified whom he most hoped to be like in a few years' time. Eliciting his 'constructions' relating to his family members and his school experiences brought the following bipolar constructs:

Lazy _____ A vision in life/has money
Drinks _____ Does sport
Unfit _____ Plays football

The educational psychologist used these bipolarities to explore where Austin would locate himself within these constructs. Austin saw the qualities on the right as his preferred poles. He discussed his aspiration for what might be, hypothetically, a good day in his life, next week and next year. He described the person he most wants to be like, and, on a scale of 1–10, rated his *desire* to reach those qualities himself, his *ability* to reach them and his next step towards this.

A week later, they met again, to review the work that was done in the first week. Austin said he did not know this much about himself before and explored ways of dealing with those peers he found threatening and frustrating, guided by his desire to reach his goals.

A week later, his mentor reports to the educational psychologist that Austin had begun attending again, and that Austin has been cooperating well with his instructors and his peers. A month later, and 3 months later, the news was still good, and Austin progressed through his end-of-year assessments successfully. Discussion identified that Austin was more 'centred'. He seemed more confident of himself, and was not thrown off course by the comments or jibes of his peers.

The key to this small-scale intervention was exploration of Austin's worldview, bringing his *core construing* to the fore and allowing him to become aware of aspects of this, to review it and to develop new behaviours.

Above all, behaviour is a form of social interaction, and cognitive approaches allow us to view *difficult behaviour* in ways that permit greater exploration of the meaning of that behaviour for the individuals involved. This notion, that any behaviour is a phenomenon that is subject to the perceptions and interpretations of others, leads us to consideration of an influential strand of research. A rich seam of investigation has been that which aims to understand the differing perspectives, and in particular the differing *attributions*, adopted regarding difficult behaviour in the classroom.

Studies of attribution and attributional style have focused upon the likely norms of particular groups involved. This has importance for the work of the educational psychologist in respect of trying to forge a way forward within difficult scenarios.

ATTRIBUTION THEORY

Attribution theory is concerned with how individuals invoke causes and explanations for various phenomena and the effects of these cognitions on their behaviour. Forsterling (2001) draws attention to the two subfields of research into the attribution of causation: attribution theories, which are concerned with the different *antecedent conditions* to *causal attributions*, and attributional theories, which focus upon the *psychological consequences* of such attributions. A key figure in the study of causal

The contribution of Bernard Weiner

Weiner's major contribution has been to relate attribution theory to school learning. Through a series of studies employing factor analytic methods, Weiner (1986, 2000) identified three dimensions along which most attributions for successes and failures were found to lie:

1   locus (whether the cause was internal or external to the person);
2   stability (whether the cause is fixed or can vary);
3   controllability (whether the person is able to control the cause).

So, for example, if a student (or a teacher or parent) attributed some success or failure to luck, this would be an external, unstable and uncontrollable cause. On the other hand, an attribution of effort could be categorised as internal, stable and controllable.

Weiner's framework has been enormously influential in areas other than educational psychology, including clinical, health and sports psychology (Graham and Folkes, 1990).

Weiner also investigated the relationship between causal attribution and help-giving, finding that teachers were more likely to feel sympathy towards a student and be willing to help that student learn appropriate ways of behaving if they attributed the misbehaviour to causes outside the student's control (Reyna and Weiner, 2001).

Summarising the contribution made by Weiner's research and other studies within the framework he developed, Woolfolk Hoy and Weinstein (2006) state that:

> When teachers assume that student failure is attributable to forces beyond the student's control, they tend to respond with sympathy and avoid giving punishments. If, however, the failures are attributed to a controllable factor, such as lack of effort, the teacher's response is more likely to be anger; retribution and punishments may follow.
>
> (p. 203)

attribution within educational contexts, both in terms of the nature of attributions in themselves and in their links to behaviour such as blaming and help-giving, has been Bernard Weiner (see Focus Box 10.1).

Causal attribution and challenging behaviour

Attribution theory has been applied to a variety of theoretical and practical problems (Hewstone, 1983). Within the educational literature, much work has focused on the relationship between a pupil's attributional style and academic attainment (Weiner, 1986). Weiner's studies make an understanding of causal attribution around challenging behaviour central to the search for effective interventions. Various research studies offer insight into the causal attributions made by teachers, students and parents for difficult behaviour in schools. The focus becomes a search to uncover obstacles, in the form of blaming, and interventions, and to identify ways forward where the parties involved may be attributing differently, and with some force.

Teachers' attributions for challenging behaviour

Studies have demonstrated that teachers tend to view parents and home circumstances as mostly to blame for difficult pupil behaviour in schools. Croll and Moses (1985) found that junior schoolteachers attribute misbehaviour in schools to parents in 66 per cent of cases. A later survey (Croll and Moses, 1999) obtained similar results, with teachers attributing 'emotional and behavioural difficulties' to home factors in 52 per cent of cases. The Elton Report (DfES,1989), cited above, concluded that parents and home factors were judged in schools to be the major causes of difficult behaviour.

A further study, by Miller (1995), found that teachers who had been able to successfully intervene with difficult behaviour, through the support of an educational psychologist, located the origins of pupils' difficulties in factors under the control of parents in 71 per cent of cases, thus fulfilling Weiner's preconditions for 'blame'. A similar finding also emerged from a study that again showed home factors to be judged the biggest contributory factor to classroom misbehaviour (Miller and Black, 2001). Some evidence suggests, however, that these more global patterns can become watered down when dealing with specific instances, where, in relation to a particular child and their parent, less blame is found (Brank et al., 2006).

Students' attributions for challenging behaviour

The common finding that teachers attribute the responsibility for challenging behaviour in schools primarily to home and parent factors is in contrast to the causal attributions made by students for the challenging behaviour of their peers. Miller et al. (2000) examined students' attributions and found four factors reflecting 'fairness of teacher's actions', 'pupil vulnerability', 'adverse family circumstances' and 'strictness of classroom regime'. The first two of these factors were also seen as more significant contributors to pupil misbehaviour. In an almost comical reversal, Kelsey et al. (2004) investigated students' explanations for when college teachers misbehave and found that these students applied an interpretive framework in which they view the teacher, not external factors or they the students themselves, as the primary cause of teacher misbehaviours.

A study by Tony (2003) of 384 Hong Kong students in the junior forms of secondary schools demonstrated the link between causal attributions and actual behaviour with the finding that an external orientation of locus of control and a passive pattern of attribution remained significant predictors of discipline problems when other factors were held constant. This contrasts somewhat with the finding from Elliott's study (1996) that there was very little relationship between behaviour and locus of control in 237 children specifically judged to have emotional and behavioural difficulties. Lambert and Miller (2010) investigated the temporal stability and predictive validity of pupil causal attributions in secondary schools, finding that there was temporal stability for a factor they termed 'culture of misbehaviour', representing the 'excitement, power, and peer recognition misbehaviour can bring in the classroom' (p. 609), for pupils between Years 7 and 10. In contrast to the earlier evidence, they also made the interesting finding that this factor correlated positively with better behaviour by pupils, as rated by their teachers. This may be of significance in informing whole-school interventions by psychologists aiming to support the promotion of positive behaviour across school.

In summary, students' attributions for challenging behaviour in schools can tend towards a focus on causes external to themselves, such as teachers' unfairness and pupils' hostile intent, or to aspects of the perpetrator's vulnerability (an internal attribution, but one beyond the actor's control). In addition, causal attributions that are external and beyond the control of the actor are significant predictors of discipline problems. A particular form of these, the attribution of hostile intent towards peers, is found to be strongly associated with aggressive behaviour, as noted above.

Parents' attributions for challenging behaviour

Generally, and not specifically in relation to behaviour within school, Johnston et al. (1992) cite research linking parents' attributions for children's behaviour to their affective and behavioural responses to that behaviour (e.g. Dix et al., 1989). Dix and colleagues found that the misbehaviour of older children was more likely to be attributed by mothers to personality factors and seen as intentional than was that of younger children. In addition, if the child was judged to be responsible for (or in control of) the behaviour, then parents were much more likely to choose 'power-assertive' methods of discipline. Cornah (2000) used a vignette and questionnaire study with mothers of children around 9 years of age to look explicitly at attributions made towards their own, and other people's, children. When mothers were explaining their own child's difficult-to-manage behaviour, they reported this as being caused by factors that were less stable and less global than when they explained similar behaviours in other children. Cornah argues that this may be an extension of the self-serving attributional bias by mothers into what she terms a 'child-serving bias'.

Turning to studies of behaviour specifically within a school context, Phares et al. (1996) investigated the perceptions of parents of the development and treatment of pupils considered to have behavioural difficulties. Parents were shown one of four vignettes and were asked to rate the responsibility the mother, father, child and teacher had for the development of the child's problem, and the responsibility to intervene. Overall, parents and children were viewed as more responsible for the development and treatment of problems than were teachers. However, for younger children, parents and teachers were seen as more responsible.

Snyder et al. (2005) reported a longitudinal study of 268 children and their families during kindergarten and first grade. In this, parent discipline practices were ascertained from 4 hours of coding of parent–child interactions, whereas maternal attributions about child behaviour were assessed by means of a structured interview. This study found that ineffective maternal discipline and the interaction of ineffective discipline and hostile attribution predicted growth in child·conduct problems at home during kindergarten and first grade. Of particular interest, changes in teacher-reported and observed child conduct problems at school during this period were predicted by growth in conduct problems at home and by the interaction of ineffective discipline and hostile attribution.

Miller *et al.* (2002) examined the factor structure of parents' attributions for challenging behaviour in schools. Factor analysis of a questionnaire with the same items as in a students' questionnaire (Miller *et al.*, 2000) indicated that parents' attributions for misbehaviour were best represented by three factors – *fairness of teacher's actions*, *pupil vulnerability* to peer influences and adverse family circumstances, and *differentiation of classroom demands and expectations*, the first two factors being seen as more significant contributors to pupil misbehaviour than the third.

In summary, in studies examining group trends, parents (usually mothers in the reported studies) appear to make different attributions for their own and for other people's children (at least at around 9 years of age). Parents tend to see the causes of their own children's misbehaviour as less stable (not occurring at all times) and less global (not appearing in a wide variety of contexts) than that of others' children. In the latter instance, parents attribute misbehaviour of older children as due to personality factors and judge it to be intentional in nature. The difficult behaviour of younger children (other people's) at school is seen as being caused by both teachers and parents, but teachers are not judged to contribute for older children.

Generalisability of attributional patterns

These studies must be interpreted carefully in the light of research that demonstrates the likely influences of various cultural and social processes and unique influences upon each situation in question. For example, Ho (2004), examining the causal attributions for student behaviour, found that Chinese teachers emphasised family factors, whereas Australian teachers placed greater importance on ability. Ho interpreted these findings in cultural terms, attributing these differences to individualistic and collectivist values likely to be influencing the two different groups. Potential cultural influences may also be found in Poulou and Norwich's study (2000), in which Greek elementary teachers perceived school and teacher factors as causal of students' emotional and behavioural difficulties, in contrast with UK data.

Another study suggests that seemingly very minor alignments in terms of group membership can still exert an influence. Guimond *et al.* (1989) studied university students in the final year of a social sciences degree and found them to attribute more importance to situational factors and less to dispositional factors than did social science students at earlier levels of education and students in other areas at all levels, providing results consistent with a micro-cultural interpretation of attributional diversity. Gender too has been shown to exert subtle influences, in a study examining the attributions, emotions and attribution–emotion associations of a large group of primarily middle-class, European American college students (MacGeorge, 2004).

Finally, there is some evidence to suggest that the general patterning of attributional norms identified in previous research may not be at work with the same potency when parties are making judgements about particular, *individual* cases. A vignette-based study of parent, teacher and pupil responses to a hypothetical scenario where a teacher was assaulted by a pupil found differential patterns, according to the specific features of the situation: namely, whether the teacher had undertaken a physical intervention with the pupil prior to the event. The findings here included that of greater concordance between parents and teachers in their judgements than in other studies, suggesting that situation–specific features, that is, events that precede judgements, may influence the more global patterns of attribution that have been identified elsewhere in the literature (Lawrence *et al.*, 2010).

So, although attributional research identifies general areas of agreement between the parties, and some persisting clashes that are likely to exacerbate tensions and difficult relationships, it is important to be aware of the possibilities of individual variance. The practising educational psychologist will be alert to the attributions that various parties are *likely* to be making (*attributional styles*) and will work to avoid the mutual blaming and scapegoating this risks. They will, however, remain aware that subtle factors of identity and culture will have a bearing, as do individual cognitions regarding features of the situation, leading to potential variations in *situation-specific attributions*.

CASE STUDY 10.2

Attributions in school: spotting the patterns

Isaac, aged 10 years and in Year 5 of his primary school, was drawn to the attention of the school's educational psychologist. He was reportedly showing behaviours that were difficult for his teacher to manage. He might call out, hit other children with no provocation or refuse to undertake his set work. He might interrupt the class teacher when she spoke to the rest of the class, or remove the work other children were doing. Gradually, he seemed to show increasingly high levels of aggression to his peers.

The school's headteacher felt he was an able pupil, and that the school should be able to 'reach' him. The headteacher did feel, however, that Isaac's mother seemed to undermine everything that his staff tried to do for Isaac. When he was in trouble and receiving sanctions for difficult behaviour, she seemed intent on finding another child to blame or challenging the class teacher's sense of fairness when she found that it was her child, not others, who was repeatedly in trouble.

Isaac's class teacher was increasingly frustrated by his effect upon her class and her ability to teach. She felt some relief on the days he was absent. Having spoken with his mother, she began to form the view that Isaac was lying to his mother about what took place in school, and that his mother was not able to control him at home or back the school up. She felt Isaac was indulged, that he was not emotionally needy, but simply not bothering to turn his behaviour around. In short, she felt unable to teach and was exasperated.

Isaac's mother was very troubled by the way in which the school seemed to pick on her son and to single him out for fixed-term exclusions, when incidents involving him also involved other children. She wanted her only son to do well in school and to achieve professional standing in life. Her experience was that the school system was weighted against certain children, and boys in particular.

- What are some of the attributions being made by the different parties in the above example?
- What lines of action should the educational psychologist consider taking in order to move this scenario forward?

USING ATTRIBUTION THEORY IN CASES OF CHALLENGING BEHAVIOUR

Attribution retraining

Attribution retraining, as the name implies, involves strategies that aim to help an individual make different types of causal attribution for their own behaviour, usually away from external and uncontrollable ones. Working with children or young people, this might include focus upon the individual's attribution of the hostile intent of others or the unfairness of teachers – and towards some element of internal and controllable causation. Cognitive approaches explored above, such as CBT or PCP, can hold the key to this with a young person, focusing upon the attributions they make regarding peers or teachers (Ruttledge and Petrides, 2012). Attribution retraining may also take place in work with adults, although Wiley *et al.* (2012) note that this may be a difficult enterprise with teaching staff, where long-term sociocultural influences are in play (Wiley and Siperstein, 2011). Nevertheless, they highlight the need for attributional work, if larger-scale, whole-school policies are to have buy-in from staff groups. They note that, whereas many parenting programmes include an element of attributional retraining on a more systematic basis over time, the work of educational psychologists has not tended to focus on this domain with staff (Wiley *et al.*, 2012). More common has been the piecemeal tackling of such attributional patterns through consultative practice.

Ecosystemic consultation

When the causal attributions of those involved lead to blaming, another form of causation can come into play – that of perpetuating 'the problem', whatever its original causes. Various consultative models aimed at the reconciliation of these diverse perspectives of home and school can be found in the literature. Conjoint consultation (Sheridan and Bovaird, 2012), ecobehavioural consultation (Gutkin, 1993), joint systems consultation (Dowling and Osborne, 1994) or ecosystemic consultation (Miller, 2003) are versions of collaborative consultation typically involving the relevant adults from the home and school environments. In the UK, the work of Elsie Osborne has been influential in showing the elements needed for a consultative review of the various perspectives upon a problem (Dowling and Osborne, 2002). Opening and exploring perspectives lead to resolution. It has been argued that the applied skills of the educational psychologist are needed to lead this collaborative exploration, Miller's study (2003) identifying the interpersonal skills displayed by psychologists (see Focus Box 10.2) that can enable a shift in unhelpful attributions on the part of teachers and parents.

FOCUS 10.2

TABLE 10.2 Examples provided by teachers of skills displayed by educational psychologists during ecosystemic consultation

Skill displayed by educational psychologist	Example
Providing a model of emotional self-regulation	'She seemed calm and always positive . . . she would never get cross'
Problem analysis	'The most valuable thing for us is for somebody to listen to our problems, like talking it through and trying to help us see one thing at a time'
Focused questioning	'I think the way she questioned me . . . I think I almost discovered something of what I was doing myself, and probably I didn't even know I was doing it'
Displaying sensitivity to role boundaries	'I don't think she was trying to teach me my job or whatever'
Helping to reframe causal attributions	'[Mother] had caused so many problems here. She's a very bristly lady, very much on the ball, but in her own way she really did care for Barry. Maybe not the way that you and I would care for our children but she did . . . she really was a caring mum'
Reattribution with respect to locus of attribution	'He helped us see that it wasn't all in the home, that there were things we were doing in school that weren't helping as well'
Reattribution with respect to stability of attribution	'One thing that stood out in my mind was when I said, "we just can't communicate with this boy", and she said, "well, maybe you haven't found a way yet"'
Reattribution with respect to controllability of attribution	'We had been feeling helpless really, but she helped us feel that there were things we were able to put in place that would move things forward'

Source: Adapted from Miller, 2003

The small sample of skills illustrated here contribute crucially to the formation and maintenance of a working alliance in which attributions of blame can gradually be replaced by respect for the positive contributions that each party is able to make in these most contentious and emotionally demanding of circumstances. It is worth noting that such work remains part of the wider ecosystem of the school, influenced by the organisation's culture in relation to the management of behaviour difficulties. A study of the relationship of teacher self-efficacy to their sense of responsibility for intervening with behaviour (Gibbs and Powell, 2012) reflected on the apparent influence of teachers' *collective self-efficacy* to intervene with factors deemed by them to be external influences upon pupil behaviour. Their finding, that this collective self-efficacy, alone in their study, may negatively correlate with rates of pupil exclusion from school, is grounds for their commentary that it is important to promote whole-school approaches to interventions for behaviour, and to see individually focused work as part of a wider staff ecology in attributions towards managing behaviour.

PSYCHODYNAMIC INFLUENCES IN MANAGING BEHAVIOUR SCHOOLS

Providing a counterbalance to the perspectives upon difficult behaviour thus far reviewed, psychodynamic, humanistic and person–centred approaches as explanations for behaviour focus upon the internal life of the individual and give rise to consideration of mental health and well-being. In this century, schools have increasingly become viewed as sites where well-being is the flip side of the coin regarding questions of difficult behaviour, and they are seen as holding a responsibility for ensuring the positive well-being of pupils (Rait *et al.*, 2010; Banerjee *et al.*, 2014). Positive mental health is now viewed as a precondition for positive behavioural engagement (Wolpert *et al.*, 2013). From a survey exploring provision to promote the well-being of pupils in school, there is evidence, however, that the nature of such programmes is variable, nationally, and that the focus upon *preventive* programmes may be underdeveloped (Vostanis *et al.*, 2013).

ATTACHMENT THEORY

Attachment theory (Bowlby, 1969), originally seen as the preserve of clinicians, is one example of an approach rooted in psychodynamic perspectives that has played a role in offering explanations of behaviour in school in recent times. Positing the importance of the early attachment process between caregiver (mother) and child, attachment theory proposes that this early relationship supports the development of a notional 'internal working model' as a function of that early relating, through which our social and emotional experience of the world can be processed and responded to (Geddes, 2006). The patterning of those early relationships and subsequent experiences, particularly in early childhood development, is seen as contributing to the development of an attachment pattern that is either *secure* or *insecure*, with some key manifestations of this latter category (although others have been developed or identified by theorists): *anxious, avoidant, ambivalent* or even *disorganised* patterns are considered to be found where the adult care-giving is not able to generate responses in either a sufficiently consistent or appropriate manner to allow the infant or child to develop appropriate confidence in that relating pattern from which to explore the world. A wide research literature underpins the way in which early attachment patterns can be identified (Ainsworth *et al.*, 1978), how they may develop (Crittenden and Dallos, 2009), with what influences (Coleman, 2003) and their implications for later life (Fonagy, 2003).

Various psychologists have explored the contribution of attachment theory to pupil and school functioning (Geddes, 2006; Bergin and Bergin, 2009; Boom *et al.*, 2010; Verschueren and Koomen, 2012). The theory has held two key lines of influence in explanations of school behaviour. First, a student's early experience of attachment processes and their current familial relationship patterns can be considered to influence a young person's relating to adults and peers in school and, therefore, potentially constitute an influence upon their behavioural responses. Second, the concept of attachment can be translated into the school environment and argued to be a developmental need for all children, highlighting the responsibility of teaching staff to provide positive and secure relationships that, although primarily informed by the instructional nature of the environment, reflect a student's need for strong positive relationships in school (Boorn et al., 2010). This latter aspect propels us towards consideration of how relationships are built within school and to potentially micro-analyse teacher–pupil dynamics and how these may, or may not, build a pupil's positive sense of the relationships with adults in school (Swinson, 2010; Spilt et al., 2011).

Swinson and Knight (2007) illustrated the effects of positive verbal teacher feedback, even for those pupils showing more significantly difficult behaviour. Pupils themselves report the significance of positive adult relationships in school for them, and this can contribute to a pupil's sense of engagement and correlate with achievement (Roorda and Koomen, 2011). It is interesting to consider this phenomenon in terms of 'teacher contact', as is done by Korthagen and colleagues (Korthagen, 2014), where small verbal contacts through the school day are seen as distinct from teacher–pupil relationships. Such contacts, however, form the substrate for the relationships referred to in the literature, and they also represent the type of contact often described in the ABA literature – brief contacts, issuing of instructions, verbal guidance – which together constitutes the moulding of behaviour. Clunies-Ross et al. (2008) put forward the double value of preventive approaches to classroom management in promoting both positive behaviour and relationships. In contrast, reactive approaches contain stress risks for the adult and certainly, for pupils, represent a less effective approach to shaping behaviour and, once again, relationships. Attachment to school has become an area of theoretical interest too (Cooper, 2008), with evidence that a pupil's more general sense of relating to school, known as school belonging (Hazel et al., 2013) can help to promote positive engagement (Hirschfield and Gasper, 2011).

The contribution of attachment is most marked, arguably, in the literature underpinning nurture groups, small-group, school-based provisions, located within mainstream schools, for children whose behaviour is significantly challenging, where it is hypothesised that attachment-based provision can support and remediate the development of the insecurely attached child (Bennathan and Boxall, 2000; Boxall, 2002). Such groups, ideally, are staffed by a trained teacher, with teaching assistant support, and work in a restorative way, aiming to support the well-being and functioning of vulnerable young people, through offering a flexible, warm climate for their learning, where adults respond according to the developmental level of the child, and where the creation of positive, calm relationships is a focus.

Attachment theory has been amplified and differentiated to a very considerable extent over recent decades (Cassidy and Shaver, 2008) and has, therefore, been able to bring increasingly fine-tuned understanding to a range of topics in human relating, including those of disrupted, difficult or lost attachments. Despite attachment theorising perhaps risking deterministic views of a child's functioning ('Freddie has an attachment disorder' might, in a hasty context, be taken to be information that is used incautiously, or without the fuller insights of how attachments are mediated and influenced), its potential contribution to understanding difficult behaviour in schools is very significant.

Psychodynamic insights, such as attachment-based theories, together with developmental psychology, have highlighted the importance of understanding typical development of children when aiming to support those with challenging behaviour or aiming to supply positive and nurturing school environments. The internal life of the individual is no longer seen as an adjunct to behaviour, but as integrally bound up with it. Thus, the development of prosocial skills, of emotion regulation and problem-solving, and of empathy, for example, are all areas understood to be significant in the psychosocial functioning of the child, and their promotion is seen as constituting a 'preventive' approach to behaviour difficulties in schools (Durlak and Weissberg, 2011), and, according to some evidence, as having the additional benefit of enhancing academic achievements. Durlak and Weissberg (2011) note the comprehensive evidence for such programmes, in various configurations. In the UK, a policy initiative known as SEAL (the social and emotional aspects of learning), initiated during the past decade, aimed to promote these features in children as individuals, in groups, in classrooms and at a whole-school level. Although evaluations indicate that only an early stage of progress in promoting ambitious outcomes was reached (Humphrey, 2013), there is nevertheless strong evidence for the positive effects of interventions at various levels, including multicomponent interventions, allowing for a whole-school focus, as well as class and group.

CONCLUSIONS

We have reviewed the various guises in which psychology offers a theoretical and applied contribution to understanding difficult behaviour in schools. The field contains a vast literature, and the overview here is necessarily cut to scale. It has not been possible to explore in depth the influences of the systems approaches or systemic theories on behaviour difficulties and change that interest many educational psychologists, nor review in detail the *methods* and *means* by which educational psychology aims to bring about change in schools, such as consultation. That, in summary, is another story: that of the process of supporting behaviour change among adults in school and the community. Here, we have primarily reviewed the contribution of behavioural approaches, the influences of cognitive theories upon psychological practice, particularly the area of attribution theory, and of one set of psychodynamic insights upon practice. As we have seen, there are multiple possible influences that can be brought to bear to explore and intervene with difficult classroom behaviour. The domain is one where theoretical psychology has prospered, creating many conduits to successful interventions: evidence-based practice.

SUMMARY OF MAIN ISSUES ADDRESSED IN THIS CHAPTER

- There are three main types of ABA strategy – differential reinforcement of alternative response, differential reinforcement of the omission of a response and differential reinforcement of lower rates of responding. LaVigna (2000) concluded that differential reinforcement of the omission of a response is generally the most effective for classroom settings, but needed to be accompanied by a programme that directly taught positive behaviours.

- A spectrum of possible classroom reinforcers has been posited, and strategies should always aim towards children being able to find classroom and school experiences intrinsically motivating.
- Studies have demonstrated that aspects of young children's classroom behaviour can be influenced by teachers employing a carefully developed system that combines the use of praise, ignoring and clear statements of classroom rules.
- Sanctions and punishments have become widely associated in the public mind with ABA, although they are problematic when trying to achieve behaviour change.
- Practice in ABA has seen an evolution from a focus upon 'on-task' behaviour encouraged by changed consequences to a concern with more socially and academically useful behaviour and a greater focus on environmental antecedents, and on positive behaviour supports.
- Functional behaviour assessment (FBA) has utility in the reviewing and supporting of individual cases of difficult behaviour in schools.
- Cognitive approaches have been found to play a helpful role in supporting individual change in school and in group-based interventions to support social and behavioural development in children.
- Personal construct psychology has also played a role, as a cognitive approach, in helping practitioners gain insight into the cognitions of those involved in situations of difficult behaviour.
- Attribution theories are concerned with the antecedent conditions to causal attributions, and attributional theories focus upon psychological consequences of these.
- Three dimensions along which causal attributions can be located are important: locus, stability and controllability. Teachers appear more willing to help students whose misbehaviour they attribute as beyond the student's control.
- Factor analytic studies have demonstrated that teachers, students and parents may make different causal attributions for the causes of difficult behaviour in schools. Students appear to conflict with teachers by attributing difficult behaviour to teacher unfairness, with which parents concur. Teachers and students, however, are in agreement that, 'pupil vulnerability' is a major cause. Teachers and parents, meanwhile, both identify 'adverse home circumstances' as a major cause, whereas students do not.
- A robust significant association between children's 'hostile attribution of intent' towards peers and their aggressive behaviour has been demonstrated, implicating the process of attribution further in this additional form of challenging behaviour in schools.
- Ecosystemic consultation is a method adopted by some educational psychologists, involving joint working with the young person and also his or her teacher(s) and parent(s). Research attests to positive outcomes from this form of consultation.

- Psychodynamic approaches and other theories supporting provision for the well-being of all pupils in school have been influential recently.

SAMPLE ESSAY TITLES

1 What are the possible advantages of using applied behaviour analysis in educational settings?
2 Applied behaviour analysis is, in essence, an elaborate system of 'carrots and sticks'. Discuss.
3 How might educational psychologists use attribution theory to help them in their work around challenging behaviour in schools?
4 How can a range of psychological theories support the work of an educational psychologist in schools?

KEY CONCEPTS AND TERMS

- Applied behavioural analysis
- Classroom management
- Social reinforcement
- Rules, praise and ignoring

- Antecedents
- Consequences
- Differential reinforcement
- Reinforcers
- Cognitive behavioural approaches

- Causal attributions
- Attachment theory
- Preventive reactive approaches
- Ecological systems theories

RECOMMENDATIONS FOR FURTHER READING

Journal articles

Crittenden, P.M. and Dallos, R. (2009). All in the family: Integrating attachment and family systems theories. *Clinical Child Psychology and Psychiatry*, *14*(3), 389–409.

Gable, R.A., Hester, P.H., Rock, M.L. and Hughes, K.G. (2009). Back to basics: Rules, praise, ignoring, and reprimands revisited. *Intervention in School and Clinic*, *44*(4), 195–205.

Greig, A. (2007). A framework for the delivery of cognitive behaviour therapy in the educational psychology context. *Educational and Child Psychology*, *24*(1), 19–35.

Henderling, J. and Lepper, M.R. (2002). The effects of praise on children's intrinsic motivation: A review and synthesis. *Psychological Bulletin*, *128*(5), 774–95.

Marchant, M., Heath, M.A. and Miramontes, N.Y. (2012). Merging empiricism and humanism: Role of social validity in the school-wide positive behavior support model. *Journal of Positive Behavior Interventions*, *15*(4), 221–30.

Miller, A., Ferguson, E. and Moore, E. (2002). Parents' and pupils' causal attributions for difficult classroom behaviour. *British Journal of Educational Psychology, 72*, 27–40.

Rait, S., Monsen, J.J. and Squires, G. (2010). Cognitive behaviour therapies and their implications for applied educational psychology practice. *Educational Psychology in Practice, 26*, 105–22.

Snyder, J., Cramer, A., Afrank, J. and Patterson, G.R. (2005). The contributions of ineffective discipline and parental hostile attributions of child misbehaviour to the development of conduct problems at home and school. *Developmental Psychology, 41*(1), 30–41.

Spilt, J., Koomen, H. and Thijs, J. (2011). Teacher wellbeing: The importance of teacher–student relationships. *Educational Psychology Review, 23*, 457–77.

Weiner, B. (2000). Interpersonal and intrapersonal theories of motivational form an attributional perspective. *Educational Psychology Review, 12*, 1–14.

Books and book chapters

Brophy, J. (2006). History of research on classroom management. In C.M. Evertson and C.S. Weinstein (eds), *Handbook of Classroom Management*. London: Lawrence Erlbaum.

Landrum, T.L. and Kauffman, J.M. (2006). Behavioural approaches to classroom management. In C.M. Evertson and C.S. Weinstein (eds), *Handbook of Classroom Management*. London: Lawrence Erlbaum.

Miller, A. (2003). *Teachers, Parents and Classroom Behaviour: A psychosocial approach*. Maidenhead, UK: Open University Press.

Wiley, A., Tankersley, M. and Simms, A. (2012). Teachers' causal attributions for student problem behavior: Implications for school-based behavioral interventions and research. In B.G. Cook, M. Tankersley and T.J. Landrum (eds), *Classroom Behavior, Contexts, and Interventions (Advances in Learning and Behavioral Disabilities, Vol 25)*. Bingley, UK: Emerald, pp. 279–300.

Woolfolk Hoy, A. and Weinstein, C.S. (2006). Student and teacher perspectives on classroom management. In C.M. Evertson and C.S. Weinstein (eds), *Handbook of Classroom Management: Research, practice and contemporary issues*. London: Lawrence Erlbaum.

REFERENCES

Ainsworth, M.D., Blehar, M., Waters, E. and Wall, S. (1978). *Patterns of Attachment: A Psychological study of the strange situation*. Hillsdale, NJ: Lawrence Erlbaum.

Allday, R.A., Nelson, J.R. and Russel, C.S. (2011). Classroom-based functional behavioral assessment: Does the literature support high fidelity implementation? *Journal of Disability Policy Studies, 22*(3), 140–9.

Apter, B., Arnold, C. and Swinson, J. (2010). A mass observation study of student and teacher behaviour in British primary classrooms. *Educational Psychology in Practice, 26*(2), 151–71.

Banerjee, R., Weare, K. and Farr, W. (2014). Working with 'Social and Emotional Aspects of Learning' (SEAL): Associations with school ethos, pupil social experiences, attendance, and attainment. *British Educational Research Journal, 40*(4), 718–42.

Bannister, D. and Fransella, F. (1986). *Inquiring Man: Theory of personal constructs*. London: Croom Helm.

Bannister, D. and Fransella, F. (2013). *Inquiring Man: Theory of personal constructs*. London: Routledge.

Bennathan, M. and Boxall, M. (2000). *Effective Intervention in Primary Schools: Nurture groups*. London: Routledge.

Bergin, C. and Bergin, D. (2009). Attachment in the classroom. *Educational Psychology Review*, *21*(2), 141–70.

Boorn, C., Hopkins Dunn, P. and Page, C. (2010). Growing a nurturing classroom. *Emotional and Behavioural Difficulties*, *15*(4), 311–21.

Bowlby, J. (1969). *Attachment and Loss, Volume I: Attachment*. New York. Basic Books.

Boxall, M. (2002). *Nurture Groups in School: Principles and practice*. London: SAGE.

Brank, E., Hays, S. and Weisz, V. (2006). All parents are to blame (except this one): Global versus specific attitudes related to parental responsibility laws. *Journal of Applied Social Psychology*, *36*(11), 2670–84.

Bronfenbrenner, U. and Morris, P.A. (2006). The bio-ecological model of human development. In R.M. Learner and W. Damon (eds), *Handbook of Child Psychology (6th edn): Vol 1, Theoretical Models of Human Development*. Hoboken, NJ: John Wiley, pp. 793–828.

Brophy, J. (2006). History of research on classroom management. In C.M. Evertson and C.S. Weinstein (eds), *Handbook of Classroom Management*. London: Lawrence Erlbaum.

Burland, R. (1979). Social skills as the basis for coping strategies in school. *Proceedings of the 1979 DECP Annual Course*. British Psychological Society.

Canter, L. and Canter, M. (1976). *Assertive Discipline: A take-charge approach for today's educator*. Seal Beach, CA: Lee Canter.

Canter, L. and Canter, M. (1992). *Lee Canter's Assertive Discipline: Positive behaviour management for today's classroom*. Santa Monica, CA: Canter.

Cassidy, J. and Shaver, P.R. (2008). *Handbook of Attachment: Theory, research, and clinical applications* (2nd edn). New York: Guilford.

Chalk, K. and Bizo, L. (2004). Specific praise improves on-task behaviour and numeracy enjoyment: A study of year four pupils engaged in the numeracy hour. *Educational Psychology in Practice*. *20*(4), 335–51.

Chisholm, B., Kearney, D., Knight, G., Little, H., Morris, B. and Tweddle, D. (1986). *Preventive Approaches to Disruption: Developing teaching skills*. Basingstoke. Macmillan Education.

Clunies-Ross, P., Little, E. and Kienhuis, M. (2008). Self-reported and actual use of proactive and reactive classroom management strategies and their relationship with teacher stress and student behaviour. *Educational Psychology*, *28*(6), 693–710.

Cole, R.L., Treadwell, S., Dosani, S. and Frederickson, N. (2012). Evaluation of a short-term, cognitive-behavioral intervention for primary age children with anger-related difficulties. *School Psychology International*, *34*(1), 82–100.

Coleman, P.K. (2003). Perceptions of parent–child attachment, social self-efficacy, and peer relationships in middle childhood. *Infant and Child Development*, *12*, 351–68.

Cooper, P. (2008). Nurturing attachment to school: Contemporary perspectives on social, emotional and behavioural difficulties. *Pastoral Care in Education, 26*(1), 13–22.

Cornah, D. (2000). Explaining children's behaviour. *Special Children*, 38–9.

Crittenden, P.M. and Dallos, R. (2009). All in the family: Integrating attachment and family systems theories. *Clinical Child Psychology and Psychiatry, 14*(3), 389–409.

Croll, P. and Moses, D. (1985). *One in Five*. London. Routledge and Kegan Paul.

Croll, P. and Moses, D. (1999). *Special Needs in the Primary School: One in five?* London. Continuum.

De Castro, B.O., Veerman, J.W., Koops, W., Bosch, J.D. and Monshouwer, H.J. (2002). Hostile attribution of intent and aggressive behavior: A meta-analysis. *Child Development, 73*(3), 916–34.

Deci, E.L., Koestner, R. and Ryan, R.M. (2001). Extrinsic rewards and intrinsic motivation in education: Reconsidered once again. *Review of Educational Research, 71*(1), 1–27.

Department for Education (2011). Getting the simple things right: Charlie Taylor's behaviour checklists. www.education.gov.uk (accessed 20 February 2014).

Department for Education (2012). A profile of pupil exclusions in England. Education Standards and Research Divison. www.education.gov.uk (accessed 20 February 2014).

Department for Education and Employment (DfEE) (1999). *Social Inclusion: Pupil support* (Circular 10/99). London: DfEE.

Department for Education and Employment (DfEE) (2000). *Home–School Agreements. Guidance for schools*. London: DfEE.

Department for Education and Science (DfES) (2001). *Code of Practice on the Identification and Assessment of Children with Special Educational Needs*. London: DfES.

Department for Education and Science (DfES) (2007). *School Discipline and Pupil-behaviour Policies: Guidance for schools*. London: DfES.

Department for Education and Science (DfES) (1989). *Discipline in Schools (The Elton Report)*. London: HMSO.

Dix, T., Ruble, D.N. and Zambarabno, R.J. (1989). Mothers' implicit theories of discipline: Child effects, parent effects and the attribution process. *Child Development, 60*, 1373–91.

Dowling, E. and Osborne, E. (1994). *The Family and the School: A joint systems approach to problems with children* (2nd edn). London: Taylor & Francis.

Dowling, E. and Osborne, E. (2002). *The Family and the School: A joint systems approach to problems with children*. London: Taylor & Francis.

Dunlap, G., Kincaid, D., Horner, R.H., Knoster, T. and Bradshaw, C.P. (2014). A comment on the term 'positive behavior support'. *Journal of Positive Behavior Interventions, 16*(3), 133–6.

Durlak, J. and Weissberg, R. (2011). The impact of enhancing students' social and emotional learning: A meta-analysis of school-based universal interventions. *Child Development, 82*(1), 405–32.

Eccles, C. and Pitchford, M. (1997). A functional approach to behaviour problems. *Educational Psychology in Practice, 13*(2), 115–21.

Elliott, J. (1996). Locus of control in behaviourally disordered children. *British Journal of Educational Psychology, 66*(1), 47–57.

Fonagy, P. (2003). The development of psychopathology from infancy to adulthood: The mysterious unfolding of disturbance in time. *Infant Mental Health Journal, 24*(3), 212–39.

Forsterling, F. (2001). *Attribution: An introduction to theories, research and applications.* Hove, UK: Psychology Press.

Fransella, F. (ed.) (2003). *International Handbook of Personal Construct Psychology.* Chichester, UK: Wiley.

Fransella, F. (2005). *The Essential Practitioner's Handbook of Personal Construct Psychology.* Chichester, UK: Wiley.

Frederickson, N., Jones, A.P., Warren, L., Deakes, T. and Allen, G. (2013). Can developmental cognitive neuroscience inform intervention for social, emotional and behavioural difficulties (SEBD)? *Emotional and Behavioural Difficulties, 18*(2), 135–54.

Fuggle, P., Dunsmuir, S. and Curry, V. (2013). *CBT With Children, Young People and Families.* London: SAGE.

Gable, R.A., Hester, P.H., Rock, M.L. and Hughes, K.G. (2009). Back to basics: Rules, praise, ignoring, and reprimands revisited. *Intervention in School and Clinic, 44*(4), 195–205.

Galvin, P., Mercer, S. and Costa, P. (1990). *Building a Better Behaved School.* Harlow, UK: Longman.

Geddes, H. (2006). *Attachment in the Classroom.* London: Worth.

Gibbs, S. and Powell, B. (2012). Teacher efficacy and pupil behaviour: The structure of teachers' individual and collective beliefs and their relationship with numbers of pupils excluded from school. *The British Journal of Educational Psychology, 82*(4), 564–84.

Goodwin, D.W. and Coates, T.J. (1976). *Helping Students Help Themselves. How you can put behaviour analysis into action in your classroom.* Englewood Cliffs, NJ: Prentice-Hall.

Graham, S. and Folkes, V.S. (1990). *Attribution Theory. Applications to achievement, mental health and interpersonal conflict.* Mahwah, NJ: Lawrence Erlbaum.

Greig, A. (2007). A framework for the delivery of cognitive behaviour therapy in the educational psychology context. *Educational and Child Psychology, 24*(1), 19–35.

Guimond, S., Begin, G. and Palmer, D.L. (1989). Education and causal attributions: The development of 'person-blame' and 'system-blame' ideology. *Social Psychology Quarterly, 52*(2), 126–40.

Gutkin, T.B. (1993). Moving from behavioral to ecobehavioral consultation: What's in a name? *Journal of Educational and Psychological Consultation, 4*, 95–9.

Halonen, A., Aunola, K., Ahonen, T. and Nurmi, J.-E. (2006). The role of learning to read in the development of problem behaviour: A cross-lagged longitudinal study. *The British Journal of Educational Psychology, 76*(3), 517–34.

Harding, E. and Atkinson, C. (2009). How EPs record the voice of the child. *Educational Psychology in Practice, 25*(2), 125–37.

Hardman, C. (2001). Using personal construct psychology to reduce the risk of exclusion. *Educational Psychology in Practice, 17*(1), 41–51.

Harrop, A. and Swinson, J. (2007). The behavioural approach in schools: A time for caution revisited. *Educational Studies, 33*(1), 41–52.

Harrop, L.A. and McNamara, E. (1979). The behavioural workshop for classroom problems. A re-appraisal. *British Journal of In-Service Education, 1*(1), 47–50.

Hart, R. (2010). Classroom behaviour management: Educational psychologists' views on effective practice. *Emotional and Behavioural Difficulties, 15*(4), 353–71.

Hastings, N. and Wood, K.C. (2002). *Reorganizing Primary Classroom Learning.* Maidenhead, UK: Open University Press.

Hazel, C., Vazirabadi, G.E. and Gallagher, J. (2013). Measuring aspirations, belonging, and productivity in secondary students: Validation of the student school engagement measure. *Psychology in the Schools, 50*(7), 689–704.

Henderlong, J. and Lepper, M.R. (2002). The effects of praise on children's intrinsic motivation: A review and synthesis. *Psychological Bulletin, 128*(5), 774–95.

Hewstone, M. (1983). *Attribution Theory: Social and functional extensions.* Oxford, UK: Blackwell.

Hirschfield, P.J. and Gasper, J. (2011). The relationship between school engagement and delinquency in late childhood and early adolescence. *Journal of Youth and Adolescence, 40*(1), 3–22.

Ho, I.T. (2004). A comparison of Australian and Chinese teachers' attributions for student problem behaviours. *Educational Psychology, 24*(3), 375–91.

Horner, R.H., Carr, E.G., Halle, J., McGee, G., Odom, S. and Wolery, M. (2005). The use of single-subject research to identify evidence-based practice in special education. *Exceptional Children, 71*(2), 165–79.

Humphrey, N. (2013). Making the most out of school-based prevention: Lessons from the social and emotional aspects of learning (SEAL) programme. *Emotional and Behavioural Difficulties, 18*(3), 248–60.

Johnston, C., Patenaude, R.L. and Inman, C.A. (1992). Attributions for hyperactive and aggressive child behaviours. *Social Cognition, 10*(3), 255–70.

Kearney, A. (2007). *Understanding Applied Behavior Analysis: An introduction to ABA for parents, teachers, and other professionals.* London: Jessica Kinglsey.

Kelly, G.A. (1963). *A Theory of Personality: The psychology of personal constructs.* New York: Norton.

Kelsey, D.M., Kearney, P., Plax, T.G., Allen, T.H. and Ritter, K.J. (2004). College students' attributions of teacher misbehaviours. *Communication Education, 53*(1), 1–17.

Korthagen, F. (2014). Teacher–student contact: Exploring a basic but complicated concept. *Teaching and Teacher Education, 40*, 22–32.

Kounin, J.S. (1970). *Discipline and Group Management in Classrooms.* New York: Holt, Rinehart & Winston.

Lambert, N. and Miller, A. (2010). The temporal stability and predictive validity of pupils' causal attributions for difficult classroom behaviour. *British Journal of Educational Psychology, 80*(4), 599–622.

Landrum, T.L. and Kauffman, J.M. (2006). Behavioural approaches to classroom management. In C.M. Evertson and C.S. Weinstein (eds) (2006). *Handbook of Classroom Management.* London: Lawrence Erlbaum.

LaVigna, G. (2000). *Alternatives to Punishment.* New York: Irvington.

LaVigna, G.W. and Willis, T.J. (2012). The efficacy of positive behavioural support with the most challenging behaviour: The evidence and its implications. *Journal of Intellectual & Developmental Disability, 37*(3), 185–95.

Lawrence, C., Rees, J. and Ferguson, E. (2010). Group-based evaluations for pupil-on-teacher violence: The impact of teacher intervention strategy. *Journal of Community & Applied Social Psychology, 20,* 377–89.

Levy, A. and Kahan, B. (1991). *The Pindown Experience and the Protection of Children.* Stafford, UK: Staffordshire County Council.

Maag, J.W. (2012). School-wide discipline and the intransigency of exclusion. *Children and Youth Services Review, 34*(10), 2094–100.

MacGeorge, E.L. (2004). Gender differences in attributions and emotions in helping contexts. *Behavioural Science, 48*(3), 175–82.

McNamara, E. and Harrop, L.A. (1981). Behaviour modification in the secondary school: A rejoinder to Wheldall and Austin. *Occasional Papers of the DECP, 5*(2), 60–3.

Madsen, C.H., Becker, W.C. and Thomas, D.R. (1968). Rules, praise and ignoring: Elements of elementary classroom control. *Journal of Applied Behavioural Analysis, 1*(2), 139–50.

Marchant, M., Heath, M.A. and Miramontes, N.Y. (2012). Merging empiricism and humanism: Role of social validity in the school-wide positive behavior support model. *Journal of Positive Behavior Interventions, 15*(4), 221–30.

Mathews, S., McIntosh, K., Frank, J.L. and May, S.L. (2013). Critical features predicting sustained implementation of school-wide positive behavioral interventions and supports. *Journal of Positive Behavior Interventions.* DOI: 10.1177/1098300713484065

Merrett, F. and Blundell, D. (1982). Self-recording as a means of improving behaviour in a secondary school. *Educational Psychology, 2,* 147–57.

Merrett, F. and Wheldall, K. (1978). Playing the game: A behavioural approach to classroom management in the junior school. *Educational Review, 30*(1), 41–50.

Miller, A. (1995). Teachers' attributions of causality, control and responsibility in respect of difficult pupil behaviour and its successful management. *Educational Psychology, 15,* 457–71.

Miller, A. (2003). *Teachers, Parents and Classroom Behaviour. A psychosocial approach.* Maidenhead, UK: Open University Press.

Miller, A. and Black, L. (2001). Does support for home–school behaviour plans exist within teacher and pupil cultures? *Educational Psychology in Practice, 17*(3), 245–61.

Miller, A., Ferguson, E. and Byrne, I. (2000). Pupils' causal attributions for difficult classroom behaviour. *British Journal of Educational Psychology, 70,* 85–96.

Miller, A., Ferguson, E. and Moore, E. (2002). Parents' and pupils' causal attributions for difficult classroom behaviour. *British Journal of Educational Psychology, 72,* 27–40.

Mueller, C. and Dweck, C. (1998). Praise for intelligence can undermine children's motivation and performance. *Journal of Personality and Social Psychology, 75*(1), 33–52.

Ofsted (2005). The Annual Report of HM's Chief Inspector of Schools 2003/4. DfES: London.

O'Neill, S. and Stephenson, J. (2010). The use of functional behavioural assessment for students with challenging behaviours: Current patterns and experience of Australian practitioners. *Australian Journal of Educational & Developmental Psychology, 10,* 65–82.

Parsons, C. (2005). School exclusion: The will to punish. *British Journal of Educational Studies, 53,* 187–211.

Phares, V., Ehrbar, L.A. and Lum, J.J. (1996). Parental perceptions of the development and treatment of children's and adolescents' emotional/behavioural problems. *Child and Family Behaviour Therapy*, *18*(4), 19–36.

Poulou, M. and Norwich, B. (2000). Teachers' causal attributions, cognitive, emotional and behavioural responses to students with emotional and behavioural difficulties. *British Journal of Educational Psychology*, *70*(4), 559–81.

Rait, S., Monsen, J.J. and Squires, G. (2010). Cognitive behaviour therapies and their implications for applied educational psychology practice. *Educational Psychology in Practice*, *26*, 105–22.

Rathel, J.M., Drasgow, E., Brown, W.H. and Marshall, K.J. (2013). Increasing induction-level teachers' positive-to-negative communication ratio and use of behavior-specific praise through e-mailed performance feedback and its effect on students' task engagement. *Journal of Positive Behavior Interventions*. DOI: 10.1177/1098300713492856

Ravenette, T. (1997). *Selected Papers. Personal construct psychology and the practice of an educational psychologist*. London: Whurr.

Rennie, E.N.F. (1980). Good behaviour games with a whole class. *Remedial Education*, *15*, 187–90.

Reyna, C. and Weiner, B. (2001). Justice and utility in the classroom: An attributional analysis of the goals of teachers' punishment and intervention strategies. *Journal of Educational Psychology*, *93*, 309–19.

Roorda, D. and Koomen, H. (2011). The influence of affective teacher–student relationships on students' school engagement and achievement: A meta-analytic approach. *Review of Educational Research*, *81*(4), 493–529.

Ruttledge, R. and Petrides, K. (2012). A cognitive behavioural group approach for adolescents with disruptive behaviour in schools. *School Psychology International*, *33*(2), 223–39.

Ryan, R.M. and Deci, E.L. (2000). Self-determination theory and the facilitation of intrinsic motivation, social development, and well-being. *The American Psychologist*, *55*(1), 68–78.

Sheridan, S. and Bovaird, J. (2012). A randomized trial examining the effects of conjoint behavioral consultation and the mediating role of the parent–teacher relationship. *School Psychology Review*, *41*(1), 23–46.

Skinner, B. (1953). *Science and Human Behavior*. New York: Simon & Schuster.

Snyder, J., Cramer, A., Afrank, J. and Patterson, G.R. (2005). The contributions of ineffective discipline and parental hostile attributions of child misbehaviour to the development of conduct problems at home and school. *Developmental Psychology*, *41*(1), 30–41.

Spilt, J., Koomen, H. and Thijs, J. (2011). Teacher wellbeing: The importance of teacher–student relationships. *Educational Psychology Review*, *23*, 457–77.

Squires, G. (2001). Using cognitive behavioural psychology with groups of pupils to improve self-control of behaviour. *Educational Psychology in Practice*, *17*, 317–35.

Squires, G. (2010). Countering the argument that educational psychologists need specific training to use cognitive behavioural therapy. *Emotional and Behavioural Difficulties*, *15*(4), 279–94.

Squires, G. and Caddick, K. (2012). Using group cognitive behavioural therapy intervention in school settings with pupils who have externalizing behavioural difficulties: An unexpected result. *Emotional and Behavioural Difficulties*, *17*, 25–45.

Sterzer, P. and Stadler, C. (2009). Neuroimaging of aggressive and violent behaviour in children and adolescents. *Frontiers in Behavioral Neuroscience*, *3*(35), 1–8.

11 School bullies

Are they also victims?

Susan Birch and Norah Frederickson

CHAPTER SUMMARY

Recent surveys have consistently identified bullying as an important issue in relation to the well-being of children and young people. Although bullying can occur in a range of contexts and now, with cyberbullying, through an increasing number of media, in this chapter we will focus primarily on 'traditional' bullying occurring at school. School bullies are typically portrayed as large, oafish thugs, and the popular image of victims of bullying is of physically weak, sensitive and timid individuals. However, psychological research introduced in this chapter has shown that both these popular stereotypes are oversimplifications. Some school bullies are also victimised, and the incidence of negative circumstances and outcomes associated with bullying for all involved is very much higher than for pupils not involved. Theories of bullying range across explanations at the levels of the individual, family, peer group and school system. A wide range of interventions have been developed accordingly, although rigorous evaluation is lacking in most cases, and some have aroused controversy. In particular, there is disagreement over intervention programme principles for children who bully, and it is here that the overlap between bullies and victims has particular implications. In addition, at the end of the chapter, there will be an opportunity for you to explore briefly whether research around the 'traditional' forms of bullying may inform our developing understanding of cyberbullying.

LEARNING OUTCOMES

When you have studied this chapter, you should be able to:

1 describe the principal theories of *traditional bullying* and the research evidence relating to them;
2 critically evaluate the main assessment and intervention approaches used in relation to bullying behaviour in schools;
3 debate key theoretical and professional controversies in this research area, drawing on recent psychological literature.

BULLYING: AN INTRODUCTION

The extent to which bullying plays a part in our society is difficult to quantify. Hansen *et al.* (2012) state that worldwide prevalence estimates for bullying *victimisation* in school-aged children vary widely, between 5.3 per cent and 50 per cent. Monks *et al.* (2009) suggest that this variability is influenced by how bullying is defined, including the frequency level (once a month, once a week, etc.) and the time frame (in the last month, the last six months, etc.). The Tellus4survey (Chamberlain *et al.*, 2010), which collected the views of 253,755 children and young people in Years 6, 8 and 10 in the UK, found that nearly half of children and young people had been bullied at school at some point in their lives, and 29 per cent had been bullied in the previous year. Clearly, these estimates fall at the top of the prevalence range suggested by Hansen *et al.* (2012).

Although media reports have tended to suggest that the incidence of bullying is increasing, Rigby and Smith (2011) have suggested an alternative position. They carried out a review of international studies published between 1990 and 2009 where data collection was repeated, in one place and from equivalent samples, and suggested that, in fact, 'it appears that the prevalence of bullying among young people is generally decreasing; although in a minority of countries, this may not be the case' (p. 451).

ChildLine's report, 'Can I tell you something?' (ChildLine, 2014), hit the headlines in the UK in January 2014, drawing attention to the sharp rise in the incidence of both cyberbullying and racist bullying, (as reported by children contacting ChildLine). In relation to racist bullying, the ChildLine report noted a 69 per cent increase on the previous year in the number of children and young people contacting the helpline saying that they had been called, among other insults, a terrorist or a bomber, or had been told to 'go back where they came from' (p. 41). The report noted an 87 per cent rise between 2011–12 and 2012–13 in contacts made by children related to cyberbullying. Requests for support and advice were made in relation to how to deal with being bullied via social-networking sites, chatrooms, online gaming sites, or via mobile phones. The NSPCC website, highlighting key findings from the report, noted that, 'Young people have told ChildLine that the 24 hour nature of online bullying means there's no escape and can lead to very serious feelings of isolation, low self-esteem and in a few desperate cases, even suicide' (NSPCC, 8 January 2014).

Rigby and Smith (2011) suggest that their review findings relating to cyberbullying are less conclusive than for traditional bullying, as, in 2009, they were only able to locate two studies using a repeated-measures design to explore prevalence trends. They go on to suggest that longitudinal studies will be particularly important, as developments in technology are likely to facilitate an increase in the means by which young people can engage in cyberbullying, and there may, therefore, be 'a corresponding rise in its prevalence' (p. 451).

There is also an increasing awareness of bullying for lesbian, gay and bisexual young people in schools. Stonewall's recent *The School Report* (Guasp, 2012), a survey of 1,145 young people carried out in 2006, states that 65 per cent of the lesbian, gay and bisexual young people in British schools responding had experienced direct homophobic bullying, and 35 per cent of lesbian and gay pupils did not feel safe or accepted at school. The report also suggested a disquieting lack of action on the part of schools, with only a quarter of the young people reporting that their school had said that homophobic bullying was wrong.

Bullying is, therefore, widespread, frequently occurring and diverse in character. Having been bullied at school has been shown to be related to elevated risks of childhood and young adult psychiatric disorders (Copeland *et al.*, 2013), and even having been part of a peer group characterised by bullying and/or victimisation has been shown to be related to significant negative outcomes, such as poorer levels of well-being, behaviour and academic achievement (Gutman and Brown, 2008). It is, therefore, a topic of great importance in education, in schools, as well as in society as a whole.

WHAT IS BULLYING?

Although there is no universally agreed definition of bullying, most authors agree on its key features, described as the 'double IR' (Orpinas and Horne, 2006):

- I – imbalance of power
- I – intentional
- R – repeated over time.

Can you identify each of these elements in the following definition of bullying? It is one of the most widely used definitions in research studies with children and was adapted for use in the UK from the pioneering work of Olweus in Norway:

> We say a child or young person is being bullied, or picked on when another child or young person, or a group of children or young people, say nasty and unpleasant things to him or her. It is also bullying when a child or a young person is hit, kicked, threatened, locked inside a room, sent nasty notes, when no one ever talks to them and things like that. These things can happen frequently and it is difficult for the child or the young person being bullied to defend himself or herself. It is also bullying when a child or young person is teased repeatedly in a nasty way. But it is not bullying when two children or young people of about the same strength have the odd fight or quarrel.
>
> (Whitney and Smith, 1993; reproduced by permission
> of Taylor & Francis)

The DfE's July 2014 advice for headteachers, staff and governing bodies, describes bullying as follows:

> Bullying is behaviour by an individual or group, repeated over time, that intentionally hurts another individual or group either physically or emotionally. Bullying can take many forms (for instance, cyber-bullying via text messages or the internet), and is often motivated by prejudice against particular groups, for example on grounds of race, religion, gender, sexual orientation, or because a child is adopted or has caring responsibilities. It might be motivated by actual differences between children, or perceived differences. Stopping violence and ensuring immediate physical safety is obviously a school's first priority but emotional bullying can be more damaging than physical; teachers and schools have to make their own judgements about each specific case.
>
> (DfE, 2014, p. 6)

This paragraph (which stood alone in the July 2013 guidance) is now followed by an account of the importance of an imbalance of power between the perpetrator and the victim. Hence, the DfE's current definition of bullying does recognise the three features making up the 'double IR' (Orpinas and Horne, 2006). This *power imbalance* is described by Juvonen and Graham (2004) as the single most critical characteristic of a bullying relationship, whereby the victim is unable to prevent or stop the aversive behaviour. Power in children's groups is not only based on differences in physical size and strength and associated access to resources. It may also be based on social attention-holding ability and success in forming affiliative relationships (Hawker and Boulton, 2001). Hence, different types of 'traditional' bullying are distinguished, based on the type of power that is being abused:

- physical – hitting, kicking, taking belongings (resource-holding potential);
- verbal – name calling, insulting, making offensive remarks (social attention-holding power);
- relational – spreading nasty stories about someone, exclusion from social groups, being made the subject of malicious rumours (affiliative relationships/sense of belonging).

It can be seen that cyberbullying may overlap here, in terms of both the second and third bullet points, as an alternative mode of delivering a 'type' of bullying.

Clear distinctions are sometimes claimed – for example, relational bullying has been branded 'girls' bullying'. However, there appear to be complex interactions between pupil characteristics and prevalence of type of bullying. For example, from a meta-analysis, Archer (2004) reported that girls were only found to be more involved in relational aggression in samples above 11 years, where peer ratings were used, whereas boys were more likely to engage in physical bullying than girls across all ages.

WHO ARE THE BULLIES?

Which pupils are identified as bullies depends to some extent on the assessment method used, although gender differences are commonly reported, with boys being more likely to be identified as bullies (e.g. Copeland *et al.*, 2013). Four main methods for identifying bullying behaviour can be described, as shown in Method Box 11.1 (see Pellegrini, 2001; Cornell *et al.*, 2006).

METHOD 11.1

Self-reports

Children are typically presented with a definition of bullying and asked to rate the frequency with which they have been involved over a specified period, in either bullying or being bullied. For example, the *Peer Relations Questionnaire* (Rigby and Slee, 1998) contains a six-item bully scale and a five-item victim scale. Items such as 'I am part of a group that goes around teasing others' and 'I get picked on by others' are rated on a four-point scale, ranging from 'never' to 'very often'.

These self-report questionnaires are usually anonymous to encourage honesty. Even then, there may be effects of social desirability biases, as pupils may resist endorsing responses that involve admitting to an unfavourable self-presentation.

Peer assessments

These methods generally involve surveying a classroom of pupils, asking each to identify classmates who meet behavioural descriptions characteristic of bullies and victims. Peer-assessment methodologies are well established in the literature on *social competence*, and, in some cases, existing instruments have been extended to collect data on bullying. For example, Nabuzoka and Smith (1993) extended the 'Guess who' peer-assessment method developed by Coie *et al.* (1982), adding:

- a bully – someone who often picks on other children or hits them, or teases them or does other nasty things to them for no good reason;
- a bullying victim – someone who often gets picked on or hit or teased or has nasty things done to them by other children for no good reason.

Salmivalli (1999) has developed a set of scales (the participant role scales) that collect information on the roles children may play in bullying incidents. These include:

- bully (five items): active, initiative-taking, leader-like behaviour;
- assistant (two items): active, but more follower than leader-like;
- reinforcer (four items): inciting the bully, providing an audience etc.;
- defender (six items): sticking up for or consoling the victim;
- outsider (four items): doing nothing in bullying situations, staying away;
- victim (one item): 'gets bullied', needs to be nominated by 30 per cent of same-sex classmates to be classified as a victim.

Teacher questionnaires

Smith (2004) points out that these are generally considered less reliable than self- or peer reports, as teachers are often unaware of much of the bullying that is occurring, for example in the playground. However, at younger ages, for example in nursery school, the balance of preference shifts in favour of teacher reports, both because child reports may be less reliable and because younger children are more closely supervised, and so teachers are likely to be better informed.

Observation

This method is primarily used with preschool or primary-aged children, although rarely, as data collection and analysis are very time consuming (for examples, see Craig et al., 2000; Black and Jackson, 2007). It is little used with older children for several reasons. Older children range over a much wider geographical area during their break times at school, when such observations are typically conducted, making data collection difficult. Much relational bullying will be very difficult to observe, and, with physical and verbal bullying, the presence of an adult observer is very likely to greatly decrease the incidence of bullying.

Pellegrini and Bartini (2000) compared different methods of identifying bullies and victims and reported low-to-moderate correlations between them. Juvonen et al. (2001) found that, compared with peer assessments, self-report measures of victimisation better predicted psychological adjustment problems (depressive symptoms and low self-worth), whereas peer assessments better predicted low social acceptance. They argue that the most appropriate assessment technique will depend on the goal of an investigation – 'to understand peer harassment as a social problem, as a personal predicament, or both' (p. 120).

ARE SOME BULLIES ALSO VICTIMS OF BULLYING AT SCHOOL?

Of direct relevance to the question asked in the title of this chapter is the consistent finding that a proportion of the children identified as bullies are also identified as victims. Solberg et al. (2007) reported data from over 18,000 Norwegian pupils, aged 11–15 years, who completed a self-report measure. They were given a definition of bullying very similar to that used by Whitney and Smith (1993; see above) and were asked how often they had been bullied or had taken part in bullying in the previous 2–3 months in school. Response options were:

- option 1 – I haven't;
- option 2 – only once or twice;
- option 3 – two or three times a month;
- option 4 – once a week;
- option 5 – several times a week.

Table 11.1 shows how cut-off scores on this measure were used to classify pupils. Across the whole sample, 9.5 per cent were classified as victims, 4.6 per cent as bullies, and 1.9 per cent as *bully–victims*. Hence, close to 30 per cent of bullies were also victims.

Copeland *et al.* (2013) looked at the categorisation of bullying behaviour in their population-based sample of 1,420 children, assessed annually between the ages of 9 and 16 years. They reported that 21.6 per cent of participants were victims only, 5 per cent were bullies only, and 4.5 per cent were both bullies and victims (68.9 per cent were neither). Hence, in Copeland's US sample, approximately 50 per cent of bullies were also victims. In this study, both the child and the primary caregiver were asked whether the child had been bullied or teased or had bullied others in the previous 3 months, as part of a wider assessment, and either being bullied or bullying was counted if either the child or parent reported this at any assessment. Hence, levels may be higher than in the previous study, where self-report alone and a more structured approach appear to have been used.

Bully–victims have been increasingly recognised in the research as a particularly vulnerable group, exhibiting a range of social, emotional and behavioural difficulties. Indeed Copeland *et al.* describe bully–victims as 'the most troubled children' (2013, p. 424). They have consistently been described as anxious, irritable, hot-tempered and prone to start fights and to exhibit retaliatory, or reactive, aggression (Olweus, 1978; Schwartz *et al.*, 1997). There are contrasts between this pattern of behaviour and the behaviour both of 'pure bullies' and 'pure victims'. Non-victimised bullies are not characterised by overtly angry, disregulated behaviour, but tend to exhibit organised and goal-directed, or proactive, aggression. Victims of bullying who are not also bullies are described as non-aggressive, shy, passive and submissive (Olweus, 1978, 1991).

The suggestion that bully–victims may represent an especially high-risk group is supported by a number of findings, one example being that they have been found to experience higher levels of depression than either bullies or victims (Swearer *et al.*, 2001). A bully–victim cycle has been described, for example by Ma (2001), who investigated both pupil-level and school-level influences. The suggestion inherent in the cycle, that these pupils may first have been bullied and then imitated the bullying behaviour they experienced, has gained media attention following the finding from retrospective analyses of school shootings in the United States (Anderson *et al.*, 2001; Vossekuil *et al.*, 2002; Wike and Fraser, 2009) that a considerable proportion (50–70 per cent) of the perpetrators had been bullied at school, and 30 per cent had a record of violence prior to the attack. 'These bullied youth may represent the "provocative" or "aggressive" victims described in recent studies on bullying behaviour, who often retaliate in an aggressive manner in response to being bullied. This group represents a particularly high risk population' (Anderson *et al.*, 2001, p. 2702).

TABLE 11.1 Categories of bully, victim and bully–victim, as defined by Solberg *et al.* (2007)

		Had taken part in bullying	
		Options 3, 4 & 5	*Options 1 & 2*
Had been bullied	*Options 3, 4 & 5*	Bully–victim	Victim
	Options 1 & 2	Bully	Not involved

Source: Solberg *et al.*, 2007

WHY DOES BULLYING OCCUR?

A wide variety of different theories have been advanced to explain bullying behaviour. In this section, we will begin by exploring an overarching *ecological systems theory* framework before going on to consider *sociocognitive deficit* theories, theories of family influence and group process theories, aspects of which interlink and each of which could be seen to fit under the umbrella of an ecological systems framework.

Ecological systems theories

A number of authors (Olweus, 1993; Sharp, 1999; Swearer and Espelage, 2004) argue that bullying can only be adequately understood by means of a multilevel analysis.

> In a nutshell, bullying does not occur in isolation. Young people involved in bullying in school often experience multiple problems and bullying is encouraged or inhibited as the result of complex relationships between the individual, family, peer group, school, community, and culture.
>
> (Swearer and Espelage, 2004, p. 3)

Hong and Espelage (2012) present an ecological systems analysis of risk factors associated with bullying and victimisation in school, using Bronfenbrenner's ecological systems theory (Bronfenbrenner and Ceci, 1994), which conceptualises an individual's social environment as five interrelated systems:

- A *microsystem* is a pattern of activities, roles and interpersonal relationships experienced by a child in a particular setting where they are directly involved. The classroom, home and playground are three examples of settings where the child regularly interacts with others.
- A *mesosystem* describes the relationships between two or more settings in which the child actively participates. Disagreement between a child's teacher and parents about how to deal with bullying in the playground would be an example at this level.
- An *exosystem* is a setting where the child is not directly involved, but it affects or is affected by what happens in settings that do involve the child. A local authority's policy on bullying would be an influence on schools in the area and would be influenced by events in schools, such as high-profile media reports on instances of bullying.
- The *macrosystem* refers to the influence of cultural and subcultural mores and belief systems. Societal attitudes to bullying and common features of its representation in the media would be factors at this level.
- The *chronosystem*, which Hong and Espelage (2012) refer to as the consistency or change of the individual and the environment over the life course, is particularly discussed in relation to family structures and how these may adversely affect children in terms of the development of problematic behaviours, including bullying.

Hong and Espelage (2012) go on to discuss a range of risk factors for bullying behaviours at each level, as illustrated in Figure 11.1.

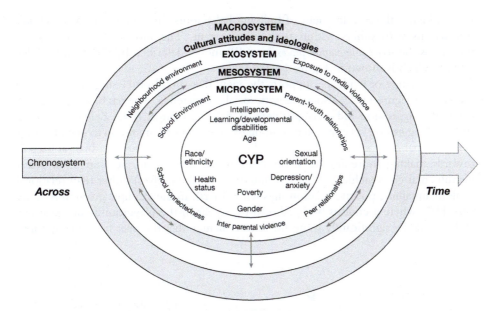

FIGURE 11.1 Ecological systems analysis of factors associated with bullying and victimisation in school

Source: Based on Hong and Espelage, 2012

Compared with the volume of research on individual-level factors in bullying, less work to date has been done on ecological factors that are associated with bullying. Doll *et al.* (2004) reviewed the associations of two sets of classroom-level variables with lower levels of bullying:

- the quality of social relationships (including pupil–pupil, pupil–teacher and teacher–parent);
- individual pupil responsibility in the classroom (including support for pupil self-control, self-efficacy and self-determination).

Payne and Gottfriedson (2004) summarised research on a range of school factors found to be related to bullying, in particular teacher interest and responsiveness, and pupil attitude, cooperativeness and alienation. Lower levels of bullying were found in schools where teachers were likely to discuss bullying with pupils, recognise bullying behaviour, show interest in stopping bullying and actually intervene in bullying incidents. More negative pupil attitudes to bullying were also associated with lower levels of the behaviour. Pupil cooperativeness was negatively correlated with bullying and victimisation, whereas pupil alienation and low levels of involvement in school increased the likelihood of involvement in bullying.

Sociocognitive deficit theories

Theories focusing on sociocognitive deficits have drawn on models used to account for aggressive behaviour more generally. They aim to explain how within-child factors may influence the development of bullying behaviours through affecting the child's interactions with others within their microsystem. The most influential of these theories is the *social information processing* (SIP) model described by Crick and Dodge (1994), which is shown in Figure 11.2.

A wide range of evidence supports the view that skilful processing at each of the six stages in Figure 11.2 is associated with social competence, whereas biased processing can lead to aggression and social problems (Crick and Dodge, 1996; Zelli *et al.*, 1999). At Step 1, aggressive, as opposed to non-aggressive, children are found to encode fewer benign social cues, attending preferentially to hostile cues. There is a bias, at Step 2, towards making more hostile attributions of intentions and, at Step 3, to select instrumental goals (achieving desired outcomes for themselves) rather than relational goals (maintaining positive relationships with others). In the example given in Activity Box 11.1, where a child is bumped into by a peer in the playground, an aggressive child would be significantly more likely to conclude that the peer had knocked into

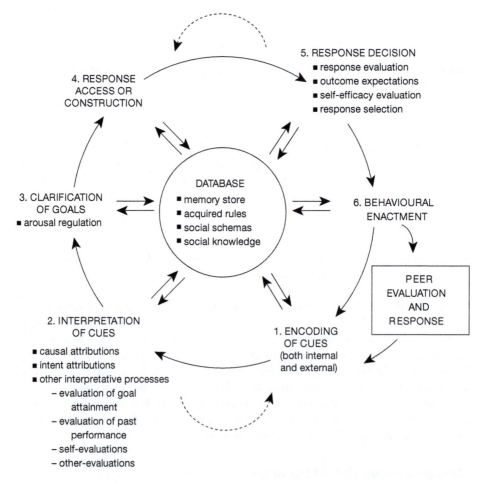

FIGURE 11.2 Social information processing model

Source: Crick and Dodge, 1994, p. 76

ACTIVITY 11.1

It is a busy playtime on a primary school playground. An 8-year-old boy is involved in a game of tag with a group of his friends. They are weaving in and out of football players and skipping girls. One of the boys bumps into another as he runs to get away from the 'chaser', and the football the second boy is holding is knocked from his hands. What happens next?

- The first boy calls back 'sorry', and the second boy shrugs it off, smiles and retrieves his football. Both games continue.
- *Or,* the boy who has lost his football shouts angrily, runs after the first boy, grabs his jumper and flings him to the ground.

Think what might have been going on for each of these two boys at each stage of Crick and Dodge's model (see Figure 11.2), in each scenario.

Can you relate this model to a scenario from your own recent experience?

them on purpose, with the intention of hurting them or of making them lose their ball, and would be more likely to select the goal of hurting the boy to teach them not to aggress in the future. Aggressive children generate fewer prosocial responses at Step 4, and, at Step 5, they evaluate aggressive responses more favourably, expecting that positive outcomes will result. They also feel more self-confident in their ability to enact the aggressive behaviour successfully at Step 6.

It is disputed whether bullying, as distinct from other forms of aggression, is caused by sociocognitive deficits in processes such as those depicted in the model. Instead, Sutton *et al.* (1999a, p. 118) argued that, 'Many bullies may in fact be skilled manipulators, not social inadequates'. Drawing attention to the social nature of bullying, Pepler and Craig (1995) reported that peers are present in some 85 per cent of bullying episodes. They also highlighted subtler, relational bullying, and they argued that some bullying seems to require a high level of sociocognitive skill. They investigated one type of sociocognitive skill in particular, *theory of mind* (ToM) abilities. ToM (which was discussed in detail in Chapter 9) involves the ability to attribute mental states, such as beliefs, desires and intentions, to others and to predict behaviour accordingly. Sutton *et al.*'s study explored the performance of bullies, victims, outsiders and other roles (as assessed using the peer-nominated participant role scale described earlier) on cognitive false-belief tasks and on emotion-based false-belief tasks. They found that bullies scored higher than any other participants on both versions of the tasks (except the non-involved outsider role).

Although various authors (e.g. Sutton *et al.*, 1999b, 2001; Arsenio and Lemerise, 2001) have debated whether bullies should be regarded as socially competent or not, there is substantial agreement on a variety of issues, such as the need to consider different groups of bullies and the potential explanatory value of the SIP model in relation to each. Sutton *et al.* (1999a) acknowledged that investigation of different types of child who bully others was indicated. Drawing on the finding that bullies had higher scores than victims and controls on the psychoticism scale of the Eysenck personality questionnaire (Slee and Rigby, 1993), they suggested that, 'It may be the aggressive, hot headed reactive bully–victims who fit the traditional picture of the social skills deficient bully, while proactive aggressors may be more cold and calculating, actually possessing rather good social cognition' (Sutton et al., 1999a, p. 123).

In a more recent exploration of ToM abilities and bullying behaviour, Shakoor et al. (2012), in a longitudinal twin study, explored whether 12-year-olds, reported by self, teachers or mothers to be involved in bullying, either as victims, bullies or bully–victims, had had poor ToM when previously assessed at the age of 5 years. They found that adolescents who had been involved in bullying had significantly poorer ToM at the age of 5 years compared with adolescents not involved with bullying, the effect being strongest for bully–victims. They went on to conclude that, 'Poor ToM in childhood appears to be a robust developmental marker for later victim or bully–victim status' (p. 258), and they highlighted that poor ToM may affect children's social relationships and their likelihood of developing either victim or bully–victim status. They reflected that, where children find it difficult to understand others' perspectives and to decode social cues, they may then rely on their own direct experiences. Where these are negative, these may then lead children to interpret ambiguous situations in a negative light, leading to an aggressive response, rather than a more accepting or neutral response. Hence, both victims and bully–victims would have social information processing deficits in perceiving and interpreting social cues at the early stage of the model proposed by Crick and Dodge (1994) (see Figure 11.2), whereas proactive bullies may show skills in these areas, but have different goals and means of achieving them at the later stages of the model.

Arsenio and Lemerise (2001) also suggested that attention to goals is warranted and that proactively aggressive bullies may be characterised by a focus on instrumental goals rather than relational goals. They also support the 'cold and calculating' characterisation of proactive bullies, suggesting a lack of empathy to account for why they are undeterred by others' distress in their pursuit of instrumental goals. Parallels are drawn with research by Blair showing that children who are rated by their teachers as high on callous/unemotional behaviour (psychopathic traits) are less able than age mates to recognise specific emotions in others, namely sadness and fear, but not, for example, happiness. Sadness and fear are the very emotions, mediated by brain activity in the amygdala, the recognition of which is thought to play a central role in inhibiting aggression (see Blair et al., 2006, for a review of work in this area). Hence, deficient emotional, rather than cognitive, processing may be implicated in some bullying behaviour. Viding et al. (2009) went on to investigate whether higher levels of callous unemotional (CU) traits are indeed associated with higher levels of both direct and indirect bullying in a group of 11–13-year-olds. Participants were asked to complete self-report questionnaires about CU traits and psychopathology, including conduct problems, alongside peer report measures of both direct and indirect bullying. They reported that higher levels of CU traits were associated with increased levels of direct bullying, and that CU traits and conduct problems should be seen as related but also as 'distinct entities in mediating the susceptibility of children to bully others directly' (p. 471). It was the combination of both sets of traits (CU traits and conduct problems) that could be seen to put children at a particularly high risk for engaging in both direct and indirect bullying.

Theories of family influence

These theories consider family relationships or processes that may cause or exacerbate bullying behaviour, again within the child's microsystem.

Social learning theory holds that bullying behaviour is acquired through modelling and reinforcement of behaviour, and that early experience is particularly influential. A range of supportive evidence suggests higher levels of hostility and punitive responses by parents towards children who bully (Bowers *et al.*, 1994). For example, Olweus (1994) reports high levels of physical aggression and emotional hostility in interactions between parents of bullies and their children. In addition, such parents tend not to set limits to their child's aggression, so that it is often successful in achieving the child's goals. This contrasts with the parenting style of victims' mothers, which is described as over-involved and overprotective (Bowers *et al.*, 1994; Olweus, 1994).

Much of this research has been correlational and so open to alternative interpretations – maybe parents of bullies are reacting to their children's behaviour. However, the results of a longitudinal study by Schwartz *et al.* (1997) suggest that parental behaviour is instrumental in the development of bullying in some children. They carried out assessments of boys and their home environments, first when the boys were preschoolers and again when they were 8–10 years of age. Bully or victim status was established by peer assessment in school on items such as 'gets picked on' and 'says mean things'. Physical abuse, domestic violence, maternal hostility and harsh discipline in the early home environment were associated with later bully–victim status. The early home environments of bullies who were not also victims were not characterised by physical abuse or harsh treatment, although aggressive models and parental conflict were often present. In this study, the home environments of victims who were not also bullies did not differ from those of children not involved in bullying. However Schwartz *et al.* (1997) point out that they did not assess overprotective parenting.

Attachment theory (Bowlby, 1969) posits that early caregiver–child interactions lead to the development of an 'internal working model' that is used to guide future relationships. A number of different types of caregiver–child interaction pattern, or attachment style, have been described. They are typically identified through the 'strange situation procedure' (Ainsworth *et al.*, 1978), in which a 10–24-month-old infant is briefly separated from their parent in an unfamiliar setting and then reunited with them. Three patterns of behaviour were originally identified, indicative of different attachment styles:

- *Secure* – these infants were happy to see the parent when reunited. If they had been distressed when the parent had left, they settled on the parent's reappearance and re-engaged in absorbed play or exploration.
- *Insecure–avoidant* – these infants typically showed little distress on separation and, when the parent reappeared, they moved or turned away, engaging in play and ignoring the parent.
- *Insecure–resistant/ambivalent* – these infants were very distressed on separation and, when the parent returned, they tended both to seek contact and reject it when offered.

More recently, attention has focused on a fourth category, *disorganised attachment*, shown by 10 per cent of infants as they try and fail to develop an organised pattern of behaviour in response to a highly dysfunctional parenting style or care environment, instead exhibiting a variety of unusual and contradictory responses. Strong associations are reported between disorganised attachment, problems in regulating emotions, behaviour problems in school and psychopathology in adolescence (Green and Goldwyn, 2002). This suggests that further investigation of how early dysfunctional parenting and disorganised attachment relationships relate to future bully–victim status would be valuable.

Group process theories

Rather than regarding bullying as the actions of deviant individuals, these theories seek to identify the functions that may be served by bullying in social groups. *Social dominance theory* will be considered as one example of this approach. Nishina (2004) suggests that bullying behaviour could serve particular social functions that may have been adaptive in evolutionary terms. It is argued that groups with clearly established dominance hierarchies are likely to be more successful, both because within-group conflict will be minimised and because good organisation will lead to higher levels of success in between-group conflicts. Although it is possible to establish one's social dominance by prosocial as well as coercive means, Nishina suggests that 'bistrategic controllers' who use both strategies may be the most successful and admired by others.

Research with primates suggests that, within stable group hierarchies, there is little need for within-group aggression, and the relative disadvantages of being low ranking (in terms, for example, of access to resources) are attenuated. On this analysis, bully–victims are children who refuse to 'accept their place' in a group and challenge higher- as well as lower-status individuals. It is suggested that it is the group-destabilising potential of this behaviour and the group discomfort generated as a result that lead to these individuals being disliked and rejected by peers. It is also suggested that involvement in the bullying of someone outside a group can create feelings of belonging within the group and so represent a strong motivational force.

Nishina stresses that this kind of analysis should not be used to excuse bullying as being a part of human nature. Rather, it may be helpful in explaining why the behaviour appears pervasive and difficult to eradicate. It may also suggest ways in which the school environment can impact on the incidence of bullying. For example, the ways in which adults in the school establish their dominance over the children might be expected to influence how dominance hierarchies among children are established, both directly through the systems of rules and sanctions in place and indirectly through modelling. It suggests that action against bullies is unlikely to be effective if it does not address the role others play in the bullying, or are perceived to play (Rigby, 2005), in particular in providing social reinforcement to the bully.

WHICH BULLYING INTERVENTIONS ARE EFFECTIVE?

Ecological systems theories have had a major impact on the design of interventions, and it is typically recommended that bullying should be tackled through consistent implementation of strategies at organisational, group and individual levels (Sharp, 1999, p. 5):

- Staff and students working together to develop a clear set of guidelines for everybody which specify what bullying is and what they should do when they know or suspect it is going on.
- Long-term curriculum work about bullying and other forms of antisocial behaviour, including teaching students how to manage personal relationships assertively and constructively.
- Peer-led approaches, such as peer counselling and buddying, to offer support to pupils who are new to the school or who are feeling lonely, rejected or victimized.
- Direct intervention strategies when bullying has occurred or is suspected of occurring. Problem solving approaches which involve all students, including those who have been indirectly involved, are most effective. Early involvement of parents is recommended. Follow-up over time is always needed to check that the bullying has not resumed.

Thompson and Smith (2011) further categorise anti-bullying interventions into proactive strategies (designed to prevent bullying happening through contributing to an anti-bullying school ethos) and reactive strategies (those employed to respond directly to bullying when it happens). Relating this framework to Sharp's model above, we can see that the first three approaches would be seen to be proactive, and the final approach, reactive.

International research indicates that multilevel intervention, modelled on the approach developed by Olweus (1993) in Norway, usually leads to reductions of around 5–20 per cent in victimisation rates (Smith, 2004). This contrasts with the 50 per cent reduction in the original Olweus study. Ttofi and Farrington (2011) present the findings of a systematic review and meta-analysis of forty-four programme evaluations. They report decreases in bullying of 20–23 per cent on average and decreases in victimisation of 17–20 per cent, that is, broadly in line with the reductions reported by Smith (2004). They then identified and coded the constituent elements of the programmes, before using these codes to then analyse the effectiveness of twenty different programme elements. They found that the following were elements associated with a decrease in bullying: parent training/meetings/information for parents, classroom management, classroom rules and teacher training, having a whole-school anti-bullying policy, school conferences, disciplinary measures and improved playground supervision. The number of elements, duration and intensity of the programme were also important, and they hypothesised that, 'a considerable period of time is needed in order to build up an appropriate school ethos that efficiently tackles bullying' (Ttofi and Farrington, 2011, p. 45).

In terms of effectiveness for reducing victimisation, the most important elements were reported to be disciplinary methods, parent training/meetings, videos and cooperative group work. Of particular note for educational psychologists is the finding that work with peers was associated with a significant increase in victimisation (and a non-significant increase in bullying). Work with peers was defined as 'the formal engagement of peers in tackling bullying' (p. 43), and approaches such as peer mediation, peer mentoring and encouraging bystander intervention were included here. Hence, these approaches would not be recommended on the basis of that review, despite the use of peer support strategies by a significant proportion of UK schools.

A critical factor to consider here may be the emphasis or context for the involvement of peers. It is the abdication of responsibility to peers that is counter-indicated, rather than the involvement of peers within a coherent, multilayered, whole-school approach.

The recommendation, in Sharp's last bullet point above, that problem-solving approaches involving all affected pupils should be used in response to incidents of bullying would appear consistent with the literature discussed in the previous section in relation to social information processing and group processes. Examples of such approaches that are commonly used by educational psychologists are the *no blame/support group approach* (see Young, 1998) and the method of shared concern (Pikas, 2002; Rigby, 2005). However, this recommendation has proved controversial (Smith, 2001). An article in *The Guardian* in January 2006 recounted, 'Council chiefs admitted today they were considering dropping a controversial policy of not blaming bullies in schools for their actions – following a scathing attack by the prime minister'. Tony Blair had commented in the House of Commons that bullying should be punished, so that the children can be 'made to learn the harm that they are doing' (Guardian Unlimited, 2006).

However, as discussed earlier, the existence of particularly vulnerable bully–victims can make a focus on punishing bullies problematic, especially as it is the reactively aggressive bully–victims who are most likely to come to teachers' attention for *punishment*. Use of the imbalance of power that exists between teachers and pupils to punish bully–victims might be predicted to risk reinforcing counterproductive messages to this group. Even proactively aggressive bullies, who are not also victims, are already more alienated from school and have been more exposed to aggressive models at home. It is difficult to see how a punitive approach might be expected to have a positive effect, and indeed (R.J.R., not Tony) Blair *et al.* (2006) review studies suggesting that children who show psychopathic tendencies, as proactively aggressive bullies appear to do, are more responsive to reward than to punishment.

By contrast, success is more likely with a social problem-solving approach that makes clear what behaviour is expected, puts in place a system of rewards and sanctions and works with the peer group to ensure that congruent consequences are operating at the group and organisational levels. In particular, despite exhortations to tell adults (e.g. 'Don't suffer in silence', DfES, 2002), children who are being bullied are often reluctant to seek help from school staff and are more likely to do so when there is an anti-bullying whole-school climate, where fears of inaction, ridicule or reprisal are likely to be minimised (Unnever and Cornell, 2004; Wang *et al.*, 2013).

Juvonen and Graham (2004, p. 249) argue that:

> Unless an interventionist has a clear theory about what causes bullying, it is difficult to avoid what has come to be called a 'laundry list' approach . . . a little bit of everything and not much of anything specific to the targeted behavior.

Given the range of levels at which influences on bullying have been identified, it can be seen that multicomponent programmes are likely to be needed. If appropriate theories are drawn on at each level, it is argued that a coherent set of proposals can be developed. Rigby (2004) offers an analysis of the implications for intervention in schools of key current theories of bullying, which should assist educational psychologists working with schools on bullying prevention, or with children who bully.

In their practice, educational psychologists will be collecting information on the type of bullying behaviour that is occurring and drawing on psychological theory and research to generate and test hypotheses about the causes of this bullying within the particular school situation. The results of this assessment will inform the selection of appropriate interventions and further collection of data, in order that the interventions implemented can be evaluated.

Bullying is a young area of psychological research, and there are still many gaps in the knowledge base, particularly in relation to the effectiveness of interventions with different groups of children involved in bullying and, most recently, in relation to cyberbullying. Given the 'youthfulness' of this particular area of research, the problem-solving framework or process outlined above may need to be taken back a stage. How much is known about the theory underlying cyberbullying? Are educational psychologists aware of the issues, and to what extent are their interventions based in psychological theory and research?

Bauman (2013) highlights that having a clear understanding of the theoretical underpinnings of cyberbullying and whether it is a variation of bullying rather than a unique phenomenon will have implications for the design of both intervention and prevention strategies. However, she also highlights that, although teachers may feel unprepared to tackle cyberbullying, 'a well-designed and rigorously tested program, perhaps integrated with some direct instruction on cybersafety, should be examined' (p. 254).

ACTIVITY 11.2

To what extent is cyberbullying an extension of traditional bullying, or is it something different?

- Smith *et al.* (2008) defined cyberbullying as 'an aggressive intentional act carried out by a group of individuals using electronic forms of contact, repeatedly and over time against a victim who cannot easily defend him or herself' (p. 376).
- *Cyberbullying: Safe to learn: Embedding anti-bullying work in schools* (DCSF, 2007) highlights the following as being important factors in cyberbullying:
  - anonymity of the cyberbully versus a 'traditional' bully;
  - lack of immediate feedback from the victim – less opportunity for either party to resolve the misunderstanding;
  - more likely to take place across different age groups, e.g. school children targeting a teacher;
  - number of potential bystanders and the ease with which bystanders can become perpetrators, by passing on or showing others (possibility of an alternative terminology of 'accessories' being used);
  - omnipresent – nowhere is safe;
  - time – it can be difficult to stop and difficult to control.

To what extent can you identify the elements from Smith *et al.*'s definition (2008) and from the DCSF guidance, in the following extract, taken from *The Guardian* online?

Do you know where your children go online?

> Sexting, bullying and getting round security settings . . . young people tell
> Olivia Gordon what really happens on the internet

Thirty years ago, children were taught never to accept sweets from strangers, but the equivalent modern message, about staying safe online, doesn't seem to be getting through. For all its positives, the online world is full of potential hazards to young people. Sexting, bullying and sexual approaches from strangers are online dangers modern teenagers routinely face. And adults' knowledge of what young people are doing online is often vague and complacent.

[. . .]
Khushal Shah, 17 [Names have been changed]
From *London*
Hours online a day *Three*
Online devices *Smartphone, desktop, laptop, tablet*
Age when first went online *15*

When I was 14, I came into school one day and my friend said: 'Welcome to Facebook'. Someone had made a fake account in my name. There were things on my profile that were Photoshopped, like my face on a nude picture of someone else. And abusive comments towards others, about people's mums for example – sexual remarks. It was very disturbing. Someone was using my account to bully others in my name.

I felt so ashamed by what was on there. A lot of people stopped talking to me. I felt like an outcast. Finally my friends made me go to my teachers and parents to talk about it. They didn't know you could do such a thing or what you could do about it. Eventually Facebook got the account deactivated, and found the IP address and who had done it. I was told it was someone I knew, someone in my year group. Their parents were told, but I never found out who it was. That anonymity for the bully, it's like there's a screen protecting them from everything. It gives them power.

I have got Facebook now and I'm on a few other social networking sites, but before I go on, the first thing I check is the privacy settings.

As well as doing my A-levels, I'm now a trained cybermentor for the charity BeatBullying's chatroom. If anyone is in trouble, I private message them and try to help. I hear about bullying on Facebook, Twitter, Myspace, BBM, WhatsApp, Snapchat: there are so many sites and they keep changing. Cyberbullying's evolving. It's happening with younger and younger people, because they are growing up with this technology. I've been in touch with children as young as 11 being cyberbullied.

A lot of people think, 'How can I tell my parents?' Parents should make sure their child knows they can come to them for anything. They shouldn't just tell the child to turn the screen off or deactivate the account. They should guide them into confidently confronting the attack.

I want to become a psychologist when I finish school.

(Olivia Gordon, Saturday 9 November 2013, theguardian.com, ©Guardian News & Media Ltd 2013. Reproduced with permission)

Bauman (2013) highlights, not only that cyberbullying can be seen as 'bullying perpetrated with digital technology' (p. 248), but that it also has unique features, some of which are reflected in the DCSF's guidance (2007). She cites research by Mishna *et al.* (2012) that highlights the large overlap between cyberbullying and *cybervictimisation* as evidence for cyberbullying being a unique phenomenon (with 27.5 per cent of youths identified as being both cyberbullies and cybervictims). On the other side of the debate, she cites evidence to suggest that it is the 'behaviour rather than the method of delivery which is the critical factor' (p. 250) and the findings that the implementation of an anti-bullying programme containing no cyberspecific content appeared to lead to a decrease in the incidence of cyberbullying (Salmivalli *et al.*, 2011).

Reread the extract above. To what extent do theories of traditional bullying help us to understand cyberbullying?

SUMMARY OF MAIN ISSUES ADDRESSED IN THIS CHAPTER

- Bullying and cyberbullying are a significant cause for concern, both in education and within society as a whole. Recent reports and research link both bullying and cyberbullying to mental health difficulties.
- The central characteristic in definitions of bullying is an imbalance of power that makes it very difficult for the target of aversive behaviour to prevent or stop it.
- Self- and peer reports of bullying and victimisation are the most frequently used methods of identification and assessment. The preferred method will depend on the purpose of the assessment.
- Findings from large national samples of school pupils indicate that approximately one-third of those who bully are also bullied. These 'bully–victims' may represent a population at particularly high risk of negative emotional and social outcomes.
- Among the theories advanced to explain bullying, the following have been most influential:
  - ecological systems theories, which consider a multilevel analysis of bullying to be essential, where whole-school ethos interacts with individual-level variables to determine whether bullying will occur;
  - sociocognitive deficit theories: different types of bully may be characterised by different types of problem with cognitive and/or emotional processing;
  - social learning theory and attachment theory: the leading theories of family influence on bullying;

- social dominance theory: described as an important group process theory of bullying.
- Preventative programmes in schools draw largely on well-researched, moderately effective multilevel approaches. However, there is considerable controversy about the most effective direct-intervention strategies to employ when bullying has occurred. Politicians 'talking tough' advocate punishment, although psychological theory and research suggest that this may be unsuccessful or counterproductive with particular groups of pupils. A need for further research is highlighted, on which bullying interventions work, for whom, under what circumstances and whether effective anti-bullying programmes, alongside information and teaching about Internet safety, will also be effective in reducing cyberbullying.

KEY CONCEPTS AND TERMS

- Bullying
- Cyberbullying
- Victimisation
- Cybervictimisation
- Power imbalance
- Bully–victim

- Social information processing model
- Sociocognitive deficit
- Social learning theory
- Theory of mind
- Attachment theory

- Social dominance theory
- Ecological systems theory
- No blame approach
- Punishment

RECOMMENDATIONS FOR FURTHER READING

Journal articles

Bauman, S. (2013). Cyberbullying: What does research tell us? *Theory into Practice*, *52*(4), 249–56.

Hong, J.S. and Espelage, D.L. (2012). A review of research on bullying and peer victimization in school: An ecological system analysis. *Aggression and Violent Behavior*, *17*(4), 311–22.

Ma, X. (2001). Bullying and being bullied: To what extent are bullies also victims? *American Educational Research Journal*, *38*, 351–70.

Rigby, K. (2004). Addressing bullying in schools. Theoretical perspectives and their implications. *School Psychology International*, *25*(3), 287–300.

Stassen Berger, K. (2007). Update on bullying at school: Science forgotten? *Developmental Review*, *27*, 90–126.

Ttofi, M.M. and Farrington, D.P. (2011). Effectiveness of school-based programs to reduce bullying: A systematic and meta-analytic review. *Journal of Experimental Criminology*, *7*, 27–56.

Veenstra, R., Lindenberg, S., Huitsing, G., Sainio, M. and Salmivalli, C. (2014). The role of teachers in bullying: The relation between antibullying attitudes, efficacy, and efforts to reduce bullying. *Journal of Educational Psychology*. Available online at http://dx.doi.org/10.1037/a0036110 (accessed 28 November 2014).

Books and other publications

DfES (2000). *Bullying – Don't suffer in silence. An anti-bullying pack for schools*. London: DfES. Available online at http://publications.teachernet.gov.uk/eOrderingDownload/DfES %200064%20200MIG479.pdf (accessed 28 November 2014).

Smith, P. (2014). *Understanding School Bullying: Its nature and prevention strategies*. London: SAGE.

SAMPLE ESSAY TITLES

1 Are traditional bullies skilled manipulators or social inadequates?
2 Compare and contrast the success of different theories in explaining bullying behaviour.
3 Should bullies be punished? What can psychology contribute to this debate?
4 Is cyberbullying just another 'type' of bullying?

REFERENCES

Ainsworth, M.S., Blehar, M.C., Waters, E. and Wall, S. (1978). *Patterns of Attachment: A psychological study of the strange situation*. Hillsdale, NJ: Lawrence Erlbaum.

Anderson, M., Kaufman, J., Simon, T.R., Barios, L., Paulozzi, I., Ryan, G., Hammond, R., Modzeleski, W., Feucht, T., Potter, L. and The School-Bar Associated Violent Deaths Study Group (2001). School-associated violent deaths in the United States, 1994–1999. *Journal of the American Medical Association, 286*(21), 2695–702.

Archer, J. (2004.) Sex differences in aggression in real-world settings: A meta-analytic review. *Review of General Psychology, 8*(4), 291–322.

Arsenio, W.F. and Lemerise, E.A. (2001). Varieties of childhood bullying: Values, emotion-processing and social competence. *Social Development, 10*, 59–73.

Bauman, S. (2013). Cyberbullying: What does research tell us? *Theory Into Practice, 52*(4), 249–56.

Black, S.A. and Jackson, E. (2007). Using bullying incident density to evaluate the Olweus Bullying Prevention Programme. *School Psychology International, 28*(5), 623–38.

Blair, R.J.R., Peschardt, K.S., Budhani, S., Mitchell, D.G.V. and Pine, D.S. (2006). The development of psychopathy. *Journal of Child Psychology and Psychiatry, 47*(3/4), 262–75.

Bowers, L., Smith, P.K. and Binney, V. (1994). Perceived family relationships of bullies, victims and bully/victims in middle childhood. *Journal of Social and Personal Relationships, 11*(2), 215–32.

Bowlby, J. (1969). *Attachment and Loss* (Vol 1). New York: Basic Books.

Bronfenbrenner, U. and Ceci, S.J. (1994). Nature–nurture reconceptualized in developmental perspective: A bioecological model. *Psychological Review, 101*(4), 568.

Chamberlain, T., George, N., Golden, S., Walker, F. and Benton, T. (2010). *Tellus4 National Report* (National Foundation for Educational Research, Research Report: DCSF-RR218). London: DCSF.

ChildLine (2014). *Can I Tell You Something? What's affecting children in 2013* (ChildLine Review of 2012–13. NSPCC). Available online at www.nspcc.org.uk/news-and-views/latest-news/2014/childline-report/can-i-tell-you-something_wda100359.html (accessed 10 January 2014).

Coie, J.D., Dodge, K.A. and Coppotelli, H. (1982). Dimensions and types of social status: A cross-age perspective. *Developmental Psychology, 18(4)*, 557–70.

Copeland, W.E., Wolke, D., Angold, A. and Costello, E.J. (2013). Adult psychiatric outcomes of bullying and being bullied by peers in childhood and adolescence. *JAMA Psychiatry, 70(4)*, 419–26.

Cornell, D.T., Sheras, P.L. and Cole, J.C.M. (2006). Assessment of bullying. In S.R. Jimerson and M. Thurlong (eds), *Handbook of School Violence and School Safety from Research to Practice.* Mahwah, NJ: Lawrence Erlbaum.

Craig, W.M., Pepler, D.J. and Atlas, R.(2000). Observations of bullying in the playground and in the classroom. *School Psychology International, 2(1)*, 22–36.

Crick, M.R. and Dodge, K.A. (1994). A review and reformulation of social information-processing mechanisms in children's social adjustment. *Psychological Bulletin, 115(1)*, 74–101.

Crick, M.R. and Dodge, K.A. (1996). Social information processing mechanisms on reactive and proactive aggression. *Child Development, 67(3)*, 993–1002.

Department for Children, Schools and Families (DCSF) (2007). *Cyberbullying: Safe to learn: Embedding anti-bullying work in schools.* London: DCSF. Available online at www.kidscape. org.uk/media/83407/safe_to_learn_embedding_anti-bullying_work_in_schools.pdf (accessed 10 May 2014).

Department for Education (DfE) (2014). *Preventing and Tackling Bullying: Advice for headteachers, staff and governing bodies* (March). Available online at www.gov.uk/government/ uploads/system/uploads/attachment_data/file/368340/preventing_and_tackling_bullying_ october14.pdf (accessed 28 November 2014).

DfES (2002). *Bullying – Don't suffer in silence. An anti-bullying pack for schools.* London: DfES. Available online at http://publications.teachernet.gov.uk/eOrderingDownload/DfES% 200064%20200MIG479.pdf (accessed 28 November 2014).

Doll, B., Song, S. and Siemers, E. (2004). Classroom ecologies that support or discourage bullying. In D.L. Espelage and S.M. Swearer (eds), *Bullying in American Schools: A social-ecological perspective on prevention and intervention.* Mahwah, NJ: Lawrence Erlbaum, pp. 1–12.

Green, J. and Goldwyn, R. (2002). Annotation: Attachment disorganization and psycho-pathology: New findings in attachment research and the potential implications for developmental psychopathology in childhood. *Journal of Child Psychology and Psychiatry, 43(7)*, 835–46.

Guardian Unlimited (2006, 4 January). Council may drop 'no-blame' bullying policy. Available online at www.theguardian.com/education/2006/jan/04/schools.uk1 (accessed 10 May 2014).

Guasp, A. (2012). *The School Report: The experiences of gay young people in Britain's schools in 2012.* London: Stonewall.

Gutman, L.M. and Brown, J. (2008). *The Importance of Social Worlds: An investigation of peer relations* (Centre for Research on the Wider Benefits of Learning, Institute of Education,

Research Brief, DCSF-WBL-06–08). London: DCSF. Available online at www.gov.uk/government/publications/the-importance-of-social-worlds-an-investigation-of-peer-relationships (accessed 28 November 2014).

Hansen, T.B., Steenberg, L.M., Palic, S. and Elklit, A. (2012). A review of psychological factors related to bullying victimization in schools. *Aggression and Violent Behavior, 17*(4), 383–7.

Hawker, D.S. and Boulton, M.J. (2001). Sub-types of peer harassment and their correlates: A social dominance perspective. In J. Juvonen and S. Graham (eds), *Peer Harassment in School.* New York: Guilford.

Hong, J.S. and Espelage, D.L. (2012). A review of research on bullying and peer victimization in school: An ecological system analysis. *Aggression and Violent Behavior, 17*(4), 311–22.

Juvonen, J. and Graham, S. (2004). Research-based interventions on bullying. In C.E. Sanders and G.D. Phye (eds), *Bullying: Implications for the classroom.* San Diego, CA: Elsevier Academic Press, pp. 229–55.

Juvonen, J., Nishina, A. and Graham, S. (2001). Self-views versus peer perceptions of victim status among early adolescents. In J. Juvonen and S. Graham (eds), *Peer Harassment in School.* New York: Guilford.

Ma, X. (2001). Bullying and being bullied: To what extent are bullies also victims? *American Educational Research Journal, 38,* 351–70.

Mishna, F., Khoury-Kassabri, M., Gadalla, T. and Daciuk, J. (2012). Risk factors for involvement in cyber bullying: Victims, bullies and bully–victims. *Children and Youth Services Review, 34*(1), 63–70.

Monks, C.P., Smith, P.K., Naylor, P., Barter, C., Ireland, J.L. and Coyne, I. (2009). Bullying in different contexts: Commonalities, differences and the role of theory. *Aggression and Violent Behavior, 14*(2), 146–56.

Nabuzoka, D. and Smith, P.K. (1993). Sociometric status and social behaviour of children with and without learning difficulties. *Journal of Child Psychology and Psychiatry, 34*(8), 1435–48.

National Society for the Prevention of Cruelty to Children (NSPCC) (2014). [website] www.nspcc.org.uk/news-and-views/latest-news/2014/childline-report/can-i-tell-you-something_wda100359.html (accessed 10 May 2014).

Nishina, A. (2004). A theoretical review of bullying: Can it be eliminated? In C.E. Sanders and G.D. Phye (eds), *Bullying: Implications for the classroom.* San Diego, CA: Elsevier Academic Press.

Olweus, D. (1978). *Aggression in the Schools: Bullies and whipping boys.* Washington, DC: Hemisphere (Wiley).

Olweus, D. (1991). Bully/victim problems among school children: Basic facts and effects of a school-based intervention programme. In D.J. Pepler and K.H. Reuben (eds), *The Development and Treatment of Childhood Aggression.* Hillsdale, NJ; Erlbaum, pp. 411–48.

Olweus, D. (1993). *Bullying at School.* Oxford, UK: Blackwell.

Olweus, D. (1994). Annotation: Bullying at school: Basic facts and effects of a school-based intervention programme. *Journal of Child Psychology and Psychiatry, 35,* 1171–90.

Orpinas, P. and Horne, A.M. (2006). *Bullying Prevention: Creating a positive school climate and developing social competence.* Washington, DC: American Psychological Association.

Payne, A.A. and Gottfriedson, D.C. (2004). Schools and bullying: School factors related to bullying and school-based bullying interventions. In C.E. Sanders and G.D. Phye (eds), *Bullying: Implications for the classroom*. San Diego, CA: Elsevier Academic Press, pp. 159–76.

Pellegrini, A.D. (2001). Sampling instances of victimization in middle school: A methodological comparison. In J. Juvonen and S. Graham (eds), *Peer Harassment in School. The plight of the vulnerable and victimized*. New York: Guilford, pp. 125–44.

Pellegrini, A.D. and Bartini, M. (2000). An empirical comparison of methods of sampling aggression and victimization in school settings. *Journal of Educational Psychology, 92*(2), 360–6.

Pepler, D.J. and Craig, W.M. (1995). A peek behind the fence: Naturalistic observations of aggressive children with remote audio visual recording. *Developmental Psychology, 31*(4), 548–53.

Pikas, A. (2002). New developments of the shared concern method. *School Psychology International, 23*(3), 307–26.

Rigby, K. (2004). Addressing bullying in schools. Theoretical perspectives and their implications. *School Psychology International, 25*(3), 287–300.

Rigby, K. (2005). Why do some children bully at school? The contribution of negative attitudes towards victims and the perceived expectations of friends, parents and teachers. *School Psychology International, 26*(2), 147–61.

Rigby, K. and Slee, P.T. (1998). *The Peer Relations Questionnaire (PRQ)*. Point Lonsdale, Australia: The Professional Reading Guide.

Rigby, K. and Smith, P.K. (2011). Is school bullying really on the rise? *Social Psychology of Education, 14*(4), 441–55.

Salmivalli, C. (1999). Participant role approach to school bullying: Implications for interventions. *Journal of Adolescence, 22*, 453–9.

Salmivalli, C., Kärnä, A. and Poskiparta, E. (2011). Counteracting bullying in Finland: The KiVa program and its effects on different forms of being bullied. *International Journal of Behavioral Development, 35*(5), 405–11.

Schwartz, D., Dodge, K.A., Pettit, G.S. and Bates, J.E. (1997). The early socialization of aggressive victims of bullying. *Child Development, 68*(4), 665–75.

Shakoor, S., Jaffee, S.R., Bowes, L., Ouellet-Morin, I., Andreou, P., Happe, F., Moffitt, T.E. and Arseneault, L. (2012). A prospective longitudinal study of children's theory of mind and adolescent involvement in bullying. *Journal of Child Psychology and Psychiatry, 53*(3), 254–61.

Sharp, S. (1999). Bullying behaviour in schools. In N. Frederickson and R.J. Cameron (eds), *Psychology in Education Portfolio*. Maidenhead, UK: NFER-Nelson.

Slee, P.T. and Rigby, K. (1993). The relationship of Eysenck's personality factors and self esteem to bully-victim behaviour in Australian schoolboys. *Personality and Individual Differences, 14*(2), 371–3.

Smith, P.K. (2001). Should we blame the bullies? *The Psychologist, 14*(2), 61.

Smith, P.K. (2004). Bullying: Recent developments. *Child and Adolescent Mental Health, 9*(3), 98–103.

Smith, P.K., Mahdavi, J., Carvalho, M., Fisher, S., Russell, S. and Tippett, N. (2008). Cyberbullying: Its nature and impact in secondary school pupils. *Journal of Child Psychology and Psychiatry, 49*(4), 376–85.

Solberg, M.E., Olweus, D. and Endresen, I.M. (2007). Bullies and victims at school: Are they the same pupils? *British Journal of Educational Psychology, 77*, 441–64.

Sutton, J., Smith, P.K. and Swettenham, J. (1999a). Bullying and 'theory of mind': A critique of the 'social skills deficit' view of anti-social behaviour. *Social Development, 8*(1), 117–27.

Sutton, J., Smith, P.K., and Swettenham, J. (1999b). Social cognition and bullying: Social inadequacy or skilled manipulation? *British Journal of Developmental Psychology, 17*(3), 435–50.

Sutton, J., Smith, P.K. and Swettenham, J. (2001). 'It's easy, it works and it makes me feel good': A response to Arsenio and Lemerise. *Social Development, 10*(1), 74–8.

Swearer, S.M. and Espelage, D.L. (2004). Introduction: A social–ecological framework of bullying among youth. In D.L. Espelage and S.M. Swearer (eds), *Bullying in American Schools: A social–ecological perspective on prevention and intervention*. Mahwah, NJ: Lawrence Erlbaum, pp. 1–12.

Swearer, S.M., Song, S.Y., Cary, P.T., Eagle, J.W. and Mickleson, W.T. (2001). Psychosocial correlates in bullying and victimization: The relationship between depression, anxiety and bully/victim status. *Journal of Emotional Abuse, 2*, 95–121.

Thompson, F. and Smith, P.K. (2011). *The Use and Effectiveness of Anti-bullying Strategies in Schools* (Research Report DFE-RR098). London: DfE.

Ttofi, M.M. and Farrington, D.P. (2011). Effectiveness of school-based programs to reduce bullying: A systematic and meta-analytic review. *Journal of Experimental Criminology, 7*, 27–56.

Unnever, J.D. and Cornell, D.G. (2004). Middle school victims of bullying: Who reports being bullied? *Aggressive Behaviour, 30*(5), 373–88.

Viding, E., Simmonds, E., Petrides, K.V. and Frederickson, N. (2009). The contribution of callous-unemotional traits and conduct problems to bullying in early adolescence. *Journal of Child Psychology and Psychiatry, 50*(4), 471–81.

Vossekuil, B., Fein, R.A., Reddy, M., Borum, R. and Modzeleski, W. (2002). The final report and findings of the safe school initiative: Implications for the prevention of school attacks in the United States. Washington, DC: US Secret Service and US Department of Education.

Wang, C., Berry, B. and Swearer, S.M. (2013). The critical role of school climate in effective bullying prevention. *Theory Into Practice, 52*(4), 296–302.

Whitney, I. and Smith, P.K. (1993). A survey of the nature and extent of bullying in junior/middle and secondary schools. *Educational Research, 35*(1), 3–25.

Wike, T.L. and Fraser, M.W. (2009). School shootings: Making sense of the senseless. *Aggression and Violent Behavior, 14*(3), 162–9.

Young, S. (1998). Support group approach to bullying in schools. *Educational Psychology in Practice, 14*, 32–9.

Zelli, A., Dodge, K.A., Lochman, J.E., Laird, R.D. and Conduct Problems Prevention Research Group (1999). The distinction between beliefs legitimizing aggression and deviant processing of social queues: Testing measurement validity and the hypothesis that bias processing mediates the effects of beliefs on aggression. *Journal of Personality and Social Psychology, 77*(1), 150–66.

12 Coping with life by coping with school?

School refusal in young people

Anthea Gulliford and Andy Miller

CHAPTER SUMMARY

In this chapter, we explore psychological explanations for what may be happening when a young person avoids attending school. Terms such as school phobia, school refusal, persistent *and* chronic non-attendance *and* truancy *will be reviewed.*

The particular focus here is the form of school non-attendance known as school refusal, sometimes called school phobia. Considering a range of theoretical formulations for school refusal behaviour will lead us to understand how these in turn influence interventions. The literature guides us to a particular focus upon the role of anxiety in school refusal behaviour, and in turn upon cognitive behavioural approaches that may help to remediate this.

We shall acknowledge the significant influence of family and school contexts upon a young person refusing to attend school, and explore what this may imply for the practitioner. Above all, the individual and varying nature of the problem presentation for school refusal will be acknowledged. An example from educational psychology casework is presented to illustrate a multisystemic approach to school refusal-based problems.

LEARNING OUTCOMES

When you have studied this chapter, you should be able to:

1 describe the major theoretical formulations that have attempted to account for chronic non-school attendance;
2 explain how these link to various intervention approaches;
3 identify those aspects of case presentations that may have significant implications for assessment and intervention with school refusers;
4 justify the selection of components of effective intervention plans for school refusers.

WHAT IS SCHOOL PHOBIA?

School refusal can be a challenging phenomenon for professionals to intervene with, and at very least concerning, if not upsetting, for families and others involved around such cases. Typically, a case involving a young person who will not attend school is complex, with many features or layers of the scenario to attend to (Kearney, 2008a). This complexity is mirrored in the definitions used over the years to describe such behaviours, and exploring these is a starting point.

The terms school refusal, school phobia, school non–attendance, and truancy, can all appear to represent similar elements of differing phenomena. Kearney (2003) has argued that different sets of professionals are often 'not on the same page' when addressing school refusal, partly through the disparity that exists in terms of fundamental concepts such as definition, assessment and treatment: the terms – and perhaps approaches – adopted often depending upon a professional's identity and perspective (Kearney and Graczyk, 2014).

As a useful starting point Kearney (2008a) allows us to distinguish between *problematic* and *non-problematic* attendance, with the implication that short-lived or even pre-arranged non-attendance, for example through illness, does not require our focus in the same way. We should be mindful, however, of the hidden risks of such behaviours, and of the swift pathways that may lead towards *problematic attendance*, once a young person has ceased even temporarily attending school (Christenson and Thurlow, 2004; Lehr *et al.*, 2004; Hickman *et al.*, 2008).

Another conceptual distinction can be drawn. There are those young people who choose not to attend school through various kinds of disaffection, typically *without the knowledge of their parents or carers* (Blagg and Yule, 1984; Blagg, 1987), behaviour that meets the description of truancy or, in its more extreme form, *dropout* (Christenson and Thurlow, 2004). Others, on the other hand, may refuse to attend for reasons related to possible generalised or social anxieties or emotional distress regarding a feature of the school environment, *with the awareness of their parents or carers* (Blagg and Yule, 1984; Ingul and Nordahl, 2013), who meet the description of school refusal *or* sometimes school phobia. Although the difficulty of parents or carers in asserting influence over a *truant* child is sometimes noted (Thomas *et al.*, 2011; Heyne *et al.*, 2013), it can also be seen as a feature of school refusal or phobia (Chapman, 2007; Ollendick and Benoit, 2012).

School phobia has been described as distinct from school refusal, as a matter of degree or alternatively as a discrete phenomenon, where, aligned to the literature on phobias (Carr, 2006), a child is considered to hold a specific fear regarding something, perhaps an activity or a part of the building, within the school setting (Hersov, 1977; Chitiyo and Wheeler, 2006). Interestingly, Torrens Armstrong and colleagues consider whether anxious or fearful behaviours can, in fact, be easily discriminated by school staff, or whether the distinction between school refusal and school phobia can be given legitimacy by those who may see the behavioural response as unreasonable (Torrens Armstrong *et al.*, 2011). In this chapter, the interchangeable use of the terms school phobia and refusal are accepted. Focus Box 12.1 offers Blagg's definitions of key terms (1987).

Criteria used by Blagg (1987) for distinguishing between school phobia, truancy and other non-attendance

Criteria for defining school phobia (from Berg *et al.*, 1969)	Severe difficulty in attending school, often resulting in prolonged absence
	Severe emotional upset, which may involve such symptoms as excessive fearfulness, temper tantrums, misery or complaints of feeling ill, without obvious organic cause, when faced with the prospect of going to school
	Pupil remains at home with the knowledge of parents during school hours
	Absence of significant antisocial disorders such a juvenile delinquency, disruptiveness and sexual activity
Criteria for defining truancy (from Blagg and Yule, 1984)	Absent from school without good reason on at least five occasions in one term
	Pupil shows no evidence of a marked emotional upset accompanying the non-attendance at school
	Pupil is absent without the parents' permission or approval, the majority of time off being spent away from home. Parents sometimes aware of the non-attendance, but unable to exert any influence over their child
Criteria for defining other poor attenders (from Blagg and Yule, 1984)	Absent from school without good reason on at least five occasions in one term
	Pupil shows no evidence of a marked emotional upset accompanying the non-attendance at school
	Remaining at home with knowledge and permission of parents (possibly kept at home deliberately to help with an ill or 'needy' parent)

FOCUS 12.1

Over time, prominence has been given to explanations that address the *emotional component* of school refusal, linking school refusal to the ever-growing literature on anxiety in childhood and adolescence (Carr, 2008, 2009; Chitiyo and Wheeler, 2006), guiding us to the need for insights into the way in which the child interacts with their environment in instances of school refusal. Hughes *et al.* (2010), for example, note the way in which the rewarding or aversive features of the environment may subtly maintain a child's refusal to attend school.

Locally generated nomenclature among educational psychologists and local authorities in Britain seems to vary: for example, 'emotionally based school refusal' can be found in West Sussex, and 'anxiety related school attendance difficulties' in Nottinghamshire. By and large, the term school phobia has less currency with practitioners, if not the academic community, where it may be seen as outdated and potentially overly specific (Thambirajah *et al.*, 2007).

Nuttall and Woods (2013) remind us of the heterogeneity of each case involving a young person refusing to attend school, and, for some practitioners, definitions and distinctions within the term school refusal may appear over-categorical. We can do well by being mindful of school refusal as a description of behaviour, rather than a categorical description of a static quality of a young person (Pellegrini, 2007). An accepted and helpful delineation of school refusal is to consider two constituent components: the *emotional* and *behavioural* aspects (Thambirajah *et al.*, 2007), and this may guide practitioners' approaches to understanding and intervening with distinct facets of each school refusal concern. To further analyse the individual features of each case, some authors have urged a focus upon the *functional consequences* of the behaviours in question (Kearney and Silverman, 1993, 1999), whereas others have recommended a focus upon the school (Pellegrini, 2007) or family context (Chapman, 2007; Kearney and Silverman, 1995) in which the behaviour occurs.

KEY PERSPECTIVES: THE CASE FOR A FUNCTIONAL ANALYSIS

Kearney and Silverman (1990) argued for an approach that examined the functions served by a pupil not attending school, rather than a system based on categorisation through symptoms. They suggested four main sets of reasons for non-attendance, which incorporate a number of previous formulations, some in novel rearrangements:

- *to avoid the experience of severe anxiety or fearfulness related to attending school*: one or more specific features of the school day may be feared or causing anxiety, for example, the toilets, the corridors, sitting examinations or specific lessons (often physical education lessons);
- *to avoid social situations that are feared, or that cause anxiety*: this includes problems with peers, perhaps due to bullying or name calling; social isolation at school; and problems with individual teachers (e.g. being criticised or humiliated by a teacher in front of classmates);
- *to seek attention or to reduce the feeling of separation anxiety*: Kearney and Silverman (1990) combine these different concepts, arguing that functionally they are equivalent: the young person receives positive reinforcement for their non-attendance in the shape of special attention at home;

- *to enjoy rewarding experiences that non-attendance at school may bring*: for example, this could be watching television or playing computer games at home, or associating with friends; depending on the company kept, this could lead to involvement in antisocial acts and/or criminal activities; this category, therefore, includes those children and young people usually referred to as truants.

Kearney (2007) has consolidated the usefulness of this four-function model as a way of organising, assessing and treating this population by carrying out hierarchical regression analysis and structural equation modelling. Data on 222 young people aged between 5 and 17 years and displaying school refusal were provided by the young people and their parents. Kearney found that 'behaviour function' was a better determinant of degree of school absenteeism than 'behaviour form' (i.e. extent of depressive symptoms; school-based fear; negative affectivity consisting of worry, oversensitivity, concentration problems and physiological symptoms of anxiety; *social anxiety* and generalised anxiety).

KEY PERSPECTIVES: THE CHILD AND FAMILY AND THE SCHOOL

Examining behaviour *function* guides us to attend to the familial and social context for that behaviour, towards ecological perspectives encountered elsewhere in this volume (Bronfenbrenner and Morris, 2006). Kearney (2008a) notes the potential for deep complexity in problematic school non-attendance and suggests a five-level model, to allow professionals to explore what proximal and distal factors – including *child* and *family*, *school* and *community* factors – might be involved in maintaining school refusal. Theorists have explored the question of family dynamics and how they might subtly or directly contribute to school refusal behaviours, and they have made links with a wider literature exploring parent–child interactions, information processing biases and parenting practices (Barth *et al.*, 2007; Carr, 2009; Hoglund and Leadbeater, 2004; Kearney and Silverman, 1995; Ollendick and Benoit, 2012; Schafer, 2011).

Other authors have noted factors within the school context that may play a part in the development of a school refusal problem (Lauchlan, 2003; Pellegrini, 2007; Kearney, 2008a), suggesting the need for responsive curricula, structures and social processes, that is, teaching approaches that can accommodate the specific anxieties or needs of a young person. One study highlighted how parents of school refusers particularly identify the vulnerable young person's need for two significant features in school: predictability in their environment and teacher support (Havik *et al.*, 2014). Carroll (2011) explored the peer group relationships of low attenders and reported on the apparent significance of the wider social environment for the pupil, identifying lower peer nominations in friendship preferences by peers for low attenders and highlighting the potential for cumulative vulnerabilities for school refusers, who may not have the social support that often buffers a young person's experience of school.

INCIDENCE AND EPIDEMIOLOGY OF *SCHOOL REFUSAL*

Studies yield varying *incidence* rates, depending on the nature and stringency of the definition of school refusal used. It is possible to conclude that around 1–2 per cent of the UK school aged population is a figure for the prevalence of *school refusal* (Attwood and Croll, 2006; Elliot, 1999), but one which masks a considerably higher incidence among older pupils, and among particular populations (Attwood and Croll, 2015; Chitiyo and Wheeler, 2006; Kearney, 2008b).

Berg (1996) summarised the epidemiological features of school refusal, indicating no significance of gender, social class, academic ability or attainment. He did, however, identify family position as a significant factor, with the youngest child in a family of several children more likely to be affected. It was found that parents of school refusers were often older than would otherwise be expected. Although a school child of any age may refuse to attend, young teenagers at about the time of transition from primary to secondary school were more likely to develop school refusal.

Onset of refusal tends to be gradual, but it *may* occur suddenly after time away from school because of illness or holidays, and in some cases it may even occur without any obvious reason. Kearney (2008b) associates the onset of school refusal behaviours with the first time a child or young person enters a new educational setting, for example, a new nursery or secondary school, highlighting times of *transition* as a potential risk. Others have noted the risks of school refusal following a critical incident or traumatic event (Torrens Armstrong *et al.*, 2011).

Internal features of the young person will be reviewed below, but it is now accepted that there is a strong relationship between social anxiety and school refusal (Ingul and Nordahl, 2013). Berg noted that, for some young people, although not all, there may be an associated social impairment, leading to their avoidance of contact with other children (Berg, 1996).

Taking an ecological perspective on school refusal requires a focus on the contexts in which it occurs. Lauchlan (2003) notes school features that may be associated with the onset and severity of chronic non-attendance as including:

- an environment in which there are high occurrences of bullying, truancy and disruption;
- a school setting or streaming policy that results in the pupil being grouped with a number of disaffected and troublesome peers;
- a school where teacher–pupil relationships are excessively formal, impersonal and/or generally hostile;
- where toilets, corridors and playground areas are not monitored carefully by staff, perhaps because such duties are not seen as their responsibility.

CONSEQUENCES OF SCHOOL REFUSAL

Information about the *long-term outcomes* for young people who exhibit features of school refusal varies (McShane *et al.*, 2004), depending on a range of factors, including whether treatment interventions have been taken up, and their type, and also the particular characteristics of the young people involved, for example, the presence of comorbid mental health difficulties or academic difficulties. There are, though, obvious potential educational *correlates*, such as lowered academic attainment, reduced performance at public examinations and, consequently, reduced career options (Carroll, 2010). Elsewhere, regression analyses have identified school refusal as a key risk factor for self-harm and other risk behaviours associated with adolescence, for example risky sexual behaviour, substance use and attempting suicide (Guttmacher *et al.*, 2002; Hallfors *et al.*, 2002; Denny *et al.*, 2003; Almeida *et al.*, 2006; Chou *et al.*, 2006; Henry and Huizinga, 2007).

School refusal may also be correlated with long-term problems in adulthood, including marital, occupational and economic difficulties, anxiety disorders, depression, alcoholism and antisocial behaviour (Kearney, 2008b; Dembo *et al.*, 2013).

UNDERSTANDING SCHOOL REFUSAL: THE GROWTH OF THE CONCEPT OF ANXIETY

At the outset of this field, attempts at understanding and treatment were made by psychiatric personnel who drew on psychodynamic and other theories in their search for a conceptualisation of school refusal. Three types of explanation were originally offered: based on separation anxiety, anxiety about aspects of schooling and other social anxieties.

Explanations in terms of separation anxiety derive from psychoanalytic thinking and were first advanced by Johnson *et al.* (1941). In this formulation, separation anxiety was seen as a product of an unresolved mother–child dependency relationship in which an excessively strong mother–child attachment resulted in a reluctance on the part of a child to leave the home. Later papers (for example, Estes *et al.*, 1956) provided a more detailed account of the dynamic nature of the development of what was then seen as a type of neurosis. In addition to the early dependency relationship, separation issues were also thought to be founded on an inadequate fulfilment of the mother's emotional needs within an intimate adult relationship. It was posited that, as a result of an interplay of hostility and dependency, and as a consequence of subconscious mechanisms of displacement and projection, a level of anxiety about separation developed in the child to an acute degree. (Refer to Fonagy, 2010, for a fuller discussion of the insights psychoanalytic theory can provide us with, and how these might relate to attachment and separation theorising.)

An alternative psychoanalytic approach, suggested by Berry *et al.* (1993), focused on the child's feelings of *omnipotence*. In this theory, the child developed a grandiose opinion of him or herself that, when challenged in school by realities that confront the child's limitations, lead to avoidance of school and staying at home, where parents further reinforce the distorted self-image. This interpretation might, more moderately, be considered through reflection upon family dynamics, where parents or carers may have struggled to successfully assert rules and boundaries.

A very broad range of familial and parenting approaches can constitute successful ones, but Baumrind's (2005) model of parenting styles posits three core modes of parenting: authoritative, authoritarian and permissive. The first of these is the one that enables harmony and appropriate rule setting and has been associated with more contented youth development (Baumrind, 2005) and with lower levels of anxiety in children (Ginsburg *et al.*, 2005).

Studies of factors associated with school refusal have noted familial relationships as a potential area for assessment and intervention, with some features noted as potentially contributing to school refusal, such as marital discord (Kearney and Bates, 2005) or rule setting within the family (Kearney and Silverman, 1995). Models of social anxiety in youth have also explored the effects of parent–child interactions upon the development of anxiety (Ollendick and Benoit, 2012). Overall, the literature indicates to a practitioner the importance of exploring the influences of family and parenting in school refusal.

A third view, deriving from a behavioural viewpoint and, more specifically, from within *classical conditioning*, was that of *school-focused anxiety*, noted above as school phobia, in which some particular features of the school environment, such as the size of buildings, the strictness of some teachers, the difficulty of some lessons and tasks or the potential embarrassment associated with using the toilet or changing for physical education activities become the source of fear and anxiety.

A fourth formulation was that of social anxiety, a more specific form of school-based anxiety centring specifically on interactions with others and incorporating fears of being rejected, isolated or bullied, and an inability to make friends. A sense of psychological safety is important for children and young people, and there is evidence that social anxiety can play a significant role in the development and maintenance of school refusal behaviours for some young people (Coplan and Prakash, 2004; Ingul and Nordahl, 2013).

Consider the brief case study presented in Activity Box 12.1. It is a real case, disguised to preserve confidentiality.

Some aspects of Martin's case – the persistent and apparently unexplained nature of his absence, the somatic complaints in the early morning and his intense fearfulness when the possibility of a return to school was discussed – figure centrally in the original description presented by Broadwin (1932) in the first description of a form of school non-attendance seemingly characterised by fearful responses.

In the classic 'clinical presentation' of school phobia put forward by Hersov (1977), Hersov noted the overt signs of anxiety or panic in such cases, despite encouragement or persuasion by parents, with the young person unable to complete the journey to school, or perhaps even unable to leave the home. Blagg (1987) noted the potential presence of various somatic complaints, aches and pains or nausea, for example, which might dissipate once the need to attend school was lifted.

MAKING SENSE OF SCHOOL REFUSAL/PHOBIA

The concerns for students such as Martin may challenge practitioners. School staff may feel stress, through disquiet about missed lessons, their inability to 'get to the bottom of the problem' or challenged relationships with the family (Blagg, 1987). They may feel disappointment when a student promises to begin attending again on a certain date and then fails to do so, or may even doubt the reality of the underlying anxieties (Torrens Armstrong *et al.*, 2011). The role of the educational psychologist can be to support those concerned – family, staff and other professionals – through reframing and problem-solving, using psychologically informed models, as well as some of the careful consultation approaches described earlier in this volume (see Chapters 1 and 10, for example).

ACTIVITY 12.1

Case study: Part 1: The initial presentation

Martin was a young person in Year 3, aged 7 years, whose non-attendance at school was a great concern to a worried and newly in post headteacher. Martin had, for around the past 4 months, gradually reduced his attendance at school and, by the later part of the Spring Term of Year 3, had moved from being a sporadic attender to not attending school at all. The headteacher had recently called a meeting between Martin's parents and an education welfare officer, who had advised the parents that Martin really must attend school or face strong consequences.

Martin's mother noted that he had had a bout of flu in the Autumn Term. She stated that she felt it would be difficult for Martin to attend school now, because, although he was generally well again, he often reported feelings of nausea in the morning that began when he was brushing his teeth.

When Martin was brought into the school playground by his mother the morning following the meeting, he cried and clung to his mother, refusing to leave her. Eventually, they left to return home. After a telephone call between his mother and the headteacher later that day, it was agreed that Martin's mother would try once again, the following morning, but this time with the class teacher present to coax Martin into school.

The next day, the same thing happened, with Martin refusing this time to even enter the school playground and attempting to kick a teaching assistant who hoped to prise him away from his mother. These visits left his mother emotionally drained, and Martin appeared distressed. Teaching staff were concerned about the effect on other pupils.

The headteacher sought the advice of the educational psychologist, asking what kind of emotional distress could be causing Martin to refuse to enter school, and how to help with this problem.

A summary of information from the school included the following further details:

- Martin was young for his year group, having an August birthday.
- His father has lost his job the previous summer and was now at home during the day with Martin's mother, who was a homemaker.
- Martin was the youngest of three children. The older sister and brother, 15 and 17, respectively, were living at home, his brother attending college, and his sister attending school.
- His parents were very anxious that, as there was no wage earner in the home, they should not be prosecuted for failing to bring their son to school.

Activity

Consider your initial response to the following questions:

1 What hypotheses might plausibly explain Martin's behaviour?
2 Why might it be desirable for Martin to return to school?
3 Why might it be undesirable for Martin to return to school?

ACTIVITY 12.2

Case study: Part 2: Further assessment information and the initial formulation

A meeting was convened between the psychologist, Martin's parents and the school's special needs co-ordinator (SENCo), to discuss Martin's situation.

Following a broad-ranging discussion with Martin's parents, the educational psychologist explored a number of questions with them. This revealed:

- Martin had been unwell in October, and his attendance had fallen from 93 per cent in September to 43 per cent by December.
- During January and February, Martin's attendance dropped significantly. By March, he was refusing to enter school.
- Martin's parents had felt concerned when he entered Year 3 that he would not be able to keep up with the academic pace expected, where they perceived the work as more formal and demanding.
- Martin's academic attainments were at the lower end of the range of his class.
- Martin, his parents felt, was an easy child and good company at home. Martin's sister, they noted, was very helpful around the home, helping with Martin's needs. After two older children, Martin had been a much-longed-for third child.
- Martin's father stated that, although the loss of his job was upsetting, the family kept him busy at home.
- Martin's nausea in the mornings led his mother to take him to the family doctor, who felt that there was no underlying cause. His mother said that, once Martin had had a snack mid morning, he seemed to recover. She felt that it was important, if he were to attend school, to make sure that someone could offer him this same support at break times.
- The school noted that Martin did not seem to have many friendships. He seemed not to enjoy outdoor play, and lunchtimes often saw him seeking to help out in the classroom.

Activity

Consider the comments above on the clinical presentation of school phobia; the criteria used by Blagg for distinguishing between school phobia, truancy and other non-attendance; and the epidemiological aspects of school refusal.

1 Identify the theoretical explanations of school refusal behaviour that might hold relevance as explanations of Martin's behaviour.
2 From the information given so far, generate a number of explanatory hypotheses for Martin's behaviour and order them in terms of their likelihood.

INTERVENTION APPROACHES

Each of the key formulations outlined above can be linked to specific interventions. Considering the early conceptualisations of school refusal behaviour, Blagg (1987) reviewed early treatment studies based on a traditional psychodynamic approach, beginning with a study published by Jung in 1911 and ranging through a number that reported the use of psychoanalysis, either with children alone or mother and child together, with some courses of treatment lasting for up to 3 years. Blagg also referred to a series of interventions, the first published in 1948, in which children and young people were treated by hospital admission, as an in-patient, typically on a psychiatric ward. More recent thinking within child and adolescent psychiatry has emphasised the need for a rapid return to school wherever possible (Goodman and Scott, 2002), with the possibility of individual psychotherapy to explore more persistent anxieties being offered, once the child is back in school (Black and Cotterell, 1993). By 1993, Black and Cotterell were reporting that, in the British context, in-patient treatment of school refusal was most uncommon. In terms of efficacy, King and Bernstein (2001) have pointed out that neither play therapy nor psychodynamic psychotherapy treatments for school refusal have been subjected to rigorous evaluation. It is only more recently that the outcomes of family therapy have been investigated, with some evidence of its probable efficacy (Carr, 2009).

From a behavioural psychology orientation, *systematic desensitisation* approaches were located within a classical conditioning framework and attempted to help the young person overcome the anxiety by reciprocal inhibition (Wolpe, 1954), that is, the teaching of behaviours antagonistic to the anxiety, such as controlled breathing or imagining pleasant activities. Such treatments either took place entirely in the child's imagination or *in vivo*, where some or all of the treatment would be carried out in the presence of the anxiety-producing stimuli, perhaps in the early morning before school departure or, if it were possible to arrange, at school itself.

As an alternative to systematic desensitisation approaches, some behaviour therapists found the use of *emotive imagery* to be a powerful alternative. Galloway and Miller (1978), two educational psychologists, reported on the case of an 11-year-old boy who regularly refused to go to school on certain mornings. Interviews with the boy and his mother revealed that he was fearful of showering after games and physical activities. A programme of systematic desensitisation, using imagined shower scenes followed up by reciprocal inhibition training *in vivo*, enabled the boy to improve his attendance and take showers at school after a total of seven treatment sessions.

Flooding or *implosion* is a procedure for confronting the maximally feared situation, usually in imagination, directly rather than after graded exposure, as in most desensitisation approaches. Blagg (1987) cautioned that real-life confrontation of maximal fears – flooding – was a highly demanding and stressful treatment, not least as a result of the '*extinction* spike', a temporary accentuation of the fear, as an early phase of classical extinction. For this reason and others, Blagg suggested that, if used at all, flooding should be used as one part of a more complex, composite approach.

From an *operant conditioning* stance, approaches have attempted to alter reinforcement contingencies by attempting to maximise the reinforcement for being in school, by creating *positive, reinforcing* experiences within the school. Conversely, attention has been paid to the need to avoid *positive reinforcement* for school refusal, such as activities of choice being pursued by a young person. Approaches within this paradigm have noted, too, the need to decrease *negative reinforcement* – avoidance of unpleasant stimuli for the child (Kearney and Albano, 2004). These considerations ultimately highlight the potential significance of school ecology as part of a child's school refusal (Lauchlan, 2003; Nuttall and Woods, 2013).

The 'rapid response' approach

Blagg (1987) gave guidelines for attempting to ensure a rapid return to school. His work was distinctive for its time in combining theoretical insights from both a psychodynamic and a behavioural perspective (including some rudiments of early CBT). He set out practical advice on information gathering, assessment and problem formulation and addressed the complex challenges of putting into practice multilevel plans that required a number of parties to work together, often under conditions of high emotion and stress.

Blagg evaluated this *rapid response* approach by comparing the use of this behavioural approach with young people against those receiving home tuition and psychotherapy, and against sixteen young people who were hospitalised (Blagg and Yule, 1984). The authors concluded that the rapid response approach achieved a better outcome, in terms of a maintained return to school, than the comparative treatment groups – and than any other reported study at that time dealing with young people in the 11–16 age range. More recently, Grandison (2011) has highlighted the need for ensuring longer-term maintenance and follow-up support from practitioners in achieving successful interventions and attendance patterns.

INTERVENTION APPROACHES EMPLOYING COGNITIVE BEHAVIOURAL THERAPY

Among all of the approaches, *cognitive behavioural therapy* (CBT), which aims to mediate the anxiety-based features of school refusal, has a particularly strong evidence base (Heyne *et al.*, 2011; Seligman and Ollendick, 2011; Maric *et al.*, 2013). CBT uses cognitive restructuring and behavioural tasks to intervene with automatic thoughts and maladaptive behaviours, highlighting the relationship between behaviour and the environment in developing new behavioural repertoires (Chu *et al.*, 2013; Fuggle *et al.*, 2013; Fujii *et al.*, 2013; Heyne *et al.*, 2013). Heyne *et al.* (2005) set out a CBT-based approach to school refusal that involves a coherent and comprehensive range of assessment and intervention components, drawing concurrently on child, parent and teacher perspectives and actions. They recommend assessment approaches and materials that enable a case formulation to be made on the basis of the following types of information:

- individual factors (e.g. learning history, cognitions, somatic symptoms, social skills, academic difficulties and comorbid mood problems);

- family factors (e.g. parental anxiety/depression and response to non–attendance); and
- school factors (e.g. teacher support and isolation in the playground).

The guidance incorporates features from earlier interventions, such as the use of relaxation training procedures and the strong emphasis on securing a rapid return to school wherever possible (Blagg, 1987), but its distinctive component is the *cognitive* element of the therapy. This is deemed essential because events may be processed in a distorted manner by emotionally distressed school refusers. In essence, this aspect of CBT aims to modify 'maladaptive cognitions in order to effect change in the young person's emotions and behaviour, mobilising them towards school attendance' (Heyne *et al.*, 2005, p. 331). These authors draw on their previous work in which the process of conducting cognitive therapy is aided by what they term the 'Seven Ds':

- *describing* the cognitive therapy model;
- *detecting* cognitions (e.g. 'I know the teacher doesn't like me because she raises her voice');
- *determining* which cognitions to address;
- *disputing* maladaptive cognitions;
- *discovering* adaptive cognitions or *coping* statements;
- *doing* between-session practice tasks;
- *discussing* the outcome of the tasks (from Heyne and Rollings, 2002).

CBT with anxious school refusers has now moved beyond the question of 'does it work?' to 'how does it work?' and 'for which groups, through which processes?' (Heyne *et al.*, 2011). A study by Layne and colleagues explored specific responses to CBT and highlighted the need to attend to pre-intervention variables in young people, again bringing into relief the heterogeneity within school-refusal populations (Layne *et al.*, 2003). For example, when other variables had been factored out, better post-treatment attendance was reported among males (Layne *et al.*, 2003). It is also a consistent finding that older pupils respond less well to CBT, and this extends to CBT with school refusers (Heyne *et al.*, 2013). The suggestion is that the entrenchment of the issues is more marked by later adolescence, though other influential factors have also been proposed to explain this finding, for example the capacity of older young people to resist parental pressure to conform (Maric and Heyne, 2012; Heyne and Sauter, 2013; Maric *et al.*, 2013). Overall, CBT appears to offer a robust mechanism through which to intervene with young people, but the story regarding the specific responses of specific groups of school refusers is likely to continue to be developed (Kearney and Graczyk, 2014).

A 'SCHOOL-FOCUSED' APPROACH

In contrast, authors who have reminded us of the value of an ecological perspective on the issue of school refusal (Lauchlan, 2003; Hoglund and Leadbeater, 2004; Pellegrini, 2007; Lyon and Cotler, 2009) guide the practitioner to explore adjustments and adaptations to the school environment that will allow a young person to enter school more ably. Kearney (2008a) suggests that conceptualising a five-level model of intervention may help professionals. These comprise combinations of *child*, *parent and family*, *peer and school*, and *community* levels of intervention. This points the way to *multi-systemic* interventions, that is, those with *multiple* goals at various levels of the problem. This approach has been identified in other areas of need as potentially helpful in intervening with problems involving an individual interacting with their environment (Barth *et al.*, 2007). Several authors echo this, illustrating how behaviour change must be addressed in the multiple social and physical contexts in which it occurs (Lauchlan, 2003; Lyon and Cotler, 2009).

It is challenging enough to encourage a school to adapt its prosocial environment for the benefit of all students (Banerjee *et al.*, 2013), but more complex still to encourage an organisation to make such changes in support of a single individual. Nevertheless, the rationale for considering indicated adaptations to the school's psychosocial environment is robust. There is evidence within educational research that a positive school climate can positively correlate with attainment and outcome for students (Reyes *et al.*, 2012). An interesting area of research is that of 'school engagement' (Appleton, 2008; Furlong and Christenson, 2008; Reschly and Huebner, 2008), which has identified a student's sense of belonging and identification with school – *engagement* – as a significant variable correlating positively with achievement: this indicates that a student's sense of school engagement can be supported by a positive climate, one where relationships are fostered between pupils and between pupils and staff (refer to Chapters 10 and 13 for further exploration of these ideas).

Promoting engagement is the flip side of the coin when aiming to reduce absenteeism, then. Within the educational psychologist role, one can contrast the need to respond to established problems with the need to promote the environments that prevent them. Kearney and Graczyk (2014), therefore, argue for a tiered response to problems of school attendance that distinguishes between provision that is universal (preventative), targeted (identifying and working with those at risk) or specialist (reacting to those already displaying a problem) by supporting the practitioner in finding their selected focus for intervention work. This notion has already been touched upon the chapters upon managing behaviour in schools (Chapter 10) and on approaches to bullying (Chapter 11).

ACTIVITY 12.3

Case study: Part 3: The intervention

The educational psychologist undertook a number of further steps, drawing together elements of an ecologically informed programme:

- In a second meeting with Martin's parents, the educational psychologist explored the current situation at home. Martin's mother began to notice that nausea only occurred on days when he believed he was going to school and came to understand that this might be a symptom of anxiety.
- In a cognitive-behavioural-focused session, Martin revealed his worries about isolation at school.

- His father was determined that Martin should now start catching up on his work and told Martin that any time at home in the week would be spent working on school tasks, rather than watching television. As Martin had real strengths in art and design, his father agreed to offer Martin the chance to earn some model-building time at home, at weekends, with him. Finally, both parents saw that Martin needed to show more age-appropriate independence in the home, and his sister was to be helped to see the need to do less for her sibling.
- The educational psychologist worked with Martin himself, where he talked about disliking playtimes. His talk showed that he felt vulnerable to other pupils and what he called name calling, and being left out. He also worried about his work in class and said he could not understand what he needed to do when the teacher had explained things to the class. Although he was adamant that he did not wish to return to school, exploration of Martin's construing of the world levered open dissonances, where it became evident that he wanted to be someone who was well liked, with many friends. He also wanted to become good at art.
- Following this, an in-depth consultation took place with the class teacher and the school SENCo, to ensure that the (a) academic and (b) social environment of the classroom and school were ones that Martin could access. A personalised learning plan was drawn up to address his needs as a learner returning to the classroom. The means to include his interest in construction and art in the curriculum were reviewed, as were the ways in which additional adult supports could be made available to him, according to need, without this becoming too evident to his peers. Martin was to use a traffic-light system to indicate to the teacher if he felt things were too tricky for him and required additional explanation. At break times, similarly, a teaching assistant on general duties would provide a 'mentor' role for Martin, to enable him to talk with them, or help out with tasks within school.
- Discussing how to make the transition into the school building easier for Martin, it was agreed that, if he entered the building before other children arrived, he would find this easier, avoiding the hurly-burly of the cloakroom. This was arranged with school staff, using the pretext that Martin had additional 'monitor' responsibilities to catch up on since his absence.
- Only through consultation did the staff become aware of the extent of Martin's social isolation from his immediate peer group. It was agreed that a focus upon his 'social inclusion' in school was appropriate, aiming to support his development of peer relationships and foster a greater social identity within the class group, as well as enhancing his own sense of self-efficacy within school. The range of activities included buddying systems for break times, structured choice activities led by Martin, co-operative learning tasks within the classroom and peer tutoring for younger children. Opportunities for Martin to take responsibilities within the school day were identified, and a review of the class-based reward system ensured that it aimed to build Martin's *intrinsic*

motivation to attend school, rather than to see reinforcement through rewards as the key.

Activity

1 Identify sources within the literature reviewed in this chapter for as many elements in the intervention plan as you can.
2 Identify which aspects of the plan seem most 'theory driven' and which might be more concerned with (probably very necessary) practical arrangements and the efficient use of resources.
3 Decide also upon other aspects of interventions described in this chapter that might have been profitably incorporated into the plan.

ACTIVITY 12.4

Case study: Part 4: The outcome

• The week following consultation with staff, Martin attended school for four full days, and a pattern of attendance swiftly returned. He continued to have a high number of absences throughout that year, some through small ailments and 1 week away from school for the death of a grandparent. However, in Year 4, Martin achieved attendance of over 90 per cent.

• A series of review dates were set, to allow all involved to draw in relevant information on Martin's attendance progress and make any indicated adaptations to his programme. It was noted by the educational psychologist that, despite good success with this programme, some real care should be taken on Martin's transition to secondary school, aged 11, to ensure that any social or learning needs could be carefully accommodated.

COPING WITH LIFE BY *COPING* WITH SCHOOL?

Coping with adverse life events or pressures is a major requirement for maintaining adaptive functioning and has been recognised, together with the presence of *protective factors*, as the mechanism for reducing the risk of future mental health problems. This has been captured by the term *resilience*, where an extensive range of psychological research has been undertaken (Masten and Obradovic, 2006). Of interest here is the notion within resiliency theory that some capacity to withstand adversity is necessary in order to develop or demonstrate resilience, and that this in turn may *enhance* resilience. Coping successfully with one situation hypothetically strengthens an individual's ability to cope in the future. A failure to cope with a complex setting such as school may, therefore, have potentially serious, long-term correlates, as various outcome studies have shown. It is of great importance that children and young people are supported to develop the complex social and organisational skills required to mange educational environments (Place *et al.*, 2002).

SUMMARY OF MAIN ISSUES ADDRESSED IN THIS CHAPTER

- A set of symptoms that came to be taken as indicative of 'school phobia' was first reported in the literature over 70 years ago.
- Early conceptualisations divided school refusers into school phobics, truants and others, although later studies suggested that school refusal was a far more heterogeneous concept.
- For school refusal with strong emotional and somatic components, there are no differences in the incidence rates between boys and girls, different social classes, and different levels of ability or academic attainment. There are, however, higher incidences reported for the youngest of several children in a family, for children of older parents, for those around the age for transferring from primary to secondary levels of schooling, and for those with other social impairments.
- Incidence rates vary depending on the stringency of the definition adopted; using fairly strict criteria, the overall incidence within the child population is 1–2 per cent.
- Early theoretical formulations were developed within psychodynamic thinking and within behavioural psychology, the former utilising the concepts of separation anxiety and omnipotence, and the latter focused on school and other more social anxieties formed through classical and operant conditioning.
- A range of discrete treatment approaches were developed from these formulations: psychotherapeutic child and family counselling and hospitalisation from within psychodynamic and medical traditions, and systematic desensitisation, emotive imagery, flooding or implosion and contingency management from within behavioural psychology.
- Interventions grounded in cognitive behaviour therapy have an evidence base indicating their efficacy, and further information continues to emerge about how this works for specific groups of school refusers.
- A *functional analysis* of school refusal has been promoted as helpful, and subsequent research has suggested that this may be the most useful way of organising, assessing and treating this population.
- *Family dynamics* are seen as important to explore, linked to the question of separation anxiety, potentially, or to issues of the *functional effects of school refusal.*
- Multi-systemic responses are seen to be useful, allowing attention to be paid to differing features of the child's *ecology*: family, school and community.
- A *rapid return* to some form of school attendance where at all possible is indicated as a treatment priority. Educational psychologists have developed such approaches, often incorporating multi-element interventions that pay due attention to school-based triggering and maintaining factors, supporting with follow-up.

- The evidence for the long-term outcomes of school refusal is likely to be confounded by a number of factors. It is possible to identify that school refusal unaddressed, especially if it is comorbid with other mental health difficulties such as depression, has the potential to correlate with significant difficulties in adult life, including mental health difficulties.
- The ability to cope with complex and sometimes challenging social situations such as school may serve to strengthen an individual's ability to cope with other testing life circumstances.

KEY CONCEPTS AND TERMS

- School phobia
- School refusal
- Non-attendance
- Truancy
- Incidence
- Separation anxiety
- Omnipotence
- School-focused anxiety

- Social anxiety
- Classical conditioning
- Operant conditioning
- Systematic desensitisation
- Emotive imagery
- Flooding, implosion
- Extinction

- Functional analysis
- Cognitive behavioural therapy
- Rapid response
- Long-term outcomes of school refusal
- Coping
- Protective factors

RECOMMENDATIONS FOR FURTHER READING

Journal articles

Chitiyo, M. and Wheeler, J. (2006). School phobia: Understanding a complex behavioural response. *Journal of Research in Special Educational Needs, 6*(2), 87–91.

Kearney, C.A. (2008a). An interdisciplinary model of school absenteeism in youth to inform professional practice and public policy. *Educational Psychology Review, 20*(3), 257–82.

Kearney, C.A. (2008b). School absenteeism and school refusal behavior in youth: A contemporary review. *Clinical Psychology Review, 28*, 451–71.

Lyon, A.R. and Cotler, S. (2009). Multi-systemic intervention for school refusal behavior: Integrating approaches across disciplines. *Advances in School Mental Health Promotion, 2*(1), 20–34.

Reschly, A. and Huebner, E. (2008). Engagement as flourishing: The contribution of positive emotions and coping to adolescents' engagement at school and with learning. *Psychology in the Schools, 45*(5), 419–31.

Books and book chapters

Blagg, N. (1987). *School Phobia and its Treatment.* London: Croom Helm.

Elliot, J.G. and Place, M. (2004). *Children in Difficulty: A guide to understanding and helping* (2nd edn). London: Routledge, Chapter 3.

SAMPLE ESSAY TITLES

1 Is school refusal a unitary concept? If it is not, what are the implications for interventions?

2 To what extent do various conceptualisations of school refusal lead to intervention approaches that educational psychologists might employ?

3 A headteacher consults you, the educational psychologist, about an able pupil who has suddenly begun to refuse to attend school. The headteacher has been unable to persuade the pupil to return and has begun to feel very frustrated and manipulated. Write a letter to the head putting this behaviour into a psychological context.

REFERENCES

Almeida, M.D.C.C., Aquino, E.M. and Barros, A.P.D. (2006). School trajectory and teenage pregnancy in three Brazilian state capitals. *Cadernos de saúdepública, 22*(7), 1397–409.

Appleton, J. (2008). Student engagement with school: Critical conceptual and methodological issues of the construct. *Psychology in the Schools, 45*(5), 369–86.

Attwood, G. and Croll, P. (2006). Truancy in secondary school pupils: Prevalence, trajectories and pupil perspectives. *Research papers in education, 21*(4), 467–84.

Attwood, G. and Croll, P. (2015). Truancy and well-being among secondary school pupils in England. *Educational Studies, 41*(1–2), 14–28.

Banerjee, R., Weare, K. and Farr, W. (2013). Working with 'Social and Emotional Aspects of Learning'(SEAL): Associations with school ethos, pupil social experiences, attendance, and attainment. *British Educational Research Journal, 40*(4), 718–42.

Barth, R.P., Greeson, J.K.P. and Guo, S. (2007). Changes in family functioning and child behavior following intensive in-home therapy. *Children and Youth Services Review, 29,* 988–1009.

Baumrind, D. (2005). Patterns of parental authority and adolescent autonomy. *New Directions for Child and Adolescent Development, 108,* 61–9.

Berg, I. (1996). School avoidance, school phobia and truancy. In M. Lewis (ed.), *Child and Adolescent Psychiatry: A comprehensive textbook* (2nd edn). Baltimore, MD: Williams & Wilkins.

Berg, I., Nichols, K. and Pritchard, C. (1969). School phobia – Its classification and relationship to dependency. *Journal of Child Psychology and Psychiatry, 10,* 123–41.

Berry, G., Injejikian, M.A. and Tidwell, R. (1993). The school phobic child and the counsellor: Identifying, understanding and helping. *Education, 114*(1), 37–45.

Black, D. and Cottrell, D. (1993). *Seminars in Child and Adolescent Psychiatry*. London: Gaskell, Royal College of Psychiatrists.

Blagg, N. (1987). *School Phobia and its Treatment*. London: Croom Helm.

Blagg, N. and Yule, W. (1984). The behavioural treatment of school refusal – A comparative study. *Behaviour Research and Therapy*, *22*(2), 119–27.

Broadwin, I.T. (1932). A contribution to the study of truancy. *Orthopsychiatry*, *2*, 253–9.

Bronfenbrenner, U. and Morris, P.A. (2006). The bio-ecological model of human development. In R.M. Learner and W. Damon (eds), *Handbook of Child Psychology (6th edn): Vol 1, Theoretical Models of Human Development*. Hoboken, NJ: John Wiley, pp. 793–828.

Carr, A. (2006). *The Handbook of Child and Adolescent Clinical Psychology: A contextual approach*. London: Routledge.

Carr, A. (2008). *What Works with Children, Adolescents, and Adults? A review of research on the effectiveness of psychotherapy* [Google ebook]. London: Routledge.

Carr, A. (2009). The effectiveness of family therapy and systemic interventions for child-focused problems. *Journal of Family Therapy*, *31*, 3–45.

Carroll, H. (2010). The effect of pupil absenteeism on literacy and numeracy in the primary school. *School Psychology International*, *31*(2), 115–30.

Carroll, H. (2011). The peer relationships of primary school pupils with poor attendance records. *Educational Studies*, *37*(2), 197–206.

Chapman, G. (2007). *School Refusal Behavior: The relationship between family environment and parenting style*. Las Vegas: University of Nevada.

Chitiyo, M. and Wheeler, J. (2006). School phobia: Understanding a complex behavioural response. *Journal of Research in Special Educational Needs*, *6*(2), 87–91.

Chou, L.C., Ho, C.Y., Chen, C.Y. and Chen, W.J. (2006). Truancy and illicit drug use among adolescents surveyed via street outreach. *Addictive Behaviors*, *31*(1), 149–54.

Christenson, S.L. and Thurlow, M.L. (2004). School dropouts: Prevention considerations, interventions, and challenges. *Current Directions in Psychological Science*, *13*(1), 36–9.

Chu, B.C., Skriner, L.C. and Zandberg, L.J. (2013). Shape of change in cognitive behavioral therapy for youth anxiety: Symptom trajectory and predictors of change. *Journal of Consulting and Clinical Psychology*, *81*(4), 573–87.

Coplan, R. and Prakash, K. (2004). Do you 'want' to play? Distinguishing between conflicted shyness and social disinterest in early childhood. *Developmental Psychology*, *40*(2), 244–58.

Dembo, R., Briones-Robinson, R., Barrett, K., Winters, K.C., Schmeidler, J., Ungaro, R.A., Karas, L., Belenko, S. and Gulledge, L. (2013). Mental health, substance use, and delinquency among truant youths in a brief intervention project: A longitudinal study. *Journal of Emotional and Behavioral Disorders*, *21*(3), 176–92.

Denny, S.J., Clark, T.C. and Watson, P.D. (2003). Comparison of health-risk behaviours among students in alternative high schools from New Zealand and the USA. *Journal of Paediatrics and Child Health*, *39*(1), 33–9.

Elliott, J.G. (1999). School refusal: Issues of conceptualisation, assessment, and treatment. *Journal of Child Psychology and Psychiatry, and Allied Disciplines*, *40*, 1001–12.

Estes, H.R., Haylett, C.H. and Johnson, A.L. (1956). Separation anxiety. *American Journal of Psychotherapy*, *10*, 682–95.

Fonagy, P. (2010). *Attachment Theory and Psychoanalysis*. London: Karnac.

Fuggle, P., Dunsmuir, S. and Curry, V. (2013). *CBT with Children, Young People and Families*. London: SAGE.

Fujii, C., Renno, P., McLeod, B.D., Lin, C.E., Decker, K., Zielinski, K. and Wood, J.J. (2013). Intensive cognitive behavioral therapy for anxiety disorders in school-aged children with autism: A preliminary comparison with treatment-as-usual. *School Mental Health, 5*(1), 25–37.

Furlong, M. and Christenson, S. (2008). Engaging students at school and with learning: A relevant construct for all students. *Psychology in the Schools, 45*(5), 365–8.

Galloway, D. and Miller, A. (1978). The use of graded *in vivo* flooding in the extinction of children's phobias. *Behavioural Psychotherapy, 6*, 7–10.

Ginsburg, G., Grover, R. and Ialongo, N. (2005). Parenting behaviors among anxious and non-anxious mothers: Relation with concurrent and long-term child outcomes. *Child & Family Behavior Therapy, 26*(4), 23–41.

Goodman, R. and Scott, S. (2002). *Child Psychiatry*. Oxford, UK. Blackwell.

Grandison, K.J. (2011). School refusal: From short stay school to mainstream. Unpublished thesis, University of Birmingham.

Guttmacher, S., Weitzman, B.C., Kapadia, F. and Weinberg, S.L. (2002). Classroom-based surveys of adolescent risk-taking behaviors: reducing the bias of absenteeism. *American Journal of Public Health, 92*(2), 235–7.

Hallfors, D., Vevea, J.L., Iritani, B., Cho, H., Khatapoush, S. and Saxe, L. (2002). Truancy, grade point average, and sexual activity: A meta-analysis of risk indicators for youth substance use. *Journal of School Health, 72*(5), 205–11.

Havik, T., Bru, E. and Ertesvåg, S.K. (2014). Parental perspectives of the role of school factors in school refusal. *Emotional and Behavioural Difficulties, 19*(2), 131–53.

Henry, K.L. and Huizinga, D.H. (2007). School-related risk and protective factors associated with truancy among urban youth placed at risk. *The Journal of Primary Prevention, 28*(6), 505–19.

Hersov, L. (1977). School refusal. In M. Rutter and L. Hersov (eds), *Child Psychiatry. Modern approaches*. Oxford, UK: Blackwell.

Heyne, D. and Rollings, S. (2002). *School Refusal*. Oxford, UK: BPS Blackwell.

Heyne, D., King, N. and Olendeck, T.H. (2005). School refusal. In P. Graham (ed.), *Cognitive Behaviour Therapy for Children and Families* (2nd edn). Cambridge, UK: Cambridge University Press.

Heyne, D., Sauter, F.M., Widenfelt, B.M. van, Vermeiren, R.R.J.M. and Westenberg, P.M. (2011). School refusal and anxiety in adolescence: Non-randomized trial of a developmentally sensitive cognitive behavioral therapy. *Journal of Anxiety Disorders, 25*(7), 870–8.

Heyne, D., Sauter, F.M., Ollendick, T.H., Van Widenfelt, B.M. and Westenberg, P.M. (2013). Developmentally sensitive cognitive behavioral therapy for adolescent school refusal: Rationale and case illustration. *Clinical Child and Family Psychology Review, 17*(2), 191–215.

Hickman, G., Bartholomew, M. and Mathwig, J. (2008). Differential developmental pathways of high school dropouts and graduates. *The Journal of Educational Research, 102*(1), 3–14.

Hoglund, W. and Leadbeater, B. (2004). The effects of family, school, and classroom ecologies on changes in children's social competence and emotional and behavioral problems in first grade. *Developmental Psychology, 40*(4), 533–44.

Hughes, E.K., Gullone, E., Dudley, A. and Tonge, B. (2010). A case-control study of emotion regulation and school refusal in children and adolescents. *The Journal of Early Adolescence, 30*(5), 691–706.

Ingul, J.J.M. and Nordahl, H.H.M. (2013). Anxiety as a risk factor for school absenteeism: What differentiates anxious school attenders from non-attenders? *Annals of General Psychiatry, 12*(1), 25.

Johnson, A.M., Falstein E.I., Szurek, S.A. and Svendsen, M. (1941). School phobia. *American Journal of Orthopsychiatry, 11*, 702–11.

Kearney, C.A. (2003). Bridging the gap among professionals who address youths with school absenteeism: Overview and suggestions for consensus. *Professional Psychology: Research and Practice, 34*(1), 57–65.

Kearney, C.A. (2007). Forms and functions of school refusal behaviour in youth. *Journal of Child Psychology and Psychiatry, 48*(1), 53–61.

Kearney, C.A. (2008a). An interdisciplinary model of school absenteeism in youth to inform professional practice and public policy. *Educational Psychology Review, 20*(3), 257–82.

Kearney, C.A. (2008b). School absenteeism and school refusal behavior in youth: A contemporary review. *Clinical Psychology Review, 28*, 451–71.

Kearney, C.A. and Albano, A.M. (2004). The functional profiles of school refusal behavior. Diagnostic aspects. *Behavior Modification, 28*(1), 147–61.

Kearney, C.A. and Bates, M. (2005). Addressing school refusal behavior: Suggestions for frontline professionals. *Children & Schools, 27*(4), 207–16.

Kearney, C.A. and Graczyk, P. (2014). A response to intervention model to promote school attendance and decrease school absenteeism. *Child & Youth Care Forum, 43*, 1–25.

Kearney, C.A. and Silverman, W.K. (1990). A preliminary analysis of a functional model of assessment and intervention of school refusal behaviour. *Behaviour Modification, 149*, 340–66.

Kearney, C.A. and Silverman, W. (1993). Measuring the function of school refusal behavior: The School Refusal Assessment Scale. *Journal of Clinical Child Psychology, 22*(1), 85–96.

Kearney, C.A. and Silverman, W. (1995). Family environment of youngsters with school refusal behavior: A synopsis with implications for assessment and treatment. *The American Journal of Family Therapy, 23*(1), 59–72.

Kearney, C. and Silverman, W. (1999). Functionally based prescriptive and nonprescriptive treatment for children and adolescents with school refusal behavior. *Behavior Therapy, 30*(4), 673–95.

King, N. and Bernstein, G.A. (2001). School refusal in children and adolescents: A review of the past ten years. *Journal of the American Academy of Child and Adolescent Psychiatry, 40*, 197–205.

Lauchlan, F. (2003). Responding to chronic non-attendance: A review of intervention approaches. *Educational Psychology in Practice, 19*(2), 133–46.

Layne, A.E., Bernstein, G.A., Egan, E.A. and Kushner, M.G. (2003). Predictors of treatment response in anxious-depressed adolescents with school refusal. *Journal of the American Academy of Child and Adolescent Psychiatry, 42*(3), 319–26.

Lehr, C., Sinclair, M. and Christenson, S. (2004). Addressing student engagement and truancy prevention during the elementary school years: A replication study of the check and connect model. *Journal of Education for Students Placed at Risk, 9*(3), 279–301.

Lyon, A. and Cotler, S. (2009). Multi-systemic intervention for school refusal behavior: Integrating approaches across disciplines. *Advances in School Mental Health Promotion, 2*(1), 20–34.

McShane, G., Walter, G. and Rey, J.M. (2004). Functional outcome of adolescents with 'school refusal'. *Clinical Child Psychology and Psychiatry, 9*(1), 53–60.

Maric, M. and Heyne, D. (2012). The role of cognition in school refusal: An investigation of automatic thoughts and cognitive errors. *Behavioural and Cognitive Psychotherapy, 40*(3), 255–69.

Maric, M., Heyne, D.A., MacKinnon, D.P., van Widenfelt, B.M. and Westenberg, P.M. (2013). Cognitive mediation of cognitive-behavioural therapy outcomes for anxiety-based school refusal. *Behavioural and Cognitive Psychotherapy, 41*(5), 549–64.

Masten, A.S. and Obradovic, J. (2006). Competence and resilience in development. *Annals of the New York Academy of Sciences, 1094,* 13–27.

Nuttall, C. and Woods, K. (2013). Effective intervention for school refusal behaviour. *Educational Psychology in Practice, 19*(4), 347–66.

Ollendick, T.H. and Benoit, K.E. (2012). A parent–child interactional model of social anxiety disorder in youth. *Clinical Child and Family Psychology Review, 15*(1), 81–91.

Pellegrini, D.W. (2007). School non-attendance: Definitions, meanings, responses, interventions. *Educational Psychology in Practice, 23*(1), 63–77.

Place, M., Hulsmeier, J., Davis, S. and Taylor, E. (2002). The coping mechanisms of children with school refusal. *Journal of Research in Special Educational Needs, 2*(2), 1–10.

Reschly, A. and Huebner, E. (2008). Engagement as flourishing: The contribution of positive emotions and coping to adolescents' engagement at school and with learning. *Psychology in the Schools, 45*(5), 419–31.

Reyes, M., Brackett, M.A., Rivers, S.E., White, M. and Salovey, P. (2012). Classroom emotional climate, student engagement, and academic achievement. *Journal of Educational Psychology, 104*(3), 700–12.

Schafer, R. (2011). The relationship between the functions of school refusal behavior and family environment. Unpublsihed thesis, University of Nevada, Las Vegas.

Seligman, L.D. and Ollendick, T.H. (2011). Cognitive-behavioral therapy for anxiety disorders in youth. *Child and Adolescent Psychiatric Clinics of North America, 20*(2), 217–38.

Thambirajah, M., Grandison, K. and De-Hayes, L. (2007). *Understanding School Refusal: A handbook for professionals in education, health and social care.* London: Jessica Kinglsey.

Thomas, J.M., Lemieux, C.M., Rhodes, J.L.F. and Vlosky, D.A. (2011). Early truancy intervention: Results of an evaluation using a regression discontinuity design. *Children and Youth Services Review, 33*(9), 1563–72.

Torrens Armstrong, A.M., McCormack Brown, K.R., Brindley, R., Coreil, J. and McDermott, R.J. (2011). Frequent fliers, school phobias, and the sick student: School health personnel's perceptions of students who refuse school. *Journal of School Health, 81*(9), 552–9.

Wolpe, J. (1954). Reciprocal inhibition as the main basis of psychotherapeutic effects. *Archives of Neurological Psychiatry, 72,* 205–26.

13 School ethos and student identity

When is wearing a uniform a badge of honour?

Tony Cline

CHAPTER SUMMARY

In this chapter, you will examine different ways of describing a school's ethos and culture and different ways of investigating them. We will reflect on how the ethos of a school is expressed in its day-to-day life. A school exists for its pupils. The chapter will also examine how an institution's ethos may impinge on the experiences of its students and the development of their identities as academic learners.

LEARNING OUTCOMES

When you have studied this chapter, you should be able to:

1 explain and evaluate different strategies for investigating a school's ethos;
2 analyse how a school's ethos may influence the development of its students' identities as academic learners;
3 describe how educational psychologists can work to ameliorate the impact of school ethos on students in difficult situations.

FOCUS 13.1

Newspaper report: School uniform in Scotland

In February 2005, Scotland's first minister, Jack McConnell, made an outspoken attack on what he saw as the damage caused by liberal values in education. Among other things, he said, a large number of Scottish schools had got rid of school uniform over the years. On 2 March, *The Scotsman* newspaper invited two public figures to debate the issue.

John Wilson, education director in East Renfrewshire, 'Scotland's most successful education authority', wrote in support that he considered uniform important in their local authority. He said that they encouraged schools to promote it as part of their approach to an education based firmly on attainment, achievement and inclusion. Uniform helped promote the unity and ethos of a school, and that, in turn, promoted the learning within. Security was boosted by making strangers not in uniform easier to spot. They had always said that they would meet private-sector schools on their own ground. They thought that part of the attraction that those schools had for parents was their emphasis on uniform. So, as part of their strategy of encouraging local children to go to their local schools at the heart of their communities, they promoted uniform.

Judith Gillespie, convener of the Scottish Parent Teacher Council, opposed school uniforms, saying that, 'School uniform means what it says on the tin – everyone looks the same'. There was nothing new about this denial of difference. When she herself had moved to a secondary school in the 1950s, she had quickly identified the teachers' hypocrisy over school uniform. The argument from adults was that school uniform ends competition and means that one cannot tell the rich from the poor. She could see that that was nonsense: 'Rich kids had uniform that looked smart and fitted, while those of us with less money made do with second-hand stuff or, worse, home-made gear that never fitted properly'. The competition simply moved to areas that escaped adult attention. What she valued now more was the chance to express individualism, to experiment with clothes and to work out an individual identity.

DEFINING SCHOOL ETHOS

The tension between individuality and uniformity in schools is fundamental to their function in society: their task of preparing children for adulthood can only be achieved if they are successful simultaneously in managing large groups and responding to individual needs. In the 1960s and 1970s, the fashionable view among psychologists (reflected in the Plowden Report on primary education; Plowden Committee, 1967) was that schools made little difference. It was thought that home factors exerted much more influence on children's achievements at school than school factors did. In sociology, too, the influence of schools was played down. Sociologists tended to locate the causes of unequal educational outcomes in basic inequities in the structure of society. A research team led by Michael Rutter, who presented that outline of earlier thinking (Rutter et al., 1979, pp. 1–2), sought to challenge it. They gave their book the title *Fifteen Thousand Hours* to reflect the fact that, between the age of 5 and 16, young people spend that amount of time in school. Does it make a difference which school it is? Clearly, John Wilson of East Renfrewshire thinks it does and thinks that school uniform can help each school to impress its ethos on its students. Did the findings obtained by Rutter's team support him?

In what has become a classic study, they collected performance data for twelve inner London secondary schools and undertook extensive observations and interviews in each school. They mostly concentrated on specific events and behaviours, although there were some interview questions on more general attitudes and values (see Method Box 13.1). They suggested that, in many cases, individual actions by members of staff might have been less important in their own right than 'in the part they play in contributing to a broader school ethos or climate of expectations and modes of behaving'. Their defence of the focus on specific actions was that they hoped to identify what sorts of action teachers and pupils could take to establish an improved ethos if needed (Rutter et al., 1979, pp. 55–6). Here are some of their findings:

- The schools differed markedly in the behaviour and attainments shown by their pupils.
- Although the schools differed in the proportion of children with difficult behaviour or low attainments that they admitted, these differences did not wholly account for the variations between schools in their pupils' later behaviour and attainment.
- The variations between schools in different forms of outcome for their pupils were reasonably stable over periods of at least 4 or 5 years.
- In general, though with some exceptions, schools' overall performance was at a fairly similar level across the various measures of outcome. That is, schools that did better than average in terms of the children's behaviour in school tended also to do better than average in terms of examination success and low rates of delinquency.
- These differences in outcome between schools were not due to such physical factors as the size of the school, the age of the buildings or the space available; nor were they due to broad differences in administrative status or organisation. Some schools obtained good outcomes in spite of what seemed to be poor premises, and successful schools had a range of types of administrative arrangement.
- Some of the factors that had an influence on pupil outcomes were open to modification by the staff, rather than fixed by external constraints. Examples included the degree of academic emphasis, teacher actions in lessons, the availability of incentives and rewards, and the extent to which children were able to take responsibility within the classroom.
- Other factors that were shown to have an influence on pupil outcomes were outside teachers' immediate control. The most important factor of this kind was the academic balance of the schools' intakes.

Another finding, crucial for the purposes of this chapter, was that:

> The association between the *combined* measure of overall process and each of the measures of outcome was much stronger than any of the associations with individual process variables. This suggests that the cumulative effect of these various social factors was considerably greater than the effect of any of the individual factors on their own. The implication is that the individual actions or measures combine to create a particular *ethos*, or set of values, attitudes and behaviours which will become characteristic of the school as a whole.
>
> (Rutter *et al.*, 1979, pp. 177–9)

Controversially, they argued that, although their data had been collected at one point in time:

> The total pattern of findings indicates the strong probability that the associations between school process and outcome reflect in part a causal process. In other words, to an appreciable extent children's behaviour and attitudes are shaped and influenced by their experiences at school and, in particular, by the qualities of the school as a social institution.
>
> (p. 179)

They concluded that a measure was required of how a school functions as a whole as a social organisation. This process is discussed in Method Box 13.1.

The report by Rutter and his colleagues attracted a great deal of interest when it was published. There were critical reviews both of its statistical analyses (e.g. Goldstein, 1980) and of its 'managerial' focus (Burgess, 1980). For example, the team's conclusions about the management of pupils were described as being 'grounded in the worst traditions of behaviouristic experimental social psychology' (Pateman, 1980). Nonetheless, the study had a seminal influence on educational research, and its main findings were confirmed in later studies of other types of school (e.g. Mortimore *et al.*, 1988, on primary schools) and schools in different systems (see Part 1, Section 2, of Townsend, 2007). A major tradition of research on *school effectiveness* grew from the interest generated by the London study and others at that time and a parallel tradition of professional work on *school improvement* (Reynolds, 2010).

For our purposes in this chapter, the most serious weakness of the study was its pragmatic collation of unrelated variables to create a measure of 'school ethos'. The implicit assumption was made that there will be a consistent relationship in any organisation between inputs and outputs, and that this relationship can be discovered through correlating a wide range of input and output measures and identifying the most significant connections. There was no attempt to develop a coherent theoretical account of how that relationship operated in the schools that were studied, a task that was left to later researchers (Scheerens, 2013).

Critics have argued that there are complex forces in play in the life of an organisation such as a school that cannot be adequately captured by a *reductionist* strategy of measuring factors such as those listed in Method Box 13.1. In a complex human system, what matters is not just what happens, but how participants interpret what happens –

METHOD 13.1

Treating behavioural process variables as a means of measuring school ethos

Rutter *et al.* (1979) did not set out with a theoretical model of school ethos. Noting that they had not found a suitable instrument for their purposes in the earlier research literature, they developed a list of diverse school process variables that, 'seemed potentially relevant to the pupils' progress'. They emphasised those variables that applied to the pupils as a whole group, rather than those that applied only to smaller subgroups with special needs or special problems. The following list shows a sample selected from every fifth item in the schedule of forty-six process measures that they eventually used:

- *Work on walls*: Each room that was visited to administer pupil questionnaires and to observe third-year lessons was assessed on a five-point scale: 0 = nothing on walls; 4 = all possible areas covered.
- *Subjects taught*: Each teacher who was interviewed was asked which subjects they taught. A school's score was the percentage of teachers who taught across subject areas, rather than having a specific specialist subject.
- *Teachers' interventions in third-year classrooms*: This was the percentage of teacher observation periods when teachers were dealing with pupils' behaviour, for example curbing unacceptable behaviour.
- *Detentions*: Pupils responded to a questionnaire item asking how many times they had been kept in detention since the previous September.
- *Pupils caring for resources*: Observations were made during third-year lessons as to whether pupils brought and took away resources for learning, such as books, folders and exercise books.
- *Staff's late arrival at school*: An item in the questionnaire for teachers asked whether anyone else was aware if staff arrive late for school.

As noted above, the research team argued that items of this kind did not affect pupil outcomes directly, but by their combination in an overall impact through an institutional ethos. Their reasons were, first, that most of the individual process variables had only an indirect connection with the outcomes with which they were associated, such as school attendance. Second, the same teacher actions had different effects in different schools. For example, if a teacher left children on their own in one school, they might get on with their work, whereas, in another school, they would become involved in disruptive behaviour. Third, some of the variables did not bear on individual pupils directly, but on the state of the buildings or the conditions of the staff group (pp. 182–3). They showed that the schools' overall scores for school process variables correlated highly with pupil behaviour scores (r = 0.92) and showed substantial, though slightly less strong, correlations with academic attainment ($r = 0.76$), overall attendance ($r = 65$) and recorded delinquency ($r = -0.68$).

ACTIVITY 13.1

- Discuss what assumptions are made in the argument summarised in the last paragraph in Method Box 13.1.
- In the light of the information that is given here, can you suggest an operational definition of 'school ethos' that might have been employed by the research team? (Remember that an operational definition is a definition that describes as specifically as possible the precise elements and procedures involved in solving a research problem.)

what shared ideas they apply to the routines and events that characterise the institution, what 'culture' dominates it, and whether some of those who are involved resist the dominant culture. Classic – and more recent – quantitative research on school effectiveness is seen as failing to identify causal mechanisms and failing to take account of irregular and inconsistent processes within open systems (Wrigley, 2004). Later, we will examine an alternative approach to investigating the culture or ethos of a school, but first, we need to consider the other construct that appears in the title of the chapter.

THE DEVELOPMENT OF IDENTITY AS A STUDENT

Infants in the first few months of life do not appear to be self-conscious, but, by the age of 2, they develop a sense of themselves as a person and, in their third year, they begin to be able to draw on the standards and rules that prevail in their society in order to evaluate their own behaviour. They may show embarrassment when they see a gap between what they are doing and what is expected of them, and they begin to experience further emotions such as pride, shame and guilt (Lewis, 2002). As they start to move more and more outside the immediate ambit of their home, they are exposed to a wider range of people and need to develop a sense of their own *social identity*, as distinct from that of others. Questions such as 'Who am I?' are answered, in part, by categorising themselves as members of groups with which they can identify. Their perception of themselves is influenced by comparing themselves with the increasing range of people around them and by evaluating those comparisons in the light of how they see the others judging them (Erikson, 1968). For most children, school is a key arena for important developments in identity formation. In that context, Schachter and Rich (2011) adopted the following definition for the concept of 'identity':

the individual's dynamic self-understandings and self-definitions used to structure, direct, give meaning to and present the self, that are negotiated intra- and interpersonally across the lifespan within sociocultural contexts, along with the psychosocial processes, meaning-systems, practices and structures that regulate their continued development.

(p. 223)

Children develop various social identities as they move into school and middle childhood, for example in relation to gender. However, they do not simply opt to be in one differentiated group or another (e.g. 'the boys' or 'the girls'). The process is more complex than that, as they learn about the various definitions of masculinity and femininity that are available and position themselves in relation to these possibilities within their groups. Lloyd and Duveen (1992) proposed that, as children encounter new social representations of gender after starting school, they reconstruct the social gender identities that they had developed during the preschool years. They observed children in reception classes in four schools over an extended period. For our purposes, an important finding in their ethnographic study of four schools was that the way reception class teachers organised their classrooms constrained the ways in which gender identities were expressed there. It might be expected that traditionally minded teachers would encourage their pupils to adopt traditional sex roles in their play in the classroom, for example by giving boys 'male' toys to play with. This is not what happened. The process did not involve teachers imposing their vision of sex roles on the young pupils in their charge. It was, rather, that patterns of play and gender role affiliation were influenced by the way that the classrooms were run. Gender differentiation appeared to be most marked in those classrooms where the teacher allowed more time for peer-organised activities, which, for example, allowed a small group of girls in one school to define their femininity through the exclusion of boys from their play. Classroom organisation and ethos had a paradoxical impact: the regime imposed by the more 'progressive' teachers allowed more scope for the expression of traditional gender identities than the regime of the more 'conservative' teachers did. If we are looking for the effects of school ethos on student identity, we should not expect a simple imposition of the one on the other.

INTERNALISED EXPECTATIONS

A key stage in this process, according to Duveen, is that children first learn how others see them and then gradually internalise these expectations and take a position in relation to them (Duveen, 2001). In a series of studies employing a quite different type of methodology, Bennett and Sani (2011) have investigated how the process of *internalisation* may occur. They have sought to show that the development of social identities does not just involve learning to categorise oneself in terms of group membership, but also includes subjectively identifying with the group. One key process appears to be self-stereotyping (i.e. thinking of oneself as a person who shows the stereotypical features of members of the group in question). Crucially for our purposes, they showed that this process can be affected by context. For example, in one study (Bennett and Sani, 2008, Study 2), a female experimenter asked children to rate themselves on twelve carefully selected trait adjectives: four were seen as traditionally 'masculine' (brave, big, strong, tough), four were seen as 'feminine' (friendly, clean, helpful, polite), and four were thought to be neutral (quiet, shy, small, tidy). These trait descriptors, which had been tested for their supposed properties in a pilot study, were presented in random order to ninety-three participants aged 5, 7 and 10 years old. First of all, in a 'neutral context' condition, children were simply asked for each adjective: 'Do you think you are very (adjective), quite (adjective) or not at all (adjective)?' Three weeks later, in the 'gendered context' condition, the children were seen again and went through the same procedure. However, this time, before describing themselves, they responded to the same twelve adjectives with respect to the *gender outgroup*. For example, girls were told, 'I want to know what you think boys are like'. Following this, the same procedure as above was employed, that is, children were asked to consider *themselves* with respect to the same adjective set. The researchers were interested in the results for those adjectives that related to their assumed ingroup identity (e.g. for boys, traits such as bravery and strength, and for girls, traits such as kindness and gentleness). The key question was: would the children make stronger self-attributions of those attributes associated with their own group when gender identity had been made salient for them than when it was not? The results indicated that boys judged themselves to be bigger, braver and stronger in the gendered condition than in the neutral condition, whereas girls showed no such differences between the two conditions. The authors considered various possible explanations for this finding: perhaps it reflects greater pressures on boys than girls to conform to gender norms; perhaps the particular list of adjectives used in this study enabled the characterisation of masculinity more effectively than it did femininity; at a more general level, perhaps male identity may be more readily defined through trait adjectives than is the case for female identity. They suggested that a future replication study could employ gender-related behaviours rather than gender-related single terms.

Experimental strategies of the kind outlined above necessarily simplify the process that is being studied. Bennett and Sani acknowledged that the internalisation of social identities is almost certainly not an all-or-none affair as their methodology implied: 'we fully accept that future research should examine the *extent* to which specific identities are internalized' (2008, p. 74). However, their findings confirmed, in line with their theoretical position, that boys' self-conceptions in relation to girls (the gender outgroup) are not inflexible and can be affected by social context. The subtle ways in which that context can vary in schools are partly captured by the concept of school ethos, as studied by Rutter's team and their successors.

Although the development of gender identity is significantly affected by experiences at school, the most intensive impact of these experiences in their first years in school seems likely to be on children's sense of themselves as a learner, their academic self-concept. Of course, school ethos and teacher behaviour are not the only factors. Thus, a case study of a 7-year-old girl who thought of herself as good at maths suggested that she based this, not only on what her teacher had written in a report, but also on what her father had said about her and on comparisons that had been made at home with one of her sisters (Abreu and Cline, 2003, pp. 24–5). The key psychological construct in this process has sometimes been termed *reflected appraisal*, children's beliefs about what their parents, teachers and peers think about them with respect to school achievement. Survey evidence, as well as case-study evidence, has indicated that reflected appraisals predict what children themselves will see as their own level of academic ability in each subject area. The evidence also suggests that these mechanisms continue to operate into adolescence (Bouchey and Harter, 2005).

Abreu (1995) has used the concept of *valorisation* to describe the process by which some kinds of activity are given high status within the school curriculum, while others are not. She studied illiterate farmers in a sugar-cane farming community in north-east Brazil and showed how they employed sophisticated traditional methods of calculation to work out acreage and crop yield in their irregularly shaped fields. However, neither they nor their children treated these low-status calculations as 'real'

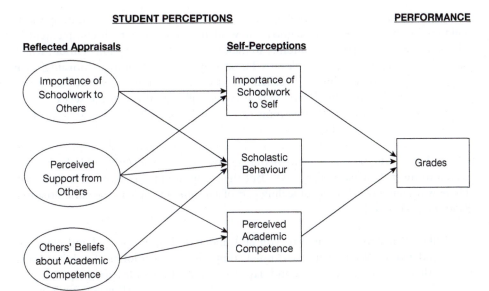

FIGURE 13.1 Model proposed by Bouchey and Harter (2005) to describe the processes underlying maths/science achievement. ('Others' includes mothers, fathers, teachers and classmates)

mathematics, a term they reserved for the mathematics taught at school. The internalisation of reflected appraisals in school depends, in part, on the valorisation of the sources of these appraisals (Abreu and Cline, 2003). The ways in which that process operates in a school will no doubt be influenced by its ethos.

Influence of school ethos

In the decades since the publication of *Fifteen Thousand Hours*, more evidence has accumulated showing that the ethos and culture of a school have a significant impact on a range of aspects of student identity and behaviour, independently of such variables as the composition of the student population. Some of the research has focused on mainstream schools. For example, West *et al.* (2004) carried out a longitudinal study of forty-three secondary schools in the west of Scotland and showed that, after adjusting for pupil and family characteristics, there remained a school effect on the likelihood of a child taking up excessive smoking or drinking. In this context, other researchers have highlighted the role that a school's ethos can play in promoting a 'sense of belonging' among pupils in a mainstream secondary school. This may then reduce the felt need to use drugs as a route to membership of a peer group of students who are disconnected from the main institutional markers of status in the school (Fletcher *et al.*, 2009). Exploring the relationship between school ethos and pupils' sense of belonging further looks likely to be a fruitful vein of research in this field.

Some research has focused on the differences in ethos between mainstream schools and various types of independent establishment. For example, Rivers and Soutter (1996) found that children who had been the victims of bullying in mainstream schools left the status of victim behind after moving to a Rudolph Steiner school with a non–

competitive, group-centred ethos. Creese *et al.* (2006) found that Gujarati-speaking children had been enabled to negotiate new identities as learners in complementary schools run by the Gujarati community in their town. In these part-time schools, which the children attended once a week on a Tuesday evening or a Saturday morning, their linguistic repertoire as bilingual speakers was seen as important in a way that it was not in the mainstream schools that they attended full time through the week.

Burden (2005) studied the learning careers of boys with dyslexia at a specialist boarding school and found that many who had had a sense of failure and embarrassment in their mainstream schools had developed what Burden called 'dyslexic pride' in that school. In part, the boys had been encouraged by the easy availability of help that was geared to meet their particular needs. But there appeared to be more to it than that. There was a sense of *belonging*, of feeling part of a group of people in the same situation. Keith (aged 12) said:

> I liked that people listened to you and understand how you feel and everyone was the same. We looked at the usual comprehensive school but I didn't want to go there 'cos I'd be different and have to go out of class for extra help.
>
> (Burden, 2005, p. 54)

The impact of school ethos on the development of students' identities as learners is often indirect: it gives a message about the kind of person who is valued in this community and facilitates a process by which students come to think that they are that kind of person.

It is no accident that some of the most persuasive research on the impact of school ethos on student identity has focused on small schools with an unusual and well-defined purpose. In the most effective of the schools, the teachers shared common goals and benefited from a strong consensus about the methods employed in the school to pursue those goals (Rivers and Soutter, 1996; Creese *et al.*, 2006). In many large mainstream schools, those conditions may not apply. The institution is a highly complex organisation, with diverse and sometimes competing subcultures. Groups of teachers and groups of pupils find themselves isolated from one another. Pupils develop their identities as learners across disparate departments and subcultures, finding those identities affirmed in some settings and challenged or undermined in others. Such schools are fragile organisations that lack the cohesion and strength to support their members – staff or pupils. In the next section, we will examine how educational psychologists can contribute when a school's ethos has many negative features.

CAN A SCHOOL'S EDUCATIONAL PSYCHOLOGIST INFLUENCE ITS ETHOS?

It has long been argued that, to have greatest impact, educational psychologists should place more emphasis on work aimed at the organisation, policy and structure of schools than on work with individual pupils (Gillham, 1978). Sometimes this arises as a result of a direct request for action at the school level. Bettle *et al.* (2001) described the support provided to a school that was in great difficulties by a team from the local authority's educational psychology service. The school, which was in a socially deprived area in Buckinghamshire, a relatively prosperous shire county, provided for children aged 7–11 years of age. After an official inspection, it had been placed in *special measures*. This was a category used by Ofsted inspectors when 'a school is failing or is likely to fail to give its pupils an acceptable standard of education'. After being placed in this category, the school was required to produce an action plan setting out a proposed response to the inspection report (Department for Education, 1993). In addition, at that time, the local authority (LA) had to produce a commentary on the school's plan and a statement of the action that it proposed to take to support the school. In this case, the school's educational psychologist, as a member of the LA staff, was asked by the new headteacher to give extra time in order to process a higher number of formal assessments of special educational needs (50 per cent of the pupils in the school were on the special educational needs register).

> The Chief Psychologist discussed this with the Headteacher and consequently they agreed that, given the key issues identified in the Action Plan, the Service should support specific initiatives relating to improving behaviour management or learning across the school. The time for this would best be accommodated . . . from time earmarked by the service for project work with schools, and a joint planning meeting was therefore held in order to discuss possible pieces of work.
> (Bettle *et al.*, 2001, p. 56)

The school's link educational psychologist also participated in a task force that gave attention to special educational needs in the school, but this account will focus on the project initiative.

In an initial discussion, the headteacher highlighted what he called 'ethos in the school' as a key area for work, specifically a high level of conflict and hostility between pupils. It was agreed that this should be the focus of the educational psychologist and her colleagues, who would support the school to develop a more supportive and caring ethos among students. 'The Headteacher felt that many of the pupils needed to learn fundamental skills for getting along with others, valuing others as well as themselves, and feeling secure and cared for in their school environment' (p. 57). The educational psychologists' contributions included investigating staff and pupil perceptions, feedback to staff, training and evaluation. The key point of interest here is the focus of their initial data collection. They did not attempt direct observations, but focused instead on learning how the situation in the school was perceived by different groups of participants. Their approach was guided by *soft systems methodology*, an approach to the analysis of ill-structured problem situations of this kind that was developed on the basis of action research (Frederickson, 1993; Checkland and Poulter, 2010). This initial phase of the team's work is summarised in Method Box 13.2.

In challenging contexts in different countries, the transformation of school ethos may be a crucial element in the creation of a more peaceful and equal society. It is possible for educational psychologists to contribute to that process, alongside other school support professionals. For example, in the Western Cape Province in South Africa, the role of school psychologists in the past focused mainly on the assessment of individual learners' difficulties with a view to placement in special classes and special schools. This shifted to the provision of psycho-educational and psychotherapeutic/counselling support within a whole-school context as part of an institution-level

METHOD 13.2

Investigating stakeholders' perceptions as a means of measuring school ethos

Two educational psychologists spent half a day in the school, administering the questionnaires with classes of pupils and interviewing the staff. The staff interviews explored such questions as how they felt the children got along with each other in their individual classes and in the school. Staff were asked what had been tried before, and what kinds of support they felt would be most useful in the future. Pupils in each year group completed two questionnaires – the *My Class Inventory Short Form* (which surveys perceptions of the classroom learning environment, resulting in scores for constructs such as group cohesiveness and group friction) and the *Life in Schools Checklist* (which surveys perceptions of positive and negative events in school and results in scores such as a bullying index and a general aggression index). The educational psychology team aimed to assist the staff group to 'unfreeze', that is identify and accept the reasons for organisational change in the school. They kick-started the process by feeding back the data from this initial investigation at a staff meeting in the form of a *rich picture*: see Figure 13.2.

FIGURE 13.2 A 'rich picture' of the school situation that emerged from the educational psychologists' consultations there

Source: Bettle *et al.*, 2001. ©Taylor & Francis. Reproduced with permission

---

ACTIVITY 13.2

- Discuss what assumptions are made in the portrayal of the school's 'behaviour ethos' that is conveyed in that picture.
- In the light of the limited information that is given here, can you suggest an operational definition of 'school ethos' that might have been employed by the educational psychology team?
- Compare the conclusions you have drawn from the data in this method box with the conclusions you drew in Method Box 13.1. What do any differences between the two tell you about differences in the ways school ethos has been conceptualised in these two reports?

---

support team. The explicit goal was to help a school to develop a more inclusive ethos. In her account of the change, Daniels (2010) gives the example of psychologists' response to the effects of gang violence on a group of schools:

> At first psychologists would go in time after time to do trauma debriefing with teachers and learners. Then it was decided to have workshops with the staff on identifying what had helped to make them resilient despite working under very challenging circumstances; valuing and spreading these practices; teaching skills to manage conflict; and envisioning short, medium and long term strategies to change the situation in the school and community.
>
> (p. 638)

Over time, the emphasis moved to building capacity in the schools, while continuing to draw on the strengths of a multidisciplinary support network. The group's slogan was 'None of us is as smart as all of us'.

Sometimes, the need for a psychologist's intervention across a school as a whole emerges from observation during the course of individual work, rather than as a result of an explicit request. This is illustrated in Case Study 13.1 below.

CASE STUDY 13.1

Change in Newbridge School

A day special school in a metropolitan area, which we will call Newbridge School, faced multiple challenges with a falling roll, changing patterns of admission, pupils with increasingly complex needs that were not always well understood by staff who had served in the school for many years, low staff confidence and frequent expressions of parental concern. A 'well-being' survey of staff showed low staff morale, divided staff teams and little team ethos. They reported little sense of control and a culture where there was little support – either formally or informally. There was mistrust between staff groups and a general feeling that they did not all pull together under pressure. After consultation with a new headteacher and senior management team, the school's educational psychologist agreed to meet with each class teacher and carry out a class observation, to provide positive feedback and agree next steps to develop their practice. Recurring themes emerged from discussions and observations, and a series of whole-staff training sessions were delivered to target areas for development. Feedback was also given to the senior management team, so that key issues that emerged could be addressed. Links were made with the speech and language therapists, and observations were shared, so that consistent messages could be given to class teams. Workshops were arranged for parents, and team problem-solving sessions were designed to create support plans for specific pupils who were causing concern.

At the end of the year when this intervention took place, the annual staff survey was repeated. Previously, the results had placed the school, when compared with other special schools, in the very lowest category for school ethos, including staff morale, with all scores well below average. A year later, when the survey was repeated, all scores were in the 'strength' range (over 3.5 on a 5-point scale), with many in the 'excellent' range (over 4). In feedback to the educational psychology service at the end of the year, the headteacher commented that the psychologist had 'played a very active role in the process of school improvement, supporting teachers through lesson observations, training, consultation and work with parents'. The headteacher also commented that, 'as a special school, the educational psychologist has had to work with class teams and at a whole school level so her influence has been widespread throughout the school'.

CONCLUSION

The concept of a school's 'ethos' refers to something vague and ill defined – its 'feeling' or 'character' as an organisation. It is possible to draw on analyses of organisational culture to clarify the concept. A school's culture encompasses the norms, values and expectations shared by staff and pupils, alongside the traditions and routines of the establishment that express those values. It can be thought of as operating at different levels of visibility – overt behaviour, structures and processes ('artefacts'), explicit ideals, goals and aspirations ('espoused beliefs and values') and basic underlying assumptions that determine perceptions, thoughts, feelings and behaviour (Schein, 2010). The school's overall ethos is the result of all this – 'the ambience that is felt at a school as a result of its cultural history; past, present and ever changing' (Solvason, 2005, p. 86). As we noted above, there may be distinct subcultures and microcultures in different parts of a complex institution such as a school. These may cohere within a strong, cohesive organisational culture, with clear leadership and a set of shared goals and values across the school, or differing subcultures may co-exist, with varying degrees of harmony and tension (Martin, 1992). The way in which the ethos of a particular establishment is experienced by its staff and pupils will depend on many factors, including the size and type of school and perhaps its history and functions.

Within the framework of educational psychology, a school cannot be understood by focusing solely at a single level, whether that is the whole school or the communal context, group settings such as classrooms, the family or the individual. Schools exist for the sake of their pupils and to serve a community by preparing its youngest members for their roles in adult society. There is a need to operate at multiple levels. The greatest challenge appears to lie in learning how factors at different levels interact. How do elements of a school's ethos and culture influence the personal development of its students? In his article for *The Scotsman* with which this chapter began, John Wilson saw the relationship as simple: symbols such as a uniform will help to 'promote the unity and ethos of a school and that, in turn, promotes the learning within'.

Once the complexity of the relationship between school ethos and student identities is fully understood, it becomes difficult to predict when wearing a uniform will be a badge of honour for students. In her article for *The Scotsman*, Judith Gillespie recalled a school prize-giving she had recently attended. She had been 'impressed at the inventiveness of some youngsters in managing to turn an ordinary shirt and tie into a fashion statement'. Those individuals chose to flaunt an alternative identity on an occasion when their *academic identity* was supposed to be on show. No doubt their satisfaction in doing so will have been enhanced because they were able to transform the 'official' uniform for that purpose. This reinforces the interactive analysis that considers both the institutional ethos and the individual as an active participant in construing it. Students' identities are developed, not by adopting their school's ethos as it is presented to them, but by trying out various ways of positioning themselves in relation to it.

SUMMARY OF MAIN ISSUES ADDRESSED IN THIS CHAPTER

- Schools differ markedly in the outcomes they achieve with their pupils, even when variations in pupil intake are taken into account.
- These differences between schools have been attributed to their overall ethos or culture, rather than to specific policies or individual staff actions.
- In the classic study that yielded those findings (Rutter *et al.*, 1979), *behavioural process variables* were treated as a means of measuring school ethos.
- That approach has been criticised as reductionist on the grounds that the complex forces that are in play in the life of an organisation such as a school cannot be adequately captured by such measures.
- The development of social identities is stimulated when children move more and more outside the immediate ambit of their home and are exposed to a wider range of people.
- The reflected appraisals of others such as teachers and parents influence children's own academic self-perceptions in the subject areas to which they relate, but that influence does not have a uniformly decisive impact on individuals' self-definition.
- The evidence for a powerful impact of school ethos on the development of students' identities as learners is strongest in small schools that have a well-defined mission and values that are widely shared among members of the school community.

- In a range of situations, practising educational psychologists have given attention to school ethos as a factor in some children's difficulties.
- Interventions in schools with serious problems have included projects based on 'soft systems methodology'. The analysis of school ethos in this strategy focuses on the perceptions of stakeholders and aims to influence their behaviour by changing the way that they view the situation.
- Other strategies, which focus on *staff development*, have also been employed by educational psychologists in this context.
- If research and professional practice in educational psychology are to be effective, a *multilevel focus* is required that gives attention, not only to psychological processes at the communal, small-group, family and individual levels, but also to the ethos and culture of a school as a whole.

KEY CONCEPTS AND TERMS

- School ethos
- School culture
- Behavioural process variables
- Reductionist
- Social identity
- Internalisation
- Reflected appraisal

- Valorisation
- Academic identities
- School in special measures
- Soft systems methodology
- Rich picture

- Staff development
- Multilevel focus of educational psychology

RECOMMENDED FURTHER READING

Journal articles

Bennett, M. and Sani, F. (2011). The internalisation of group identities in childhood. *Developmental Science, 56*(1), 117–24.

Bettle, S., Frederickson, N. and Sharp, S. (2001). Supporting a school in special measures: Implications for the potential contribution of educational psychology. *Educational Psychology in Practice, 17*(1), 53–68.

Daniels, B. (2010). Developing inclusive policy and practice in diverse contexts: A South African experience. *School Psychology International, 31*(6), 631–43.

Books and book chapters

Checkland, P. and Poulter, J. (2010). Soft systems methodology. In M. Reynolds and S. Holwell (eds), *Systems Approaches to Managing Change: A practical guide*. London: Springer-Verlag, pp. 191–242. Available online at https://crawford.anu.edu.au/public_policy_community/

content/doc/2010_Checkland_Soft_systems_methodology.pdf (accessed on 17 November 2013).

Lloyd, B. and G. Duveen (1992). *Gender Identities and Education: The impact of starting school.* Hemel Hempstead, UK: Harvester Wheatsheaf.

Rutter, M., Maughan, B., Mortimore, P., Ouston, J. and Smith, A. (1979). *Fifteen Thousand Hours: Secondary schools and their effects on children.* Wells, UK: Open Books.

SAMPLE ESSAY TITLES

1 Can school ethos be measured?
2 Assess the nature of the relationship between a school's ethos and its students' self-image.
3 You are the educational psychologist serving a large secondary school that has decided to liberalise its rules about school uniform. Drawing on what you know of psychological research in this area, design a research study to investigate the impact of this change on the development of student identities.

REFERENCES

Abreu, G. de (1995). Understanding how children experience the relationship between home and school mathematics. *Mind, Culture and Activity: An International Journal, 2*(2), 119–42.

Abreu, G. de and Cline, T. (2003). Schooled mathematics and cultural knowledge. *Pedagogy, Culture and Society, 11*(1), 11–30.

Bennett, M. and Sani, F. (2008). Children's subjective identification with social groups: A self-stereotyping approach. *Developmental Science, 11*, 69–75.

Bennett, M. and Sani, F. (2011). The internalisation of group identities in childhood. *Psychological Studies, 56*(1), 117–24.

Bettle, S., Frederickson, N. and Sharp, S. (2001). Supporting a school in special measures: Implications for the potential contribution of educational psychology. *Educational Psychology in Practice, 17*(1), 53–68.

Bouchey, H.A. and Harter, S. (2005). Reflected appraisals, academic self-perceptions, and math/science performance during early adolescence. *Journal of Educational Psychology, 97*(4), 673–86.

Burden, R. (2005). *Dyslexia and Self-Concept: Seeking a dyslexic identity.* London: Whurr.

Burgess, T. (1980). What makes an effective school? In B. Tizard *et al.* (eds), *Fifteen Thousand Hours: A discussion.* London: University of London Institute of Education.

Checkland, P. and Poulter, J. (2010). Soft systems methodology. In M. Reynolds and S. Holwell (eds), *Systems Approaches to Managing Change: A practical guide.* London: Springer-Verlag, pp. 191–242. Available online at https://crawford.anu.edu.au/public_policy_community/content/doc/2010_Checkland_Soft_systems_methodology.pdf (accessed on 17 November 2013).

Creese, A., Bhatt, A., Bhojani, N. and Martin, P. (2006). Multicultural, heritage and learner identities in complementary schools. *Language and Education, 20*(1), 23–43.

Daniels, B. (2010). Developing inclusive policy and practice in diverse contexts: A South African experience. *School Psychology International, 31*(6), 631–43.

Department for Education (1993). *Schools Requiring Special Measures.* Circular No. 17/93. London: DfE.

Duveen, G. (2001). Representations, identities, resistance. In K. Deaux and G. Philogène (eds), *Representations of the Social: Bridging theoretical traditions.* Oxford, UK: Blackwell, pp. 257–70.

Erikson, E.H. (1968). *Identity: Youth and crisis.* New York: Norton.

Fletcher, A., Bonell, C., Sorhaindo, A. and Strange, V. (2009). How might schools influence young people's drug use? Development of theory from qualitative case-study research. *Journal of Adolescent Health, 45*(2), 126–32.

Frederickson, N. (1993). Using Soft Systems Methodology to rethink special educational needs. In A. Dyson and C. Gains (eds), *Rethinking Special Needs in Mainstream Schools: Towards the year 2000.* London: David Fulton, pp. 1–21.

Gillham, B. (1978). Directions of change. In B. Gillham (ed.), *Reconstructing Educational Psychology.* London: Croom Helm, pp. 11–23.

Goldstein, H. (1980). Critical notice of *Fifteen Thousand Hours. Journal of Child Psychology and Psychiatry, 21*(4), 364–6.

Lewis, M. (2002). Early emotional development. In A. Slater and M. Lewis, *Introduction to Infant Development.* Oxford, UK: Oxford University Press, pp. 192–209.

Lloyd, B. and Duveen, G. (1992). *Gender Identities and Education: The impact of starting school.* Hemel Hempstead, UK: Harvester Wheatsheaf.

Martin, J. (1992). *Cultures in Organizations: Three perspectives.* New York: Oxford University Press.

Mortimore, P., Sammons, P., Stoll, L., Lewis, D. and Ecob, R. (1988). *School Matters: The Junior Years.* Wells, UK: Open Books.

Pateman, T. (1980). Can schools educate? *Journal of Philosophy of Education, 14*(2), 139–48. 'Lightly revised' version available at www.selectedworks.co.uk/schooleducation.html (accessed 8 August 2007).

Plowden Committee (1967). *Children and their Primary Schools (The Plowden Report).* London: HMSO.

Reynolds, D. (2010). *Failure-free Education: The past, present and future of school effectiveness and school improvement.* London: Routledge.

Rivers, I. and Soutter, A. (1996). Bullying and the Steiner School ethos: A case study analysis of a group-centred educational philosophy. *School Psychology International, 17*(4), 359–77.

Rutter, M., Maughan, B., Mortimore, P., Ouston, J. and Smith, A. (1979). *Fifteen Thousand Hours: Secondary schools and their effects on children.* Wells, UK: Open Books.

Schachter, E.P. and Rich, Y. (2011). Identity education: A conceptual framework for educational researchers and practitioners. *Educational Psychologist, 46*, 222–38.

Scheerens, J. (2013). The use of theory in school effectiveness research revisited. *School Effectiveness and School Improvement: An International Journal of Research, Policy and Practice, 24*(1), 1–38.

Schein, E.H. (2010). *Organizational Culture and Leadership* (4th edn). San Francisco: Jossey Bass.

Solvason, C. (2005). Investigating specialist school ethos . . . or do you mean culture? *Educational Studies*, *31*(1), 85–94.

Townsend, T. (ed.) (2007). *International Handbook of School Effectiveness and Improvement*. Dordrecht, Netherlands: Springer.

West, P., Sweeting, H. and Leyland, A. (2004). School effects on pupils' health behaviours: Evidence in support of the health promoting school. *Research Papers in Education*, *19*(3), 261–91.

Wrigley, T. (2004). 'School effectiveness': The problem of reductionism. *British Educational Research Journal*, *30*(2), 227–44.

Index